STUDIES IN THE GRAMMAR AND LEXICON OF NEO-ARAMAIC

Studies in the Grammar and Lexicon of Neo-Aramaic

Edited by Geoffrey Khan and Paul M. Noorlander

https://www.openbookpublishers.com

All external links were active at the time of publication unless otherwise stated and have been archived via the Internet Archive Wayback Machine at https://archive.org/web

Updated digital material and resources associated with this volume are available at https://doi.org/10.11647/OBP.0209#resources

Semitic Languages and Cultures 5.

ISSN (print): 2632-6906
ISSN (digital): 2632-6914

ISBN Paperback: 978-1-78374-947-8
ISBN Hardback: 978-1-78374-948-5
ISBN Digital (PDF): 978-1-78374-949-2
ISBN Digital ebook (epub): 978-1-78374-950-8
ISBN Digital ebook (mobi): 978-1-78374-951-5
ISBN Digital (XML): 978-1-78374-952-2
DOI: 10.11647/OBP.0209

Cover image: Women in the village of Harbole, south-eastern Turkey (photograph taken by Brunot Poizat in 1978 before the village's destruction).
Cover design: Anna Gatti

CONTENTS

GLOSSING ABBREVIATIONS ix

CONTRIBUTORS xi

PREFACE xvii

ABSTRACTS xxi

Eugene Barsky and Sergey Loesov

A History of the Intransitive Preterite of Ṭuroyo: from a Property Adjective to a Finite Tense 1

Paul M. Noorlander

Towards a Typology of Possessors and Experiencers in Neo-Aramaic: Non-Canonical Subjects as Relics of a Former Dative Case 29

Dorota Molin

The Jewish Neo-Aramaic Dialect of Dohok: Two Folktales and Selected Features of Verbal Semantics ... 95

Geoffrey Khan

Verbal Forms Expressing Discourse Dependency in North-Eastern Neo-Aramaic 143

Eran Cohen

Conditional Patterns in the Jewish Neo-Aramaic Dialect of Zakho 195

Michael Waltisberg

Language Contact and Ṭuroyo: The Case of the Circumstantial Clause 221

Ivri Bunis

The Morphosyntactic Conservatism of Western Neo-Aramaic despite Contact with Syrian Arabic 235

Steven E. Fassberg

On the *Afel* Stem in Western Neo-Aramaic 287

Ariel Gutman

The Re-Emergence of the Genitive in North-Eastern Neo-Aramaic 301

Lidia Napiorkowska

Modelling Variation in the Neo-Aramaic Dialect of Azran with Articulatory Phonology 319

Aziz Tezel

On the Origin of Some Plant Names in Ṣūrayt/ Ṭūrōyo in Ṭūr ʿAbdīn 335

Eugene Barsky and Yulia Furman

Remarks on Selected Exponents of the 208-Swadesh List in Ṭuroyo 353

Hezy Mutzafi

Neo-Aramaic Animal Names... 389

Alexey Lyavdansky

A Corpus-Based Swadesh Word List for Literary Christian Urmi (New Alphabet Texts) 415

Aziz Emmanuel Eliya Al-Zebari
(in collaboration with Anjuman M. Sabir)

Lexical Items Relating to Material Culture in the NENA Dialects of the Aqra Region 443

Salam Neamah Hirmiz Hakeem

Arabic Loanwords in the Neo-Aramaic Dialect of Ankawa.. 469

Sina Tezel

Language Loss in the Ṣūrayt/Ṭūrōyo-speaking Communities of the Diaspora in Sweden...................... 487

INDEX 505

GLOSSING ABBREVIATIONS

A	Arabic
ACC	accusative
ACT	active
ALV	alveolar
ALVPAL	alveopalatal
AOR	aorist
ART	article
ARTP	Articulatory Phonology
ATTR	attribute
CAUS	causative
CLF	classifier
CLO	closure
COMP	complementiser
CONJ	conjunction
CONN	connective
COP	copula
CRIT	critical
CST	construct state (head of attributive annexation)
DAT	dative
DEF	definite (article)
DEIX.COP	deictic copula
DEM	demonstrative
DEP	dependent (marker of dependent clause or noun phrase)
DET	determined state
DIST	distal demonstrative
DM	discourse marker
DOM	differential object marking
ERG	ergative
EXIST	existential
EZ	ezafe
F	feminine
FOC	focus
FPL	feminine plural
FS	feminine singular
FUT	future
GEN	genitive
GLO	glottis
GN	geographic name
H	Hebrew
HAB	habitual
IMP	imperative
IMPF	imperfect
IND	indicative
INDEF	indefinite
INDET	indetermined state
IPFV	imperfective
IRR	irrealis
K	Kurdish
LAB	labial
LNK	linker
M	masculine

MEDP	mediopassive
MOD	modal
MPL	masculine plural
MS	masculine singular
N	neuter
NEG	negative
NMLS	nominalisation
NOM	nominative
NPL	neuter plural
NPSFX	nominal suffix
NPST	non-past
NS	neuter singular
PAL	palatal
PASS	passive
PC	prefix conjugation
PERS	personal
PFV	perfective
PHAR	pharyngeal
PL	plural
PN	personal name
PN	proper noun
POSS	possessive
PRET	preterite
PROG	progressive
PRON	pronoun
PRS	present
PST	past
PTCP	participle
PVB	preverbal modifier
QAM	*qam* pre-verbal prefix
QĀTL	Arabic *qātel* paradigm (historical active participle)
QATTĪL	*qaṭṭīl* adjective
QŌTL	Western Neo-Aramaic *qōṭel* paradigm (historical active participle)
QTĪL	*qṭīl* adjective and resultative participle
QTL	*qatal* and *qṭal* suffix conjugations in Arabic and Western Neo-Aramaic respectively
REFL	reflexive
REL	relative
RES	resultative
S	singular
SBJV	subjunctive
SC	suffixing conjugation
TB	tongue body
TT	tongue tip
UVU-PHAR	uvular-pharyngeal
VEL	velum
VOC	vocative
YQTL	*yiqtol* prefix conjugation in Arabic and Western Neo-Aramaic

CONTRIBUTORS

Eugene Barsky (PhD, St Tikhon's Orthodox University of Humanities, Moscow, 2010) researched the Book of Ezra in his PhD thesis. His current work focuses on the grammar of Aramaic and the history of the Bible. His previous publications on Neo-Aramaic relate to the lexicon of Ṭuroyo and Mlaḥso.

Sergey Loesov (PhD, Russian State University for the Humanities, Moscow, 1994) is a professor at the National Research University 'Higher School of Economics' (Moscow). His research publications concern the following main fields: history of Aramaic, Neo-Aramaic dialectology, history of Akkadian and morphosyntax of Akkadian.

Paul M. Noorlander (PhD, Leiden University, 2018) is a Rubicon Fellow at Leiden University seconded to the University of Cambridge. His current work focuses on the documentation of endangered Neo-Aramaic dialects originally spoken in Turkey and coordinating the development of the online NENA database and NENA digital corpus. His PhD thesis was on the typology of alignment in Neo-Aramaic. He has worked on Semitic languages from a comparative-historical perspective and on diachronic developments in Aramaic in particular, including detailed syntactic studies of Late Antique Aramaic varieties. His research interests and published work also involve tense-aspect-mood, word order and contact between Neo-Aramaic and neighbouring languages such as Iranian and Armenian.

Dorota Molin is a PhD student (2018–2021) in Middle Eastern Studies at the University of Cambridge, working on North-Eastern Neo-Aramaic. She obtained her MPhil degree at Cambridge for a dissertation on Biblical Hebrew quotations in the Aramaic incantation bowls in the context of Biblical Hebrew pronunciation traditions. She is interested in comparative dialectology and its contribution to understanding diachrony (e.g., grammaticalisation). She has also published on contact between Modern Hebrew and Negev Arabic and worked as a research assistant on a forthcoming Diplomatic Edition of Mishna-Codex Kaufmann (A50). She holds a BA degree in Hebrew and Arabic (Cambridge).

Geoffrey Khan (PhD, School of Oriental and African Studies, London, 1984) is Regius Professor of Hebrew at the University of Cambridge. His research publications focus on three main fields: Biblical Hebrew language (especially medieval traditions), Neo-Aramaic dialectology and medieval Arabic documents. He is the general editor of *The Encyclopedia of Hebrew Language and Linguistics* and is the senior editor of *Journal of Semitic Studies*. His most recent book is *The Tiberian Pronunciation Tradition of Biblical Hebrew*, 2 vols, Cambridge Semitic Languages and Cultures 1 (University of Cambridge & Open Book Publishers, 2020).

Eran Cohen (PhD, Hebrew University of Jerusalem, 2002) is a professor of linguistics at the Hebrew University of Jerusalem. His work is mainly descriptive and comparative, covering various phases and registers of several languages—Akkadian, Neo-Aramaic, Biblical and Modern Hebrew, as well as various aspects of comparative linguistics of Semitic. The domains covered in his work are syntax and macro-syntax, including such topics as information structure, the functional analysis of verbal systems (tense, aspect and modality, as well as its functions in narrative), the structure of narrative, conditional structures and relative clauses. Recent research topics include interrogative markers in Semitic, the diachrony of epistemic particles from a comparative perspective, genitive constructions in Semitic, conditional constructions in Semitic and manner demonstratives.

Michael Waltisberg (PhD, Marburg, 2008; Habilitation, Marburg, 2014) is currently Privatdozent at the Philipps-University of Marburg, and is employed at the University of Heidelberg as interim Professor for Semitic Linguistics. He has worked on the Semitic language family as a whole in a comparative and typological perspective, with a particular focus on issues of syntax and semantics. His main contributions are in the fields of Classical Arabic and several pre-modern and modern Aramaic varieties. He is currently participating in a project on the information structure of Syriac (Middle Aramaic).

Ivri Bunis (PhD, Hebrew University of Jerusalem, 2018) is a post-doctoral Research Associate in the Department of Middle Eastern Studies at the University of Cambridge. He wrote his PhD thesis on the morphosyntax of Jewish Palestinian Aramaic of the Byzantine period. His research interests include Aramaic historical linguistics, Late Western Aramaic, Rabbinic Hebrew in contact with Aramaic and Western Neo-Aramaic in contact with Syrian Arabic.

Steven E. Fassberg (PhD, Harvard University, 1984) is Caspar Levias Professor of Ancient Semitic Languages at the Hebrew University of Jerusalem. His research has focused on Northwest Semitic, Aramaic dialectology and the Hebrew of the First and Second Temple periods. His publications in the field of Neo-Aramaic include *The Jewish Neo-Aramaic Dialect of Challa* (Brill, 2010). His latest book is *An Introduction to the Syntax of Biblical Hebrew* (Bialik Institute, 2019).

Ariel Gutman (PhD, University of Konstanz, 2016), researched Neo-Aramaic dialects for his PhD thesis in Konstanz, where he was an Associate Fellow of the Zukunftskolleg Interdisciplinary Institute. He is also an alumnus of the Hebrew University of Jerusalem, the Sorbonne Nouvelle University and the École Normale Supérieure of Paris. He has conducted linguistic fieldwork in France, in Israel and in West Papua, Indonesia. His research interests and publications are in the fields of Syriac Philology, Neo-Aramaic dialectology, Child Language Acquisition and Natural Language Processing. He is currently working as a software engineer specialising in computational linguistics at Google in Zurich.

Lidia Napiorkowska (PhD, University of Cambridge, 2013) researched the Diyana-Zariwaw dialect of Neo-Aramaic for her PhD thesis. Her postdoctoral project involved further documentation of rare Neo-Aramaic dialects in Iraqi Kurdistan, Sweden and Great Britain. She is now a lecturer at the Department of Hebrew Studies, Warsaw University, where she combines teaching Modern Hebrew with her research interests in phonology, language contact and comparative Semitic studies.

Aziz Tezel is a Researcher Emeritus in Semitic Languages. His research focuses on etymological problems, borrowings, quadriradical verbal formations, flora and the *bgdkft*-consonants. His book publications include *Comparative Etymological Studies in the Western Neo-Syriac (Ṭūrōyo) Lexicon* (Uppsala University, 2003).

Yulia Furman (PhD, Russian State University for the Humanities, Moscow, 2017) is an Alexander von Humboldt fellow at the Freie Universität Berlin. Her PhD thesis was on a 7th-century Syriac universal history by John bar Penkaye. Her research interests include Neo-Aramaic languages, the grammar of Classical Syriac and the history of Syriac literature. Her current project deals with the lexical and grammatical aspect of the Ṭuroyo verb.

Hezy Mutzafi (PhD, Tel Aviv University, 2001) is Professor of Semitic Linguistics in the Department of Hebrew Language and Semitic Linguistics, Tel Aviv University. His research and publications focus on Neo-Aramaic dialectology, in particular North-Eastern Neo-Aramaic regional varieties and Neo-Mandaic. His latest book is *Comparative Lexical Studies in Neo-Mandaic* (Brill 2014).

Alexey Lyavdansky is a lecturer of Classical Hebrew and Aramaic at the Institute for Oriental and Classical Studies, National Research University Higher School of Economics (Moscow). His research and publications focus on Neo-Aramaic, Babylonian Aramaic and Classical Hebrew. Currently, he is leading a project to create an electronic corpus of literary Christian Urmi Neo-Aramaic. He is also undertaking documentation of the Neo-Aramaic dialects in Russia.

Aziz Emmanuel Eliya Al-Zebari (PhD, Salahaddin University, Erbil, 2018) is a lecturer in the English Department of the Catholic University of Erbil, Iraq. He was born in the village of Upper Gerbish in the area of Nekhla, North of Aqra. For his PhD thesis he documented the Neo-Aramaic dialect of the Aqra region.

Salam Neamah Hirmiz Hakeem (PhD, Salahaddin University, Erbil, 2010) focuses on three main fields of research: sociolinguistics, text analysis and pedagogy. He teaches Syriac in the Department of Syriac of Salahaddin University. He is a native speaker of the Ankawa dialect of Neo-Aramaic and has researched the impact of Arabic on this dialect and its sociolinguistics motivations.

Sina Tezel (PhD, Uppsala University, 2011) is Senior Lecturer in Semitic Languages at the University of Uppsala. Her PhD thesis was on Arabic loanwords in Ṣūrayt/Ṭūrōyo. Her current research focuses on comparative Semitics, loanwords, language contact, the *bgdkpt*-consonants and neologisms.

PREFACE

The Neo-Aramaic dialects are modern vernacular forms of Aramaic, which has a documented history in the Middle East of over 3,000 years, the earliest inscriptions being datable to approximately 1,000 BCE. The Neo-Aramaic dialects that have survived down to modern times are generally classified into four subgroups:

1. Western Neo-Aramaic (south-western Syria)
2. Central Neo-Aramaic (south-eastern Turkey West of the Tigris), represented by varieties of Ṭuroyo (also known as Ṣurayt) in Ṭur ʿAbdin and the dialect of Mlaḥso
3. North-Eastern Neo-Aramaic (northern Iraq, south-eastern Turkey and western Iran), generally known as NENA
4. Neo-Mandaic (south-western Iran)

The Neo-Aramaic dialects are clearly closely related to the written forms of Aramaic of earlier periods. The Neo-Aramaic subgroups can be correlated broadly with dialectal divisions that are reflected in pre-modern written Aramaic sources from the first millennium CE onwards particularly during Late Antiquity, which are sometimes referred to collectively as 'Middle Aramaic' or 'Late (Antique) Aramaic'. Central Neo-Aramaic, North-Eastern Neo-Aramaic and Neo-Mandaic are related to the eastern branch of pre-modern Aramaic, e.g. Classical Syriac, Classical Mandaic and Jewish Babylonian Aramaic, whereas Western Neo-Aramaic is related to the western branch, e.g. Jewish and Christian Palestinian Aramaic and Samaritan Aramaic. No Neo-Aramaic subgroup, however, could be considered a direct descendent of the attested forms of the literary pre-modern Aramaic varieties.

Nine of the papers in this volume focus on NENA dialects, five concern Ṭuroyo varieties, two focus on Western Neo-Aramaic and one compares all three subgroups.

https://doi.org/10.11647/OBP.0209.18

Due to upheavals in the Middle East over the last one hundred years, thousands of speakers of Neo-Aramaic dialects have been forced to migrate from their homes or have perished in massacres. As a result, the dialects are now highly endangered. The study and documentation of these dialects is thus of prime concern not only for the preservation of the speakers' oral heritage but also for their identity. A number of contributors to this volume are native speakers of Neo-Aramaic (Aziz Tezel, Sina Tezel, Aziz Al-Zebari, Salam Hakeem). We hope this Open Access volume will be a source of inspiration for speakers to take pride in their linguistic heritage and seek ways to contribute to its preservation.

In recent years research on the Neo-Aramaic dialects has been flourishing. This has resulted in the documentation of many endangered dialects and the discovery of many fascinating aspects of linguistic variation and change. The dialects exhibit a remarkable diversity in all aspects of grammar. Moreover, the considerable depth of attestation of Aramaic from earlier periods provides evidence for pathways of change. For these reasons the research of Neo-Aramaic is of importance for more general fields of linguistics, in particular language typology and historical linguistics.

The papers in this volume represent the full range of research that is currently being carried out on Neo-Aramaic dialects and advance the field in numerous ways. Many of them originated as papers presented at the last two international conferences of Neo-Aramaic (Warsaw 2016, organised by Lidia Napiorkowska, and Uppsala 2018, organised by Eleanor Coghill and Sina Tezel). The contributions to the volume cover a wide range of topics, including studies of phonology, morphology, syntax and lexicon. A large proportion of them, however, focus on syntax or lexicon. In order to allow linguists who are not specialists in Neo-Aramaic to benefit from the papers, the examples are fully glossed. Abbreviations for the glosses can be found at the beginning of the volume.

Several of the papers investigate the historical development of verbal syntax (Eugene Barsky and Sergey Loesov, Dorota Molin, Geoffrey Khan, Ivri Bunis), dative subjects (Paul Noorlander), verbal stem morphology (Steven Fassberg) and nominal case morphology (Ariel Gutman). These papers demonstrate that Neo-Aramaic varieties are indispensable for the study of the historical development of Aramaic. Its long history is not only remarkable but also is instructive for understanding language change in general. The volume contains detailed case studies of, for instance, the shift from adjectives into verbs (Eugene Barsky and Sergey Loesov), from dependent into main clauses (Geoffrey Khan), dative into nominative subjects (Paul Noorlander), reanalysis of causatives as intransitives (Steven Fassberg) and the cyclic reinvention of case marking (Ariel Gutman).

Since the Neo-Aramaic dialects are so diverse, each variety requires a detailed description in its own right. Narrative texts like folktales are invaluable for preserving an endangered language without a written culture of its own. Moreover, they facilitate the study of language use in context. Detailed synchronic descriptions of language use in this volume include studies on non-canonical subject marking across Neo-Aramaic varieties (Paul Noorlander) and Tense-Aspect-Mood in NENA, particularly the negation of the future and continuous aspect (Dorota Molin), modality and discourse dependency (Geoffrey Khan) and conditional constructions (Eran Cohen). Dialectal variation is a challenge for linguistic analysis. One paper (Lidia Napiorkowska) applies an articulatory phonological model to describe the phonological variation in a highly endangered NENA dialect. Such synchronic variation points to diachronic processes in progress and holds important clues for the limitations of grammaticalisation (Dorota Molin), the reanalysis of modal verbal forms (Geoffrey Khan) and internal motivations besides language interference (Lidia Napiorkowska).

Neo-Aramaic variation has often arisen due to dialect mixing or contact. Syntax is particularly prone to change due to language contact. Since they belong to linguistic-religious minorities, Neo-Aramaic speakers are necessarily bi- or multilingual. Arabic-Aramaic contact is the particular focus of two papers pertaining to Ṭuroyo (Michael Waltisberg) and to Western Neo-Aramaic (Ivri Bunis), both of which show the complexities of such language contact situations. While pattern replication may seem evident, it cannot be easily identified using current frameworks of contact (Michael Waltisberg). Prolonged bilingualism among linguistic minorities can even show unexpected resilience against contact-induced change (Ivri Bunis). Two papers address central issues of morphological structures concerning verbal derivation in Western Neo-Aramaic (Steven Fassberg) and the genitive in NENA (Ariel Gutman). While the reanalysis of causative stem formations in Western Neo-Aramaic cannot be attributed to language contact with Arabic (Steven Fassberg), the re-emergence of the genitive in NENA is partially due to convergence with Kurdish (Ariel Gutman).

The papers on lexicon make important contributions to documenting particular semantic fields in various dialects, e.g. plant names (Aziz Tezel), animal names (Hezy Mutzafi) and material culture (Aziz al-Zebari). The papers of Aziz Tezel and Hezy Mutzafi also discuss the etymology of the items in the semantic fields they are concerned with. Two papers (Eugene Barsky and Yulia Furman, Alexey Lyavdansky) examine the profile of the core lexicon with a view to establishing historical relationships by applying the Swadesh list.

The final two papers in the volume focus on features of Neo-Aramaic dialects that reflect their attrition and incipient loss, in one case (Salam Hakeem) in northern Iraq, which is the historical heartland of Aramaic, and in the other (Sina Tezel) among the younger generations of Neo-Aramaic speakers in the diaspora communities of Europe.

We are very grateful to Open Book Publishers for all their efficient help. Their open-access initiative will allow this publication to be widely read not only by scholars but also by members of the Neo-Aramaic-speaking communities in the Middle East and in the diaspora throughout the world.

The Editors, Cambridge, June 2020

ABSTRACTS

Eugene Barsky and Sergey Loesov examine the history of the Semitic nominal pattern **qaṭṭīl* (*$C_1aC_2C_2\bar{i}C_3$) in terms of its evolving grammatical semantics. The **qaṭṭīl* form is a Central Semitic innovation, which became fully productive in old Aramaic as a adjective denoting properties (e.g. *ʿammīq* 'deep', *ḥakkīm* 'wise'), marginalising the inherited property adjective patterns **qaṭil* (*$C_1aC_2iC_3$) and to some extent also **qaṭīl* (*$C_1aC_2\bar{i}C_3$). It eventually became the past tense stem of intransitive verbs in Ṭuroyo. The paper traces in detail the history of the verbalisation of **qaṭṭīl*, drawing on a corpus-based study of Classical Syriac.

Paul M. Noorlander presents a study of subject-like possessors and experiencers in Neo-Aramaic. These are expressed through person affixes on verbs and verboids that historically go back to a dative preposition—the marker of recipients. Based on a cross-dialectal study of their clause structure, the paper argues that these arguments are non-canonical subjects whose morphosyntax is still reminiscent of their original recipient-like function. The identical marking of the agent of past perfective verbs and these non-canonical subjects are likely to be ultimately historically related and part of the overall typology of the language area, since some of these constructions have close parallels in Iranian languages.

Dorota Molin presents two folktales from the hitherto unstudied NENA dialect of the Jews of Dohok (north-western Iraq) accompanied by linguistic glosses, translation and comments on a few grammatical features. There is a link to an audio recording of the texts. These folktales are followed by a survey of selected TAM features in this dialect. The asymmetric distribution of the realis habitual preverb (*k*-) between past and non-past is likely to be due to an incomplete grammaticalisation of this preverb. The resultative construction is lexically restricted, indicating that it is not a full perfect in this dialect. The use of the progressive/ continuous is also very restricted compared to other dialects.

Geoffrey Khan examines various verbal forms in NENA dialects that are used to express discourse dependency. The common feature of all these forms is that they express some kind of cognitive continuity from what precedes without there being syntactic subordination. There is a discussion of the various contexts in which the forms are used and of the possible pathways of their historical development. The forms expressing discourse dependency include *bət-qaṭəl*, *qam-qaṭəl* and narrative subjunctive *qaṭəl*. It is argued that *bət-qaṭəl* with this function developed from a future form in apodoses to conditional constructions. Evidence is presented from dialects in the Cudi region to support the hypothesis that the *qam-qaṭəl* form originally expressed an immediate future. The origin of the narrative subjunctive is identified in the subjunctive of dependent purpose clauses.

Eran Cohen presents a description and discussion of the various conditional phenomena in the Jewish Neo-Aramaic dialect of Zakho. He explains and exemplifies the different conditional types—ordinary, speech-act, inferential, and concessive-conditionals. The paper identifies two patterns expressing ordinary conditionals, with and without a conditional particle, and examines the strutures of counterfactual conditionals. Narrative conditionals are compared with counterfactuals and their function is explained vis à vis other clause types. Finally, the co-occurrence of conditionals with other epistemic expressions is analysed.

Michael Waltisberg develops an earlier paper (Waltisberg 2013) on the circumstantial clause of Ṭuroyo, where it was argued that the circumstantial clause both formally and semantically is a direct replication of the corresponding Arabic construction. The present article resumes this discussion by adducing more data from neighbouring Arabic dialects as well as from other Middle Aramaic and Neo-Aramaic varieties. This results in a slightly different and less clearcut conclusion concerning the impact of language contact. The paper demonstrates the methodological issues that must be taken into account when attempts are made to identify syntactic replication across closely related languages.

Ivri Bunis examines aspects of language contact between Western Neo-Aramaic and Syrian Arabic. The genetic relationship between Western Neo-Aramaic and Syrian Arabic and the retention of the older Aramaic suffix and prefix conjugations in Western Neo-Aramaic have left the latter with a verbal morphology very similar to Syrian Arabic. Both languages, however, diverge in how their cognate verbal forms express TAM. The divergences between the languages were originally due to independent development, most likely before the intensive contact between them. The paper argues that given the close and prolonged contact of Western Neo-Aramaic with Arabic, the divergences between the two languages also reflect significant conservatism in Western Neo-Aramaic.

Steven E. Fassberg draws attention to a noteworthy feature of the morphology of Maʕlula Western Neo-Aramaic whereby some *Afel* verbs correspond to *Peal* intransitive verbs in older Aramaic. 1st form intransitive Arabic loans also show up in Maʕlula in *Afel*. The shift may have begun in Late Western Aramaic, when there was a retraction of stress followed by the creation of prosthetic vowels resolving word-initial consonantal clusters. Speakers possibly reinterpreted *Peal Vqtel* (< **qatila*) forms as *Afel* verbs. Such a reanalysis would have been reinforced by the overlap between the two stems in expressing state and condition.

Ariel Gutman draws attention to a case of cyclic morphological change in Neo-Aramaic. In its earliest attested stages, Aramaic had already lost the Proto-Semitic case system, as only vestiges of an oblique case are found in an ancient inscription. Yet starting in the 17th century CE, one can observe a process which leads to the re-emergence of genitive and oblique case markers in certain Neo-Aramaic dialects, facilitated by Kurmanji language contact. This cycle is accompanied by another cyclic change, namely the decline and re-creation of an apocopate construct state marking of nouns.

Lidia Napiorkowska uses Articulatory Phonology (ArtP) to model phonological variation in the NENA dialect of Azran. ArtP construes speech production as composed of gestures that may shift in time and magnitude. This approach explains palatalisation and fronting of pronunciation encountered in Azran as a result of gestural overlap, thus identifying an internal motivation for variation in addition to possible language contact influence. Moreover, employing a dynamic model provides insights into the phonology–phonetics interface and has implications for establishing conventions of transcription

Aziz Tezel presents material from his ongoing research of plant names in Ṭuroyo (Ṣurayt) and their background. The discussion here focuses on some plants whose names are either of obscure origin or have undergone changes. Taking the corresponding names in Syriac and other earlier languages of the region into consideration, proposals are made for the origin of the names of the plants concerned, with a brief description of their uses in the local culture. Comparisons to corresponding names in NENA are made. An account of dialectal differences is given. Some borrowings from neighbouring languages are identified.

Eugene Barsky and Yulia Furman study selected concepts from the 208-Swadesh list in Ṭuroyo: BIRD, HEAD, HUSBAND, MAN (MALE), MAN (HUMAN BEING), SUN, WIFE and WOMAN. This is based on fieldwork conducted in Germany in 2016 among the Ṭuroyo-speaking community and a published field corpus gathered in the 1960s. Each concept and its possible exponents are presented together with a discussion of their distribution in the corpus and in the modern language. The results of the study reveal diachronic change and dialectal diversity in the usage of the exponents in question.

Hezy Mutzafi examines animal names in various Neo-Aramaic dialects, from Western Neo-Aramaic in south-eastern Syria to Neo-Mandaic in south-western Iran. A large number of modern Aramaic animal names—mostly of inherited Aramaic origin and hitherto unattested—are discussed. Among these are lexical innovations that were moulded by processes of word-formation. Some other animal names, supposed to be related to the Christian Urmi dialect, are shown to have nothing to do with genuine Neo-Aramaic speech, but are rather Syriac classicisms interpolated into Bible translations and dictionaries.

Alexey Lyavdansky presents a basic word list for literary Christian Urmi Neo-Aramaic together with etymologies and a discussion of problematic issues. This study, which uses a variant of the Swadesh list of 110 basic words, is the first research outcome of a project that has created an electronic corpus of literary Christian Urmi based on the texts published in the Soviet Union between 1929 and 1938 (Novij Alfavit). With some exponents being uncertain (having two possible variants), the statistical results demonstrate that more than 90 percent of the exponents have reliable Aramaic etymologies. Four meanings have exponents that originate from Persian. The exponents of two meanings have Kurdish etymologies. Six exponents have no clear etymology.

Aziz Emmanuel Eliya Al-Zebari presents lexical material relating to material culture from the NENA dialects of the Aqra region. These dialects can be classified broadly into those of the villages lying to the North of the Aqra mountain and those of the inhabitants of the region to the South of the mountain. Those lying to the North are situated in an area known as Nexla and include the villages of Dinarta, Upper Gerbish and Sanaye. The dialect area lying to the South of the Aqra mountain includes the town of Aqra and the villages of Kherpa, Kharjawa, Nuhawa, Barrake, Sharmen and Malaberwan. The lexical items that are presented are classified into the follow semantic fields: (§1.) Buildings and Structures, (§2.) Containers, (§3.) Instruments and Tools, (§4.) Agriculture, (§5.) Sewing, Weaving and Spinning, (§6.) Hunting, (§7.) Fires, (§8.) Clothes and Fabrics.

Salam Hakeem identifies and classifies the types of Arabic loanwords that currently occur in the spoken Neo-Aramaic dialect of Ankawa. He examines the reasons for the extensive use of such loanwords by the younger generation. It is shown that although the main contact language in Ankawa is now Kurdish, Arabic continues to have a greater impact on the Neo-Aramaic dialect than Kurdish. The reasons for this are identified as the influence of education, which was entirely in Arabic until the last decade, social media, in which Arabic is still the dominant means of communication, and the recent displacement of many Arabic-speaking Christians from Mosul to Ankawa.

Sina Tezel discusses language loss in communities speaking Ṭuroyo (Ṣurayt) in the diaspora in Sweden. She examines the challenges of new social and cultural terminology. There is a loss of the regional dialectal diversity of Ṭuroyo with consequent dialect mixing. Many lexemes are falling from use and the semantic range of lexemes is contracting. Also under threat is culturally-specific idiomatic phraseology. Such incipient loss of the language is, moreover, reflected by codeswitching in the speech of the younger generations.

A HISTORY OF THE INTRANSITIVE PRETERITE OF ṬUROYO: FROM A PROPERTY ADJECTIVE TO A FINITE TENSE[1]

Eugene Barsky and Sergey Loesov

1. Research Question

The ultimate source of inspiration for the present study is our ambition to offer a detailed description of the history of the Aramaic verbal system. A key event in this history is what Goldenberg used to call 'the morphological revolution', i.e. the shift, within Eastern Aramaic, from the Middle Aramaic[2] verbal systems to those of Modern Aramaic. In the course of this shift, Eastern Aramaic gave up the inherited suffix conjugation[3] (**qatala*) and the prefix conjugation (**yaqtulu*) and developed a new repertoire of verbal forms, all of whose bases were deverbal adjectives in earlier stages of Aramaic's history.

We start our historical investigation with Ṭuroyo, since the verbal system of this language, with its two Preterites, *qaṭəl*-Preterite for most intransitive verbs of the G-stem vs. L-Preterite *qṭəlle* for transitive ones, seems to be more conservative than that of North-Eastern Neo-Aramaic (NENA). It may represent

1 The research was supported by RFBR grant 19-012-00475.

2 The term 'Middle Aramaic' is used in this paper to refer both to unwritten varieties of Aramaic spoken throughout the 1st millennium AD and the literary registers of those that were committed to writing during the same period (Jewish Palestinian Aramaic, Syriac, Mandaic, etc.).

3 With the exception of Neo-Mandaic, which retained the suffix conjugation.

 https://doi.org/10.11647/OBP.0209.01

a stage that used to exist in some of the ancestor languages of NENA as well.[4]

Various studies have attempted to establish how the Eastern Aramaic L-Preterite *qṭəlle* developed historically.[5] As far as we know, however, there have been no corpus-based studies of the diachronic pathway that led to the *qaṭəl*-Preterite of Ṭuroyo, i.e. how the Central Semitic adjective **qaṭṭīl* became verbalised.

In Aramaic, **qaṭṭīl* started as an adjective expressing permanent properties and ended up being the base of various verbal forms in the past tense domain. The functional range of **qaṭṭīl* in the modern Aramaic verbal system is not restricted to the G-stem intransitive Preterite of Ṭuroyo. **Qaṭṭīl* is the Perfect of both transitive and intransitive verbs in Mlaḥsó (Jastrow 1994, 45, 52f.). Moreover, in certain village varieties of Ṭuroyo (in particular, Midən and Kfarze), **qaṭṭīl* is the base for the Passive Preterite of III-y verbs. Thus, in these villages, the Passive Preterite of the verb *ḥzy* is *ḥazi* ('he was seen') rather than *ḥze*.[6] The latter form exists in Midyat and some village dialects. This has been inherited directly from the Middle Aramaic ancestor of Ṭuroyo, while the former (*ḥazi*) developed within Ṭuroyo by analogy with the 1 f.s. and 3 f.s. intransitive Preterite forms of IIIy verbs: ***baxyono*** 'I (f.) wept' : ***ḥazyono*** 'I (f.) was seen', ***baxyo*** 'she wept' : ***ḥazyo*** 'she was seen', ***baxi*** 'he wept': x; x = ***ḥazi*** 'he was seen'.[7] In Maʿlula, a Western Neo-Aramaic variety, **qaṭṭīl* of intransitive G-stem verbs functions both as a dynamic past

4 If we adhere (as we do) to the *Stammbaum* model in historical linguistics, we cannot accept a hypothesis according to which all NENA known to us had one and the same ancestor in the Middle Aramaic period. Positing a shared ancestor for all NENA is tantamount to claiming that out of all Eastern Middle Aramaic varieties only three had produced progeny that survived into modern times: the ancestor of NENA, the ancestor of Ṭuroyo and Mlaḥsó and the ancestor of Neo-Mandaic.

5 See Coghill (2016), with exhaustive references to earlier studies.

6 See comparative paradigms in Ritter (1990, 378).

7 We owe the suggestion of this analogical development to a personal communication of Paul Noorlander.

verbal form[8] and a stative (or continuous) present tense form, depending on the lexical semantics of the root and even on the utterance context.[9]

By contrast, in both NENA[10] and Neo-Mandaic,[11] reflexes of **qaṭṭīl* have not produced new finite verb forms but rather are extant only in nominal forms (i.e., adjectives and substantives).

In this paper, we restrict the scope of the study to a comparison of the data collected from Classical Syriac and Ṭuroyo. For the Ṭuroyo data, we have drawn upon our Verb Glossary of Ṭuroyo (in progress).[12] According to our glossary of verbs, Ṭuroyo has over 200 verbal roots with a *qaṭəl*-Preterite. Around 100 of them are of Aramaic origin, the majority of the remainder are of Arabic origin.

2. Prehistory of the *Qaṭəl*-Preterite: **Qaṭṭīl* Outside Aramaic and in Early Aramaic

The Ṭuroyo *qaṭəl*-Preterite is the end product of the complete verbalisation of **qaṭṭīl*, originally a deverbal adjective pattern. This pattern (in the guise of *qaṭilo*) still continues in Ṭuroyo for adjectives, including deverbal ones, i.e. as the 'participle' of certain intransitive verbs.[13]

---

8 "Das Perfekt," according to Werner Arnold, see, e.g., Arnold (2006, 22) and Arnold (1999).

9 Compare *tarbil ḳamuʿō ti* ***šawwīlle*** 'the way of stone piles, the one **he had made**' (Arnold 2006, 68, l. 26) with *nḏōb nḥōmyin … šunyōṯun šawwīyan xanni* 'if we see … [that] their wives do so (= are also disloyal to their husbands)' (Bergsträsser 1915, 27: 16f.). See Correll (1978, 63–68) for numerous examples of this verbal form. Correll's interpretation of its grammatical meaning is unfortunately dogmatic. For him, it is "das Resultativpartizip" in virtually all contexts.

10 Nöldeke (1868, 99); Khan (2008, 411).

11 Macuch (1965, 185ff.). See also Macuch (1993, 383) (*hamīm* 'heiß'), Macuch (1993, 116: 193) (*zalīl* 'eng').

12 On the project of the Verb Glossary of Ṭuroyo, see Furman and Loesov (2015).

13 See Jastrow (1967, 117ff., 229ff.)

2.1. The Etymology of *Qaṭṭīl

Diachronically, the verbal adjective *qaṭṭīl developed as follows: *qaṭil* → *qaṭīl* → *qaṭṭīl*.[14] All three patterns have in common that they denoted property adjectives, and as a matter of fact this use is preserved for all the three patterns in various Central Semitic languages, e.g. Biblical Hebrew, Syriac, and Classical Arabic. This use as a property adjective must have been the original one for each of the three derivations in question.

In written Central Semitic languages apart from Aramaic, *qaṭṭīl is well-documented in Biblical Hebrew and Arabic. In both languages, it mostly expresses enduring properties of human beings. The respective nominals may be syntactically both substantives and adjectives, as the following lists illustrate.

Biblical Hebrew (complete list):
ʿallīz 'exultant', *ʿārīṣ* 'violent, powerful', *ʿattīq* 'old; removed, set apart' (<Aram., Wagner 1966, no. 229), *ʾabbīr* 'strong, powerful', *ʾaddīr* 'mighty', *ʾammīṣ* 'strong', *bārīᵃḥ* 'fugitive', *kabbīr* 'strong, mighty', *pārīṣ* 'burglar', *ṣaddīq* 'innocent, just', *šallīṭ* 'having power' (<Aram., Wagner 1966, no. 309), *taqqīp̄* 'mighty' (<Aram., Wagner 1966, no. 330), *yaqqīr* 'precious, dear' (hapax in Jr 31:20; < Aram.?).

Arabic (selected examples):[15]
ʿirrīḍ 'mean, malevolent', *ʿiššīq* 'lover', *ḏikkīr* 'having a retentive memory', *ḍillīl* 'steeped in deviation', *ḏ̣illīm* 'very unfair', *fiḫḫīr* 'self-important', *ḫibbīṯ* 'very bad', *ḫirrīq* 'very generous', *ḫittīr* 'one who frequently acts with treachery', *mirrīḥ* 'joyful'.

Our perusal of dictionaries shows that the lexicon of written Arabic has hardly more than some fifty tokens of the *qaṭṭīl pattern.

14 See Barth (1894, 51), Brockelmann (1908, 354), Bauer and Leander (1927, 192), Kuryłowicz (1973, §46), Fox (2003, 267 f.).

15 Note the "attenuation" *a* > *i* in the first syllable of the base. In Classical Arabic, this is a regular shift *a* > *i*/_ CCī.

2.2. **Qaṭṭīl* in Biblical Aramaic

It is in Aramaic, unlike Arabic and Biblical Hebrew, that **qaṭṭīl* first becomes a productive noun pattern that is regularly derived from verbal roots. Biblical Aramaic (BA) has twelve **qaṭṭīl* derivations, as many as Biblical Hebrew, though the Aramaic Biblical corpus is circa fifty times smaller than that of Hebrew.

**qaṭṭīl* also started its life in Aramaic as an adjective expressing permanent properties. Thus, in Biblical Aramaic, **qaṭṭīl* expresses properties, including the basic lexical items: *ʿammīq* 'deep', *ʿattīq* 'old, aged', *ḥakkīm* 'wise', *ḥassīr* 'wanting, deficient', *qaddīš* 'holy', *raḥḥīq* 'far', *saggī* 'great, much, many', *šallīṭ* 'powerful, mighty', *šappīr* 'beautiful', *taqqīp̄* 'strong, mighty', *yaqqīr* 'difficult, honourable', *yaṣṣīḇ* 'well established', *yattīr* 'extraordinary, exceeding'.

The innovative and productive nature of **qaṭṭīl* in Aramaic of the 1st millennium BC stands in sharp relief when we compare the Biblical Aramaic adjectives from the list above with their Biblical Hebrew cognates, most of which display the patterns **qaṭil*, **qaṭal*, and **qaṭul*, which are retentions from the proto-Semitic stage and no longer productive in Central Semitic: *ʿāmōq* 'deep', *ḥāḵām* 'clever, skillful', *ḥāsēr* 'one in want', *qāḏōš* 'holy', *rāḥōq* 'far', *yāqār* 'scarce, precious, valuable', *yōṯēr* 'excessive'.

Thus Biblical Hebrew adjectives derived from the same roots as BA *qaṭṭīl* adjectives were mostly formed using archaic patterns, while Biblical Hebrew *qaṭṭīl* tokens are scarce and partly borrowed from Aramaic.

Syntactically, these Biblical Aramaic nominals are used as verbal arguments, attributive adjectives and nominal predicates. The *qaṭṭīl* of Biblical Aramaic still behaves syntactically as a nominal. We find, however, one instance where a *qaṭṭīl* adjective derived from a dynamic verb inherits the argument structure of the source verb (2):

(1)	*malkū*	…	*dī*	*ṯi-šlaṭ*	*b-ḵol*
	kingdom.INDET.S		DEP	3FS-rule.PC	in-all

ʾarʿ-ā
land-DET.S

'A kingdom … that will rule in the whole earth.' (Dan 2: 39)

(2)	*w-malḵ-īn*	*taqqīp̄-īn*	*hăw-ō*	*ʿal*
	and-king-INDET.PL	mighty-INDET.PL	be.SC-3MPL	over

yərušlām	*w-šallīṭ-īn*	*b-ḵōl*	*ʿăḇār*
GN	and-rule.QATTĪL-MPL	in-all	crossing.CST.S

nahăr-ā	*w-midd-ā*	*ḇlō*	*wa-hălāḵ*
river-DET.S	and-tribute-DET.S	tribute	and-tribute.INDET.S

miṯyəheḇ	*l-hon*
to.be.given.PTCP.MS	to-3MPL

'And mighty kings were over Jerusalem, and ruling in all Beyond-the-River, and tribute, custom and toll were paid to them.' (Ezra 4: 20)

The syntagm *malḵīn … šallīṭīn b-ḵōl ʿăḇār nahărā* 'kings ruling in all Beyond-the-River' in (2) replicates the argument structure of the finite verb *šlṭ* 'have power, rule'. Both the derivation of a *qaṭṭīl* form (here *šallīṭīn*) from a fairly dynamic verb and its syntactic usage are atypical for Biblical Aramaic and foreshadow the career of *qaṭṭīl* in Middle Aramaic, which is represented in this paper by Classical Syriac.

3. **Qaṭṭīl* in Syriac

We have searched for *qaṭṭīl* tokens in the *Compendious Syriac Dictionary* (CSD, J. Payne Smith 1903) and *Peshitta* New Testament (PNT). In CSD, we have found some 180 *qaṭṭīl* lexemes whose existence seems reliable. Of these, we have found some 64 in the PNT. We have found 207 vocalised words following the *qaṭṭīl* pattern in R. Payne Smith's (1879–1901) *Thesaurus Syriacus* (TS), Sokoloff's (2009) *Syriac Lexicon* (SL) and CAL (the online *Comprehensive Aramaic Lexicon*) alongside CSD. Our principal source is CSD, where the tokens are either independent lemmata, such as *šappīr* 'fair, good, lovely' (CSD, 590), or nominal forms in verb entries, usually labelled 'part. adj.', e.g. *sallīq* (CSD, 379).

Unfortunately, these data cannot be accepted uncritically. The identification, in CSD or TS, of a form as *qaṭṭīl* rather than *qṭīl* is not always reliable. Note that J. Payne Smith employs the term 'part. adj.' in verb entries, both for *qaṭṭīl* and *qṭīl* tokens,[16] while most *qṭīl* tokens she labels as 'pass. part'. In verb entries of CSD, the meanings of nominal forms are not uniformly provided. Furthermore, we have been unable to find textual evidence for several *qaṭṭīl* tokens that appear in the dictionaries.

3.1. From Property Adjective to Verbal Adjective

A major difference between Biblical Aramaic and the Syriac NT regarding *qaṭṭīl* is that in PNT *qaṭṭīl* is formed not only from unambiguous property roots, but also from stative and dynamic verbal roots. Some of the examples are *ʾabbīḏ* 'lost, gone astray', *ʾazzīl* '(is) gone', *ʾattī* 'having come', *ʿallīl* 'having entered', *dabbīq* 'close to, cleaving', *daḥḥīl* 'fearing', *dammīḵ* 'asleep', *naḥḥīṯ* 'having gone down', *tammīh* 'amazed'. It stands to reason that these are used almost exclusively as **predicates** rather than independent nominals or attributive adjectives. Due to their semantics, they cannot be easily employed independently in specifically nominal

16 I.e. for *qṭīl* tokens with non-trivial meanings, in particular those derived from intransitive verbs.

syntactic functions. This means they were formed in order to serve as predicates in the first place, by analogy with the predicative use of the property adjective *qaṭṭīl*. Further research is required to establish the relative chronology of *qaṭṭīl* derivations, i.e. to answer the question which verbs (in terms of the four Vendlerian classes)[17] were the first to form purely predicative *qaṭṭīl* forms. We speculate, however, that it was stative verbs that were the first to produce them, by analogy with property adjectives:

ḥakkīm ʾat 'You are wise' > *tammīh ʾat* 'You are amazed'

The shared feature of the two kinds of clauses is as follows. Both were thought of as **stative**, while *tammīh ʾat* was also **resultative**, i.e., it encoded a **stative** situation that was thought of as 'having come about' rather than a **property** that 'always' existed of itself.

(3)

a.

w-ṯammīh-īn-^{h}waw		*kul-hon*
and-be.amazed.QATTĪL-MPL-PST.3MPL		all-3MPL
ʾaylēn	*d-šāmʿ-īn-^{h}waw*	*l-ęh*
DIST.PL	DEP-listen.PTCP-MPL-PST.3MPL	to-3MS

Greek original (Act 9:21 BNT):

eksista-nto	*de*	*pant-es*
be.amazed.IMPF.REFL-3PL	TOP	every-MPL

hoi	*akou-ont-es*
ART.MPL	listen.PTCP.PRS.ACT-NOM.MPL

'All those who were listening to him **were amazed**.'

---

17 I.e., stative verbs, atelic verbs, telic events (accomplishments), and punctual situations (achievements).

b.

ʾāmr-ā	*l-ęh*	*ʾa^{n}ṯṯā*	*hāy*	*mār-^{y}*	*lā*
say.SC-3FS	to-3MS	woman	VOC	lord-1S	NEG

dawlā	*l-āḵ*	***w-ḇęrā***	***ʿammīqā***
bucket	to-2MS	and-well	deep

Greek original:

leg-ei	*aut-o*	*e*	*gyn-e*
say-PRS.ACT.3S	PRON.PERS-DAT.MS	ART.NOM.FS	woman-NOM.S

Kyri-e,	*oute*	*antlem-a*	*ech-eis*
lord-VOC.MS	and.not	bucket-ACC.NS	have-PRS.ACT.2S

kai	***to***	***phrear***	***est-in***	***bathy***
and	ART.NS	well.NOM.S	be-PRS.ACT.3S	deep.NOM.NS

(Jn 4:11 BYZ)

'The woman told him, My lord, you do not even have a bucket, and **the well is deep.**'

c.

yawsep̄	*dēn*	*baʿl-āh*	***kēʾnā-^{h}wā***
PN	TOP	husband-3FS	honest-PST.3MS

Greek original (Mt 1:19 BNT):

Ioseph	*de*	*ho*	*aner*	*aut-es,*
PN.NOM	TOP	ART.DEF.MS	husband-NOM.S	PRON.PERS-GEN.FS

dikai-os	***on***
righteous-NOM.MS	be.PTCP.PRS.ACT.NOM.MS

'Joseph, her husband, **was a decent man.**'

d. *lḇūš-ęh* ***ḥewwār-ʰwā***
clothes-3MS white-PST.3MS

Greek original (Mt 28:3 BNT):

en *de* *to* *endym-a*
be.IMPF.ACT.3S TOP ART.NOM.NS garment-NOM.NS

aut-ou ***leuk-on***
PRON.PERS-GEN.MS white-NOM.NS

'His clothes **were white.**'

The predicate of (3a) has the same morphological shape *qaṭṭīl* as the predicate of (3b) and the same surface syntax as those of (3c) and (3d), while the predicative adjectives in (3c) and (3d) have morphological patterns other than *qaṭṭīl*. In (3a), *w-****ṯammīhīn-****ʰwaw* (semantically, a stative-resultative predicate) translates the Greek finite (Imperfect) form *eksistanto*, while the *qaṭṭīl*-predicate of (3b), *w-****ḇęrā ʿammīqā*** (semantically, a property adjective), translates the Greek predicative adjective (with the present-tense verbal copula) *estin bathy* 'is deep'. In (3c) and (3d), Syriac predicative property adjectives translate Greek predicative property adjectives (note that in 1d the Syriac adjective is in the determined state).

3.2. From Stative-Resultative to Dynamic Perfect

What one observes in Syriac is a verbalisation stage of *qaṭṭīl* even more advanced than that of a stative-resultative predicate: *qaṭṭīl* lexemes formed from dynamic roots **can take the kinds of verbal arguments and adjuncts that exclude a stative-resultative interpretation**. This means these forms are no longer stative-resultative nominal predicates but rather **dynamic verbal forms**. The contexts show that these verbal forms encode

past events and can express a PERFECT or ANTERIOR. They could be used as translations of past tense forms of the Greek NT texts.

Consider the following examples, which come both from translations and original texts:

(4)

w-ʾen-^{h}ū	*d-šārē-ʾnā*	*l-hon*	*kaḏ*
and-even.if	DEP-dismiss.PTCP.MS-1S	to-3MPL	while

ṣāym-īn	*l-ḇāttay-hon*	*ʿāyp-īn*	*b-ʾurḥā*
fast.PTCP-MPL	to-house.PL-3MPL	be.tired.PTCP-MPL	on-way

gēr	*ʾnāšā*	*men-hon*	***men***	***ruḥqā***	***ʾattīʾ-īn***
for	some	from-3MPL	from	distance	come.QATTĪL-MPL

Greek original (Mk 8:3 BYZ):

kai	*ean*	*apoly-s-o*	*aut-ous*
and	IF	release-AOR-SBJV.ACT.1S	PRON.PERS-ACC.MPL

nest-eis	*eis*	*oik-on*	*aut-on*
hungry-ACC.MPL	(in)to	house-ACC.MS	PRON.PERS-GEN.MPL

ekly-the-sontai	*en*	*te*	*hod-o,*
become.weary-PASS-FUT.3PL	in	ART.DAT.FS	way-DAT.FS

tin-es	*gar*	*auton*	***apo***
PRON.INDF-NOM.MPL	because	PRON.PERS-GEN.MPL	from

makrothen	***hek-asin***
far.away	come.PERF-ACT.3PL

‘And if I let them go home while they are fasting, they will faint on the way, for some of them **have come from far away**.’

(5)

w-ʾezz^{l}-aṯ	*l-ḇayt-āh*	*w-ʾeškḥ-aṯ*
and-go.SC-3FS	to-house-3FS	and-find.SC-3FS

barṯ-āh	*kaḏ*	*ramy-ā*	*b-ʿarsā*
daughter-3FS	while	lie.PTCP.PASS-3FS	on-bed

w-nappīq	*menn-āh*	*šẹʾḏ-āh*
and-go.out.QATTĪL.MS	from-3FS	demon-3FS

Greek original (Mk 7:30 BNT):

kai	*apelth-ousa*	*eis*	*ton*
and	go.away.AOR-PTCP-ACT.NOM.FS	(in)to	ART.ACC.MS

oik-on	*aut-es*	*heur-en*	*to*
house-ACC.MS	PRON.GEN.FS	find.AOR-ACT.3S	ART.ACC.NS

paidi-on	*beble-men-on*	*epi*	*ten*
child-ACC.NS	throw.PRF-PTCP.PASS-ACC.NS	on	ART.ACC.FS

klin-en	*kai*	*to*	*daimoni-on*
bed-ACC.FS	and	ART.ACC.NS	demon-NOM.NS

ekselelyth-os
get.out.PRF.PTCP.ACT-ACC.NS

'She went to her house and found that her daughter was lying upon the bed and that her demon **had gone** out of her.'

(6) *w-īṯeḇ-*^{w} *ba-spī*^{n}*ttā* *w-ʾāṯ-ēn-*^{h}*waw*
and-sit.SC-3MPL on-boat and-go.PTCP-3MPL-PST.3MPL

l-ʿeḇrā *la-ḵp̄arnaḥum* ***w-ḥešk-aṯ-***^{h}***wāṯ***
to-crossing to-GN and-be.dark.SC-3FS-PST.3FS

l-āh *w-lā* *ʾattī-*^{h}*wā* *lwāṯ-hon*
to-3FS and-NEG come.QATTĪL.MS-PST.3MS towards-3MPL

Yešūʿ
PN

Greek original (Jn 6:17 BNT):

kai *emba-nt-es* *eis* *ploi-on*
and get.into.AOR-PTCP.ACT-NOM.MPL into ship-ACC.NS

erch-onto *peran* *tes* *thalass-es*
come-IMPF.MED.3Pl on.the.other.side ART.GEN.FS sea-GEN.FS

eis *Kapharnaoum.* *kai* ***skoti-a*** ***ede***
into GN and darkness-NOM.FS already

egegon-ei *kai* *oupo* *elelyth-ei*
take.place.PLUPRF-ACT.3S and not.yet come.PLUPERF-ACT.3S

pros *aut-ous* ***ho*** ***Iesous***
to PRON-ACC.MPL ART.NOM.MS PN

‘And they sat in a boat and were going to Capernaum. And it became dark, and **Jesus had not** (yet) **come** to them.’

(7) *lā* *ṣḇā* *d-ne-rʿī-w*^{hy}
NEG want.SC.3MS DEP-3MS-meet.PC-ACC.3MS

meṭṭol *d-lā* *ne-ṯʾešeḏ* *dmā* *da-ṯray-hon*
in.order.that DEP-NEG 3MS-shed.PC blood DEP-2-3MPL

gabb-ē *ʾellā* *šaddar* *l-ęh* *b-yaḏ* *Rup̄inā*
side-PL but send.SC.3MS to-3MS by-hand PN

w-p̄aqd-ęh *d-ʾen-*^{h}*ū* *d-ʿal*
and-command.SC.3MS-ACC.3MS DEP-now.if DEP-on

tḥomā *ʾīṯ-aw*^{hy} *Qawwaḏ* *wa-ʿḏakkēl* ***lā***
border COP-3MS PN and-until.now NEG

ʿabbīr *l-ḇēṯ* *r*^{h}*omāy-ē* *ne-ttel*
cross.QATTĪL.MS to-territory Greek-PL 3MS-give.PC

l-ęh *dahḇā* *ne-šrī-w*^{hy}
to-3MS gold 3MS-send.away.PC-ACC.3MS

'(Anastasius) was unwilling to meet him (Qawad) in battle, that blood might not be shed on both sides; but he sent him money by the hand of Rufinus, to whom he gave orders that, if Qawad was on the frontier and **had not yet crossed over** into the Greek territory, he should give him the money and send him away.' (JS 46)

(8) *šūrā* *dēn* *d-Baṭnan Qasṭrā* *d-ḇa-Srug*
wall TOP DEP-GN DEP-in-GN

d-nappīl-^{h}*wā* *wa-mtarraʿ*
DEP-collapse.QATTĪL.MS-PST.3MS and-break.down.PTCP.PASS.MS

kull-ęh	*ʾeṯbannī*	*w-eṯḥaddaṯ*	*ba-šqāl*
all-3MS	rebuild.SC.3MS	and-restore.SC.3MS	by-care

ṭaʿnā	*d-Ewlogis*	*hegmōnā*	*d-Urhāy*
decision	DEP-PN	governor	DEP-GN

‘And the wall of Batnan-Qastra in Serug, which **had collapsed** into ruin, was completely rebuilt and restored by the decision of Eulogius, the governor of Edessa.’ (JS 83)

(9)

ʾap̄en	*lā*	*ʾamīṯ-ęh*	*b-mawtā*
though	NEG	kill.SC.3MS-ACC.3MS	with-death

kyānāyā	*ʾellā*	*b-haw*	*da-ḥṭīṯā*
natural	but	with-DIST.MS	DEP-sin

mayyīṯ-ʰwā
die.QATTĪL.MS-PST.3MS

Though he (God) did not kill him (Adam) with natural death, he **had** still **died** a death of sin (IshGn 064).[18]

In (4) *men ruḥqā ʾattīʾīn*, the adjunct ***men ruḥqā*** ‘from afar’ corroborates a dynamic past interpretation of *ʾattīʾīn*. The same applies to (5) *w-nappīq* ***mennāh*** *šęʾḏāh*. In (6), the two Greek pluperfects (*skotia ede egegonei* and *oupo eleluthei... ho Iesous)* were rendered differently in Syriac. The first one was translated with Preterite + *hwā* (*ḥeškaṯ-ʰwāṯ lāh*), the second by *qaṭṭīl* + *hwā* (*lā ʾattī-ʰwā*). This is because Syriac *ḥaššīḵ* denoted a property with the senses ‘obscure, under a cloud, in darkness, ignorant’

18 I.e., Mar Ishodad of Merv believes that Adam had died a spiritual death of sin even before he left the Garden of Eden.

(CSD, 162), and, therefore, would be inappropriate in this text as a rendering of a dynamic event. In (7), *wa-ʿd̲akkēl lā ʿabbīr l-b̲ēt̲ rʰomāyē*, besides the endpoint of crossing, there is a phasal particle *ʿd̲akkēl* 'not yet', well known for its propensity to combine with a PERFECT. In (8), *šūrā ... d-nappīl-ʰwā ... kulleḥ ʾet̲banni*, the form *nappīl-ʰwā* clearly has an eventive pluperfect force. In (9), *b-haw da-ḥṭīt̲ā mayyīt̲-ʰwā*, the predicate is clearly dynamic.

Thus, *qaṭṭīl* predicates in (4)–(9) are not stative but rather past dynamic (eventive, fientive). Semantically, they are perfects, not resultatives, as we consider (with mainstream functional typology) the RESULTATIVE to be a sub-class of stative situations but the PERFECT to encode dynamic situations.[19]

So, the Syriac evidence for dynamic *qaṭṭīl* points to a 'mature' Perfect, which is employed as both an absolute and a relative tense: i.e., in narrative, a *qaṭṭīl*-Perfect has a reference point different from speech time. In other words, our Syriac *qaṭṭīl*-Perfect can function as both a shifter (or 'deictic') PERFECT and as a PLUPERFECT.[20] In the latter case, it may have an appropriate marker *-(h)wā*,[21] which, as we have seen, may be used with all kinds of nominal predicates in Syriac.

Symmetrically, another innovative construction, *qṭīl leḥ*, provides both active PERFECT and analytical PLUPERFECT for Syriac transitive verbs:[22]

19 We use small caps for linguistic universals, such as PERFECT or PASSIVE.

20 Or as a verb form employed to introduce 'nachgeholte Information' [recovered information], to use an elegant term of Harald Weinrich (1985).

21 It anticipates relative tense markers in Modern Aramaic, which are etymologically related to this *-hwā*.

22 See also numerous examples in Bar-Asher Siegal (2014) and Coghill (2016, 306–27).

(10) *hānnā* *dēn* *meddem* *da-snē* ***lā***
PROX.MS TOP something DEP-wicked NEG

ʿḇīḏ ***l-ẹh***
do.QTĪL.MS to-3MS

Greek original (Lk 23:41 BNT):

hout-os *de* ***oud-en*** *atop-on*
PRON.DEM-NOM.MS TOP PRON.INDEF-ACC.NS wrong-ACC.NS

epraks-en
do.AOR-ACT.3S

'But this one has done nothing bad'

(11) *šḇāḇ-aw^{hy}* *dēn* *w-ʾaylēn* *da-**ḥzē-^{h}wā***
neighbour.PL-3MS TOP and-DIST.PL DEP-see.QTĪL.MS-PST.3MS

l-hon *men* *qḏīm* *d-ḥāḏar-^{h}wā*
to-3MPL from former DEP-beg.PTCP.MS-PST.3MS

ʾāmr-īn-^{h}waw *lā-^{h}wā* *hānnaw* *haw*
say.PTCP-MPL-PST.3MPL NEG-be.SC.3MS PROX.MS DIST.MS

d-yāṯeḇ-^{h}wā *w-ḥāḏar*
DEP-sit.PTCP.MS-PST.3MS and-beg.PTCP.MS

Greek original (Jn 9:8 BNT):

hoi *oun* *geiton-es* *kai* ***hoi***
ART.NOM.PL TOP neighbour-NOM.MPL and ART.NOM.PL

theor-ount-es *aut-on* *to*
see-PTCP.PRES.ACT-NOM.MPL PRON-ACC.MS ART.ACC.NS

proteron	*hoti*	*prosait-es*	*en*
earlier	that	beggar-NOM.MS	be.IMPF.3S

e-leg-on:	*ouch*	*hout-os*	*est-in*
IMPF-say-3PL	not	PRON.DEM-NOM.MS	be-PRS.3S

ho	*kathe-men-os*	*kai*	*prosait-on*
ART.NOM.MS	sit-PTCP.PRS-NOM.MS	and	beg-PTCP.PRS.NOM.MS

'His neighbours and those who **had formerly seen** him begging said, "Isn't this the [same man] who used to sit and beg?"'

These sentences should not be interpreted as passive, since the agents are given prominence by special particles (in both the originals and translations) and by the context.[23] The fact that corresponding verbal forms in the Greek original are active transitive further supports this.

Thus, one could surmise that Classical Syriac might have had a Perfect tense roughly comparable with German or Italian. This Perfect would have had two shapes depending on the respective verb's value of transitivity. In the individual Syriac corpora we have perused, the dynamic *qaṭṭīl* is predominantly derived from intransitive telic verbs of motion, though even in such verbs it is rare. The data of our sample are as follows:

- Aphrahat, *Demonstrations* (written in 337–345 C.E.), 77,505 words. 2 verbs with dynamic *qaṭṭīl*: *ʾbd* 'perish' (2 tokens), *npl* 'fall' (1 token). Total: 3 tokens.[24]
- Peshitta New Testament (PNT) (composed perhaps in the 5th century C.E.), 101,479 words. 4 verbs with dynamic *qaṭṭīl*: *ʾty* 'come' (3 tokens), *ʿll* 'enter' (1 token),

23 In terms of pragmatics, PASSIVE is demotion (most often, deletion) of agent.

24 Aphrahat 10:194, 14:270, 19:360.

ʾbd 'perish' (4 tokens), *npq* 'go out' (1 token). Total: 9 tokens.[25]

- Eusebius, *Church History* (translated into Syriac no later than 462 C.E.), 63,194 words. 4 verbs with dynamic *qaṭṭīl*: *ʾbd* 'perish' (1 token), *ʿrq* 'flee' (1 token), *mrd* 'escape' (1 token), *nḥt* 'go down, land' (3 tokens). Total: 6 tokens.[26]
- Chronicle of Joshua Stylite (written in 507 C.E.), 15,434 words. 2 verbs with dynamic *qaṭṭīl*: *ʿbr* 'cross' (1 token), *npl* (1 token). Total: 2 tokens.[27]
- Ishodad, *Commentary on the Pentateuch* (written around 850 C.E.), 77,252 words. 10 roots with dynamic *qaṭṭīl*: *ʾty* 'come' (1 token), *ʾzl* 'go' (2 tokens), *ʿrq* 'flee' (1 token), *ʾbd* 'perish' (1 token), *myt* 'die' (1 token), *npl* 'fall' (1 token), *npq* 'go out' (1 token), *sgd* 'bow' (1 token), škn 'settle or rest upon' (1 token), *yqd* 'burn (intr.)' (1 token). Total: 11 tokens.[28]
- Bar Ebroyo, *Ecclesiastical History* (written in the 13th century C.E.), 82,373 words. 5 verbs with dynamic *qaṭṭīl*: *ʾty* 'come' (1 token), *ʾzl* (1 token), *ʿll* 'enter' (1 token), *ʿrq* 'flee' (4 tokens), *ḥrb* 'get ruined' (1 token). Total: 8 tokens.[29]

The number of dynamic *qaṭṭīl* tokens in each of the individual corpora is small, but, throughout the nine centuries of Syriac literature examined for this study, the *qaṭṭīl* pattern tends to express the PERFECT consistently in the context of essentially the same tightly-knit group of telic/punctual verbs. In more detailed terms of lexical semantics, these are, for the most part, either verbs of motion or patientive intransitives, such as *ʾbd* 'perish', *myt* 'die', and *ḥrb* 'get ruined'. This fact remains to be explained.

25 Mt 18:11; Mk 7:30, 8:3, 11:20; Lk 8:30, 15:6, 15:9, 19:10; Jn 6:17, 11:19.

26 Eusebius 52, 56, 148, 149, 210, 317.

27 JS 46, 83.

28 IshGn 64, 123, 127, 188; IshEx-Dt 8, 25, 67, 109, 117, 137.

29 BH 1:331, 1:411, 2:783, 3:23, 3:71, 3:311, 3:317, 4:429.

Moreover, throughout our corpus, the grammatical reading of individual deverbal tokens of *qaṭṭīl* still depends on the lexical semantics of the respective verb.[30] For example, in Syriac, *dammīḵ* invariably denotes 'he is asleep' (not 'he fell/has fallen asleep'). It expresses a state contemporaneous with a reference point, as observed in (12):

(12)	*w-hā*	*zawʿā*	*rabbā-^{h}wā*	*b-yammā*	*ʾaykannā*
	and-TOP	moving	great-PST.3MS	in-sea	so that

d-ʾelpā	*te-ṯkassē*	*men*	*gall-ē,*	*hū*	*dēn*
DEP-boat	3FS-be.covered.PC	by	wave-PL	3S	TOP

Yešūʿ	***dammīḵ-^{h}wā***
PN	sleep.QATTĪL.MS-PST.3MS

Greek original (Mt 8:24 BYZ):

kai	*idou,*	*seism-os*	*megas*
and	TOP	shaking-NOM.MS	large.NOM.MS

e-gen-eto	*en*	*te*	*thalass-e,*
AOR-occur-MED.3S	in	ART.DAT.FS	sea-DAT.FS

hoste	*to*	*ploi-on*	*kalypt-esthai*
so.that	ART.ACC.NS	ship-ACC.S	hide-INF.PRS.PASS

hupo	*ton*	*kymat-wn;*	*aut-os*
under	ART.GEN.NPL	wave-GEN.NPL	himself-PRON.NOM.MS

de	***e-katheud-en***
TOP	IMPF-sleep-3S

30 As against Ṭuroyo, where all finite *qatəl* forms have the perfective aspectual reading. Thus, *daməx* is 'he slept', 'he fell asleep', see below.

'And look, a great commotion arose in the sea, so that the boat was being covered by waves. But he, Jesus, **was asleep.'**

The predicate ***dammīḵ-ʰwā*** is a translation of the Greek Imperfect ***e-katheud-en*** 'was sleeping/asleep.'

Most importantly, this is the only token of *dammīḵ* in the standard text of the Peshitta for both OT and NT.[31] Otherwise, in this corpus, the situation 'be asleep' is rendered by the adjective *dmeḵ* for the Present (e.g., Mark 5:39 PNT) and *dmeḵ-ʰwā* for the Past (e.g., Acts 12:6 PNT). It stands to reason that the morphological form of the Syriac adjective *dmeḵ* is a reflex of the archaic pattern **qaṭil,* no longer productive in Central Semitic (see Sections 1.1. and 1.2 above). Thus, *dammīḵ* is an inner-Syriac innovation that had not existed in earlier Aramaic. The same applies to *nappīq* and *ʾattī*. By contrast, ṭuroyo *damǝx* corresponding to Syriac *dammīḵ* expresses 'he fell asleep', while *damixo*, the erstwhile determined form, means 'asleep', e.g. *ono damíxo-no* 'I am asleep'.

3.3. Summary

In sum, throughout our Syriac sample, *qaṭṭīl* derivations of intransitive **telic** verbs have the force of the PERFECT (or a PLUPERFECT when used as relative tense with a reference point in the past in narrative). Yet, their use to express these grammatical meanings is not obligatory, because *qṭal* also appears with the same functions in texts. Consider three Syriac renderings of the same Greek verse, Jn 6:17:[32]

31 The manuscript tradition has preserved a few more occurrences of *dammīḵ* where the standard text has *dmeḵ* or *dāmeḵ* (e.g., Act 12:6).

32 See Kiraz (1996, 100f.)

(13) *w-iṯeḇ*^{w} *ba-spī*^{n}*ttā w-ʾāṯēn-*^{h}*waw l-ʿeḇrā la-Ḵp̄arnaḥum w-ḥeškaṯ-*^{h}*wāṯ lāh* ***w-lā ʾattī-***^{h}***wā*** *lwāṯhon Yešūʿ* (PNT).

(PNT) ***w-lā*** ***ʾattī-***^{h}***wā***

and-NEG come.QATTĪL.MS-PST.3MS

w-iṯeḇ^{w} *ba-spī*^{n}*ttā w-ʾāṯēn-*^{h}*waw l-ʿeḇrā la-Ḵp̄arnaḥum mettol d-ḥeškaṯ-*^{h}*wāṯ lāh* ***w-lā ʾeṯā-***^{h}***wā*** *lwāṯhon Yešūʿ* (S).

(S) ***w-lā*** ***ʾeṯā-***^{h}***wā***

and-NEG come.PST.3MS-PST.3MS

w-iṯeḇ^{w} *ba-spī*^{n}*ttā w-ʾāṯēn-*^{h}*waw l-ʿeḇrā d-yamṯā la-Ḵp̄arnaḥum w-ḥeškaṯ-*^{h}*wāṯ lāh* ***w-lā ʾeṯā*** *lwāṯhon Yešūʿ* (C).

(C) ***w-lā*** ***ʾeṯā***

and-NEG come.PST.3MS

'And they sat in a boat and were going to Capernaum. And it became dark, and **Jesus had not** (yet) **come** to them.'

In PNT, the 'pluperfect' sense is rendered by the *qaṭṭīl* form, while S uses the *qṭal*, and C uses the *qṭal-wā* form.

In the Classical Syriac corpus, *qaṭṭīl* need not be restricted to derivations of telic verbs to express the PERFECT. Thus, *tammīh* sometimes has the meaning 'he became amazed', and even *yabbīš* in certain contexts seems to express 'it has dried up' (cf. Mk 11: 20 PNT). These facts will hopefully be dealt with in the course of our further research.

4. The Development from an Assumed Middle Aramaic Ancestor of Ṭuroyo to the Ṭuroyo of Today

The transition from the Middle Aramaic past-tense repertoire to the Neo-Aramaic repertoire of Ṭuroyo seems broadly straightforward. The new Perfect (*qaṭṭīl*) takes root and its use increases exponentially, and finally ousts the old Preterite (*qṭal*) to become the basic Past tense. This follows the well-known typological pathway, which is found, for example, in Western European languages like French, certain dialects of Italian and most of contemporary German.

Our aim is to trace the development of the Ṭuroyo verbal system in as much detail as possible. This study is still in progress. For the moment, we have undertaken a comparison of *qaṭṭīl* formations found in CSD with approximately one hundred Ṭuroyo verbs of Aramaic origin that have *qaṭəl*-Preterites. It stands to reason that Proto-Ṭuroyo was not identical to Edessan Syriac, yet we have no better starting point for a diachronic study of Ṭuroyo than Syriac.

We have found around 50 overlaps between the two groups of verbs. Some 50 intransitive Syriac verbs with *qaṭṭīl* attested in CSD have direct correspondences in Ṭuroyo and have a *qaṭəl*-Preterite, while the rest of them (i.e., approximately 130 verbs with *qaṭṭīl*-derivations) are not in our Verb Glossary of Ṭuroyo and, therefore, most probably have not survived into this language.

The surviving verbs can be neatly divided into two semantic groups: motion and state-and-property (including body posture). In the table below, we present 14 Ṭuroyo motion verbs with Aramaic etymology out of 50 in total. The leftmost column of the table provides glosses of Syriac verbs whose *qaṭṭīl* forms stand in the next column. In the Ṭuroyo column, we adduce special glosses for Ṭuroyo when the meanings do not match the Syriac ones and we give the Preterite forms of the etymologically related Ṭuroyo verbs.

Table 1: Syriac and Ṭuroyo Correspondences of *Qaṭṭīl

Gloss	Syriac	Ṭuroyo
go	*ʾazzīl*	*azzé*
come	*ʾattī*	*aṯi*
go down	*naḥḥīṯ*	*naḥət*
fall	*nappīl*	*nafəl*
go out	*nappīq*	*nafəq*
go up	*sallīq*	*saləq*
flee, escape	*ʿarrīq*	*ʿarəq*
escape	*pallīṭ*	*faləṭ*
stand up	*qayyīm*	*qayəm*
run	*rahhīṭ*	*rahəṭ*
quiver	*raʿʿīl*	*raʿəl*
be in motion, tremble	*zayyīʿ*	*zayəʿ* **'fear'**
sink	*ṭabbīʿ*	*ṭawəʿ* also **'fall asleep'; 'set'** (sun)
cross	*ʿabbīr*	*ʿabər* **'enter'**

Also worth mentioning is the Syriac verb *rkb* 'mount, bestride, ride (a horse)'. CSD (541) only mentions *rḵīḇ* and not the expected **rakkīḇ*. Cognate verbs in Ṭuroyo include ***raku/roku*** 'to get on, to mount (vehicle, horse *ʿal*)'; ***raxu/roxu*** 'ride, mount (horse)'. Note also *lawišo* 'wearing, clothed', while CSD (235) records *lḇīš* rather than **labbīš*.

Thus, as far as the correspondences of geminated R_2-stops in Ṭuroyo go, we have *ʾattī* vs. *aṯi*, *ṭabbīʿ* vs. *ṭawəʿ*, *ʿabbīr* vs. *ʿabər*. Additional relevant examples from our comparative list include *yattīḇ* 'sitting, seated' (CSD, 198f.) vs. *yatu* 'he sat down', *sabbīʿ* 'full, satisfied' (CSD, 358) vs. *sawəʿ* 'he became full/satiated', and *rabbīʿ* (CSD, 526: "pass. part." of *rḇaʿ* 'lie down, couch; recline') vs. *rawəʿ* 'it lied down, rested (animals)', *rakkīḵ* 'soft, gentle' (CSD

540) vs. *rakəx* 'it became soft',[33] *rattīḵ* 'fervent, enthusiastic' (CSD 552) vs. *raṯəx* 'to seethe'. The behaviour of second radical stops vs. spirants appears to be unpredictable.[34] This means that, e.g., *aṯi* is not an immediate reflex (or a direct descendent) of *ʾattī*. The implication is that the *qaṭəl*-Preterite was derived directly from the 'new' (Neo-Aramaic) root at a certain stage of development, and in no instance is it a continuation of the corresponding Syriac *qaṭṭīl* form.

Our preliminary conclusions are as follows.

We do not know whether *qaṭṭīl* became an inflectional form that was available for every intransitive verb in the ancestor of Ṭuroyo. (This is a possibility we have been entertaining for a long time in the course of our research.) Due to a lack of adequate Syriac textual corpora at our disposal, it is difficult to identify textual examples even for the 180 *qaṭṭīl* lexemes recorded in CSD.

Since, phonologically, numerous tokens of the Ṭuroyo Preterite *qaṭəl* and the deverbal adjective *qaṭilo* do not go back directly to the corresponding forms attested in Syriac, we believe that all the inflectional forms of Ṭuroyo verbs were derived at a certain period synchronically from the new roots, whether of Aramaic or Arabic origin. This means that we can neither prove nor refute the existence of a Middle Aramaic stage at which a productive finite form of *qaṭṭīl* of intransitive verbs existed. Finally, the diachronic background for plosive or spirant realisation of etymological stops in Ṭuroyo has to be studied in its own right, as a step forward in the reconstruction of Proto-Ṭuroyo.

Abbreviations

Bibliographical Abbreviations

Aphrahat *The Homilies of Aphraates, The Persian Sage.* Edited by W. Wright. Vol. 1. The Syriac Text. 1869. London: Williams and Norgate.

33 On this verb, see Furman and Loesov (2016, 41).

34 See also Jastrow (2015, 240).

BH	*Gregorii Barhebrœi Chronicon Ecclesiasticum.* Ediderunt Joannes Baptista Abbeloos et Thomas Josephus Lamy. 1872. T. 1. Lovanii: Peeters; 1874. T. 2. Parisiis: Maisonneuve, Lovanii: Peeters; 1877. T. 3. Parisiis: Maisonneuve, Lovanii: Peeters.
BNT	*Nestle-Aland Novum Testamentum Graece.* 1994. Stuttgart: Deutsche Bibelgesellschaft.
BYZ	*The New Testament in the Original Greek: Byzantine Textform.* Compiled and Arranged by Maurice A. Robinson and William G. Pierpont. Southborough: Chilton Book Publishing. 2005.
C	Curetonian Gospels
CAL	Comprehensive Aramaic Lexicon, http://cal.huc.edu/
CSD	Payne Smith, Jessie. 1957. *A Compendious Syriac Dictionary. Founded upon the Thesaurus Syriacus of R. Payne Smith, D. D.* Edited by J. Payne Smith (Mrs. Margoliouth).
Eusebius	*The Ecclesiastical History of Eusebius in Syriac.* Edited from the Manuscripts by William Wright and Norman McLean. 1898. Cambridge: The University Press.
IshGn	*Commentaire d'Išoʿdad de Merv sur l'Ancient Testament. I. Genèse.* Édité par J.-M. Voste et Ceslas van den Eynde. 1950. Louvain: Secrétariat du CorpusSCO.
IshEx-Dt	*Commentaire d'Išoʿdad de Merv sur l'Ancient Testament. II. Exode-Deutéronome.* Édité par Ceslas van den Eynde. 1958. Louvain: Secrétariat du CorpusSCO.
JS	*The Chronicle of Joshua the Stylite, composed in Syriac A.D. 507.* Translated by W. Wright. 1882. Cambridge: The University Press.
PNT	Peshitta New Testament. 1979. ܟܬܒܐ ܕܕܝܬܩܐ ܚܕܬܐ in ܟܬܒܐ ܩܕܝܫܐ ܗ̄. ܟܬܒܐ ܕܕܝܬܩܐ ܥܬܝܩܬܐ ܘܚܕܬܐ. Damascus: Syrian Patriarchate of Antioch and all the East.
S	Syriac Sinaiticus Gospels
SL	*A Syriac Lexicon.* A Translation from the Latin, Correction, Expansion, and Update of C. Brockelmann's Lexicon Syriacum: Michael Sokoloff. 2009. Indiana: Eisenbrauns, Piscataway: Gorgias Press.
TS	Payne Smith, Robert. 1879–1901. *Thesaurus Syriacus.* T. I–II. Oxonii: E Typographeo Clarendoniano.

Glossing Abbreviations not in the Leipzig Glossing List

CST	construct state
DEP	dependent, i.e. the marker of an embedded clause or the dependent within a noun phrase
DET	determined state
GN	geographic name
INDET	indetermined state
PC	prefix conjugation
PN	proper noun
SC	suffix conjugation

References

Arnold, Werner. 1999. 'Das Verbum in den neuwestaramäischen Dialekten'. In *Tempus und Aspekt in den Semitischen Sprachen: Jenaer Kolloquium zur semitischen Sprachwissenschaft*, edited by Norbart Nebes, 1–8. Wiesbaden: Harrasowitz Verlag.

———. 2006. *Lehrbuch des Neuwestaramäischen.* Wiesbaden: Harrasowitz Verlag.

Bar-Asher Siegal, Elitzur A. 2014. 'From a Non-Argument-Dative to an Argument-Dative: The Character and Origin of the Qṭīl Lī Construction in Syriac and Jewish Babylonian Aramaic'. *Folia Orientalia* 51: 59–101.

Barth Jacob. 1927. *Die Nominalbildung in den semitischen Sprachen.* Leipzig: J. C. Hinrichs'sche Buchhandlung.

Bauer, Hans and Leander, Pontus. 1927. *Grammatik des Biblisch-Aramäischen.* Halle.

Bergsträsser, Gotthelf. 1915. *Neuaramäische Märchen und andere Texte aus Maʿlūla.* Leipzig: F. A. Brockhaus.

Brockelmann, Carl. 1908. *Grundriss der vergleichenden Grammatik der semitischen Sprachen.* Berlin: Verlag von Reuther & Reichard.

Coghill, Eleanor. 2016. *The Rise and Fall of Ergativity in Aramaic: Cycles of Alignment Change.* Oxford: Oxford University Press.

Corell, Christoph. 1978. *Untersuchungen zur Syntax der neuwestaramäischen Dialekte des Antilibanon* (Maᶜlūla, Baḫᶜa, Ǧubbᶜadīn).

Fox, Joshua. 2003. *Semitic Noun Patterns*. Winona Lake: Eisenbrauns.

Furman, Yulia and Sergey Loesov. 2015. 'Studies in the Ṭuroyo Verb'. In *Neo-Aramaic and its Linguistic Context*, edited by Geoffrey Khan and Lidia Napiorkowska, 1–28. Piscataway.

———. 2016. 'Notes on Historical Morphology of Turoyo'. *Babel und Bibel* 9:37–53.

Jastrow, Otto. 1967. 'Laut- und Formenlehre des neuaramäischen Dialekts von Miḏin im Ṭur 'Abdin'. Inaugural-Dissertation. Bamberg, 1967.

———. 2015. 'Language Contact as Reflected in the Consonant System of Ṭuroyo' in *Semitic Languages in Contact*, edited by Aaron Michael Butts, 234–50. Leiden.

Khan, Geoffrey. 2008. *The Neo-Aramaic Dialect of Barwar*. Vol. 1–3. Leiden, Boston: Brill.

Kiraz, George Anton. 1996. *Comparative Edition of the Syriac Gospels: Aligning the Sinaiticus, Curetonianus, Peshîṭtâ and Ḥarklean Versions*. Vol IV. Leiden, New York, Köln: Brill.

Kuryłowicz, Jerzy. 1973. *Studies in Semitic Grammar and Metrics*. London: Curzon Press.

Loesov, Sergey. 2013. 'A New Attempt at Reconstructing Proto-Aramaic (Part II)'. In *Proceedings of the 14th Italian Meeting of Afroasiatic Linguistics*, edited by Alessandro Mengozzi and Mawro Tosco, 91–106.

Macuch, Rudolf. 1965. *Handbook of Classical and Modern Mandaic*. Berlin: Walter de Gruyter.

———. 1993. *Neumandäische Texte Im Dialekt von Ahwāz*. Wiesbaden: Harrassowitz.

Nöldeke, Theodor. 1868. *Grammatik der neusyrischen Sprache: am Urmia-See und in Kurdistan*. Leipzig: T. O. Weigel.

Ritter, Hellmut. 1990. *Ṭūrōyo: Die Volkssprache der syrischen Christen des Ṭūr ʿAbdîn. C: Grammatik. Pronomen, „sein, vorhanden sein', Zahlwort, Verbum*. Stuttgart: Franz Steiner Verlag.

Wagner, Max. 1966. *Die lexikasischen und grammatikalischen Aramaismen im alttestamentlichen Hebräisch*. Berlin: Verlag Alfred Töpelmann.Weinrich, Harald. 1985. *Tempus: Besprochene und erzählte Welt*. Stuttgart: Kohlhammer.

TOWARDS A TYPOLOGY OF POSSESSORS AND EXPERIENCERS IN NEO-ARAMAIC: NON-CANONICAL SUBJECTS AS RELICS OF A FORMER DATIVE CASE

Paul M. Noorlander

Introduction[1]

Predicative possessors and impersonal experiencer constructions are encoded by the dative preposition *l-* across Semitic languages, in addition to Aramaic, Hebrew (e.g. Berman 1982) and Syrian Arabic (e.g. Cowell 1964; Al-Zahre and Boneh 2010, 250). Like most non-European languages, Semitic languages do not have a designated possession verb. Predicative possessors equivalent to English *have* are based on locational expressions of prepositional possessor (Stassen 2009), as illustrated for Hebrew in (1a-b) below.

(1) Israeli Hebrew

PREDICATIVE POSSESSOR

a. *yeš* ***le-Dan*** *sefer*
there.is to-Dan book.MS
'**Dan has** a book.'

---

1 Preparation of this article was made possible by funding from the Dutch Research Council (NWO).

 https://doi.org/10.11647/OBP.0209.02

b. *yeš* ***l-i*** *sefer*
there.is to-me book
'**I have** a book.'

Predicative possessors are originally intransitive constructions where the existential element agrees or used to agree with the possessee. It is a common phenomenon, sometimes termed 'HAVE-drift' (Stassen 2009), that predicative possession undergoes transitivisation by assimilation of its morphosyntax to that of more typical and frequent agent-patient verb constructions because of their matching semantic-pragmatic properties (Stassen 2009, 208–43). While the agent-like possessor is still prepositional, the possessee has grammaticalised to a full-fledged object in colloquial Israeli Hebrew. It can be marked differentially by the object marker *et*, for example:

c. *yeš* *le-Dan* ***et*** ***ha-sefer***
there.is to-Dan DOM the-book.MS
'Dan has **the book**.'

d. *yeš* *l-i* ***ot-o***
there.is to-him DOM-him
'I have got him.'

Similarly, the preposition *l-* expresses the experiencer in impersonal experiencer verb constructions, as illustrated for Israeli Hebrew in (1e-f). The adjective or verb denoting the mental state is non-referential ms., while the subject-like experiencer is introduced by *l-*.

IMPERSONAL EXPERIENCERS

e. *kar* ***le-Dan***
cold.MS to-Dan
'**Dan** is cold.'

f. *kar* ***l-i***
cold.MS to-me
'**I** am cold.'

The same preposition can also mark so-called external possessors. The possessor is not dependent on the nominal possessee itself but is expressed as an affectee part of the verbal predicate, for example:

EXTERNAL POSSESSOR

g. *avad* ***le-Dan*** *ha-tik.*
lost.3MS to-Dan the-file.MS
'The file got lost **on Dan.**' (Berman 1982, 41)

h. *ima* *raxaṣa* ***le-Dan*** *et* *ha-panim.*
mom washed.3FS to-Dan DOM the-face
'Mom washed **Dan's** face (for him).' (ibid. 47)

Such prepositional arguments can also be optionally added to co-refer to the subject with various semantic nuances such as (1i) below. Such subject-coreferential datives are also known as ethic or ethical datives (*dativus ethicus*) in Semitic linguistics[2].

2 See Fassberg (2018) for a recent survey of its use in Hebrew, Arabic and Aramaic with ample references.

SUBJECT CO-REFERENTIAL DATIVE

i.	*ha-yeladim*	*histalku*	***la-hem***
	the-children	ran.away.3PL	to-them

'The kids (**upped** and) ran away.' (ibid. 51)

All of these constructions are, of course, semantically and formally related to the expression of the recipient of ditransitive constructions in denoting often highly animate, typically human affectees (e.g. Berman 1989, 49; Næss 2007, 185–208).

Such subject-like prepositional affectees have been argued to be a common trait of Northwest Semitic (e.g. Pat-El 2018). Both full nominals and pronouns are marked prepositionally in all of the constructions illustrated above. Most Semitic languages lost case inflection presumably through phonetic erosion and other forces of change such as increasing fixation of word order. Thus instead of case declensions Neo-Semitic languages use zero-marked nouns and independent pronouns as the default citation form. They developed differential marking strategies of definite nominals, including cross-referencing through pronominal affixes.[3]

Typically, the predicative possessor and the experiencer of impersonal experiencer verb constructions are marked by the same preposition *l-* and its allomorphs in Late Antique Aramaic languages such as Syriac. A key difference in Syriac is the optional use of additional 'pronominal copies'. That is, prepositional person markers that cross-reference a co-nominal. In (2a) below, for example, the prepositional possessor (*l-ḡaḇrå ḥaḏ*) is referred back to by a prepositional person marker (*l-eh*). The same holds for the experiencer in (2b).

3 See Khan (1988); Kapeliuk (1989); Rendsburg (1991); Goldenberg (1997); Rubin (2005).

(2) Classical Syriac

a.

l-ḡaḇrå	***ḥaḏ***	*ʾiṯ-wa-w*	***l-eh***
to-man.MS	one.MS	EXST-was-3MPL	to-him
tren	*bnin*		
two.M	son.MPL		

'A certain man had two sons (lit. Him were two sons).' (Luke 15:11, *Curetonian*)

b.

kery-aṯ	***l-hun***	***l-ḡaḇre***	
grieved-3FS	to-them.M	to-man.MP	
w-eṯ-beš-∅		***l-hun***	*ṭåḇ*
and-MEDP-be.bad-S.3MS		to-them.M	well

'The men were grieved and very angry (Them grieved it$_{F}$ and angered it$_{M}$).' (Genesis 34:7, *Pšiṭta*)

The possessor is stripped of its prepositional marking and becomes a zero-marked noun or pronoun, when it undergoes topicalisation. Its grammatical function as possessor or experiencer has to be resumed by the prepositional person marker such as *l-eh* in the following examples.

c.

gaḇrå	***ḥaḏ***	*ʾiṯ-wa-w*	***l-eh***
man.MS	one.MS	EXST-was-3MPL	to-him
tren	*bnin*		
two.M	son.MPL		

'A certain man had (lit. Him were) two sons.' (Luke 15:11, *Sinaiticus*)

d. ***malka***... *kery-aṯ* ***l-eh*** *saggi*

king.MS grieved-3FS to-him much

'The king (who judged Daniel) felt very sorry (lit. Him grieved it_F).' (*Aphrahat* XXI: 411.20)

Such agreement markers emerge out of topicalisation constructions through increasing obligatorisation (e.g. Givón 1976; Lehmann 1988, 62; cf. Diem 2012; Mor and Pat-El 2016) and accordingly transitivisation (see above). That is, the clause-initial position without prepositional marking is favoured for discourse topics. This position grammaticalises for 'non-canonical' subjects on the model of the 'canonical' subject in other clauses (i.e. transitivitisation) where sentence-initial position of the subject has become the default position. The remaining cross-referencing prepositional pronoun becomes effectively an inflectional cross-index like verbal affixes.

Neo-Aramaic languages have a set of person markers generally known as the L-suffixes that historically go back to such dative person markers based on the preposition *l-*. In a similar fashion as (2c-d) above, these L-suffixes are used to express the predicative possessor and impersonal experiencer, for example in the dialects of Ṭur ʿAbdin, i.e. Ṭuroyo (3a-b), and Christian dialect of Urmia, i.e. C. Urmi, (4a-b):

(3) Ṭuroyo (Kfaerze, SE Turkey; Ritter 1967–1971)

a. ***ú-həmmāl-ano*** *kət-way-**le*** *əštó-abne.*

the-carrier.MS-DEM.MS EXST-PST-him six-sons.MPL

'**This carrier** had six sons.' (63/2)

b. ***ú-bab-ayðe*** *ʿayəq-∅-**le**.*

the-father.MS-his become.upset-it.M-him

'**His father** got angry.' (60/34)

(4) C. Urmi (NW Iran; Khan 2016, transcription modified)

a. ***ʾaha*** ***malka*** *ʾət-va-**lə***

DEM.MS king.MS EXST-PST-him

⁺t̬la *bnunə*

three sons.MPL

‘**This king** had three sons.’ (A39:1)

b. ***ʾalaha*** *la* *basm-a-**lə**.*

God.MS NEG please$_{\text{IPFV}}$-it.F-him

‘It$_{\text{F}}$ does not please **God**.’ (A3:68)

This article is a comparative survey of the morphological properties of such possessors and experiencers in Neo-Aramaic, concentrating on North-Eastern Neo-Aramaic (NENA) and Central Neo-Aramaic (i.e. Ṭuroyo and Mlaḥsó). Some comparative remarks concerning Western Neo-Aramaic will also be made. The data are mostly from NENA and Ṭuroyo grammatical descriptions[4] and fieldwork I conducted personally in the diaspora

4 For ease of comparison and accessibility, the various styles of transcription have been made uniform as follows. The reduced centralised vowel ([ɪ] ~ [ə] (~ [ɯ])) sometimes represented as <i>, <ı>, <ɨ>, <ĭ>, or <ə> is represented by the single grapheme <ə>.The voiceless and voiced interdental fricatives are marked by <θ> and <ð>, respectively, (as against <ṯ>, respectively, <ḏ> in some sources), and the pharyngeal and glottal stop by <ʕ> and <ʾ> (against half rings <ʿ> and <ʾ> in some sources). Post-velar unaspirated /k̭/, in for example C. Urmi (Khan 2016), corresponding with /q/ in other dialects, is represented by <q> for simplicity’s sake. Moreover, I have taken the liberty to adapt Prym and Socin (1881) and Ritter’s (1967–1971) detailed transcription of Ṭuroyo to a phonological transcription that matches NENA more closely like that of Jastrow (1992). Emphasis and glossing are mine in examples, unless stated otherwise.

or in collaboration with G. Khan and/or D. Molin in Iraq[5] and with D. Molin in Jerusalem. There are notable differences and resemblances across Neo-Aramaic dialects, some of which go back to pre-modern Aramaic.

As the term used for these person markers already suggests, the L-suffixes are no longer prepositional in nature but have become inflectional suffixes. While their use in these constructions is still reminiscent of a formerly dative case, synchronically, they are no longer prepositional but serve to cross-index arguments in the clause. Obligatorisation of such cross-indexing is a well-known feature of the 'canonical' subject relation (e.g. Keenan 1976; Onishi 2001) contrary to objects, the marking of which remains conditioned by discourse-referential properties (e.g. Haig 2018a). Do these L-suffixes express a 'non-canonical' subject? To what extent have these L-suffixes become obligatory? And to what extent do they still interact with prepositional arguments? As we shall see, dialects have different strategies and not all of them operate on the same level as (2c-d) above.

First, we shall briefly review verbal inflection and how the recipient is expressed in ditransitive constructions. These findings are compared with the morphosyntax of predicative possessors and (impersonal) experiencer verb constructions in both subgroups of Neo-Aramaic.

1. A Synopsis of Argument Marking in NENA and Ṭuroyo

1.1. Role Reference Inversion

Verbal person marking in NENA and Ṭuroyo is considerably complex and cannot be treated in full detail here.[6] Historically, verbal inflection goes back to participial constructions that

5 Data collection in Iraq was made possible by GCRF funding.

6 Overviews of the morphosyntax in NENA and Ṭuroyo can be found in Khan (2010), Coghill (2016, 55–101), Waltisberg (2016) and Noorlander (2018b, forthcoming).

combined with clitic person markers. Two sets of person markers are used. They will be referred to as the E-suffixes and L-suffixes, which are respectively diachronically enclitic pronouns and participial agreement (E-suffixes) and prepositional pronouns based on *l* (L-suffixes). These are attached to the following inflectional bases. The imperfective base is derived from the active participle and the perfective base is derived from a verbal adjective that expressed result states. I will refer to themas *qaṭəl-* (< **qāṭel-*) and *qṭil-* respectively after the inflection of stem I strong verbs. The NENA *qaṭəl*-base corresponds to Ṭuroyo *qoṭəl-*, where **ā* has shifted to /o/ in open syllables. A so-called neuter class of mainly intransitive verbs in Ṭuroyo follows the pattern C_1*a*C_2*i*C_3 in the perfective, such as *damixo* 'she slept' for *dmx*. Historically, this goes back to a verbal adjective with a geminate second consonant, e.g. **dammīḵ* 'asleep', which should not be confused with NENA *qaṭəl-*.

Transitive clauses show a type of role reference inversion[7] conditioned by these inflectional bases (Noorlander forthcoming). The roles that the E-suffixes and L-suffixes refer to are different depending whether they attach to the imperfective or perfective base. This can be seen, for instance, in the following examples from Amidya (NW Iraq). While the L-suffixes mark the object in the *qaṭəl*-base for the verb *šmʾ* 'hear', they mark the agent in the *qṭil*-base, and *vice versa* for the E-series.

(5) Imperfective (J. Amidya, NW Iraq; Hoberman 1989, 102–04)

a. *k-šamʾ-i* *baxta*

IND-hear$_{\text{IPFV}}$-they woman

'They hear a woman.'

7 Or "agreement inversion" (Doron and Khan 2012). See also Polotsky (1979, 209; 1991, 266; 1994, 95), Hoberman (1989:96, 113), Mengozzi (2002b, 44–5), Noorlander (2018b, 119–23, 129, 408–10).

b. *k-šamʾ-i-**la**.*

IND-hear$_{IPFV}$-they-her

'They hear **her**.'

(6) Perfective (J. Amidya, NW Iraq; Hoberman ibid.)

a. *šmeʾ-lu* *baxta.*

hear$_{PFV}$-they woman

'They heard a woman.'

b. *šmiʾ-**a**-lu.*

hear$_{PFV}$-her-they

'They heard **her**.'

Prominent objects are marked differentially via cross-indexing and/or prepositional marking. The definite object in (7) below, for instance, is marked consistently by the preposition (*ʾəl*)*l*- and triggers agreement throughout the constructional *qaṭəl-/qṭil*-split. In (7a), however, the L-suffix attached to *qaṭəl*- cross-indexes the object, whereas the E-suffix attached to *qṭil*- does so in in (7b).

(7) J. Arbel (NE Iraq; Khan 1999, 288–90)

a. ***ʾəl- ləxmá*** *mapé -ni -wā* ***-le***

DOM bread.MS bake$_{IPFV}$ -they -PST -it.M

'They baked (lit. it) **the bread**.'

b. *kābrá* ***lə- ʾanne beʾé*** *zəbn* ***-i*** *-le*

man.MS DOM- DEM.PL egg.PL sold$_{PFV}$ -them -he

'The man sold (lit. them) **those eggs**.'

In addition, agent focus can be expressed optionally by means of the preposition *(e)l-* combined with the agreement through L-suffixes in Ṭuroyo. The prepositional marking of the object and the agent are both optional. Additional cross-indexing of a prominent object is also optional in Ṭuroyo.[8] Contrast (8a) with (8b) below. Type (8b) is peculiar to the dialect of Raite (Waltisberg 2016, 186f.). Both can also be lacking altogether, as illustrated in (8c). The L-suffix that expresses the agent, however, is obligatory, cf. (8d) and (8e) below. Hence optional ergative prepositional marking is always accompanied by an agent L-suffix as illustrated in (8c).

(8) Ṭuroyo (SE Turkey)

	[V	-A	-O]	[*l*→O]
a.	*k-ŭð^c^*	*-i*	***-le***	***l-u-zlām***
	IND-know$_{IPFV}$	-they	-him	DOM-the-man.M

‘They know **the man**.’ (Miden, Ritter 1967–1971, 81/49)

	[V-A]	[*l*→O]
b.	*g-ḥoze-∅*	***l-i-dăvăre***
	FUT-see$_{IPFV}$-he	DOM-the-breach.M

‘He will find **the breach** (in the wall).’ (Raite, ibid. 107/90)

	[V-A]		[O]
c.	*lo*	*k-ḥoze-∅*	***ú-aḥuno***
	NEG	PVB-see$_{IPFV}$-he	the-brother.M

‘He does not find **his brother**’ (Raite, ibid. 97/113)

8 See Waltisberg (2016, 189–90) for more examples.

	[V-A]	[*l*→A]	[O]
d.	*ḥze-**le***	***l-u-Ṭayawo***	*u-med-ano*
	saw_{PFV}-he	ERG-the-Muslim.MS	the-thing.MS-DEM.MS

'**The Muslim** saw this thing.' (ʿIwardo; ibid. 33/37)

	[A]	[V-A]	[O]
e.	***hano***	*ḥze-**le***	*u-Jorj*
	DEM.MS	saw_{PFV}-he	the-George

'**He** saw George.' (ʿIwardo; ibid. 56/106)

Thus both the nominal and verbal marking of objects is conditioned by the discourse salience of the argument. The verbal agreement with the agent, however, is obligatory. The prepositional marking of the agent is optional only in the preterite in Ṭuroyo.

1.3. Semi-Clitic L-Suffixes and Ditransitive Verbs

The L-suffixes show lingering features of their enclitic origin (Doron and Khan 2012, 231). First of all, they allow tense morphemes like *-wa-* to intervene, e.g.

(9) **C. Marga** (SE Turkey)

a. *garš-át-wa-**li***

$pull_{IPFV}$-you.MS-PST-me

'You_{FS} used to pull **me**.'

b. *griš-át-wa-**li***

$pulled_{PFV}$-you.MS-PST-I

'**I** had pulled you_{FS}.'

Secondly, verbs generally only take one object affix. There are a number of dialects, however, that allow a verb to take more than one L-suffix, i.e. to stack L-suffixes. This occurs across the constructional split illustrated above. Thus, the first L-suffix always marks the (T)heme, i.e. the entity transferred to somebody, and the second marks the (R)ecipient role in the *qaṭəl*-base inflection. Example (10) illustrates this where the first L-suffix *-nay* (i.e. *maxzən-* + *-lay* → *maxzən-nay*) expresses the T and the second L-suffix *-lux* expresses the R. This is generally only allowed when the T is third person.[9]

(10) **C. Marga** (SE Turkey)

[V-	-A	-T	-R]
maxz	*-ə́n*	***-nay***	***-lux***
show$_{\text{IPFV}}$	-I.M	-them	-you.MS

'I will show you$_{\text{MS}}$ **them.**'

In a number of dialects, a second L-suffix is added to the perfective to express the R. Thus we find perfective forms in dialects like C. Marga such as (11) below where the first L-suffix *-li* (i.e. *mər-* + *-li* → *mər-ri*) marks the A, but the second one, *-lux*, marks the R.

(11) **C. Marga** (SE Turkey)

[V	-A	-R]
mə́r	*-ri*	*-lux*
said$_{\text{PFV}}$	-I	-you.MS

'I told you$_{\text{MS}}$.'

9 This third person restriction is documented for at least the *lišana deni* dialects J. Dohok (Molin and Noorlander field notes) and J. Zaxo (Cohen 2012, 163–65), as well as C. Artun (Hertevin, Jastrow 1988, 63).

Moreover, stacking of L-suffixes may occur even when the T is marked by the E-suffixes such as *-a* in (12) below.

(12) **C. Marga** (SE Turkey)

[V	-T	-A	-R]
ṭlib	*-á*	*-lay*	*-le*
betrothed$_{\text{PFV}}$	-her	-they	-him

'They betrothed her to him.'

This is also attested for rural dialects in Ṭuroyo (cf. Ritter 1990, 75), for example:

(13) Ṭuroyo

	[V	-T	-A	-R]
a.	*húw*	*-i*	*-le*	*-lalle*
	gave$_{\text{PFV}}$	-them	-he	-them

'**He** gave them **to them**.' (Miden, Ritter 1967–1971: 73/371)

Ṭuroyo, however, prefers an unmarked set of bound person markers[10] to express third person Ts[11] when both the T and R are bound pronouns, as exemplified in (13b) below.

10 These are identical to the third person forms of the copula that historically goes back to bound person markers, e.g. e.g. *ú-dawšo basímo-yo* 'The honey is nice'.

11 See Jastrow (1985, 137–38), Waltisberg (2016, 296), Noorlander (2018b, 341–45).

[V -A -R -T: 3]

b. *hú* *-li* *-lalle* ***-yo***

gave$_{PFV}$ -I -them -it.MS

'I gave them **it**$_{M}$ (the milk).' (ibd., 75/375)

In addition, a prepositional indirect object construction is available to all persons as well as all types of full nominals. Various dialect-dependent prepositions are used to mark the R independently of the verb. The respective preposition will vary significantly across as well as within dialects. Variants of the preposition (*ʾəl)l-* still occur, such as:

(14) Ṭuroyo (Miden, SE Turkey)

a. *ʾát-tarʿone* *mər-re* ***l-ú-malko***

the-doorkeeper.MPL said$_{PFV}$-they to-the-king.MS

'The doorkeepers said **to the king**. (Ritter 1967–1971, 81/16)

The prepositional recipient NP can trigger additional agreement by L-suffixes on the verb, to illustrate:

b. *Gorgis* *k-omar-∅****-re*** ***l-áb-baqore***

Gorgis PRS-say$_{IPFV}$-he-them to-the-cowherder.MPL

'Gorgis says **to the cowherders.**' (ibid. 115/164)

Several NENA dialects, however, make use of other (novel) prepositions such as *ṭ(l)a-*, *ta-*, *ba(q)-*, *qa-* etc., for example:

(15) C. Marga (SE Turkey)

xa	*mər-re*	***ta-d-ay-xena***
one	said$_{PFV}$-he	to-LNK-DEM-other

'One said **to the other**.'

Prepositional marking of the R is preferred when the T is a first or second person pronominal affix attached to the verb and when the R is a full nominal.[12]

Thus, full nominal recipients are generally prepositional. An extra L-suffix can express pronominal recipients in both NENA and Ṭuroyo for both the *qaṭəl-* and *qṭil-*based person marking. When the verb selects an additional L-suffix, it is confined to recipients found throughout the verbal system in Ṭuroyo and several NENA dialects. Third person themes can be marked through a different, unmarked set of bound person markers.

When such additional L-suffixes of the first and second person are added to *qṭil-* in Ṭuroyo, they also express the object of monotransitive verbs, e.g. *gráš-le-**li*** 'He pulled **me**'. One cannot say ***gráš-li-**le*** for 'I pulled **him**' (e.g. Noorlander 2018b, 340). Generally, NENA dialects do not add such object L-suffixes to *qṭil-* forms. Jewish dialects in Iranian Azerbaijan, however, such as Urmi and Salamas and several Christian dialects in SE Turkey such as Bohtan (Ruma; Fox 2009), Haṣṣan (Jastrow 1997; Damsma forthcoming), Umṛa and Jənnet (Noorlander field notes) use the L-suffixes for objects throughout the *qaṭəl-/qṭil-*split, i.e. *gráš-li-**le*** 'I pulled **him**', cf. *garš-ax-**le*** 'We pull **him**'.[13]

12 See, among others, Hoberman (1989:106–10), Coghill (2010) and Noorlander (2018b, 129, 144–53, 172–74, 186–87, 395–402) for further studies of ditransitives in NENA and Waltisberg (2016) and Noorlander (2018b, 340–45) for Ṭuroyo.

13 See Noorlander (2018b, 220–30, 381, 429–30; 2019a-b; forthcoming) for a discussion.

The preterite illustrated in (6) above is known as the *šmīᶜ l-* or *qṭīl l*-construction in Aramaic studies. Historically, it goes back to the resultative participle and an agent-like argument marked by *l-* . It developed from a stative-resultative to a preterite via a perfect. Views diverge as to its exact interpretation. It has been connected with possessors, experiencers and subject co-referential datives.[14] It lies beyond the scope of this article to address this issue here. It should be noted, however, that, while a connection between these 'non-canonical' subject construction types and the *šmiᶜ l*-constructions developing into the preterite seems plausible to me in itself, we shall see that there are important distinctions. Forms like *grəš-li* 'I pulled' consist of L-suffixes that are marked for tense-aspect. They serve as inflectional agent suffixes of the preterite based on *qṭil-*. This is a notable distinction from the use of L-suffixes to express affectees, since they are found across different inflections and not just the *qṭil*-based forms. This difference is observed above for the recipient role but also extensions thereof that are the relics of a formerly dative argument.

2. Beneficiaries and Subject Co-referential L-suffixes

2.1. Beneficiaries

Apart from recipients of ditransitive verbs, L-suffixes can be added to any monotransitive verb to express an additional R-like affectee, as if it were an additional argument of the verb. The Ṭuroyo L-suffix *-lən* in (16), for example, expresses a beneficiary in a construction that is clearly derived from ditransitive constructions. The same holds for *-li* in (17) below to illustrate this for *lišana deni* dialects of NENA like J. Dohok:

14 See, among others, Noorlander (2012, 2018b, 2019a-b, forthcoming) and Coghill (2016).

(16) Ṭuroyo (Midyat, SE Turkey)

[V	-A	-R]	[T]
ftíḥ	*-le*	***-lən***	*ú-tarʿo*
opened$_{\text{PFV}}$	-he	-them	the-door.MS

'He opened the door **for them.**' (Ritter 1967–1971, 26/237)

(17) J. Dohok (NW Iraq)

[V	-A	-R]	[T]
ptə́x	*-le*	***-li***	*tăra*
opened$_{\text{PFV}}$	-he	-me	door.MS

'He opened the door **for me.**'

The T-like argument can be pronominalised through the same unmarked set as in ditransitive constructions added to the L-suffix expressing the beneficiary in Ṭuroyo, e.g.

(18) Ṭuroyo (Midən, SE Turkey)

[V	-A	-R	-T]	[T]
sə́m	*-la*	***-li***	***-yo***	*zawgo d-gŭrwe*
made$_{\text{PFV}}$	-he	-them	-it	pair of-stockings

'(From a ball of threads) she made **me** a pair of stockings.' (Jastrow 1992, 138.12)

Indeed, both the A and the R-like affectee can be *l*-marked and cross-referenced by L-suffixes.[15] The *l*-marking of the A is pragmatically conditioned (agent/narrow focus), for example:

---

15 See also Waltsiberg (2016, 195) and Noorlander (2018b, 345–53; forthcoming).

(19) Ṭuroyo (ʿIwardo, SE Turkey)

	[V	-A	-R]	[A]
mən	*sə́m*	***-le***	***-le***	***l-u-šulṭono***
what	did_{PFV}	-he	-him	to-the-sultan.MS

[R]

l-u-ʿmiro

to-the-emir.MS

'… what ***the sultan*** has done **to the emir.**' (Ritter 1967–1971, 36/87)

2.2. Subject Co-referential L-suffixes

An additional R-like argument expressed by the L-suffix can also denote an interested party, indirect affectee or benefactor that is co-referential with the subject. This is found across the verbal system for many telic dynamic verbs, including

(20) Ṭuroyo (SE Turkey)

a. imperfective:

∅-šot-ína	***-lan***	*qahwa*	*k̭elik̭e*
SBJV-$drink_{PFV}$-we	-us	coffee	an.instant
∅-məjġil-ína	***-lan***		
SBJV-MEDP.$speak_{IPFV}$-we	-us		

'Let **us** drink some coffee and have **ourselves** a chat for a moment.' (Midyat, ibid. 65/77)

b. imperative:

xu[16]	***-lux***	*fak̭o*
eat.IMP	-you.MS	bite

'Have **yourself**$_{\text{M}}$ a bite to eat!' (Midən, ibid. 75/85)

c. perfective:

damix	*-ən*	***-ne***	*b-dŭkθo*
slept$_{\text{PFV}}$	-they	-them	in-place.FS

'They slept (lit. **them**) somewhere.' (Midən, 115/97)

xí	*-le*	***-le***	*fak̭o*
ate$_{\text{PFV}}$	-he	-him	bite

'He had **himself** a bite to eat.' (Miden, 73/367)

Subject co-referential L-suffixes are not uncommon for verbs of position and motion in Ṭuroyo, e.g.

(21) Ṭuroyo (SE Turkey)

a.

yatu	*-∅*	***-le***	*əšmo*
sat$_{\text{PFV}}$	-he	-him	a.little

'**He** sat down a little.' (Miden, ibid. 77/238)

b.

qayəm	*-∅*	***-le***	***Kandar***
rose$_{\text{PFV}}$	-he	-him	Kandar

'**Kandar** stood up.' (Midyat, Prym and Socin 1881, 23.29)

---

16 *xu-lux* < *xŭl-* 'eat!' + *-lux*.

c.	*saləq*	-∅	*-le*
	ascended$_{PFV}$	-he	-him

'**He** went up.' (Midyat, Prym and Socin 1881, 117.3)

Indeed, co-referential L-suffixes have become special (stressed) inflectional endings in the high frequency motion verb *ʾzl* 'go' as well as the imperative forms of *ʾθy* 'come' in Ṭuroyo, replacing the original subject encoding. Because of this, the verb *ʾzl* has an irregular and unique inflection that is identical to the L-suffixes except for the 2pl. and 3pl., which take special endings, as shown in (22) below.

(22) Ṭuroyo inflection of *ʾzl* 'go'

	IMPERFECTIVE		PERFECTIVE	IMPERATIVE
1S	*əzz-í(-no)*	< **ʾozəl-li*	*azz-í(-no)*	
1PL	*əzz-án(o)*	< **ʾozəl-lan*	*azz-án(o)*	
2MS	*əzz-ŭ́x*	< **ʾozəl-lux*	*azz-ŭ́x*	*(i)z-ŭ́x !*
2FS	*əzz-áx*	< **ʾozəl-lax*	*azz-áx*	*(i)z-áx !*
2PL	*əzz-oxu*	< **ʾozəl-loxun*	*azz-oxu*	*(i)z-oxu !*
3MS	*əzz-é(yo)*	< **ʾozəl-leh*	*azz-é(yo)*	
3FS	*əzz-á(yo)*	< **ʾozəl-lah*	*azz-á(yo)*	
3PL	*əzz-ehən*	< **ʾozəl-lehen*	*azz-ehən*	

Presumably the final /l/ of the original root *ʾzl* played a role, yielding special endings because of the complete assimilation with the preceding /z/. The 3s forms can be enhanced with *-yo*, which mimics its use in ditransitive constructions and creates a penultimate stress as in the first person *-no* in forms like *k-əzz-i-no* 'I'm going' and *k-əzz-an-o* 'We're going'. Subject co-referential L-suffixes can even be added instead, e.g.

(23) Ṭuroyo

a. *azz* -*e* **-*le*** (* < *az-* + *-le* + *-le*)

went$_{PFV}$ -he -him

'**He** went.' (Raite, Ritter 1967–1971, 95/4)

b. *azz* -*a* **-*la*** (* < *az-* + *-le* + *-le*)

went$_{PFV}$ -she -her

'**It**$_F$ reached.' (Raite,ibid. 95/27)

Importantly, no such conjugations are attested for *ʾzl* in the closely related Central Neo-Aramaic dialect Mlaḥsó. The imperfective and imperative do not take L-suffixes, e.g. *∅-oz-ina* 'Let's go' and *iz-ewun* 'Go$_{PL}$!'. The L-suffixes function as subject markers for the preterite, e.g. preterite *azi-le* 'He went', against the perfect *azi-∅* 'He has gone' (Jastrow 1994, 156). Only the pl. imperative of *ʾsy* 'come' in Mlaḥsó, e.g. ***toxun*** 'Come$_{PL}$!' does seem to parallel Ṭuroyo ***toxu***.

Subject co-referential datives also occur in NENA dialects. This is, for instance, common in the imperative of motion verbs[17], e.g. C. Urmi *ta-**lux*** 'Come$_{MS}$!, *si-**lux*** 'Go$_{MS}$!' (Khan 2016$_{II}$:151–52). It can also combine with other verbs and verbal forms expressing a beneficiary, e.g. *šqul-**lux** xa-dana ʾərba* 'Take a sheep **for yourself**' (ibid. 152), *zon-i-**lay** mexulta* 'They buy **themselves** food', *zvun-**nux** xaql-i* 'Buy$_{MS}$ (yourself$_{MS}$) my field!' (Polotsky 1996, 37, transcription modified).

The verb *ʾzl* is also highly irregular in Christian NENA dialects in SE Turkay and northern Iraq, especially on the Mosul plain. Both the *qaṭəl*-base and *qṭil*-base take L-suffixes as subject coding, as shown in (25) below, including after the 'past convertor' *-wa*, e.g. *k-zá-wa-la* 'She used to go'. Khan (2002, 120) assumes the base *za-* is a reduced form of the infinitive *ʾəzála*. Note also that

17 See Fassberg (2018: 113, incl. fn. 61) for more examples across NENA dialects.

the imperative of *ʾθy* 'come' has similarly irregular forms inflected with L-suffixes. (The imperative of *ʾzl* does not take L-suffixes in this dialect.)

(24) **C. Qaraqosh** (NW Iraq; Khan 2002, 120, 153, 155, 122)

	IMPERFECTIVE 'go'	PERFECTIVE 'go'	cp. IMPERATIVE 'come'
1S	*za-li*	*zəl-li*	
1PL	*za-lan*	*zəl-lan*	
2MS	*za-lux*	*zəl-lux*	*ha-lux!*
2FS	*za-lax*	*zəl-lax*	*ha-lux!*
2PL	*za-lxun*	*zəl-xun*	*ha-lxu(n)!*
3MS	*za-lə*	*zəl-lə*	
3FS	*za-la*	*zəl-la*	
3PL	*za-lhən*	*zəl-hən*	

In Western Neo-Aramaic, subject co-referential L-suffixes are readily found in the imperative, e.g. *zubnu-**llxun*** 'Buy$_{\text{MPL}}$ **yourselves** (sth.)!', and are common with the verbs of motion *ʾty* 'come' and *zyl* 'go', and with the change-of-state verbs *qʿy* 'sit' and *ðmx* 'sleep, fall asleep' (Arnold 1990b, 238, cf. Spitaler 1938, 222, §196*o-p*):

(25) Western Neo-Aramaic (Maʿlula, SW Syria; Arnold 1990b:239, 174)

a. ***ni-*** *ðmox* ***-laḥ*** *šaʿθa*
we- sleep -us hour
'Let **us** sleep for an hour.'

b. *θe* -∅ ***-le***
coming -he -him
'**He is** coming.'

c.	*zli*	*-n*	*-naḥ*
	went	-we	-us

‘**We** went.’

The imperative forms of *ʾθy* ‘come’ is thus regularly fused with L-suffixes in Western Neo-Aramaic (Arnold 1990b, 173) similarly to Ṭuroyo and NENA dialects on the Mosul Plain:

(26) Imperative of ‘come’ across Neo-Aramaic

	Western (Maʿlula)	Central (Ṭuroyo)	NENA(C. Qaraqosh)
MS	*θā-x*	*(i)t-ṻx !*	*ha-lux !*
FS	*θā-š*	*(i)t-áx !*	*ha-lux !*
PL	*θa-llxun* (m), *-llxen* (f)	*(i)t-oxu !*	*ha-lxu(n) !*

Subject co-referential datives (or ethical datives) were already common with such intransitive verbs in pre-Modern Aramaic and can be considered an archaic feature in Neo-Aramaic, e.g. *qum leḵ!* ‘Arise$_{FS}$!’ *qåm-∅ l-eh* ‘He has risen’ (see Fassberg 2018; cf. Joosten 1989). Fassberg (2018), following Ullendorff, argues the so-called ethical dative reflects the colloquial language. Several scholars claim the ethical dative influenced the emergence of intransitive verbal forms inflected with L-suffixes like *qəm-li* ‘I rose’ in NENA and Mlaḥsó (Mengozzi 2002b, 44; Halevy 2008; Fassberg 2018, 115). While this is conceivable, one should note that this dative endured as additional L-suffixes in the spoken varieties and did not disappear as a result (*pace* Fassberg 2018, 116). Moreover, where the original dative pronominal is conventionalized as inflectional morphemes of the verb, it is attested across the inflectional system, and thus not an inflectional property of *qṭil-* as verbal form *per se*.

2.3. Trans-Zab Jewish Dialects: *əll*-series

A different strategy comparable with subject co-referential L-suffixes exists in the so-called Trans-Zab Jewish dialects of NENA (Mutzafi 2008b). Certain intransitive verbs can take bound person markers derived from the independent set based on the preposition *ʾəll-*, constituting a secondary LL-series. They are impersonal, dummy pronouns belonging to the 3ms. or 3fs. in intransitive predicates functioning like a middle voice marker (Mengozzi 2006). They are not co-referential with the subject but seem to express the telic endpoint, for example:

(27) J. Koy Sanjaq (NE Iraq; Mutzafi 2004, 104, 229)

a. *nə́x-li-**llaw***

rested$_{\text{PFV}}$-I-it.F

'I rested (lit. **it**$_{\text{F}}$)'

b. *ytíw-li-**llaw***

sat$_{\text{PFV}}$-I-it.F

'I sat (lit. **it**$_{\text{F}}$)'

(28) **J. Saqqiz** (W Iran; Israeli 1998, 49)

*dmíx-i-**lev***

slept$_{\text{PFV}}$-they-it.M

'They slept (lit. **it**$_{\text{M}}$)'

3. Morphosyntax of Possessors in Neo-Aramaic

Possession can be expressed in various ways in Neo-Aramaic languages (Noorlander 2018b, 154–58).[18] The focus here will be on the possessor marking strategies that are related to the original dative preposition *l-*. I should note briefly, however, that possession can be expressed adnominally by means of nominal suffixes, e.g. *bab-i* 'my father', *bab-ax* 'your$_{FS}$ father'. There also reflexes of a historical adnominal linker **ḏ* that are used to denote possession through nominal annexation,[19] e.g.

(29) Ṭuroyo (SE Turkey)

a.

í-barθo	***d-ú-***	*malko*
the-daughter.FS	of-the	king.MS

'the king's daughter'

Nouns that are marked by such a linker can also occur independently, for example as the nominal element of the predicate:

b.

í-baxč-aṯe-ste	***d-ú-***	*malko*	*-wa*
the-garden.FS-DEM.FS-FOC	of-the	king.MS	-was

'This garden **belonged to** the king', lit. 'was the king's' (Midyat, Ritter 1967–1971, 24/164).

There are independent possessive/genitive pronouns derived from this particle with augmentation, for example:

18 See Stilo and Noorlander (2015, 473–76) for an areal perspective.

19 See Gutman (this volume, cf. 2016) for an overview of such constructions.

c.	*í-gweto*	***díð-***	***i***	*-yo*
	the-chees.FS	of	my	-it.is

'The cheese is **mine!**' (Midyat, ibid. 22/2).

3.1. Possessor Marked by L-suffixes Only

Predicative possession is based in existential clauses introduced by the dialectal reflexes of the existential marker **ʾiθ-* 'there is/are'. This uninflectable particle is negated by the negator *la* (in NENA and Ṭuroyo) in a form going back to **la-yθ-* 'there is/are not', and for past tense by the suffix *-wa*, e.g. **ʾiθ-wa* 'there was/were' (in NENA and Ṭuroyo), similarly to verbs. The preverbal TAM-marker *k-* typical for the indicative-durative present is always combined with it in Ṭuroyo, e.g. *k-ito* 'There is'. Together with L-suffixes they express predicative possession, e.g. *kət-li* 'I have'. In Western Neo-Aramaic, the existential particle is reduced to *ī-* or *ū-* before L-suffixes, e.g. *ī-le* 'He has' (Arnold 1990a, 185). The negator is *čū* and the past particle is *wa* preceding the predicate, e.g. *čū-le* 'He has not', *wa ī-le* 'He had'. The L-suffix in Neo-Aramaic marks the possessor which is reminiscent of their use as markers of the recipient (i.e. 'T belongs to R').

The co-referential nominal, however, is usually not prepositional. Thus, (30a) below presents a simple existential predicate in Ṭuroyo. (30b) illustrates the additional L-suffix expressing the R-like possessor without a co-nominal referent. In (30b), the possessor NP *ú-malk-ano* 'this king' is zero-marked but the L-suffix cross-references it, indexing its role as the possessor. The unmarked set of independent pronouns is similarly used to express the possessor, as illustrated in (30c).

(30) Ṭuroyo

a.

kit	***-wo***	*malko*
EXST	-PST	king.MS

'**There once was** a king.' (Midyat, Ritter 1967–1971, 99/2)

b.

ú-malk-ano	***kit***	***-way***	***-le***	*greʿo*
the-king:MS-DEM.MS	EXST	-PST	-him	servant.MS

'This king **had** a servant' (Midyat, ibid. 99/3)

c.

ono	***kit***	***-way***	***-li***	*ʿezo*
I	EXST	-PST	-him	goat.FS

'I **had** a goat.' (ʿIwardo, ibid. 57/151)

The same holds for NENA, as illustrated below for the Christian dialect of Urmi.

(31) C. Urmi (NW Iran)

a.

ʾət	***-va***	*xa-dana*	*-málca*
EXST	-PST	a-CLF	-king.MS

'**There once was** a king.' (Khan 2016_{IV}: A 2:1)

b.

ʾaha	*malca*	***ʾə́t***	***-va***	***-lə***	*+ṯla*	*bnunə*
DEM.MS	king.MS	EXST	-PST	-him	three	sons.PL

'This king **had** three sons.' (ibid. A 39:1)

c.

ana	***ʾə́t***	***-li***	*+xabra*
I	EXST	-me	news

'I **have** news.' (ibid. A 1:37)

Possessors are generally also expressed by an L-suffix in Western Neo-Aramaic such as *ī-le* 'He has' and *ī-l* 'I have' in the following examples. The possessor co-nominal itself is zero-marked.

(32) Western Neo-Aramaic

a. ***wōθ*** *b-zamōne* *malka*

PST.EXST in-time king.MS

'Once upon a time **there was** a king.' (Arnold 1991b, 20.1)

b. *hanna* *malka* ***ī-le*** *ebra*

DEM.MS king.MS EXST-him son.MS

'This king **had** a son.' (ibid.)

c. *ana* ***ī-l*** *ḥammeš* *emʿa* *ðahb*

I EXST-me five hundred gold

'I **have** five hundred gold pieces.' (ibid. 294/296.29)

3.2. (External) Possessors Marked on Verbs

3.2.1. The Verb *hwy* 'be', 'become', 'beget'

The predicative possessor constructions are marked for particular tense, aspect and mood (TAM) values like verbs. The verb *hwy* stands in a suppletive relation to the existential markers to express other TAM categories such as the future tense and subjunctive. The verb remains impersonal like the existential marker. Its inflection is identical with the 3ms. -∅ E-suffix. The L-suffix is added to the verb, for example

(33) Ṭuroyo (Miden, SE Turkey)

Baṣuṣ	*gt-owe-le*	*abro*
Baṣuṣ	FUT-be$_{\text{IPFV}}$-him	son

‘**Baṣuṣ** will **have** a son.’ (Ritter 1967–1971, 115/309)

(34) C. Urmi (NW Iran)

ʾana	***ṱ-avi-li***	*ʾarxe*
I	FUT-be$_{\text{IPFV}}$-me	guests

‘**I** will **have** guests.’ (Khan 2016$_{\text{IV}}$, A11:1)

When L-suffixes are attached to the verb *hwy*, the construction can semantically entail a process, i.e. ‘become’, rather than a state, i.e. ‘be’. The verb can be used to convey ‘be born’. The L-suffix denotes an R-like affectee, i.e. the one who begot the child, for example:

(35) Ṭuroyo (Midyat, SE Turkey)

ú-tajər	***hawi-le***	*barθo*
the-merchant.MS	be.born-him	daughter.FS

‘The merchant **begot** a daughter’ (Ritter 1967–1971, 23/4)

(36) C. Urmi (Literary, NW Iran; Polotsky 1979, 211–12)

a.

vazir	***bət-***	***havi***	***-lə***	*brata*
vizier	FUT-	be.born	**-him**	daughter.FS

‘The vizier **will have/beget** a daughter.’

In C. Urmi, the verb takes a 3fs. L-suffix in the *qṭil*-based preterite (Khan 2016_{II}, 396) such as *vi-la-lə* ***bruna*** 'He begot a son', lit. 'It_F (impersonal) was born to him a son', below:

b.	*vazir*	***ví***	***-la***	***-lə***	*bruna*
	vizier	be.born	-it.F	**-him**	son

'The vizier **had/begot** a son.'

Pronominal objects are otherwise not marked through L-suffixes on the *qṭil*-based preterite verb in such dialects. Forms like ***grəš-la-li* for intended 'She pulled me' do not occur. The secondary L-suffix is clearly reminiscent of the stacking of L-suffixes in ditransitive constructions in dialects like C. Marga and *lišana deni* Jewish dialects, cf. (37) below. This indicates how the L-suffix is considered an R-like argument in the system and expressed by an L-suffix regardless of the inflectional base, cf. (37a) below taken from the Jewish dialect of Dohok.

(37) J. Dohok (Molin and Noorlander field notes)

a.	*hú*	***-le***	*li*	*pare*
	$gave_{PFV}$	-he	me	money.PL

'**He** gave **me** money.'

Apart from (37), examples (33)–(36) above are impersonal like the predicative possessor constructions. The verb *hwy* can also agree with the possessee in an external possessor construction. The possessor is expressed as an affectee part of the verbal predicate independently of the nominal possesee. For instance, the verb agrees with the possessee *yalunke* 'children' in (37b) below but takes an additional L-suffix to denote the possessor. The possessor is expressed as an argument of the verb.

b. ***hwé*** **-*lu*** *li* ***yalunk***-*e*

be.born$_{PFV}$ -they me child-MPL

'I begot **children**.'
(lit. **Children** were born unto me)

The verb *hwy* can also be inflected for person and combine with the L-suffix not to convey a strict sense of belonging but a broader sense of relation, i.e. 'X is/becomes Y with respect to somebody'. The construction parallels ditransitive verbs. Only in this sense can the pronominal possessee be expressed in the same way as the theme in ditransitives such as -*yo* , for example in (36b):

(38) Ṭuroyo (ʿIwardo, SE Turkey)

a. ***hat*** *∅-how* **-*at*** *-lan* *qašo*

you.S SBJV-become$_{IPFV}$ -you.S -us priest.MS

'(We want) that **you** become our priest.' (Ritter 1967–1971, 33/83)

b. *∅-howe* *-lan* **-*yo*** *qašo*

SBJV-become$_{IPFV}$ -us -it priest.MS

'(We want) you to be our priest.' (lit. to become **it** for us,—a priest) (ibid. 33/84)

The same combination can also be modal. This is recorded in Ritter's corpus of Ṭuroyo. It is accompanied by negation denoting inability, for example:

c. ***ló*** ***k-owe*** **-*li*** *-yo* *d-əzz-i-no*

NEG IND-be$_{IPFV}$ -me -it SBJV-go$_{IPFV}$-me-I

'**I cannot** go.' (ibid. 63/378)

The expression of ability through predicative possessors is also recorded in Trans-Zab Jewish varieties (e.g. Khan 2004, 311, 364), *ma ʾit-wa-lu hol-i-wa* 'What could they do?', *ʾana kwe-li* 'I will be able'.

3.2.2. External Possessors

Sporadically, L-suffixes can express a possessor-like affectee of verbal predicates akin to example (1g) from Hebrew. At least one such instance where the secondary L-suffix marks an external possessor is attested in Mlaḥsó:

(39) Mlaḥsó (Lice, SE Turkey)

ṭafloki	*mís*	*-le*	***-li***
a.child	died$_{\text{PFV}}$	-he	-me

'One child **of mine** died (on me).' (Jastrow 1994, 124.121)

Such external possessors are also attested in NENA dialects where the second L-suffix marks the R in *qṭil-*. The possessor is added as an R-like affectee in both the *qaṭəl-* and *qṭil-*based inflection such as the construction in J. Dohok given in (40). Its usage in J. Dohok does not seem to have a clear distribution. Coghill (2019, 368) notes that apart from *pyš* 'remain', it is confined to telic intransitives in C. Telkepe (NW Iraq), such as *myθ* 'die', *ʔθy* 'come' and *bry* 'happen'.

(40) **J. Dohok** (Molin and Noorlander field notes)

mə́t	*-lu*	***-li***	*yalunke*
died$_{\text{PFV}}$	-they	-me	children

'**My** children died (on me).'

An L-suffix denoting an R-like argument can be added to intransitive verbs in Ṭuroyo. It can be combined with the verbs *fyš* 'remain', *qyθ* 'hit, touch, meet', *ʾθy* 'come' and *mṭy* 'arrive'. Since these motion verbs denote movement towards an endpoint, these constructions typically convey a sense of reception, e.g.

(41) Ṭuroyo (Midyat, SE Turkey)

qayəṯ-	***-le***	*rŭmḥo*	*bə-droʿ-e*
stuck$_{\text{PFV}}$	-him	spear.FS	in-arm-his

'A spear hit **his** arm.' (lit. hit **him** in **his** arm') (Prym and Socin 1881, 141.11)

The additional L-suffix and *-yo* on the intransitive verb parallels ditransitive constructions. Compare *aθí-∅-**li-yo*** 'I received **it**' and *mšadál-le-**li-yo*** 'He sent **me it**' in (42) below.

(42) Ṭuroyo (Midən, SE Turkey)

k-	*aθi*	*-∅*	***-li***	*səsyo*	*m-ú-ʿmiro*
PERF-	came$_{\text{PFV}}$	-it.M	-me	horse.MS	from-the-emir.MS

'**I** received a horse from the emir'

aθí	*-∅*	***-li***	***-yo,***	*mšadál*	*-le*	***-li***	*-yo*
came$_{\text{PFV}}$	-it.M	-me	-it	sent$_{\text{PFV}}$	-he	-me	-it

'**I** received **it**, he sent **me it**.' (Ritter 1967–1971, 81/55)

3.2.3. Trans-Zab Jewish Dialects: *əll-* and *-la-l-*series

Occasionally, one also finds prepositional external possessors in NENA attached to the verbal base. An LL-series of person markers based on the preposition (*ʾəl*)*l-* is used to express the external possessor as illustrated for J. Arbel below.

(43) J. Arbel (NE Iraq; Khan 1999, 292)

yāle	*rāba*	***míl-lu-llaw***
children	very.much	died$_{PFV}$-they-her

'Many **of her** children died.'

Western Iranian dialects such as J. Saqqiz and J. Sanandaj use the morpheme *-la-*[20] as base for the L-suffixes to express predicative possession together with the verb 'become' (Khan 2009, 88–90, 301–02). This *la-* is possibly a relic of a former impersonal L-suffix *-la* 'it$_{F}$', i.e. *xír-la-li* 'It$_{F}$ became to me' → 'I have'. Full possessor NPs are zero-marked and can occupy pre-verbal position as illustrated in (44) below. The verbal base *xir* is invariable like the existential marker and does not agree with, for instance, indefinite plural nouns such as *puḷe* 'money' in J. Sanandaj *ʾaná hămešá puḷé xír-la-li* 'I have always had money' (Khan 2009, 302). This *lal*-series, therefore, serves as a special set of person markers, identifying their role as the most salient affectee.

(44) J. Sanandaj (W Iran; Khan 2009, A:108)

Nadər Šāh ʾAfšā́r	*raba*	*qudr-éf*
Nadir Shah Afshar	very.much	power.MS-his

xír-la-	***-le***
became$_{PFV}$-it.F	-him

'**Nadir Shah Afshar** had a lot of power.'

20 Khan (2009, 89) notes "the element *la-* is likely to be a fossilised form of a 3fs. copula form **ila*". It also possible it is an L-suffix used impersonally.

3.3. Prepositional Marking of Possessors

3.3.1. Possessor Marked by *l-* Only

The independent possessor argument is generally zero-marked in NENA. Alternative expressions do exist where the possessor is prepositional in some varieties of NENA such as J. Sulemaniyya combined with a 3ms. copula in (33b) below.

(45) J. Sulemaniyya (NE Iraq)

belá	***ʾəll-ew***	*-ye*
house.MS	to-him	-it.is.M

'The house belongs **to him**.' (Khan 2004a, 336, 362)

Similarly, sporadically, a predicative possessor can be expressed independently by means of the preposition *(e)l-* in Ṭuroyo, e.g.

(46) Ṭuroyo (SE Trukey)

i-dŭkθo	*kul-a*	***el-ŭx***	*-yo*
the-place.FS	all-her	to-you.MS	-it.is

'The whole place belongs **to you**$_{FS}$ (Midən, Ritter 1967–1971, 115/240)

Unlike the rest of Neo-Aramaic, however, the predicative possessor is always independent in Mlaḥsó. The possessor is expressed as an independent dative (pro)noun such as *eli* 'to me' in (47). The possessee controls the agreement of the verb *hwy* 'be'. Jastrow (1994) does not appear to provide examples of full nominal possessors in Mlaḥsó.

(47) Mlaḥsó (SE Turkey; Jastrow 1994, 76.19)

a. *hito* ***el-i*** *ḥosoki*

there.is to-me a.sister

'**I have** a sister.'

b. *zʿure* ***el-i*** *lo-ve* *-len*

children to-me not-were/became$_{\text{PFV}}$ -they

'**I** did not **have** children / No children were born **to me.**'

Sporadically, a full nominal possessor can also be prepositional in Western Neo-Aramaic, for example:

(48) Western Neo-Aramaic

wōθ ***l-aḥḥað*** ***ġabrōna*** *eččθa*

there.was to-one man.MS woman.FS

'**A certain man** had a wife.' (Arnold 1991b, 8.1)

Note that, in these cases, the possessor is marked only by a preposition just like the examples from Hebrew in (1).

3.3.2. Possessor Marked by *l-* and L-suffixes

The possessor can be optionally marked through the preposition *l-* in addition to the L-suffix in Ṭuroyo.[21] This includes predicative possessors such as (49a) and R-like affectees such as (49b-c).

21 See Waltisberg (2016, 125) for more examples.

(49) **Ṭuroyo** (SE Turkey)

a. *ma* *kət-le* ***l-ú-malk-ano***

Q EXST-him DAT-the-king-DEM.MS

'What does **the king** have?'
(ʿIwardo, Ritter 1967–1971: 58/3, 57/12)

b. ***l-ú-ḥakəm*** *hawi* ***-le*** *barθo*

DAT-the-overlord became$_{PFV}$ -him daughter.FS

'**The overlord** (be)got a daughter.' (ʿIwardo, Ritter 1967–1971, 59/5)

c. *aθi-le* ***l-ú-malko*** *năʿame*

came$_{PFV}$-him to-the-king.MS ostritch.FS

'**The king** received an ostrich.' (Miden, ibid. 58)

The optionality of the prepositional marking of the possessor alongside the L-suffix is reminiscent of the morphosyntax of agents in the Ṭuroyo *qṭil*-based preterite (cf. Diem 2012). This strategy to combine the preposition *l-* and L-suffixes does not occur in NENA.

3.4. Transitivisation of Possessive Constructions

Predicative possessive constructions have undergone transitivisation in NENA and Ṭuroyo in that the L-suffixes are obligatory person markers like verbal inflection. Apart from the L-suffixes, the construction remains impersonal. The possessee does not control agreement and does not trigger differential object marking. Generally speaking, even when a possessee could still be contextualised through anaphora such as where English would use a pronominal object for 'to have', it will tend to remain implicit in Neo-Aramaic. Forms like *ʾət-li* or *kət-li* could also mean 'I have it$_{F}$/it$_{M}$' or 'I have them'. This raises the question of how transitivised the predicative possessive construction are in being compatible with pronominal objects like transitive clauses in general.

There are indeed cases where the transitivisation seems to be more advanced and pronominal objects are overtly expressed. This, for instance, applies when the possessee is first or second person. First and second person pronominal objects differ across dialects. The possessee can be expressed as a pronominal object either through the unmarked set of independent pronouns, e.g.

(50) C. Shaqlawa (NW Iraq)

a. *ʾaxni* ***ʾahat*** *ʾət-an*[22]

we you.S EXST-us

'We have **YOU**$_{S}$' (Khan field notes)

This parallels the use of independent personal pronouns in transitive clauses to express focal objects, for example:

b. *ʾaxni* ***ʾahat*** *qam-xaz-əx-lux*

we you PFV-see-we-you.MS

'We saw **YOU**$_{FS}$'

If available, the possessee can also be expressed through a dedicated set of prepositional pronominal objects, e.g.

(51) C. Urmi (NW Iran)

a. *ʾaxnan* ***qatux*** *ʾət-lan*

we you EXST-us

'We have **you**$_{MS}$' (Noorlander field notes)

---

22 *ʾət-an* > **ʾət-tan* < *ʾət-lan* (through assimilation).

In the latter, the marking of the possessee clearly patterns like that of objects of *qṭil*-based preterite verbal forms where the agent is expressed by the L-suffixes, e.g.

b.	*ʾaxnan*	***qatux***	*xze-lan*
	we	you	saw$_{\text{PFV}}$-us

'We saw **you**$_{\text{MS}}$'

A few NENA dialects in SE Turkey such as Artun (Hertevin), Umṛa and Jənnet mark the object on the transitive *qṭil*-based perfective by means of additional L-suffixes, e.g. *grə́š-le-la* 'He pulled it$_{\text{F}}$'. The marking of the possessee is the same as the object in the predicative possessor construction, e.g. *ʾə́t-le-la* 'He has it$_{\text{F}}$'. It has taken over the full agent and object marking morphology of the perfective (see the examples below). When object L-suffixes like *-la* 'it$_{\text{F}}$' are added to *grəš-lax* 'You$_{\text{FS}}$ pulled', first and second person agents are marked by a special set one could call the L-E-series yielding *grə́š-lət-ta* 'You$_{\text{FS}}$ pulled it'.[23] The same transitive verbal coding occurs in the predicative possessor construction, e.g. *ʾət-lət-ta* 'You$_{\text{FS}}$ have it$_{\text{F}}$'. Moreover, these transitive constructions are used when full nominal possessees trigger differential marking. Thus the indefinite possessee in (52a) functions like an indefinite object in (52c)but the definite possessee in (52b) triggers cross-indexing like a definite object in (52d).

(52) **C. Artun** (Hertevin, SE Turkey; Jastrow 1988, 67, 160.541–542)

a.	*ana*	*lət*	***-li***	*hay*
	I	EXST	-me	knowledge.FS

'I don't have knowledge.'

23 See Noorlander (2018b, 242–49, forthcoming) for a detailed discussion of the verbal person marking in C. Artun (Hertevin).

b.	*lə́t*	*-lə́n*	***-na***	*hay*
	EXST	-I	**-it**.F	knowledge.FS

'I don't have **the** knowledge.'

c.	*ḥzé*	*-li*		*baxta*
	saw_{PFV}	-I		woman

'I saw a woman.'

d.	*ḥzé*	*-lə́n*	***-na***	*baxta*
	saw_{PFV}	-I	**-her**	woman

'I saw **the** woman.'

It should be noted, however, that this is not acceptable in the majority of dialects. Speakers of J. Dohok, for example, do not readily accept pronominalisation of the possessee in predicative possessor constructions. They disfavour expressions like ***ʾətli ʾahat* 'I have you_{FS}' and circumvent this by choosing constructions involving independent possessive pronouns akin to English 'You_{FS} are mine'.

3.5. Verboid *bas-* 'enough'

A related verboid construction in NENA based on the particle *bas-* 'enough' is generally inflected with suffixes going back to possessor-like L-suffixes that have assimilated to the preceding /s/. The possessee-like complement of the quantifier *bas*, i.e. that which is possessed in a satisfactory amount such as *xaye* 'life' below, is prepositional (*m-*), e.g.

(53) C. Barwar (NW Iraq)

bass-i	*m-xáye*
enough-me	from-life.PL

'**I have had enough** of my life' (Khan 2008a, 1241).

The original L-suffix can still be observed in the past equivalent, e.g. *bas-wa-li* 'I had had enough'. Depending on the dialect, the copula can also be added to this to express the referent of the quantifier *bass-*, e.g.

(54) C. Urmi (NW Iran)

báss	*-ux*	*-ila*
enough	-you.MS	-it.is.F

'**That**$_F$ **is** enough for you.' (Khan 2016$_{I}$, 585)

The same particle is fully inflectable for L-suffixes in Ṭuroyo, as illustrated below. Unlike (53) above, the possessee is not prepositional but zero-marked or expressed by a copula:

(55) Ṭuroyo (SE Turkey)

a.

ono	*bas*	***-li***	*áḥ-ḥay-ayði*
I	enough	-me	the-life.PL-my

'**I have had** enough with my life.' (Midən, Talay 2004, 72.144)

b.

ʿəmṛ-i	*bás*	*-li*	***-yo***
age.MS-my	enough	-me	-it.is

'I am old enough (to die).' (Midən, ibid. 50.42)

The structure is at least superficially similar to ditransitives in that the T-like person markers are identical with the copula.

4. Morphosyntax of Experiencers in Neo-Aramaic

There are numerous ways in which experiencers are encoded in Neo-Aramaic. One should note that some of the constructions discussed in what follows also have equivalent expressions in other dialects involving a different structure. In impersonal experiencer constructions, for instance, experiencers can also be expressed adnominally through agreeing possessive suffixes, e.g.

(56) C. Marga (SE Turkey)

a. ***ʾana*** *xə́mm-**i*** *-le*

I heat.MS-my -it.is.M

'I am hot.' (lit. My heat is).

b. ***d-mắni*** *-la* *qarsa*

of-whom -it.is.F cold.FS

'**Who** is cold?' (lit. Whose coldness is?)

Adnominal possession is the regular expression of the experiencer of the physiological sates of 'heat' and 'cold' in Western Iranian Jewish varieties of NENA. An adnominal possessor encodes the agreement with the experiencer on the NP denoting the sensation:

(57) J. Saqqiz (W Iran)

brat-í *qard-**ev**-ya*

daughter-my cold.FS-her-it.is.F

'**My daughter** feels cold.' (lit. Her coldness is)
(Israeli 1998, 170)

This is an areal phenomenon found across languages in West Asia, including the Neo-Aramaic speaking area.[24] It regularly features in neighbouring Iranian varieties where the experiencer is marked in the so-called 'oblique' case or through pronominal clitics that also denote the possessor and the agent in the past (Haig 2018b, 132–33, 2018c, 286–87), for example:

(58) Northern Kurdish (Behdini, NW Iraq)

min	*sar*	*e*
me.'OBL'	cold	is

'I am cold' (Haig 2018b, 132)

(59) Persian (Iran)

man	*sard-**am***	*ast*
I	coldness-my	is

'I am cold' (lit. my coldness is)

There are cases where the experiencer is expressed as the object. For example, the verb *ʿjb* 'please, like', borrowed from Arabic, takes object suffixes in Western Neo-Aramaic just like the corresponding verb in Arabic, e.g.

(60) Western Neo-Aramaic (Maʿlula, NW Syria)

ana	*aʿžb-īš-**n***
I	pleased-you.FS-me

'I like you$_{FS}$.' (Arnold 1991, 140.42)

24 See Khan (2016$_{II}$, 355–59)

It will become clear, however, that experiencers are construed as R-like affectees similarly to possessors in the previous discussion.

4.1. Experiencer Marked by L-suffixes Only

4.1.1. Transitive Verbs

Apart from beneficiaries and predicative possessors, L-suffixes can denote experiencers. In several (Christian) NENA dialects (and Ṭuroyo), verbs like I *bsm*, II/III *ʿjb* and I *hny* (variants include *nny* and *nhy*) are impersonal experiencer predicates conveying more or less the equivalent to English 'like', 'please' or 'enjoy', as illustrated for Ṭuroyo and C. Barwar below.

(61) Ṭuroyo (Mzizaḥ, SE Turkey)

aḥun-i	*bosam-∅-way-**le***	*ú-dawšo*
brother-my	was.pleasant$_{\text{IPFV}}$-it.M-PST-him	honey.MS

'**My brother** used to like honey.'

(62) C. Barwar (NW Iraq)

xon-i	*basəm-∅-wa-**le***	*duša*
brother-my	please$_{\text{IPFV}}$-it.M-PST-him	honey.MS

'**My brother** used to like honey' (Khan 2008a, B8:12)

There are other verbs across NENA dialects that display the same pattern, such as *wjj* 'care' (J. Amidya NW Iraq; Hoberman 1989, 226), *ṭwy* 'be worth, merit', *ʾby* 'want, need', *mly* 'be enough' (J. Betanure NW Iraq; Mutzafi 2008a, 88–89), *mṭy* 'deserve, lit. arrive, reach' (J. Zaxo NW Iraq; Cohen 2012, 144).

When the experiencer verb is impersonal apart from the L-suffix, it takes non-referential 3ms. or 3fs. morphology. Unlike

NENA, the verb *bsm* is stative 'was pleasant/nice' or inchoative 'became pleasant/nice' in Ṭuroyo.[25] It takes the $C_1aC_2iC_3$-pattern in the perfective typical for non-referential 3ms. morphology, for example:

(63) Ṭuroyo (SE Turkey)

a. *basəm-∅-**le**...* *íy-itawto* *d-ʿawwəl*

was.pleasant$_{PFV}$-it.M-him the-sitting.FS of-before

'**He** (lit. **Him**) enjoyed (once again) sitting idly like earlier times.' (Midən, Ritter 1967–1971, 77/219)

The stimulus can be pronominalised like themes in a ditransitive construction, such as *-yo* in the following example:

b. *ú-dawšo* *basəm-∅-**li*** ***-yo***

the-honey.FS was.pleasant$_{PFV}$-it.M -him it

'The honey—**I** (lit. **Me**) liked **it**.'(Mzizaḥ)

It would seem that there are also constructions where *-yo* is effectively non-referential. This is at least the case in fixed expressions of the following kind:

c. *ġắlabe* *kary-ó-la* ***-yo*** *ʿal* *i-səsto*

very.much upset$_{PFV}$-it.F -her it on the-mare.FS

d-ú-babo

LNK-the-father:MS

'She (lit. Her **it**) was very upset about her father's mare.' (Ritter 1967–1971, 107/121)

25 Similarly, the verb *ḥly* 'sweet', e.g. *ḥaly-o-li* 'I liked her'.

The stimulus, however, can still control agreement and be referential, as is the case with the stimulus of *lzm* 'need' (56d-e) below.

d.	*ono*	*l-mə*	*g-*	*ləzm*	***-i***	*-li*
	I	for-what	PVB-	need$_{IPFV}$	-they	-me

'What do I need **them** (i.e. gold pieces) for?' (Midən; Ritter 1967–1971, 44/146)

e.	*ú-yawmo*	*d-*	*lŭzm*	***-at***	*-lan*	*itū́x*
	the-day.MS	REL	need$_{IPFV}$	-you.S	-us	come.IMP

'Come the day we need **you**$_{S}$!' (Midyat, letter, Ritter 1990, 207)

In NENA, the *qṭil*-based form of the experiencer predicate inflects for two L-suffixes such as (64b) and (65b) below. The first represents the impersonal coding, which is expressed by the E-suffix in the *qaṭəl*-based forms in (64a) and (65a), and the second denotes the R-like experiencer in both (64a-b) and (65a-b).

(64) C. Marga (NW Iraq)

a.	***ʾana***	*basəm-∅-**li***	*ʾixala*
	I	please-it.MS-me	food.MS

'**I** like the food.'

b.	***ʾana***	*bsə́m-le-**li***	*ʾixala*
	I	pleased-it.MS-me	food.MS

'**I** liked the food.'

(65) J. Dohok (NW Iraq; Molin and Noorlander fieldnotes)

a. ***ana*** *g-ʿajəb-∅-**li*** *xabuše*

I IND-pleases$_{IPFV}$-it.M-me apples.PL

‘**I** like apples.’

b. ***ana*** *ʿjə́b-le-**li*** *xabuše*

I IND-pleases$_{IPFV}$-it.M-me apples.PL

‘**I** liked apples.’

The only example known to me where Western Neo-Aramaic has similarly grammaticalised an experiencer L-suffix is the verb ‘want’ in the dialect of Jubbʿadin. The L-suffix attaches to an uninflected form *be-*, e.g. *bē-le* (< **bʿē l-eh* ‘Him wanted’), the originally 3ms. form of the resultative participle **bʿē* of *bʿy* ‘want’ (Arnold 1990a, 192). *bēle* (like *batte* in the other Western dialects) developed under influence of the corresponding construction *bədd-o* ‘He wants’ < ‘In his wish’ in local Arabic varieties. The experiencer nominal is zero-marked and controls the agreement expressed by the L-suffix:

(66) Jubbʿadin (SW Syria)

a. *wa* ***zalmθa*** *bē-**le*** *y-ʿammar* *ðorča*

PST somebody want-him he-build place

‘**Somebody** wanted to build a house.’
(Arnold 1990b, 16.1)

b. ***hi*** *bē-**la*** *č-ʿōwet*

she want-her she-return

‘**She** wants to return.’ (ibid. 78.45)

Similar impersonal 'want' constructions occur in Ṭuroyo and NENA to convey the sense of 'need'. The L-suffix expresses the person lacking something:

(67) Ṭuroyo (SE Turkey)

kə-	*bʿe*	***-lux***	*sayfo*	*kayiso*
PVB	want	-you.MS	sword.MS	good.MS

'**You** need a good sword.' (Prym and Socin 1881, 141.25)

(68) J. Betanure (NW Iraq)

g-	*bé*	*wā*	***-leni***	*ṛāba*	*ṣiwe*
PVB	want	PST	-us	very.much	wood.PL

'**We** needed a great deal of wood.' (Mutzafi 2008a, 142.33)

4.1.2. Intransitive Verbs

The L-suffix denoting the experiencer can even be added to an intransitive predicate such as the verb *ʾty* 'come' and *ʾwr* 'pass' in C. Urmi and J. Dohok. The mental state is expressed through an NP somehow reaching the experiencer.

(69) C. Urmi (Literary NW Iran; Polotsky 1979, 212)

*+**ʾav***	*ti*	*-la*	***-lə***	*muxabən*	*d-an*
he	came$_{PFV}$	-it$_{F}$	-him	pity.FS	of-DEM.PL

taxmanyatə
thoughts:PL

'**He** was sorry for those thoughts.'

(70) J. Dohok (NW Iraq; Molin and Noorlander fieldnotes)

wə́r	*-ra*	***-li***	*xšuta*	*b-reš-i*
passed$_{\text{PFV}}$	-it.F	-me	thought.FS	in-head-my

'I thought a thought in my mind.'

Verbal experiencer predicates can comprise an NP denoting the mental state or process somehow reaching the experiencer expressed through the L-suffix as illustrated in (71). Note that in (71a) and (71b) the verb does not agree with the NP and is essentially impersonal. The key person marker being the L-suffix.

(71) Ṭuroyo (SE Turkey)

a.

*k-oθe-∅-**li***	*šanθo*
IND-comes$_{\text{IPFV}}$-it.M-me	sleep.FS

'I am sleepy.'

b.

*aθi-∅-**li***	*ḥəmto*	*qwiθo*
came$_{\text{PFV}}$-it.M-me	fever.FS	heavy.FS

'I caught a heavy fever.' (ʿIwardo; Ritter 1967–1971, 44/146)

The experiencer can be added to intransitive verbs denoting physiological states such to 'be cold' in various dialects in SE Turkey. Thus the expression 'I am cold' corresponds with:

(72) Ṭuroyo (SE Turkey)

ko-	*qoraš*	***-li***
PVB	be.cold-	-me

(73) C. Artun (Hertevin, SE Turkey)

qarəš	***-li***
be.cold-	-me

(74) C. Umṛa (SE Turkey)

qayər	***-ri***
be.cold-	-me

There are several more intransitive verbs in Ṭuroyo that can express an experiencer in this way, notably *kyw* 'get ill', e.g. *kayu-li* 'I got ill', and *nyḥ* 'get well', *nayəḥ-li* 'I got well'. The verbs *ḥrw* 'be concerned' (lit. 'get destroyed') and *ʿyq* 'get distressed' combine with an additional prepositional stimulus. The verbal form is impersonal, for example:

(75) Ṭuroyo (SE Turkey)

a.

mə	*ḥaru*	***-lax***	*min-i*
what	be.destroyed	-you.FS	from-me

'Why are **you**$_{\mathrm{FS}}$ concerned about me?' (Kfaerze, Ritter 1967–1971, 61/324)

b.

ʿayəq	***-le***	*me-ruḥ-e*
be.distressed	him	from-self-his

'**He** (lit. **Him**) was distressed about himself.' (Kfaerze, ibid. 63/7)

4.1.3. Trans-Zab Jewish Dialects: *-la-l*-series

Jewish Western Iranian varieties, such as Saqqiz and Sandanaj, have a special use of the L-suffixes added to an invariant

-la- which presumably goes back to an impersonal L-suffix (see §3.2.3). Israel (1998, 170–71) records numerous examples where verbs in the *qaṭəl*-based inflection regularly combine with experiencers expressed in this way including verbs denoting pleasure such as *bsm* 'please' as illustrated below but also verbs denoting pain *mry* 'hurt', capability *kšy* 'find difficult' and merit such as *mṭy* 'deserve' (lit. reach) and *špr* 'befit'. The construction combines with a prepositional stimulus or a clausal complement. What is striking is that the morpheme *-la-*, although presumably originally an impersonal L-suffix (i.e. *bsəm-la-li* 'It$_{F}$ pleased me'), is also required with L-suffixes denoting experiencers in *qaṭəl*-based inflection[26]:

(76) J. Saqqiz (W Iran)

la	***basə́m-la***	***-li***	*mənn-év*
not	pleases$_{IPFV}$-it.M	me	from-him

'**I** (lit. **Me**) do not like (lit. **from**) him.' (Israeli 1998, 170–71)

4.2. Prepositional Marking of the Experiencer

4.2.1. Experiencer Marked by a Preposition only

So far we have observed that the experiencer NP is zero-marked like the 'canonical' subject and only expressed through L-suffixes on the verb. Nevertheless, prepositional marking of experiencer predicates does occur in several NENA dialects, reflecting an oblique status.

It is common for physiological states. The independent *ʾəll*-series is part of fixed expressions for the sensations of heat and

26 An invariant *-le-* also occurs with *qaṭəl*-inflection in C. Telkepe, e.g. *k-ʕājəb-le-li* 'I am willing' (Coghill 2019, 39).

cold which themselves feature as nouns in this construction, for example in C. Marga:

(77) C. Marga (NW Iraq)

a. *xə́mma-yle* ***ʾəlli***
heat:MS-it.is.M **me**
'**I** am hot' (lit. **Me** is heat)

b. *qársa-yla* ***ʾəlli***
coldness.MS-it.is.F me
'**I** am cold.' (lit. **Me** is cold)

Both NENA and Ṭuroyo dialects in SE Turkey confine this construction to the experiencer of heat, as illustrated below, while the sensation of cold is expressed through a verb, cf. (72)-(74) above.

(78) Ṭuroyo (SE Turkey)

ḥémo-yo ***aʕl-i***
heat.MS-it.is upon-me

(79) C. Artun (SE Turkey)

ḥəmme-le ***lal-i***
heat.MS-it.is.M to-me

(80) C. Umṛa (SE Turkey)

ḥəmme-le ***əll-i***
heat.MS-it.is.M to-me

'**I** am hot.'

Prepositional marking of experiencers typically occurs at least in Western Iranian dialects of NENA. The R-like experiencer is prepositional in the Christian variety of Sanandaj, for instance

(81) C. Sanandaj (W Iran)

maḥkēsa	*kabər-ta*	*špēr-a*[27]	***el-ē***
story.FS	great-FS	was.pleasant$_{PFV}$-it.F	to-him

'The story pleased **him** very much.' (Panoussi 1990, 123.31)

4.2.2. Experiencer Marked by *l-* and L-suffixes

Like the agent (§1.1.) and possessor (§3.3.2.), optional *l*-marking of the experiencer does occur in Ṭuroyo, for example:

(82) Ṭuroyo (SE Turkey)

a.

*maḥat-**le***	***l-ú-rŭʿyo***	*ú-darmono*
put$_{PFV}$-he	ERG-the-shepherd.MS	the-medicine.MS
*basəm-∅-**le***	***l-ú-rŭʿyo***	
was.pleasent-it.M-him	to-the-shepher.MS	

'**The shepherd** put the medicine (there) (and) **the shepherd** liked it.' (Midyat, Prym and Socin 1881, 29.10)

b.

ġắlabe	*kary-o-**le***	***l-ú-dahba***
very.much	upset-it.F-him	to-the-beast.MS

'**The beast** got very upset.' (Raite, Ritter 1967–1971, 112/331)

27 *špēra* < *sper-ra* < *sper-la

4.3. Transitivisation of Experiencer Verb Constructions

The verb *ʕjb* 'please, like', borrowed from Arabic, is a stem III causative verb in Ṭuroyo and is ambivalent as to its orientation. The verb of liking can be directed at the R-like affectee expressed by the L-suffix, for example:

(83) Ṭuroyo (SE Turkey)

a. *hăka lo maʕjáb-le-**lax***

if NEG III:pleased$_{PFV}$-it.M-you.FS

'If **you**$_{FS}$ don't like him' (Miden, Ritter 1967–1971, 115/147)

At the same time, the verb can also have undergone complete transitivization. Its coding is not distinct from primary transitive verbs. The experiencer is expressed like an agent, for example:

b. *ú-greʕuno d-həzy-**o**-le maʕajb-**o**-le*

the-youngling.MS REL-see$_{IPFV}$-she-him III:pleased$_{PFV}$-she-him

'The young man that **she** sees (and **she**) likes' (Miden, ibid. 75/199)

This also occurs in NENA dialects. At least in the preterite, the verb that is otherwise typically impersonal can also be used with 'canonical' transitive verbal coding, for instance in C. Urmi and C. Artun (Hertevin):

(84) C. Urmi (NW Iran)

ʾina	***ʾalaha***	*bsəm-lə*
if	God	please$_{PFV}$-he

'If **God** likes (it)' (Khan 2016$_{IV}$, A3:69)

(85) C. Artun (Hertevin, SE Turkey)

ana	*gălak*	*ʿjə́b-**lən**-na*[28]	*qaḥwa*
I	very.much	please$_{PFV}$-I-it.F	coffee.FS

'**I** liked the coffee very much.'

4.4. Verboids

A few experiencer verbs have a distinct verbal base in the imperfective, comparable to the verb *ʾzl* in some NENA dialects (see Subsection 2.2), e.g. *zəl-wa-li* 'I had gone' (perfective) and *k-za-wa-li* 'I used to go' (imperfective). The verb *zdy* ~ *zdʾ* 'fear, be afraid' has a regular *qṭil*-based preterite construction, e.g. J. Betanure *zdeʾ-**li*** '**I** feared', but an impersonal *qaṭəl*-based equivalent *ṣad-*, e.g. J. Betanure *k-ṣad-**li*** '**I** fear' (Mutzafi 2008, 88), C. Barwar *ʾi-ṣad-wa-**le*** 'He was afraid' (Khan 2008a, 297–98). Both *zdeʾ-* and *ṣad-* inflect the experiencer through L-suffixes, but the preterite forms like *zdeʾ-li* 'I feared' mark the experiencer completely like the agent of transitive verbs (*xze-li* 'I saw') and the forms based on *ṣad-* mark the experiencer like other impersonal experiencer verb constructions (*basəm-li* 'I like'). One may compare this also to the experiencer verboid *qar-* 'be cold' in *lišana deni* dialects (NW Iraq), e.g. J. Dohok *ʾana qar-ri* (< **qar-li*) 'I am cold', *qar-wa-li* 'I was cold'.

28 Compare §3.4. above for the transitivisation of predicative possessors in C. Artun (Hertevin).

Conclusions

Both the possessor and experiencer nominal or independent pronoun are generally clause-initial, zero-marked and obligatorily cross-referenced by the L-suffix in both NENA, Ṭuroyo and Western Neo-Aramaic. They are arguably 'non-canonical' subjects. Only sporadically do we find purely prepositional arguments.

L-suffixes can be added to monotransitive and intransitive verbs to express an R-like affectee in similar fashion to ditransitive verbs. While the optional subject co-referential L-suffixes marking that can mark an affected subject like the middle voice or express dynamic telicity seem to be generally a common Aramaic phenomenon, they undoubtedly conventionalized to verbal inflectional morphemes in certain Neo-Aramaic languages, particularly the motion verbs **ʾzl* 'go' and **ʾty* 'come'.

Impersonal experiencer constructions tend to diverge across dialects. It is common to find that verbs of liking take 'non-canonical' subject marking besides physiological states of 'cold' and 'heat'. Dialects can prefer distinct strategies for these physical sensations. In SE Turkey, for example, the experiencer of 'cold' is expressed by L-suffixes attached to a verbal predicate, while that of 'heat' by a preposition as a complement of a nominal predicate.

The Neo-Aramaic languages have developed 'non-canonical' subject marking that exhibits similar structures as the agent in the perfective past in NENA and Ṭuroyo (e.g. *grəš-li* 'I pulled'). The 'non-canonical' subject, for instance, can be marked by both the preposition *l-* and L-suffixes in Ṭuroyo only. This closely parallels the optional ergative marking in the preterite. An important difference from agent L-suffixes in the preterite is that the L-suffixes that mark the 'non-canonical' subject are found across the inflectional system, just like other R-like affectees. Exceptions where the 'non-canonical' subject marking is confined to the imperfective are the verbs 'fear', which has a verboid base *ṣad-*, and the verb 'go', which has a base *za-*, in NENA dialects. These correspond with the 'canonical' verbal inflection in the preterite (e.g. *zəl-lan* 'We went' : *za-lan* 'Let's go!').

The scope of this paper notwithstanding,[29] the originally dative possessor (i.e. **ʾīt-wā-∅ l-eh kθāwā* lit. 'Him was a book') and experiencer subjects (i.e. **bāsem-∅-wā-∅ l-eh deḇšā,* lit. 'Him was liking honey') and subject co-referential datives (i.e. **ʾāzel-∅-wā-∅ l-eh* lit. 'Him was going') and the historically dative subject of the preterite (i.e. **qīm-∅-wā-∅ l-eh* lit. 'Him was stood' → most of NENA *qəm-wa-le* 'He had stood') are all connected.

The topical, human and subject-like referent is referred back to by L-suffixes. The L-suffixes serve as cross-indexes of the possessor and experiencer similarly as their cross-indexing of agents in the preterite. The subject co-referential datives can similarly end up as inflectional affixes (e.g. Ṭuroyo *azz-í* 'I went' < **ʾazīl-∅ l-ī* 'Me went').

One important difference, however, is that the L-suffixes of the preterite are dependent on the inflectional base *qṭil-* and have an additional TAM function. This does not apply to the other uses of the L-suffixes that were subsumed under 'non-canonical' subjects in the previous discussion that can still be more R-like. The 'non-canonical' subject marking, therefore, is role-based. It is the construal as an R-like indirect affectee that makes it favour coding distinct from the 'canonical' subject. By contrast, the agent marking through L-suffixes in the preterite is not only role-based but also TAM-based. That is, the originally dative agent is dependent on the inflectional base (*qṭil-*) and hence, generally, perfective past aspect. Occasionally, however, the 'non-canonical' subject undergoes full transitivisation and takes over 'canonical' transitive coding. Sometimes it is only the transitive morphosyntax peculiar to the *qṭil*-based preterite that is taken over, identifying the L-suffixes that mark the possessor or experiencer with those that mark the agent.

29 Cf. Noorlander (2019a-b). One can compare this to European languages like French and Dutch where HAVE can be used as a possessive verb (*J'ai du pain* 'I have some bread'), a tense-aspect auxiliary (e.g. HAVE-perfect *J'ai mangé du pain* 'I ate some bread') and an experiencer verb (lit. *J'ai froid* 'I am cold', lit. 'I have cold').

Nevertheless, it is also clear that in many cases where the L-suffix is used as an extension of an R-like affectee the suffix can maintain characteristics of a ditransitive construction. These subject-like affectees are still treated like recipients, presumably as relics of their formerly dative prepositional marking. This is evident in the stacking of L-suffixes to the *qṭil*-base in NENA where the first L-suffix is impersonal and the second L-suffix denotes the R-like affectee. Impersonal experiencers thus resemble the predicative possessor construction based on the invariable existential marker (cf. Polotsky 1979, 209–10), yet, since they are verbal, they select the regular verbal affixes, even L-suffixes expressing the impersonal agent in the *qṭil*-based forms (e.g. *ʕjəb-le-le ʾalaha* 'It$_{M}$ pleased God'). Pronominalisation of the stimulus can be expressed by the unmarked set of bound person markers (also serving as the copula) like *-yo* in Ṭuroyo, which are confined to third person themes in ditransitive clauses.

The topicalisation and hence zero-marking of the NP became increasingly obligatory and original independent prepositional pronouns have undergone complete verbalisation in most cases. L-suffixes, while originally prepositional and independent of the verb, exhibit a tendency to convert into verbal person markers and sustain referential continuity with the most topical argument in sometimes otherwise largely impersonal predicates.

Both more conservative and more innovative patterns are found in Neo-Aramaic. Dialects also have the option to withstand the proclivity to convert a topicalised affectee into a 'non-canonical' subject. A dialect may still prefer to retain prepositional marking as a viable alternative besides verbal person marking or it may prefer an oblique status throughout for such arguments. In the end, each dialect 'can do its own thing' and a uniform category of 'subject' is not always readily identifiable.

References

Any data not cited are based on the author's notes from fieldwork individually or in collaboration with G. Khan and/or D. Molin.

Al-Zahre, Nisrine and Nora Boneh, 2010. "Coreferential Dative Constructions in Syrian Arabic and Modern Hebrew'. *Brill's Annual of Afroasiatic Languages and Linguistics* 2: 248–82.

Bar-Asher, Elitzur A. 2008. 'The Origin and the Typology of the Pattern "qtil li" in Syriac and Babylonian Aramaic'. In *Sha'arey Lashon: Studies in Hebrew, Aramaic, and Jewish Languages in Honor of Moshe Bar–Asher* II, edited by Aharon Maman, Steven Fassberg and Yohanan Breuer, 360–92. In Hebrew. Jerusalem: Bialik Institute.

———. 2011. 'On the Passiveness of one Pattern in Jewish Babylonian Aramaic—A Linguistic and Philological Discussion'. *Journal of Semitic Studies* 56: 111–43.

———,. 2014. 'From a Non-Argument-Dative to an Argument Dative: The Character and Origin of the *Qṭil Li* Construction in Syriac and Jewish Babylonian Aramaic'. *Folia Orientalia* 51: 59–101.

Berman, Ruth A. 1982. 'Dative Marking of the Affectee Role: Data from Modern Hebrew'. *Hebrew Annual Review* 6: 35–59.

Coghill, Eleanor. 2010. 'Ditransitive Constructions in the Neo-Aramaic Dialect of Telkepe'. In *Studies in Ditransitive Constructions: A Comparative Handbook*, edited by Andreĭ L'vovich Mal'chukov, Martin Haspelmath, and Bernard Comrie, 221–42. De Gruyter.

———. 2014. 'Differential Object–Marking in Neo–Aramaic'. *Linguistics* 52: 335–64.

———. 2016. *The Rise and Fall of Ergativity in Aramaic: Cycles of Alignment Change.* Oxford (etc.): Oxford University Press.

———. 2019. 'Grammatical relations in Telkepe Neo-Aramaic'. In *Argument Selectors: A new perspective on grammatical relations*, edited by Alena Witzlack-Makarevich and Balthasar Bickel, 349–98. Amsterdam: Benjamins.

Cohen, Eran. 2012. *The Syntax of Neo–Aramaic: The Jewish Dialect of Zakho.* Piscataway, NJ: Gorgias Press.

Cole, Peter, Wayne Harbert, Gabriella Hermon and Shikaripur N. Sridhar. 1980. 'The Acquisition of Subjecthood'. *Language* 56: 719–43.

Comrie, Bernard. 1982. 'Syntactic—Morphological Discrepancies in Maltese Sentence Structure'. *Communication and Cognition* 15 (3/4): 281–306.

Cowell, Mark W. 1964. *A Reference Grammar of Syrian Arabic*. Washington, D.C.: Georgetown University Press.

Damsma, Alinda. forthcoming. *The Neo-Aramaic Dialect of Haṣṣan*.

Diem, Werner. 2012. *Vom Status pendens zum Satzsubjekt: Studien zur Topikalisierung in neueren semitischen Sprachen*. Wiesbaden: Harrassowitz.

Doron, Edit and Geoffrey Khan. 2012. 'The Typology of Morphological Ergativity in Neo-Aramaic'. *Lingua* 122: 225–40.

Fassberg, Steven. 2018. 'The Ethical Dative in Aramaic'. *Aramaic Studies* 16: 101–16.

Fox, Samuel E. 2009. *The Neo-Aramaic Dialect of Bohtan*. Gorgias Neo-Aramaic Studies 9. Piscataway, NJ: Gorgias Press.

Givón, Talmy. 1976. 'Topic, Pronoun and Grammatical Agreement'. In *Subject and Topic*, edited by Charles N. Li, 151 – 85. New York: Academic Press.

Goldenberg, Gideon. 1997. 'Conservative and Innovative Features in Semitic Languages'. In *Afroasiatica Neapolitana*, edited by Alessandro Bausi and Mauro Tosco, 3–21. Studi Africanistici. Serie Etiopica 6. Napoli: Istituto Universitario Orientale.

Greenblatt, Jared. 2011. *The Jewish Neo-Aramaic Dialect of Amədya*. Leiden: Brill.

Gutman, Ariel. 2008. 'Reexamination of the Bare Preterite Base in the Jewish Neo-Aramaic Dialect of Zakho'. *Aramaic Studies* 6 (1): 59–84.

Haig, Geoffrey. 2018a. 'The Grammaticalization of Object Pronouns: Why Differential Object Indexing is an Attractor State'. *Linguistics* 56 (4): 781–818.

———. 2018b. 'Northern Kurdish (Kurmanjî)'. In *The Languages and Linguistics of Western Asia. An Areal Perspective*, edited by Geoffrey Haig and Geoffrey Khan, 106–58. Berlin: De Gruyter.

———. 2018c. 'The Iranian Languages of Northern Iraq'. In *The Languages and Linguistics of Western Asia. An Areal Perspective*, edited by Geoffrey Haig and Geoffrey Khan, 267–304. Berlin: De Gruyter.

Halevy, Rivka. 2008. 'Grammaticalization 'Chains' of the Subject–Coreferential Dative in Semitic and Elsewhere'. *New Reflections on Grammaticalization*, Leuven 17–19/07/2008. Conference presentation.

Hoberman, Robert. D. 1989. *The Syntax and Semantics of Verb Morphology in Modern Aramaic: A Jewish Dialect of Iraqi Kurdistan*. American Oriental Series 69. New Haven, Connecticut: American Oriental Society.

Hopkins, Simon. 1989. 'A Tale in the Jewish Neo–Aramaic Dialect of Naγada (Persian Azerbaijan)'. *Jerusalem Studies in Arabic and Islam* 12: 243–81.

Israeli, Yafa. 1998. *The Jewish Neo–Aramaic Dialect of Saqqiz (Southern Kurdistan)*. Ph.D. Thesis. In Hebrew. Jerusalem. Hebrew University of Jerusalem.

Jastrow, Otto. 1985. *Laut- und Formenlehre des neuaramäischen Dialekts von Mīdin im Ṭūr ʿAbdīn*. Wiesbaden: Harrassowitz.

———. 1988. *Der neuaramäische Dialekt von Hertevin (Province Siirt)*. Semitica Viva 3. Wiesbaden: Harrassowitz.

———. 1992. *Lehrbuch der Ṭuroyo–Sprache*. Semitica Viva Didactica 2. Wiesbaden: Harrassowitz.

———. 1994. *Der neuaramäische Dialekt von Mlaḥsô*. Semitica Viva 14. Wiesbaden: Harrassowitz.

Joosten, Jan. 1989. 'The Function of the So-called Dativus Ethicus in Classical Syriac'. *Orientalia* 58: 473–92.

Kapeliuk, Olga. 1989. 'Some Common Traits in the Evolution of Neo-Syriac and of Neo-Ethiopian'. *Jerusalem Studies in Arabic and Islam* 12: 294–320.

Keenan, Edward L. 1976. 'Towards a Universal Definition of Subject'. In *Subject and Topic*, edited by Charles N. Li, 303–33. New York: Academic Press.

Khan, Geoffrey. 1988. *Studies in Semitic Syntax*. Oxford: Oxford University Press.

———. 1999. *A Grammar of Neo–Aramaic: The Dialect of the Jews of Arbel*. Leiden: Brill.

———. 2002. *The Neo–Aramaic Dialect of Qaraqosh*. Leiden: Brill.

———. 2008a. *The Neo–Aramaic Dialect of Barwar* I–III. Leiden: Brill.

———. 2008b. *The Jewish Neo–Aramaic Dialect of Urmi*. Piscataway, NJ: Gorgias Press.

———. 2009. *The Jewish Neo–Aramaic Dialect of Sanandaj*. Piscataway, NJ: Gorgias Press.

———. 2016. *The Neo-Aramaic Dialect of the Assyrian Christians of Urmi.* Studies in Semitic Languages and Linguistics 86, I: Grammar: Phonology and morphology, II: Grammar: Syntax, III: Lexical studies and dictionary, IV: Texts. Leiden: Brill.

Lehmann, Christian. 1988. 'On the Function of Agreement'. In *Agreement in Natural Language: Approaches, Theories, Descriptions*, edited by Michael Barlow and Charles A. Ferguson, 55 – 65. Stanford, CA: Center for the Study of Language and Information.

Mengozzi, Alessandro. 2002a. *Israel of Alqosh and Joseph of Telkepe: A Story in a Truthful Language Religious Poems in Vernacular Syriac (North Iraq, 17th Century)* I: *An Anthology*. Corpus Scriptorum Christianorum Orientalium 627. Louvain: Éditions Peeters.

———. 2002b. *Israel of Alqosh and Joseph of Telkepe: A Story in a Truthful Language Religious Poems in Vernacular Syriac (North Iraq, 17th Century)* II: *Introduction and Translation*. Corpus Scriptorum Christianorum Orientalium 628. Louvain: Éditions Peeters.

———. 2006. 'Middle Markers: Neo–Aramaic and Italian Verbal Forms with a 3rd Singular Feminine Pronominal Object'. In *XII Incontro Italiano di Linguistica Camito–Semitica (Afroasiatica): Atti*, edited by Marco Moriggi, 105–15. Soviera Mannelli: Rubbettino.

Mor, Uri and Na'ama Pat-El 2016. 'The Development of Predicates with Prepositional Subjects in Hebrew'. *Journal of Semitic Studies*, 61(2): 327 – 46.

Mutzafi, Hezy. 2004. *The Jewish Neo–Aramaic Dialect of Koy Sanjaq (Iraqi Kurdistan)*. Semitica Viva 32. Wiesbaden: Harrassowitz.

———. 2008a. *The Jewish Neo–Aramaic Dialect of Betanure (Province of Dihok)*. Semitica Viva 40. Wiesbaden: Harrassowitz.

Mutzafi, Hezy. 2008b. 'Trans–Zab Jewish Neo–Aramaic'. *Bulletin of the School of Oriental and African Studies* 71 (3): 409–31.

Næss, Åshild. 2007. *Prototypical Transitivity*. Amsterdam: John Benjamins.

Noorlander, Paul M. 2012. 'Neo-Aramaic Alignment in a Historical Perspective: Some Preliminary Remarks'. *Semitics Philology Seminar*, Cambridge, 03/12/2012. Invited talk.

———. 2018a. 'Me Likes the Subject–Subject-like Properties of Experiencers and Possessors in Aramaic'. *Neo-Aramaic Languages across Space and Time.* Uppsala, 05–07/10/2018. Conference presentation.

———. 2018b. *Alignment in Eastern Neo-Aramaic Languages from a Typological Perspective.* Ph.D. Thesis. Leiden: Leiden University.

———. 2019a. 'Resultatives and Asymmetries in Aramaic Alignment Change'. *International Conference on Historical Linguistics*, Canberra, 01–05/07/2019. Conference presentation.

———. 2019b. 'One Way of Becoming Perfect? Possessive Resultatives in Semitic and Aramaic in Particular'. Semitic Philology Seminar. Cambridge, 14/10/2019. Invited talk.

———. Forthcoming. *Encounters with Ergativity and other Alignment Types in Neo-Aramaic: A Study of Dialectal Microvariation.* Studies in Semitic Languages and Linguistics. Leiden: Brill.

Onishi, Masayuki. 2001. 'Non-canonically Marked Subjects and Objects: Parameters and Properties'. In *Non–Canonical Marking of Subjects and Objects*, edited by Alexandra Y. Aikhenvald, Robert M. W. Dixon and Masayuki Onishi, 1–51. Typological Studies in Language 46. Amsterdam: John Benjamins.

Panoussi, Estiphan. 1990. 'On the Senaya Dialect'. In *Studies in Neo-Aramaic*, edited by Wolfhart Heinrichs, 107–29. Atlanta, GA: Scholars Press.

Pat-El, Na'ama. 2018. 'The Diachrony of Non-canonical Subjects in Northwest Semitic'. In *Non–Canonically Case–Marked Subjects: The Reykjavík–Eyjafjallajökull Papers.* Studies in Language Companion Series 200, edited by Jóhanna Barðdal, Na'ama Pat-El and Stephen M. Carey, 159–84. Amsterdam: John Benjamins.

Pennacchietti, Fabrizio A. 1994. 'Il Preterito Neoaramaico con Pronome Oggetto'. *Zeitschrift der Deutschen Morgenländischen Gesellschaft* 144: 259–83.

Polotsky, Hans Jakob. 1979. 'Verbs with two Objects in Modern Syriac (Urmi)'. *Israel Oriental Studies* 9: 204–27.

———. 1996. 'Notes on a Neo–Syriac Grammar'. *Israel Oriental Studies* 16: 11–48.

Prym, Eugen and Albert Socin 1881. *Der neu-aramaeische Dialekt des Ṭûr 'Abdîn.* Göttingen: Vandenhoeck & Ruprecht's Verlag.

Rendsburg, Gary A. 1991. 'Parallel Developments in Mishnaic Hebrew, Colloquial Arabic, and other Varieties of spoken Semitic'. In *Semitic Studies in Honor of Wolf Leslau*, II, edited by Alan S. Kaye, 1265–77. Wiesbaden: Harrassowitz.

Rhétoré, P. Jacques. 1912. *Grammaire de la langue Soureth ou chaldeen vulgaire, selon le dialecte de la plaine de Mossoul et des pays adjacents*. Mossoul: Imprimerie des Pères Dominicains.

Ritter, Helmut. 1967–1971. *Ṭūrōyō: Die Volksprache der syrischen Christen des Ṭūr ʕAbdîn A. Texte* I: 1967, II: 1969, III: 1971. Beirut: Steiner.

Rubin, Aaron D. 2005. *Studies in Semitic Grammaticalization*. Harvard Semitic Studies 57. Winona Lake, Indiana: Eisenbrauns.

Stassen, Leon. 2009. *Predicative Possession*. Oxford: Oxford University Press.

Stilo, Donald L. and Paul M. Noorlander. 2015. 'On the Convergence of Verbal Systems of Aramaic and its Neighbours. Part II: Past Paradigms Derived from Present Equivalents'. In *Neo-Aramaic and its Linguistic Context*, edited by Geoffrey Khan and Lidia Napiorkowska, 453–85. Piscataway, NJ: Gorgias Press.

Talay, Shabo. 2004. Ed. *Lebendig begraben: Die Entführung des syrisch–orthodoxen Priesters Melki Tok von Midən in der Südosttürkei. Einführung, aramäischer Text (Turoyo), Übersetzung und Glossar*. Studien zur Orientalischen Kirchengeschichte 29. Münster: LIT.

Waltisberg, Michael. 2016. *Syntax des Ṭuroyo*. Semitica Viva 55. Wiesbaden: Harrassowiz.

THE JEWISH NEO-ARAMAIC DIALECT OF DOHOK: TWO FOLKTALES AND SELECTED FEATURES OF VERBAL SEMANTICS

Dorota Molin

1. Introduction

This paper presents a selection of primary data from the hitherto unstudied NENA dialect of the Jews of the town of Dohok, located in north-western Iraq (this dialect is henceforth referred to as 'Jewish Dohok'). Glossing is provided for a part of the texts to ensure accessibility for readers who are not NENA specialists and notes on noteworthy linguistic features are supplied. These texts are complemented by a brief grammatical study, which is based on the texts. This study surveys selected features of verbal semantics[1] of Jewish Dohok. In particular, the study focuses on verbal forms with a grammatical function that is distinct from the function of the corresponding forms in many other NENA dialects. This demonstrates the importance of studying each dialect in its own right. The paper aims to situate the Jewish Dohok dialect typologically within the broader NENA family. In addition, it draws attention to certain less prototypical functions of the verbal forms in question. Such functions apparently reflect the subjective creative use of the tense-aspect-mood system in order to achieve a particular discourse effect.

1 The terms 'verbal semantics', 'grammatical semantics' and 'grammatical functions' are used here synonymously. These refer to the tense-aspect-mood system in its various grammatical and pragmatic applications.

 https://doi.org/10.11647/OBP.0209.03

The Jewish Dohok dialect is most closely affiliated with a group of Jewish dialects that were historically spoken West of the Great Zab River, and are known by their speakers and scholars as *Lišana Deni* ('our language'). Dialects belonging to this group were spoken also in Zakho, Amedia, Betanure, Nerwa (north-western Iraq) and Challa (south-eastern Turkey). Today, the Jewish Dohok dialect is on the verge of extinction, having only about twenty remaining active speakers. These speakers were born in the 1930s or 1940s in Dohok, or in the 1950s in Israel. As far as I know, all of them live today in Israel, mostly in the Jerusalem area.

In the following section, two folk tales are presented. I recorded these in 2018 in Castel (near Jerusalem). They were narrated by Mr Tzvi Avraham (aged 79).

The stories presented here give a taste of the rich oral literature of the NENA-speaking Jews.[2] Though stories such as the ones presented here were narrated in the Jewish community in Aramaic, many of them are likely to have been Kurdish (or Arabic) in origin (Sabar 1982, xxxii). The folktales are indeed sometimes situated in the realia of the Kurdish world—a fact illustrated in the following stories by the direct speech in lines 19 and 20 of the first story. A part of this speech is given in Bahdini Kurdish.[3] Other stories, however, appear to be distinctly Jewish, as shown by their ideological character. This was the view of the narrator himself. I have collected several stories that feature the figure of a poor, yet wise Jew, who—contrary to everyone's expectation—emerges as the hero of the story. Such folktales are apparently aimed at raising the morale of the Jews by presenting them in a very positive light (e.g. showing their resourcefulness).

2 See Aloni (2018) for the folk literature of the *Lišana Deni* Aramaic speakers. All of the other communities of the area—NENA-speaking Christians, as well as Kurdish- and Arabic-speaking communities—also possess a wealth of oral literature. These different story-telling traditions have historically undoubtedly been in contact with one another (e.g., Coghill 2009).

3 For background on the folk literature of the Aramaic-speaking Jews, see Sabar (1982) and other publications by this author.

2. The Verbal System of Jewish Dohok

In addition to their cultural value, the following folktales also attest to the complexity of the verbal system. The verbal system of Jewish Dohok, as is the case with that of other NENA dialects, can convey nuanced meanings of tense, aspect and mood, and enliven and structure the narrative, e.g., draw attention to noteworthy situations, divide story units (cf. Coghill 2009; Khan 2009). Some noteworthy forms found in the stories are used as the starting point of the grammatical survey. Reference will also be made to 'the corpus'. This is a body of Jewish Dohok texts consisting of orally-delivered personal narratives, folktales and descriptions of customs that I have collected from five different speakers.

Methodologically, this study draws from the notions of Function Grammar (Dik 1997), which maintains that the meaning of a given verbal form is context-dependent, in that it emerges from the interaction of the form with the other arguments in the context. The relevant context may be the clause or the broader discourse. In some cases a form conveys a general meaning, but the specific meaning arises from the contextual usage of the verbal form. In such cases, the verbal form is said to be 'unmarked' for the specific contextual meaning (Comrie 1976, 111–12). For example, while the future is most often 'perfective' (that is, the clause does not focus on the internal temporal composition of the situation such as its iteration or temporal duration), in Jewish Dohok, there is only one form for the expression of futurity. This means that the prototypically-future verbal form itself is aspectually unmarked and the specific aspect of the verb depends on contextual usage. A similar question of interaction between different factors contributing to 'meaning' applies to lexical semantics: sometimes—though not always—grammatical meaning interacts with lexical meaning (Comrie 1976, 41–51), suggesting that lexical meaning may also be a relevant factor in the semantics of verbs.[4]

---

4 For the application of an approach which is more structuralist in nature, see Hoberman (1989, 123–24; *Lišana Deni* dialects), and for a functional

The following overview of the verbal system will aid the reader in following the stories and the grammatical survey. Jewish Dohok has four inflectional bases: *šaqəl*, *šqəl*, *šqul* and *šqil*.[5] The *šaqəl* form is semantically the most versatile one. Its grammatical meaning is determined by a verbal prefix or its absence. In addition to these bases, the infinitive form *šqala* is also used in some constructions.

The table below presents the inventory of verbal forms, their prototypical grammatical functions and the glosses used to mark them in this paper. A category is left blank if the form is considered unmarked for that feature (i.e. it may express different values of this feature). In light of the aforementioned versatility of *šaqəl*, I have adopted a glossing system in which only the meaning-specifying verbal affixes—and not the inflectional base itself—are tagged.[6] The base itself is glossed only with the lexical meaning of the verb.

Table 1: Forms based on *šaqəl*

Form	Gloss	Tense	Aspect	Mood
Ø-šaqəl	IRR-	present, future		irrealis
	FUT/IRR-*	future		
la šaqəl	NEG IRR-			irrealis (including negative imperative)
k-šaqəl	HAB-	present		realis

study which pays special attention to discourse parameters and discourse functions of verbal forms, see Cohen (2012; Jewish Zakho dialect).

5 The default way of referring to inflectional categories of the verb in this article is by their morphological pattern—by using an exemplary verbal form from the root *š-q-l* 'to take'—rather than by their TAM functions.

6 This idea has been suggested to me by Paul Noorlander, to whom I express my gratitude for consultation in devising the glossing system.

Form	Gloss	Tense	Aspect	Mood
wəl k-šaqəl	PROG	present	progressive (non-stative?)	realis
la k-šaqəl	NEG HAB-	present		realis
		future		predictive
p-šaqəl	FUT-	future		predictive
~~la p-šaqəl~~	(no negation of *p-šaqəl*)			
qam-šaqəl**-le	PFV-	past	perfective	realis
Ø-šaqəl-wa	IRR- -PST	past		irrealis
		past	habitual	realis
k-šaqəl-wa	HAB- -PST	past	habitual	realis
p-šaqəl-wa	FUT- -PST	future in the past, past	habitual	realis

*This applies to Patterns II, III and IV (whose traditional names in Semitic philology are, respectively, 'stems II and III' and 'the quadriliteral stem'). In these forms, whic realis h always begin with *m*, the future prefix *b-/p-* has been lost after being assimilated to the following *m*, e.g.: **b-mašxən-Ø* (FUT-warm_up-he) 'he will warm up' > **m-mašxən* > *mašxən*. This has led to their merger with the *šaqəl* forms, i.e.: *Ømašxən-Ø* (IRR-warm_up-he) 'he may warm up'. In order to indicate this morphological ambiguity, all Pattern II, III and IV *šaqəl* forms and those that may have been underlyingly *p-šaqəl* are glossed as IRR/FUT.

**The alternative to *šqəlle*, used with object suffixes.

Table 2: Forms based on *šqəlle*

Form	Gloss	Tense	Aspect	Mood
šqəl-le	PFV.	past	perfective	realis
šqəl-wa-le	PFV. -PST	anterior past	perfective	realis

Table 3: Forms based on the infinitive (*šqala*)

Form	Gloss	Tense	Aspect	Mood	Resultativity
copula *bə-šqala*	in-(taking)	present	continuous (in stative verbs) continuous (non-dynamic)	realis	resultative

Table 4: Forms based on the imperative (*šqul*)

Form	Gloss	Mood
šqul	IMP.	irrealis: imperative
~~*la šqul*~~	(no negation of *šqul*)	

Table 5: Forms based on the resultative participle (šqila)

Form	Gloss	Resultativity
copula + *šqila*	RES.	resultative, experiential perfect

3. Texts with Comments on Selected Grammatical Features

3.1. Transcription and Translation Conventions

As the overview of the verbal system will have made apparent, the complexity of the meanings of verbal forms cannot be fully captured by a glossing system. The glosses that are used here, therefore, are conventional. The table above may be consulted for a more nuanced characterisation of the forms.

As for the transcription, a minimalist system is used. This assumes a phonetically predictable opposition of long vowels (open, unaccented syllables) and of short ones (elsewhere). Consequently, vowel length or shortness is only indicated when not predictable from this rule. One of the exceptions to this are monosyllabic words with *a* with an open syllable (the most common of which are *xa* 'one, a certain', *la* 'no' and verbal negator, *ma* 'what' *ta* 'for (+noun)'), which are always short. Being lexically predictable, shortness in these words is not marked. Monosyllabic prepositions and conjunctions (that is, with the exception of monophonemic ones) are transcribed as separate words. In the vast majority of cases, however, they do not carry nucleus stress, and lexical stress in them is inaudible.

Typically, only nucleus stress is marked (̀), and the end of an intonation unit is indicated by the symbol 'ˈ|'. Sometimes, however, a single intonation unit apparently has two nucleus stresses, both of which are indicated. Lexical stress is only indicated when it is not penultimate (in morphologically complex verbal forms, this typically has implications for vowel length, which is also marked).

The symbols '-' and '=' are employed in the transcription. '=' is used for enclitics. In Jewish Dohok, the only certain (i.e. phonetically verifiable) type of clitic is the present copula, so this sign is used only in those cases. The symbol '-' is used for certain units that are morphologically complex, but prosodically are one word. This is done to make the reading more transparent.

Foreign words and phrases which reflect spontaneous code-switching, rather than being loans, are marked with superscript 'H', 'A' and 'K'. These indicate, respectively, Modern Hebrew, Arabic or Bahdini Kurdish as the source. In these words, phonological detail, i.e. vowel length and lexical stress, is not indicated. Morphologically unintegrated loanwords are not parsed.

The recordings of the two stories are available online at https://nena.ames.cam.ac.uk/.

Text 1: A Man is a Wolf to a Wolf

1. *ʾəθ-wa xa-beθa d-Ø-ʿāyə̀š-Ø-wa…*ˈ

   EXIST-PST a-house REL-IRR-live-he-PST

   There was a household who used to live on…

2. *bab-ət beθa d-Ø-ʿāyəš-Ø-wa mən ṣìw-e.*ˈ

   father-GEN house REL-IRR-live-he-PST from wood-PL

   …a father of a household who used to make his living by woodcutting.[7]

3. *g-ezəl-Ø-wa go ṭùra,*ˈ *q-qāṭe-Ø-wa ṣìw-e.*ˈ

   HAB-go-he-PST in mountain, HAB-cut-he-PST wood-PL

   He used to go to the mountain and cut wood.

4. *g-meθè-Ø-wa-lu,*ˈ *Ø-dāré-Ø-wa-lu rəš xmara dìde,*ˈ

   HAB-bring-he-PST-them, IRR-place-he-PST-them on donkey his

   He would bring them, place them on his donkey

7 Sentence 2. is not its own clause, but rather a correction to sentence 1., itself unfinished. This is reflected in the translation.

5. *g-ewə́ð-Ø-wā-lu kàr-ta,*ˈ
HAB-make-he-PST-them bundle-FS

and bind them in a bundle.

6. *g-dāré-Ø-wa-lu kàr-ta*ˈ *rəš xmara dìde.*ˈ
HAB-place-he-PST-them bundle-FS on donkey his

He would put them [as] a bundle on his donkey's back.

7. *ʾu-g-nābə́l-Ø-wa-lu šùqa,*ˈ *gə-mzābə̀n-Ø-wa-lu.*ˈ
and-HAB-take-he-PST-them market, HAB-sell-he-PST-them

He would take them to the market and sell them.

8. *g-meθe-Ø-wa ʾĭxala ta yalunk-e dìde.*ˈ
HAB-bring-he-PST food. to child-PL his.

Then, he would bring food for his children.

9. *ʾu-k-eθe-Ø-wa k-əxl-i-wa*
and-HAB-come-he-PST. HAB-eat-they-PST

10. *g-ʿeš-i-wa b-ət-ʾànna,*ˈ *mən mzabon-ət ṣìw-e.*ˈ
HAB-live-they-PST in-GEN-these, from selling-GEN wood-PL.

When he came, they would eat and live on this, from the selling of the wood.

11. *xa yoma zəl-le l-ṭùra,*ˈ *b-qaṭe-Ø ṣìw-e,*ˈ
One day PFV.go-he to-mountain, FUT-cut-he wood-PL,

One day he went to the mountain—he would cut trees,

12. *xze-le xa-gùrga.*ˈ
PFV.see-he a-wolf.

and he saw a wolf.

13. *ʾaw gurga g-emər-Ø ṭa-le*
that$_M$ wolf HAB-say-he to-him
*mà wət ʾəθya?*ˈ
what COP.PRS.you$_{MS}$ RES.come.MS?
This wolf said to him 'Why have you come?'

14. *g-emər-Ø ʾana g-əb-ən*[8]*...*ˈ
HAB-say-he I HAB-want-I$_M$
g-ʿeš-ən b-ət qaṭʾ-ən[9] *ṣìw-e.*ˈ
HAB-live-I$_M$ in-GEN IRR-cut-I$_M$ wood-PL.
He said 'I want to… I make my living by woodcutting.

15. *gə-mzabn-ən-nu go šuqa*
HAB-sell-I$_M$-them in market
*ʾu-Ø-máʿăyəš-ən yalunk-e dìdi.*ˈ
and-IRR/FUT-sustain-I child-PL my
I sell it in the market and provide for my children.

16. *bə-d-è ʾana g-ʿeš-ən.*ˈ
In-GEN-this$_F$ I HAB-live-I$_M$
In this way I make my living.'

---

8 Note that the modal word is *gəbən* is followed by a realis form, though irrealis forms are standard in such contexts. These two verbs are therefore not a single construction but are separated by a hesitation. This is indicated in the translation. Indeed, it is the only attestation of such a sequence of verbs (modal verb + realis verb) in my corpus. The informant himself rejected other such constructions during an interview.

9 The activity 'woodcutting' in the construction *gʿešən bət qaṭʾən ṣìwe* in the sentence above is expressed by a finite form (literally 'I live by that I cut wood'), rather than by the infinitive *qṭaʾa* 'cutting'. The infinitive is expected here, and is in fact attested after the verb *ʿ-y-š* 'to make a living' in sentences 9–10 above: *gʿešìwa (…) mən mzabonət ṣìwe.*

17. *g-emər-Ø* *ˀana* *b-yāw-ən-nox* *kud-yom*
HAB-say-he I FUT-give-I-you every-day

xa *lira* *kurkamàna.*ˈ
one coin golden

He replied ‘Every day, I will give you one golden coin.

18. *s-i* *maṣrəf-Ø* *ta yalunk-e* *didox.*ˈ
IMP.go-you_{MS} IMP.spend-you_{CS} to child-PL your_{MS}

Go, spend it on your children.’

19. *g-emər-Ø,* ^{K}*xera xudè*^{K} *= la,*ˈ
HAB-say-he ^{K}God’s favour^{K} = COP.PRS.she

He said ‘it is ^{K}God’s favour^{K},

20. ^{K}*xera xude*^{K} *b-ət kərmànji* *g-əmr-i.*ˈ
^{K}God’s favour^{K} in-GEN Kurmanji HAB-say-they

^{K}God’s favour^{K}!’ They said it in Kurmanji.

21. *šqəl-le*[10] *lira* *kurkamana* *dide* *mən gùrga*ˈ
PFV.take-he coin golden his from wolf

He took his golden coin from the wolf

22. *ˀu-θe-le* *l-šùqa.*ˈ
and-PFV.come-he to-market.

and came to the market

10 The definite direct object *lira kurkamana dide* is not referenced with an object suffix on the verb. In the past tense in Jewish Dohok, we would expect here the following construction: *qam-šāqəl-Ø-le* (pfv-take-he-him) *lira kurkamana dide.* In NENA, definite objects are generally referenced with an object suffix on the verb itself. For a recent study on object marking in NENA, see, for instance, Coghill (2014).

23. *ʾu-zun-ne* *ta gyane* *ʾĭxala*
and-PFV.buy-he to himself food
ʾu-jull-e *ta yalunk-e* *dìde,*ˈ
and-cloth-PL to child-PL his.
and bought food for himself, and clothes for his children,

24. *ʾu-*^{A}*mabsuṭ*^{A} *mər-re* *ta bàx-t-e*ˈ
and-^{A}pleased^{A} PFV.say-he to wife-FS-his
and pleased, he told his wife

25. *wal̤l̤a* *ʾana* *xze-li* *xa-xùra*ˈ
indeed I PFV.meet-I a-friend
*go ṭura*ˈ *bale* *gùrgā=le.*
in-mountain but wolf=COP.PRS.he.
'Indeed, I met a friend on the mountain, but he is a wolf.

26. *kud-yom* *g-emər-Ø*
every-day HAB-say-he
ʾana *b-yāwən-nox* *xa* *kurkamàna.*ˈ
I FUT-give-I-you$_{M}$ one golden
"Every day"—he said—"I will give you one golden coin."

27. *ʾùd-le-li* *ʾədyo* *kurkamàna.*ˈ
PFV.make-he-me today golden.
He has given me today a golden coin.'

28. *kud-yom* *g-ezəl-Ø* *l-ṭura*
every-day HAB-go-he to-mountain

ʾu-g-ewəð-Ø	*ṣìw-e*ˈ
and-HAB-make-he	wood-PL

So every day, he goes to the mountain, cuts wood

29.

ʾu-k-eθe-Ø	*gurga*	*g-yāwəl-Ø-le*	*kurkamàna.*ˈ
and-HAB-come-he	wolf	HAB-give-he-him	golden

and the wolf comes and gives him a coin.

30.

pəš-le	*xə̀*	*yarxa,*ˈ	*trè,*ˈ	*ṭḷàha,*ˈ	*xa*	*šà-ta.*ˈ
PFV.stay-he	one	month	two,	three,	one	year-FS

One month went by, then two, three, one year.

31.

bax-t-e	*g-əmra*
wife-FS-his	HAB-say-she

waḷḷa	*hatxa*	*xə̀š*	*naša,*ˈ	*ḅə̀š=ile.*ˈ
indeed,	such	good	man	good-COP.PRS.he

His wife said ‘Indeed, what a kind man! He is good.

32.

ʾana	*g-əban*	*Ø-ʾoð-an-ne*	*qàðr-e,*ˈ
I	HAB-want-IF	IRR-MAKE-IF-him	dish-PL

I want to make some dishes for him,

33.

Ø-qaðr-an-ne	*ʾu-Ø-ʿazm-ax-le*	*kəs-lan*	*l-bèθa.*ˈ
IRR-treat-IF-him	and-IRR-invite-we-him	by-us	to-house

Let’s host him, invite him for a feast at our house.

34.

Ø-ʾoð-ax-le	*xa-ʾı̆xala*	*basìma*ˈ
IRR-MAKE-we-him	some-food	good

We shall prepare some good food for him,

35.

ʾu-^{A}Ø-mstaʿən-Ø^{A}	*go beθa*	*kəs-lan*
and-IRR/FUT-help_oneself-he	in house-MS	by-us

ʾu-Ø-doq-ax	*qàðr-e.ˈ*
and-IRR-hold-we	banquet-PL

he will enjoy himself at our house, and we will feast together.’

36.

g-emər-Ø	*ṭa-la*	*šùq-Ø-le.ˈ*
PRS-say-he	to-her	IMP.leave-you$_{CS}$-him.

gùrg-ā=le.ˈ	*ḥèwan=ile.ˈ*
wolf-COP.PRS.he	animal-COP.PRS.he

He says to her ‘Leave him alone. He’s a wolf. He’s an animal.

37.

mà	*b-aθe-Ø*	*go naš-e?ˈ*[11]	*naš-e*	*b-zàdʾ-i.ˈ*
what	FUT-come-he	in man-PL?	man-PL	FUT-fear-they

What does it mean “He will come among people”? People will be afraid.

38.

Ø-mbàrbəʿă-Ø-lu	*gurga*	*Ø-yaʾəl-Ø*	*go ma-θa.ˈ*
IRR/FUT-alarm-he-them	wolf	IRR-enter-he	in city-FS.

A wolf that enters the city will alarm them.’

11 This construction is likely to be a calque from Modern Israeli Hebrew. There, the interrogative ‘what’ can be used before future forms to express the speaker’s disapproval of the predicated eventuality, for instance, ‘what [do you mean] that he should come?!’ Incidentally, constructions such as this one are likely to be the ‘missing link’ in the grammaticalisation of interrogatives (‘what’) into negators. This development has been posited for, inter alia, *mā* in Modern Standard and some dialectal varieties of Arabic. In the present example, the meaning ‘what’ is possible, assuming an ellipsis (see translation). The implicature of this clause, however, may be understood as ‘[Surely] he won’t come!’

39. *g-əmr-a* *là,*ˈ *là,*ˈ *mar-Ø-re.* *Ø-ˀàθe-Ø.*ˈ
PRS-say-she no, no, IMP.say-you$_{CS}$-him IRR-come-he

She said 'No, no, tell him to come.'

40. *zəl-le* *g-emər-Ø* *ṭà-le,*ˈ
PFV.go-he PRS-say-he to-him

g-emər-Ø *ˀana* *l-èb-i* *Ø-ˀaθ-ən.*ˈ
PRS-say-he I NEG-can-I IRR-come-I$_{M}$

So he went and told the wolf, but he said 'I can't come.

41. *gùrgā=wən,* *k-əxl-ən* *nàš-e.*ˈ
WOLF=COP.PRS.I PRS-eat-I man-PL

I am a wolf. I eat people.

42. *b-aθ-ən* *go ma-θa* *kull-u* *Ø-mbàrbəˁ-i.*ˈ
FUT-come-I$_{M}$ in city-FS all-they IRR/FUT-alarm-they

If I come to town, everyone will be alarmed.'

43. *zəl-le* *mər-re* *ta-bax-ta* *hàtxa* *g-emər-Ø*
PFV.go-he PFV-say-he to-wife-FS such PRS-say-he

*gurga.*ˈ
wolf

So the man went and told his wife, this is what the wolf said.

44. *ˀaz* *g-əmr-a* *šud* *Ø-ˀaθe-Ø* *b-lèle,* *xə̀ška.*ˈ
so PRS-say-she let IRR-come-he in night.MS darkness

So she said 'Let him come at night, when there is darkness.'

45.

bə-d-aw	*wàxt*ˈ	*l-əθ-wa*	*beher-ùθa*ˈ.
in-GEN-that$_{M}$	time.MS	NEG-EXIST.PST	light-FS.

At that time, there were no lights.

46.

l-əθ-wa	^{A}*ʿan-ṭariq*^{A}	^{H}*menoròt.*^{H}
NEG-EXIST-PST	by way of	^{H}lamps^{H}
^{A}*kahraba*^{A}	*l-ə̀θ-wa.*ˈ	
^{A}electricity^{A}	NEG-EXIST-PST	

There was nothing like lamps. There was no electricity.

47.

xə̀ška	*wewa.*ˈ
darkness	COP.PST.he

It was dark.

48.

ʾu-pāyəš-Ø-wa		*xə̀ška,*ˈ	
and-IRR-stay-he		darkness	
kull-a	*ma-θa*	*xə̀ška*	*wawa.*ˈ
all-she	city-FS	darkness	COP.PST.she.

When it got dark, the whole city would be dark.

49.

g-əmr-a	*dammət*	*Ø-payəš-Ø*	*xə̀ška,*ˈ
PRS-say-she	when	IRR-stay-he	darkness
šud	*Ø-ʾaθe-Ø,*ˈ		
let	IRR-come-he		

She said ‘Let him come after it gets dark.

50.

beθ-Ø-an	*wele*	*bə-dumằhik*	*dət ma-θa.*ˈ
house-our	DEIX.COP.PRS.he	in-outskirts	GEN city-FS

Our house is on the outskirts of town.

51.

b-aθe-Ø	*kəs-lan*	*beθa*	*ʾu-b-àzəl-Ø.ˈ*
FUT-come-he	by-us	house	and-FUT-go-he
čŭxa	*la*	*k-xāzè-Ø-le.ˈ*	
nobody	NEG	HAB-see-he-him	

He will come straight to our house and go back. No one will see him.’

52.

g-emər-Ø	*bax-t-i*	*b-oð-a-lox-Ø*
PRS-say-he	wife-FS-my	FUT-make-she-you$_{MS}$
xa-ʿazime	*bȁš.*	
some-banquet	good.	

So he told the wolf ‘My wife will make for you a great banquet.’

53.

mər-re	*ṭa-le*	*b-àθ-ən,ˈ*	*g-emər-Ø*	*b-àθ-ən.ˈ*
PFV.say-he	to-him	FUT-come-I$_{M}$	PRS-say-he	FUT-come-I$_{M}$

He replied to him ‘I will come,’ he said ‘I will come’.

54.

g-emər-Ø,	*^{H}tov^{H},*	*b-àθ-ən.ˈ*
PRS-say-he	^{H}good^{H},	FUT-come-I$_{M}$

The wolf said ‘Well then, I will come.’

55. *θèle,ˈ baxte qam-qaðràle ʾu-ʾudla ʾĭxala basìma ṭale,ˈ*

He came, his wife showed him hospitality for him and made good food for him,

56. *ʾu-pəšle ʾāṣərta kə̀slu,ˈ xəlle, štele ʾu-muḥkèlu.ˈ*

And he stayed the evening at theirs, he ate, drank and they spoke.

57. *pəšla*[12] *drȁngi,* ˈ *g-emər ʾana b-azən l-ṭȕra.*ˈ

    It got late, [so] he says 'I will go [back] to [the] mountain.'

58. *qəmle … mӑre beθa ži zəlle qam-maxzele ʾurxa ʾu-mpə̀qle.*ˈ

    He got up … the house owner also went and showed him the way, and he went out.

59. *ʾu-ʾawa yı̄ʾəlle l-ʾòya,*ˈ *gurga ḥməlle go tӑ̀ra.*ˈ

    [As] that one entered, the wolf waited at the door.

60. *gurga ḥməlle go tӑ̀ra,*ˈ *šame ma bàmri bӑθər zəlle.*ˈ

    The wolf waited at the door to hear what they will say after he has left.

61. *baxte ži g-əmra wa̤l̤la xṑš,*ˈ *xōš xȕra ʾətlox.*ˈ

    His wife says 'Indeed, a good, good friend you have.

62. *xṑš xúrā=le ʾo gurga.*ˈ

    [A] good friend he is, that wolf.

63. *bӑle xa-məndi qȕṣur ʾibe.*ˈ

    But there is a flaw in him.'

64. *g-emər ṭala mà ʾibe qŭṣur?*ˈ

    He says to her 'What flaw is there in him?'

12 Note that it is the feminine singular subject suffix that is used non-referentially for the impersonal construction *pəšla drangi* (pfv.stay-she late 'it got late'). Indeed, the non-referential use of a feminine singular subject affix is common in NENA. Moreover, a feminine non-referential object morpheme is also attested in many NENA dialects, for instance: *ʾӑrəq-a-le* (pfv.run-her-he 'he fled'). For non-referential object affixes and likely contact dimension with Kurdish, see Mengozzi (2007).

65. *g-əmra ṭale rìxa...ˈ raba rixa là basima k-eθe mən pəmme.ˈ*

She says to him 'A smell, a lot of bad smell comes out of his mouth.

66. *rixa là basima k-eθe mən pəmme.ˈ*

A bad smell comes out from his mouth.'

67. ^{H}*ʾaz*^{H} *g-emər gùrgā=le ʾóhā=le.ˈ mà ʾoðən?ˈ*

So he says 'He is a wolf, this he is. What should I do?'

68. *šmèʾle gurga muḥkela hatxa ʾəlle,ˈ xrìwa.ˈ*

The wolf heard [how] she spoke in this way about him, maliciously.

69. *qam-dārele go nàθeˈ ʾu-qḥə̀rre,ˈ krə̀ble.ˈ*

He kept it to himself (lit. he put it in his ear), and he was upset he became angry.

70. *g-emər ʾana g-oðənnu hawùθa,ˈ ʾani k-parʾila ṭali bət xriwùθa.ˈ*

He says 'I do them a favour and they pay me back with evil.

71. *g-əmri rixa raba pīs g-napəq mən pə̀mme.ˈ*

They say "A very dirty smell comes out from his mouth."'

72. *zəlle l-ṭùra.ˈ durdət yom q-qayəm mǎre bèθa,ˈ g-ezəl ta ṣìwe.ˈ*

He went to the mountain. The next day the house owner gets up and goes for wood.

73. *gurga žiθèle,ˈ g-emər, šqullox ʾədyo ži xa lira kurkamàna,ˈ bǎle mən ʾədyo,ˈ là -k-eθət,ˈ ḥal ʾarbi yome xèta.ˈ*

The wolf came and says 'Take for yourself also today one golden coin, but from today [onwards], don't come, until forty more days.

74. *băle šqulle năra dìdox.*

But take your axe.

75. *năra didox šqùlle,ˈ g-emər, mxile go rèši,ˈ kmà ʾibox!ˈ*

Take your axe,' he says '[and] hit my head (lit. hit it on my head)[13] as [hard as] you can.

76. *ʾu-tùrre reši bət năra.ˈ*

And break my head with [the] axe.'

77. *g-emər màṭo māxənne go rešox?ˈ b-qaṭlə̀nnox?ˈ*

He says 'How [is it that] I should hit your head? Will I kill you?'

78. *g-emər là-q-qaṭləttiˈ*

He says 'You won't kill me.'

79. *g-emər ʾatta ʾan māxətte năra go rèši,ˈ ʾàn b-axlənnox.ˈ*

He says 'Now either you hit me [with the] axe on my head or I will eat you.

80. *xzi, mà gəbət?ˈ*

Look, what do you want?

81. *ʾēn là-māxətte năra go reši,ˈ ʾan b-axlə̀nnox.ˈ*

If you don't hit me on my head, I will eat you.'

13 The verb *m-x-y* 'to hit' takes as its direct object argument the noun *năra* 'axe', referred to here by the object suffix on the verb: *mx-i-le go reš-Ø-i* (imp.hit-you$_{MS}$-it on head-my) lit. 'hit it on my head', while *go reši* 'on head' is an adjunct. The same argument structure is attested with this verb in sentences 79 and 81 below.

82. *ʾaw naša ži faqìra,ˈ kma də-mṣèle, qam-māxele go rèše,ˈ* H*qam-sāləḥle*H *gurga.ˈ*

This poor man, he hit him[14] on his head as [hard as] he could [and] the wolf forgave him.

83. *ʾu-zə̀lle,ˈ gurga ži qam-yāsərre reš gyàne,ˈ brìndar=ile.ˈ*

And he went, the wolf bandaged his head—he was wounded.

84. *g-emər ṭale bas ʾarbi yoma xeta b-àθət.ˈ*

He says to him 'Only after another forty days will you come again.

85. *bas ʾarbi yoma xeta b-àθət ˈb-axlə̀nnox.ˈ*

Only, in another forty days will you come, [otherwise] I will eat you.'

86. *zə̀lle,ˈ muḥkele ta baxta, g-emər ḥāl ʾu-mā́sale didi,ˈ ʾèhā=la.ˈ*

He went and spoke to [his] wife, he says 'My situation is this.

87. *gurga mərre ṭali là-k-eθət ʾarbi yoma xeta ʾaxxa.ˈ*

The wolf told me "You will not be coming here for another forty days."'

88. H*tòv*H*.ˈ pədlu ʾarbi yòme,ˈ qəmle ʾaw naša*[15] *xa-ga-xə̀t,ˈ*

Good. Forty days passed by, the man got up once again,

---

14 In the Aramaic text, the suffix *le* 'him/it' refers to the axe, not the wolf; see note on line 75 above.

15 The word order in both of these verbal clauses is predicate—subject: *pədlu ʾarbi yòme* lit. 'passed by forty days', and *qəmle ʾaw naša* lit. 'got up that man'. Such word order occurs occasionally in Jewish Dohok—mostly with intransitive verbs, as is the case with these two verbs.

89. *zəlle l-ṭùra,ˡ zəlle xzele gùrga,ˡ g-emər ṭale, g-emər θə̆̀ ʾaxxa,ˡ*

he went to [the] mountain, he went and saw the wolf [who] says to him, he says 'Come here',

90. *g-emər θèlox,ˡ g-emər šqullox xa lira kurkamana xèta.ˡ*

he says '[since] you have come,' he says 'take for yourself another golden coin.'

91. *g-emər šrìlaˡ ʾe kafiya mən reši ʾu-xzì,ˡ duktət mxelox ʾo narà əlla.ˡ*

He says 'Untie this scarf from my head and see [the] place [which] you hit [with] that axe (lit. see [the] place you hit your axe on it).'

92. *qam-šārela mən ʿāqə̀le,ˡ wela trə̀ṣta.ˡ*

He untied it from his head (lit. mind)—it had healed.

93. *g-emər mà k-xazət?ˡ*

He says 'What do you see?'

94. *g-emər wele rešox trìṣa.ˡ*

He says 'Your head has healed!'[16]

95. *g-emər k-xàzət?ˡ g-emər šwirət*[17] *năra dìdoxˡ qam-māxətte baθər ʾarbi yòme,ˡ trə̀ṣle reši.ˡ*

He says 'Do you see?' He says 'The wound of your axe [which] you had hit—after forty days, my head has healed.

16 Note the unusual syntax: deictic copula—subject—predicate. The canonical order would be subject—copula—predicate (*rešox wele trìṣa*), or perhaps copula—predicate—subject (*wele trìṣa rešox*).

17 The etymology of this word is unknown to me.

96. *bǎle xabrət bàxtox mərra ṭali*ˈ *ḥəl mòθa*ˈ *là-g-našən-ne.*ˈ

But your wife's word, which she said to me, till death I will not forget.'

97. *g-emər mà mərra ṭalox?*ˈ

He says 'What did she say to you?'

98. *g-emər ʾaxtoxun, baxtox muḥkèloxun,*ˈ *baxtox mərra ʾo gugra xoš nàšā = le, ḅằš = ile, balé xa-rixa pi̇̀s k-eθe mən pəmme.*ˈ

He says 'You, your wife spoke, your wife said "This wolf is a good man, but a bad smell comes out of his mouth."'

99. *šwirət xàbra*ˈ *là-k-eθe nšaya.*ˈ

[A] wound [caused by a] word is not forgotten.

100. *šwirət ḍə̀rba*ˈ *naša g-našèle.*ˈ

A wound [caused by] a blow [a] man forgets.

101. *šwirət xàbra*ˈ *ḥə̀l moθa*ˈ *naša là-g-našele.*ˈ

[But] a wound [caused by a] word until death does [a] man not forget.

102. *lazəm yàʾe naša maṭo maḥke.*ˈ

A man should know how to speak.

103. *dər bằl,*ˈ *mən ʾədyo pēf*[18] *là-k-eθət l-ṭura.*ˈ

Watch out [that] from today onwards, you do not enter the mountain.

18 A Kurdish loanword, compare Jewish Zakho *pēv(a)* (Sabar 2002, 254).

Text 2: The True Lie

1. *ʾəθwa xa-ḥakòma,ˈ mərre ta dawəlta dìde—ˈ*
   There was a ruler, he said to his state—

2. *ta kùllu naše go dawəlta—ˈ*
   to all [the] people in [the] state—

3. *bə-daw wàxtˈ kud màθaˈ dawə̀lta wawa.ˈ*
   At that time, every city was [a] state.

4. *k-ṣarxíwāla dawə̀lta.ˈ*
   They used to call it a state.

5. *mərre ta dawə̀lta dide:ˈ*
   He said to his state

6. *ʾana g-əbən ta ḥukum dìdi…ˈ ta parlamèn didi—ˈ*
   'I want for my government… for my parliament…

7. *ʾana g-əbən xa…ˈ meθə́tūli xa mdagəl ṭali xa-dùgle*[19]ˈ
   I want [some]one, [I want you] to bring me [some]one who would tell me a lie

8. *la hawe-bi ʾamrənne kulle mandi mən ʾilàhā=la,ˈ*
   [so that] I could not say all things are from God,

19 In Jewish Dohok, the originally plural form *dugl-e* lie-pl has evidently been generalised to the singular, meaning 'a lie'. Contrast this with the form *dugla* in Jewish Zakho (Sabar 2002, 138).

9. *d-ʾamrənne*ˈ *ʾo dùglē=la,*[20]ˈ *ṭròṣā=wət,*ˈ *ʾo dùglē=la.*ˈ

so that I would say "This is [a] lie, you are right, this is [a] lie."

10. ᴴvᴴ-*ʾana g-yāwə́nnoxun ṭ̤là yome.*ˈ

And I give you three days.

11. *là-meθə́tūli xa mdāgəlli xa-dugle d-maṭe l-ʿāqəli,*ˈ

[If] you do not bring me [some]one [who] will tell me a lie that would be acceptable to me (lit. would enter my reason),

12. *rešoxun mafərànne.*ˈ

I will cut off your heads (lit. make them fly).

13. *b-qaṭlànnoxun,*ˈ *rešoxun b-qeṣànne.*ˈ

I will kill you, I will cut off your heads.'

14. *kullu zdèʾlu*ˈ *ʾu-zə̀llu*ˈ

All were afraid and went,

15. *məθelu naše d-ʾamri…*ˈ *mdagli dùgle.*ˈ

brought people who would say… would lie [a] lie.

16. *xa θèle,*ˈ *g-èmər*ˈ *ʾana b-amrən xa-məndi xə̀t žik.*ˈ

One [person] came [and] says 'I will tell something else too.'

20 The clause *ʾo dùglē=la* (this$_m$ lie.ms-cop.prs.she), which appears here twice, exhibits a lack of agreement between the subject and the copula. The subject (expressed by the demonstrative) is masculine singular, whereas the copula is feminine singular.

17. *ʾu-ḥakòma žik mərre,ˈ k-xāzə́tula kəsta dət-pàre,ˈ kəs dət zùze,ˈ zuzət dèhwa?ˈ*

And the ruler also said 'Do you see [the] bag of money, bag of coins, golden coins?

18. *ʾe kəsta wela mliθa zùze,ˈ*

Look, this bag is full of coins,

19. *kud də-mdagəl ṭali dùglaˈ*

[and] every[one] who would tell me a lie

20. *ʾamrən dùglē=la ʿāqəli q-qate,ˈ dùglē=la,ˈ*

[about which] I would say "My mind decides (lit. my mind cuts) [that] this is a lie,"

21. *ʾè b-yāwənna ṭale.ˈ*

I will give this to him.

22. *ʾu-ana ṭḷà yome b-yāwə́nnoxun,ˈ b-qaṭlə̀nnoxun.ˈ*

And I will give you three days, [then] I will kill you.'

23. *xa g-emər ʾana xzeli bət ʾèniˈ*

One says 'I saw with my [own] eyes

24. *xa-nàšaˈ tule rəš kanùšta.ˈ*

a man [who] sat on top of [a] broom.

25. *duqle kanùštaˈ ʾu-fərre šə̀mme.ˈ*

He seized a broom and flew into the sky.'

26. *θele kəs ḥakòma,*ˈ *g-emər ʾana hàtxa xzeli bət ʾeni.*ˈ

He came to [the] ruler [and] says 'I saw this with my own eyes.'

27. *g-èmər*ˈ *kulle məndi mən ʾilàhā=le.*ˈ

[The ruler] says 'All of this is from God.

28. *ʾilaha ʾìbe ʾaweð hatxa.*ˈ

God can do this.'

29. *xa dārele rəš kanùšta*ˈ *ʾu-màfərre*[21] *šəmme.*ˈ

Someone may put [a man] on top of [a] broom and make him fly to the sky.

30. *ʾeha lèwa dugle.*ˈ

This was not [a] lie.

31. *xa-xət θèle,*ˈ *g-emər ʾana xzeli kàlba*ˈ

Another one came and says 'I saw [a] dog

32. *yìʔəlle*ˈ *go nuqbət xmàṭa.*ˈ

[that] entered into the eye of a needle.

33. *xzèli*ˈ *yìʔəlle*ˈ *go nuqbət xmàṭa.*ˈ

I saw him [when he] entered in the eye of [a] needle.'

34. *g-emər ʾeha lèwa dugle,*ˈ

[The ruler] says 'This was not a lie.'

---

21 Note that the accent is pre-penultimate, rather than penultimate. Such accent retraction occurs sometimes in forms near the end of intonation units.

35. *g-emər ʾilaha ʾìbe ʾawəð hatxa.*ˈ

    He says 'God can do this.'

36. *ʾatta ʾo ḥakòma,*ˈ *ma d-g-əmrìle*ˈ

    Now this ruler, what[ever] they tell him,

37. *ʾawa duqle b-ʾiða dət-ʾilàha.*ˈ

    he continued to swear by God (lit. he seized the hand of God)

38. *ʾilaha ʾìbe ʾawəð.*

    [saying,] 'God can do [this].'

39. *zəllu...*ˈ *xa wewa huðaya go šùqa,*ˈ

    They went ... there was a Jew in the market (lit. one he was a Jew in the market)

40. *ṭāləbwa* ^{H}*nedavòt*^{H}*,*ˈ

    [who] he used to beg,

41. *ʿāyəšwa bət* ^{H}*nedavòt.*^{H}ˈ *g-yāwiwa ṭale ʾu-bʿāyìšwa.*ˈ

    [who] used to live off alms. They used to give him and he would live off [that].

42. *šmeʾle,*ˈ *g-emər mà-loxun ta parlament.*ˈ

    He heard [and] says 'What is [up] with you?' to the parliament.

43. *g-əmri ḥāl ʾu-mắsale ʾèha=la.*ˈ

    They say 'The situation is this.'

44. *g-ə̀mər*ˈ *nàblūli*ˈ *ʾana mdaglən ṭale xa-dùgle.*ˈ

He says 'Take me, I will tell him a lie.'

45. *Hve*H*-ʾana ži g-ə̀bən ʾāmərri*ˈ *lèwa dugle.*ˈ

And I, in fact, want him to tell me it was not a lie.

46. *ʾana g-ə̀bən ʾāmərri lewa dugle.*ˈ

I want him to tell me it was not a lie.

47. *zū́nūli xa-bàdla*ˈ *dət ḥakòme*ˈ *ʾu-náblūli l-ḥàmmam*ˈ *ʾu-xèpən*ˈ *ʾu-mbadlən ʾu-gàrʾən*ˈ *ʾu-kundā̀re*ˈ *ʾu-kullu xàθe*ˈ

Buy me a royal suit and take me to [the] bathhouse, and I shall wash, change and shave, shoes and everything new,

48. *ʾu-náblūli kəs ḥakòma,*ˈ *ʾana mdaglən ṭale xa-dugle ži*ˈ *d-ʾawa ʾàmər*ˈ *ʾe dùglē=la.*ˈ

and take me to [the] ruler, I shall tell him such a lie [that] he will say [that] it is [a] lie.

49. *ʾana g-ə̀bən ʾamər*ˈ *ʾeha dùglē=la.*ˈ

I want want him to say [that] it is [a] lie.'

50. *g-əmri ṭale* H*tòv*H.ˈ

They say to him 'Fine!'

51. *zəlle l-šùqa.*ˈ *pədlu go šùqa.*ˈ *g-emər zū́nūli šoʾa lʾìne.*ˈ

He went to the market. They passed by the market and he says 'Buy me seven big jugs,

52. *ʾu-šoʾa ḥammàre žik muθun*ˈ *ʾu-ta … d-nablilu ta ḥakòma*ˈ *ʾumaḥməlilu rèza go diwan dide.*ˈ

and also bring seven donkey drivers for … so that they can take them to the ruler and place them [in] a line in his reception room.'

53. ^{H}*tòv*$^{H'}$. *gəbe maxəlṣi b-gyànu.*ˈ *zunnu ṭale šoʾa lʾìne*ˈ *ʾu-šoʾa ḥammàre*ˈ *ʾu-zəllu kəs ḥakòma.*ˈ

Good. They want to save themselves. They bought him seven big jugs and seven donkey drivers and they went to the king.

54. *θelu kəs dargằvan*ˈ *dət ḥakòma,*ˈ *ʾanna talme ʾu-kadùne,*ˈ *talme ʾu-nàše,*ˈ

They came to the ruler's gate-keeper, [all] these vessels and jugs, vessels and people.

55. *mà ila g-əmri ʾanna ḥarrase,*ˈ *ḥarras-d go tằra.*ˈ

'What is it?' say these keepers, the keepers who [are] at [the] gate.

56. *g-əmri mălək mərre ʾaθax mdaglax xa-dùgla ṭale.*ˈ

They say '[The] king told [us that] we should come [and] tell a lie for him.'

57. *mərru ta mằlək*ˈ *flan welu ʾə̀θye,*ˈ *mdagəl xa-dùgla.*ˈ

They said to the king 'Some men have come, [one] will tell you a lie.'

58. *mălək mərre ṭàlu*ˈ *suwun muθun xà*ˈ

The king said to them 'Go, bring me someone,

59. *băle là-hawe huðaya.*ˈ

but he should not be [a] Jew.

60. *là-hawe huðaya.*ˈ

He should not be [a] Jew.'

61. *θèlu,ˈ yĭʾəllu kùlluˈ kəs mȁlək.ˈ*

    They came, they all entered into the ruler's [presence].

62. *ḥməllu go dìwan,ˈ ʾaw huðaya žìk.ˈ*

    They waited in the reception room, this Jew also.

63. *qam-maḥməllu kullu lʾine dide bət rèzaˈ ʾu-mən ḥammare baθər lʾìneˈ*

    He put all his big jugs in a line and a few of the donkey drivers behind the big jugs.

64. *ʾu-g-emər ṭale d-mȁ,ˈ mdaglət xa-dùgleˈ d-ʾana ʿāqəli qaṭe dùglē=la?ˈ*

    And [the ruler] says 'What? You [want to] tell me a lie which my mind would consider to be a lie (lit. my mind would decide it is [a] lie)?

65. *ʾamrənnox dùglē=la?ˈ*

    I should tell you it is [a] lie?'

66. *g-èmər,ˈ ḥakoma basìma,ˈ ʾana là-gə-mdaglənnox dugle,ˈ ʾana g-əmrənnox xa-məndi d-wewa tròṣa.ˈ*

    [The Jew] says 'Good ruler, I do not tell you [a] lie, I tell you something that was true.

67. *tròṣa wewa.ˈ*

    It was true.

68. *ʾana là-θeli mdaglənnox dugle.ˈ*

    I haven't come to tell [a] lie.'

69. *g-emər mà ˀətlox?*ˈ

[The ruler] says 'What have you got?'

70. *g-èmər*ˈ *k-xāzəttu ˀana lˀìne?*ˈ

[The Jew] says 'Do you see those big jugs?'

71. *g-èmər*ˈ *sawòyi*ˈ *xa-naša dolamànt wewa.*ˈ

He says 'My grandfather was a rich man.'

72. *dolamánt*ˈ *yáˁăni măre dawəlta,*ˈ *dawə̀lta ˀə́θwāle,*ˈ *ràba dolamant wewa.*ˈ

dolamant means somebody with wealth. He had wealth, he was very rich.

73. *ˀu-sawòyox*ˈ *ḥakòma wewa.*ˈ *snə̀qle,*ˈ *l-sawòyi*ˈ *mdayən-ne pàre,*ˈ *zùze,*ˈ

'And your grandfather was a ruler. He needed my grandfather to lend him money, coins,

74. *ˀu-ˀə́θwāle xa-šùla ˀāwəðwa.*ˈ

and he had a job to do.

75. *ˀu-lə̀θwālu go xazina,*ˈ

When they did not have [money] in the treasury,

76. *θele mdoyənne mən sawòyi,*ˈ *bə-dana lˀine qam-ṃāḷèwalu ṭalu zùze,*ˈ *pàre.*ˈ

he came and borrowed from my grandfather, in these big jugs, which they filled for him with golden coins, money.

77. *sawòyi*ˈ *mdoyənne tà sawoyox*ˈ *šoˀa lˀine dət zùze.*ˈ

My grandfather lent your grandfather seven big jugs of coins.

78. *ʾu-ʾatta ʾana pəšli ...*ˈ *ḥali wele twìra*ˈ *ʾu-θeli šaqlən denət sawoyi mə̀nnox.*ˈ

And now I became ... I have gone bankrupt (lit. my situation is broken) and I have come to take my grandfather's loan from you.

79. *ʾāt ḥakòma=wət*ˈ *ʾə̀tlox.*ˈ

You are the ruler [and] you have [enough].'

80. *munə̀xle ḥakoma,*ˈ *g-emər ta do nàša*ˈ *măre lʾìne,*ˈ

The ruler sighed (lit. sighed the ruler) and says to this man with [the] big jugs

81. *ʾìmal sawòyox*ˈ *xa-kalba hatxa ruwa wèwa*ˈ *dət sawoyi mằlək,*ˈ *ḥakòma*ˈ *mdayən mənne lʾine d-pàre?*ˈ

'When was your grandfather such a filthy bastard (lit. big dog) that my grandfather, the king, the ruler, would borrow from him big jugs of money?

82. *mən ʾèmal ila?*ˈ *hatxa wewa rùwa.*ˈ

Since when does such a thing happen (lit. since when is it)? He was such a great (filthy bastard).

83. *sawoyox kalba rùwa wewa.*ˈ

Your grandfather was a filthy bastard.'

84. *g-emər ṭale*ˈ *ḥakòma*ˈ *maḥki ta gyànox,*ˈ *là-mṣaʾărət sawoyi.*ˈ

[The Jew] says to him 'Ruler, speak to yourself [quietly], [but] do not curse my grandfather.

85. *ʾēn ila tròṣa*ˈ *sawoyox wele šqila mən sawoyi pàre*ˈ *ṃḷìlu ʾanna lʾìne ṭàli*ˈ *dena dìdi.*ˈ

If it is true—your grandfather had borrowed from my grandfather money—fill these big jugs for me [with the money for] my loan.

86. *ʾu-ʾēn ila dùgle,*ˈ *hàlli kəsta.*ˈ

And if it is a lie, give me a bag [of money].'

87. *ʾawa ḥakoma kràble,*ˈ *g-emər šqùl.*ˈ *qam-māxela ṣàdre,*ˈ *g-emər ʾèha*ˈ *qṭèle ʿāqəli duglē=la.*ˈ

That ruler got angry and says 'Take.' He threw the bag his way and says 'This one I accepted as a lie (lit. this one my mind has determined to be [a] lie)'.

4. Survey of Selected Functions of Verbal Forms

In this section I present a commentary on the grammatical meanings of selected verbal forms (mostly of those attested in the texts above). As remarked, the goal of this section is to highlight some of the more distinctive features of Jewish Dohok in the context of NENA, and to draw attention to certain non-prototypical, creative applications of verbal forms that are intended to create particular discourse effects.

4.1. Expression of Realis Mood through *šaqəl-wa*

The *šaqəl* form typically expresses irrealis present and future, while its past counterpart *šaqəl-wa* is prototypically past irrealis. In addition, however, *šaqəl-wa* also sometimes occurs in sentences conveying realis mood. The prototypical realis counterparts of *šaqəl* and *šaqəl-wa* have the habitual indicative prefix *k-*, thus *k-šaqəl* (present) and *k-šaqəl-wa* (past).[22]

22 Overview of the use and origin of the habitualindicative prefix across the NENA dialects can be found in Khan (2007) and in Rubin (2018,

As the previous paragraph implies, there is an asymmetry between the verbal forms: the *k-* prefix is omitted in forms conveying realis mood in the past, but in the present, such omission of the prefix is virtually unattested in the corpus.[23]

In the texts presented above, *šaqəl-wa* occurs in clauses that can be identified as subordinate relative clauses (though asyndetic), as well as in main clauses (examples 2/39–40 and 1/4 below respectively):

2/39–41[24]

*xă wewa huðaya go šùqa*ˈ

There was a Jew in the market

Ø-ṭāləb-Ø-wa	*ᴴnedavòtᴴ*,
IRR-ask-he-PST	ᴴalmsᴴ,

'[who] used to beg,'

1/4

*g-meθè-Ø-wa-lu,*ˈ	*Ø-dāré-Ø-wa-lu*	*rəš*
HAB-bring-he-PST-them	IRR-place-he-PST-them	on

*xmara dìde…*ˈ
donkey his…

'He would bring them [and] place them on his donkey…'

57:130–39), who presents some alternative reconstuctions.

23 For the past tense, a sample of the corpus (about 4000 words) was studied, and the ratio between *k-šaqəl-wa* and *šaqəl-wa* in Pattern I verbs in clauses interpreted as realis was found to be 11:1, though this ratio could be slightly different if the whole corpus were taken into account.

24 The first number refers to the text (first or second), the second indicates the line within that text.

If the absence of the habitual indicative prefix is a matter of phonetic elision, this elision is highly irregular (i.e. it is not restricted to a single phonetic environment). A more likely explanation for its absence, therefore, is linked to the original semantics of the *k*-prefix and to its process of diachronic grammaticalisation. Namely, the *k*- prefix (and its dialectal variants) most likely originated as a progressive or presentative marker (Khan 2007, 94), which was added to the base *šaqəl*, the latter subsequently becoming restricted to irrealis mood. The progressive and presentative functions are bound especially closely with the (actual) present, since they are typically used to draw attention to situations overlapping with speech time. This, in turn, suggests that the habitual indicative prefix in NENA originated in the present tense (ibid), and only later began its spread into habituality and the past tense. In light of this, it is likely that in Jewish Dohok, the *k*- prefix has not been fully grammaticalised as a marker of realis and habituality. Specifically, it does not always occur in contexts that are not directly associated with the original function of this morpheme, viz. present tense presentative or progressive. This hypothesis would explain the lack of obligatoriness of *k*- in the case of the past.

Partial grammaticalisation can also be postulated for other dialects. C. Barwar, for instance, has the realis prefix *ʾi*-. According to Khan, however, *ʾi-qaṭəl* and *ʾi-qaṭəl-wa*—in contrast to *qaṭəl* and *qaṭəl-wa*—are used to indicate 'discourse prominence'. In other words, *ʾi-qaṭəl* and *ʾi-qaṭəl-wa* forms are apparently restricted to clauses conveying a high degree of pragmatic assertiveness (Khan 2008, 590–91). The domain of assertiveness (presenting a situation as new to the listener; Cristofaro 2003, 29–33) is itself likely to be related to the actual present, which draws attention to a situation in the present that is typically assumed by the speaker to be new or surprising for the hearer. Thus, the original domain of the realis prefix is not only the actual present, but also pragmatic assertion. The synchronic distribution of the *ʾi*- prefix in Barwar may still reflect this origin.

4.2. Expression of Emphatic Negative Imperative through la *k-šaqəl* (prototypically realis)

The negative form *la k-šaqəl* is used more broadly than its affirmative *kšaqəl* counterpart, which conveys realis present. The form *la kšaqəl* negates not only the present, but also the future, which, in the affirmative, is expressed by *p-šaqəl*. Modally, these future forms convey the sense of 'near-realis'. That is, it conveys the higher-certainty, predictive type of epistemic future.[25]

This prototypical function notwithstanding, *la k-šaqəl* can also sometimes be used for an emphatic negative imperative. Prototypically, the negative imperative is expressed by the irrealis *la šaqəl*, e.g. *la Ø-aθ-ət* (NEG IRR-come-you$_{MS}$) 'do not come'.[26] One such case is attested in the texts (1/87, see below), and a few parallel examples are found elsewhere in my corpus:

1/87

là-k-eθ-ət (NEG HAB-come-you$_{MS}$) *ʾarbi yoma xeta ʾaxxa.*ˈ

'You will not be coming here for another forty days.'

^{H}ʾaz^{H} g-əmri ***là-k-eθ-etu*** (NEG HAB-come-you$_{PL}$) *mən dəšdaša,*ˈ *lazəm zonetu pantaròne.*ˈ

'So they say you won't be coming [wearing] a thawb, you have to buy trousers.'

Given that *la k-šaqəl* is typically used for predictive, 'near-realis' future, its use for a negative command is likely to be intended to have precisely that effect: it serves to present the event as almost certain. In other words, the command is so emphatic that it must certainly be obeyed. Its fulfilment may, therefore, be expressed as

25 See Akatsuka (1985) on epistemic modality as a scale.

26 For a discussion on different morphological expression of the imperative and for their various pragmatic functions in NENA, see Khan (2010, 65–70) and Hoberman (1989, 136).

if it is certain by using the predictive form. Such an interpretation fits the context of sentence 1/18, in which the wolf threatens to eat the man if he—despite the prohibition—comes again. The second sentence above is a command of a school official to his pupils, so it was uttered from a position of authority.

This function of *la k-šaqəl* also occurs in other NENA dialects. For example, native speakers of the Christian Shaqlawa dialect describe the difference between an imperative conveyed by the predictive form (corresponding to the Jewish Dohok *la kšaqəl*) and with the irrealis form (corresponding to *la šaqəl*) in the following way: 'the former means that there can be no discussion whether the command will or will not be obeyed, so it sounds much more authoritative.'[27]

4.3. Expression of the Resultative and of the Continuous Aspect (in Stative Verbs)

The resultative construction in Jewish Dohok is composed of the copula (in the 3rd person present, the deictic copula must be used) with the resultative participle *šqila,* inflected for gender and number of the subject. This is illustrated by the following constructions from the texts:

2/57

flan	***welu***	***ʾə̀θy-e,*** ˡ	*Ø-mdagəl-Ø*
some	DEIX.COP.they	RES.come-PL	IRR-lie-he

xa-dùgla.
a-lie.

'Some men have come to tell you a lie.'

2/85

sawoy-ox	***we-le***	***šqila***
grandfather-your$_{MS}$	PFV.be-he	RES.take.MS

27 Private communication with Lourd Chechman.

mən	*sawoy -i*	*pàr-e.*
from	grandfather-my	money-PL

'Your grandfather had borrowed money from my grandfather.'

In such constructions, the focus of the predication is on the persisting state that follows an event, rather than on the event itself. Such usage is confirmed by other constructions from my corpus.[28]

This, in turn, indicates that the copula + *šqila* construction in Jewish Dohok is best understood as a resultative rather than a full perfect.[29] In this dialect, it is largely used only with verbs that have a clear state following the activity—typically, stative verbs (e.g. the state of sitting following the event of sitting down). This type of usage is attested in the sentence 2/57 above (*flan welu ʾə̀θye*), where the focus is on the result of arriving. We can paraphrase: 'Some men are here.'

The only transitive verbs that can occur in the resultative construction in Jewish Dohok are possessive transitives, such as in 2/85 (*sawoyox wele šqila mən sawoyi pare*).[30] In transitive verbs such as *šqila,* the focus of the predication is on the subsequent state of having in one's possession. We can thus paraphrase: 'my grandfather had a loan.'

---

28 I am indebted to Paul Noorlander for drawing my attention to this, and for helping me test various verbs in the resultative construction during fieldwork in Jerusalem in September 2019.

29 For the distinction between the two, see (Nedjalkov 2001, 928–30). For the semantic scope of the copula + *šqila* construction in other NENA dialects, see, for instance, Khan (2008, 653–58). For a historical overview of these constructions, see Noorlander (2018, 328–31).

30 This construction is apparently past. Formally, the word *wele* can be parsed either as pfv.be-he (root *hwy*), which is one of the past copulas, or deix.cop.he, that is, the present deictic copula. Contextually, the former interpretation is more likely—if the grandfather was still alive, the king could easily check the truthfulness of the Jew's claim.

In the case of stative verbs, the resultative function overlaps semantically with the continuous aspect, which also refers to a state that is ongoing at the time of reference and had begun at some point in the past.[31] When asked to produce a sentence that includes a stative verb with continuous meaning (though typically not a verb of cognition, emotion or sensation), speakers commonly use the copula + *šqila* construction, for example:

*ʾaw naša d-**wele*** (DEIX.COP.he) ***ḥmila*** (RES.stand.MS) *kəs beθa ʾaxòni=le.* (elicitation)

'That man who **is standing** (/**has stopped**) by the house is my brother.'

By contrast, in other dialects, the copula + *šqila* construction has become a full perfect. This is the case in Christian Barwar, where copula + *šqila* can be used with the verb 'to kill' (Khan 2008, 735), there being no direct effect or state of agent resulting from the act of killing. Such perfects express a more abstract situation resulting from a previous event. The construction still does not express a specific event bound to a specific point in time, but rather the event is only an implicature. There is, however, another use of the copula + *šqila* construction in C. Barwar (as well as in the dialects that come originally from the Ṭyare region), which expresses a specific past event in narrative. This is a past perfective, though the event is presented as cognitively distant (typically in fictitious folktales). In this function, the ordinary ('enclitic') copula is used, rather than the deictic one (Khan 2008, 669).[32]

31 A similar situation is attested in languages such as Chinese or Japanese (Shirai 1998).

32 This usage, though genre-restricted, is arguably typologically the most advanced one, based on the model of diachronic change proposed by Bybee : stative > resultative > perfect > preterite (Bybee, Perkins Revere, and Pagliuca 1994, 81–82).

4.4. Expression of the Continuous Aspect

The texts presented above include no cases of verbal forms that are exclusively dedicated to the marking of continuousness.[33] Indeed, in the corpus as a whole, there are very few such forms, even though there are multiple cases of *k-šaqəl* which—contextually—clearly describe predications of a continuous nature.

In NENA dialects in general, there are two main constructions for the expression of the continuous aspect. These also commonly include the progressive function. The first—and more common one—is formed by a copula and *b*-Infinitive (in Jewish Dohok, *wele bə-šqala*), which in dialects such as Christian Urmi has been reanalysed as its own inflectional stem (Khan 2016, 185). In the second construction, a copula or a presentative particle is combined with the prototypically realis present form (in Jewish Dohok, *wal/hol/hole k-šaqəl*). In many NENA dialects, these constructions are widespread. In the more typologically advanced dialects such as Christian Urmi, Jewish Arbel and Christian Qaraqosh, the (originally) continuous construction has even been extended into non-progressive domains (e.g. habitual present or even perfective past in the narrative) (e.g., Christian Urmi—Khan 2016, vol.2, 185–200).[34]

In Jewish Dohok, however, as mentioned above, the continuous constructions are extremely rare in the corpus. This feature, as well as the restricted function and use of the resultative construction, points to the conservative character of Jewish Dohok, even in relation to the other *Lišana Deni* dialects.

---

33 Following Comrie, 'continuous' is used here to describe a state or event which is ongoing at the point of reference (Comrie 1976, 25). A continuous construction can, therefore, be used with both stative and dynamic verbs. By contrast, the term 'progressive' implies a progress, which is compatible only with dynamic verbs. The term 'continuous' is preferable here, even though many NENA grammars use the term 'progressive', since the constructions discussed here can be used in Jewish Dohok—as well as in other NENA dialects—also with stative verbs .

34 On a general discussion on the continuous (in Khan, 'progressive') constructions in NENA, see Khan (2007, 95–97).

Another noteworthy feature of Jewish Dohok is that it possesses both of the continuous constructions. These two constructions, moreover,—judging from the available data—have distinct functions.

Wele bə-šqala

This construction is only attested twice in the corpus. In both of those cases, it describes a bodily state that is not of a cognitive, emotional or sensory nature. Sentence 3f/36 below describes a state that is ongoing in the time between the Jew's visits to the king.

*mà d-g-məθele dərmane*ˈ *ˀu-mà d-g-oðiˈ* ***l-èwe bə-traṣa*** (NEG-COP. PRS.he in-healing).ˈ (3f)

'Whatever medicine they bring and whatever they do, he is not getting better.'

zəlle ^H^*misken*^H^ *ˀo huðaya l-bèθa,*ˈ ***l-ewe bə-dmàxa*** (NEG-COP.PRS.he in-sleeping)ˈ *mən zdòˀðθe.*ˈ (3f)

'The poor Jew went home, he is not sleeping for his fear.'

With other verbs, *wele bə-šqala* could not be elicited from most speakers.[35] This suggests that in Jewish Dohok *wele bə-šqala* is—in contrast to other dialects—precisely *not* a progressive construction. Rather, it conveys the non-dynamic continuous aspect, but even in this function it is highly restricted, being attested only with physical states.

In many NENA dialects, by contrast, the parallel construction with a copula + *b*-Infinitive expresses the progressive function. A situation similar to that in Jewish Dohok, however, is attested in early-NENA sources, suggesting that the situation in Jewish

35 When the speakers were presented with such a construction containing a stative verb of cognition, sensory perception or emotion, they accepted it, but said it sounded unnatural or reminiscent of another *Lišana Deni* dialect (e.g. Jewish Zakho) and rephrased it with a *k-šaqəl* form.

Dohok is a conservative one. Such early-NENA evidence is supplied by the early Christian (apparently archaising) NENA poetry from north-western Iraq (Telkepe and Alqosh), dating to the 17th-19th centuries (Mengozzi 2012). In these texts, (copula +) *b*-Infinitive is very rare, and functions as a 'circumstantial modifier or a complement of the predicate, whereas it rarely occurs in combination with the copula' (Mengozzi 2012, 34, citing Poizat 1999, 173).

Similarly, in Jewish Dohok, *wele bə-šqala* is only attested with states. In this dialect, however, those states are predicative (i.e. they contain a copula). Thus, in contrast to the early-NENA poetry, they are not necessarily presented as overlapping temporarily with the predicate of the clause, on which they are syntactically dependent. Rather, they may simply overlap with a given period of time specified by the broader context. Moreover, it remains to be seen how the continuous/progressive in NENA fits with the typical grammaticalisation paths of the progressive. Cross-linguistically, progressive constructions typically involve dynamic verbs, and—according to Bybee, Perkins, and Pagliuca (1994, 133)—often develop from (metaphorically) locative constructions.

Wəl/hol/hole k-šaqəl

In contrast to *wele bə-šqala, wəl/hol/hole k-šaqəl* is only attested with dynamic verbs in the corpus (five times in total).[36] The first element of these constructions is a presentative particle *wəl* or *hol,* or *hole* (i.e. apparently a fossilised 3MS form). Consider the following examples from the corpus:

*θela mən tàma,*ˈ *ʾay baxta* ᴴ*miskèna*ᴴˈ ***hole g-baxš-a-lu*** (PROG HAB-stir-she-them) *ṭlòxe.*ˈ (3h)

36 The association of the *wəl/hol/hole k-šaqəl* construction with lexically dynamic verbs is confirmed from interviews. Speakers showed a tendency to rephrase constructions offered by the interviewer such as **wele b-iθaya* 'he is coming' as *wəl k-eθe* 'look, he is coming'.

She came from there, that ^Hpoor^H woman, and [now] **look, she is stirring** the lentils.

*g-yāʾəl-wa go màṭbax*ˈ *k-xāpəq-wa-la g-nāšə̀q-wa-la.*ˈ *b-amrá-wā-le d-prùq-li. ʾana wəl* ***gə-mbàšlan*** (PROG HAB-cook-I),ˈ *ʾatta gəbe ʾoðan ʾixàla.*ˈ

'He used to enter the kitchen, hug her, kiss her. [But] she would tell him 'Leave me'. **Look, I am cooking**, I need to make food now.'

It is the presentative elements—*wəl, hole* or *hol*—that convey the continuous aspect. Presentative particles typically draw attention to an event that can be witnessed by the hearer. This, in turn, often has the purpose of highlighting the significance of the event. In narrative, therefore, presentatives have the effect of placing the listener in the midst of the unfolding events, as if he or she were witnessing them personally.[37] This, in turn, means that such presentative forms are likely to be used for situations that are happening in the here-and-now, and are, therefore, aspectually continuous. Still, in light of the rarity of these constructions in Jewish Dohok, it is highly unlikely that the presentative particles in constructions combined with *k-šaqəl* have been fully grammaticalised as continuous markers. Instead, these particles probably perform a discourse function (drawing attention to significant events happening in the here-and-now), which happens to overlap with a grammatical function (marking continuousness).

5. Conclusions

This paper has presented two folktales from the hitherto unstudied NENA dialect of the Jews of Dohok accompanied by linguistic glosses (for a part of text), translation and comments on a few noteworthy constructions. These stories exemplify the rich and

37 For a discussion on the function of presentative copulas and particles and their possible historical origin, see Cohen (2017).

long-standing genre of orally transmitted folktales, typical for many of the NENA-speaking communities.

These stories were followed by a brief grammatical study of a few aspects of verbal semantics, focusing primarily on features attested in the texts themselves. I concentrated especially on forms and functions that are noteworthy either from the point of view of Jewish Dohok itself, or from the perspective of NENA more broadly. I showed that the prototypically realis and predictive *la k-šaqəl* can be used for deontic modality (imperative), apparently to create a stronger imperative by presenting it as predictive ('near-realis'). I also showed that the prototypically past irrealis *šaqəl-wa* can be used for the realis past. I suggested that this is due to the incomplete grammaticalisation of the *k*-indicative habitual prefix, which is likely to have originated as a presentative-progressive marker in the present and is not yet obligatory in the past. In addition, I studied the construction copula + *šqila* (resultative participle), noting that it tends to be used only with stative and possessive transitive verbs. In light of this restriction, it should be analysed as a resultative and not as a fully-developed perfect, in contrast to many other dialects. Additionally, I showed that forms dedicated exclusively to the marking of continuousness are used only marginally. Moreover, one of them is apparently reserved for stative verbs. This is apparently a conservative feature in Jewish Dohok; which distinguishes this dialect even from the closely related dialects, such as Jewish Amedia or Jewish Zakho.

References

Akatsuka, Noriko. 1985. 'Conditionals and the Epistemic Scale'. *Language* 61 (3): 625–39.

Aloni, Oz. 2018. 'Aspects of the Oral Heritage of the Neo-Aramaic-Speaking Jewish Community of Zakho'. Ph.D. Thesis. Cambridge: University of Cambridge.

Bybee, Joan, Perkins Revere, and William Pagliuca. 1994. *The Evolution of Grammar: Tense, Aspect, and Modality in the Languages of the World*. Chicago, London: University of Chicago Press.

Coghill, Eleanor. 2009. 'Four Versions of a Neo-Aramaic Children's Story'. *ARAM Periodical* 21: 251–80.

———. 2014. 'Differential Object Marking in Neo-Aramaic'. *Linguistics* 52 (2): 335–64.

Cohen, Eran. 2012. *The Syntax of Neo-Aramaic: The Jewish Dialect of Zakho*. Gorgias Neo-Aramaic Studies. Piscataway, NJ: Gorgias Press.

———. 2017. 'The Functions of Presentative Constructions in Jewish Zakho Neo-Aramaic'. *Journal of Jewish Languages* 5 (1): 1–21.

Comrie, Bernard. 1976. *Aspect*. Cambridge: Cambridge University Press.

Cristofaro, Sonia. 2003. *Subordination*. Oxford: Oxford University Press.

Dik, Simon C. 1997. *The Theory of Functional Grammar*. 2nd ed. Berlin: De Gruyter.

Hoberman, Robert D. 1989. *The Syntax and Semantics of Verb Morphology in Modern Aramaic: A Jewish Dialect of Iraqi Kurdistan*. New Haven: American Oriental Society.

Khan, Geoffrey. 2007. 'Indicative Markers in North Eastern Neo-Aramaic'. In *XII Incontro Italiano di Linguistica Camito-Semitica*, edited by Marco Moriggi, 85–98. Soveria Mannelli: Rubbettino.

———. 2008. *The Neo-Aramaic Dialect of Barwar*. Leiden–Boston: Brill.

———. 2009. 'The Syntax and Discourse Structure of Neo-Aramaic Narrative Texts'. *ARAM Periodical* 21: 163–78.

———. 2010. 'The Expression of Deontic Modality in North-Eastern Neo-Aramaic Dialects'. In *Verbal Festivity in Arabic and Other Semitic Languages. Proceedings of the Workshop at the Unviersitätsclub Bonn on January 16, 2009*, edited by Lutz Edzard and Stephen Guth, 58–73. Wiesbaden: Harrassowitz.

———. 2016. *The Neo-Aramaic Dialect of the Assyrian Christians of Urmi*. Leiden: Brill.

Mengozzi, Alessandro. 2007. 'Middle Markers: Neo-Aramaic and Italian Verbal Forms with a 3rd Singular Feminine Pronominal Object'. In *XII Incontro Italiano di Linguistica Camito-Semitica*, edited by Marco Moriggi, 105–15. Soveria Mannelli: Rubbettino.

———. 2012. 'The Contribution of Early Christian Vernacular Poetry from Northern Iraq to Neo-Aramaic Dialectology: Preliminary Remarks on the Verbal System'. *ARAM Periodical* 24: 25–40.

Nedjalkov, Vladimir P. 2001. 'Resultative Constructions in Syntactic Typology'. In *Language Typology and Language Universals*, edited by Martin Haspelmath, 928–40. Berlin: De Gruyter.

Noorlander, Paul M. 2018. 'Alignment in Eastern Neo-Aramaic Languages from a Typological Perspective'. Ph.D. Thesis. Leiden: Leiden University.

Rubin, Aaron D. 2018. *Studies in Semitic Grammaticalization (Harvard Semitic Studies)*. Vol. 57. Leiden: Brill.

Sabar, Yona. 1982. *The Folk Literature of the Kurdistani Jews: An Anthology*. Yale Judaica Series 23. New Haven: Yale University Press.

———. 2002. *A Jewish Neo-Aramaic Dictionary. Dialects of Amidya, Dihok, Nerwa and Zakho, Northwestern Iraq*. Semitica Viva 28. Wiesbaden: Harrassowitz.

Shirai, Yasuhiro. 1998. 'Where the Progressive and the Resultative Meet: Imperfective Aspect in Japanese, Chinese, Korean and English'. *Studies in Language* 22 (3): 661–92.

VERBAL FORMS EXPRESSING DISCOURSE DEPENDENCY IN NORTH-EASTERN NEO-ARAMAIC

Geoffrey Khan

1. Introduction

In this paper I shall draw attention to the use of various verbal forms in North-Eastern Neo-Aramaic (NENA) dialects to express discourse dependency. By this I mean that certain verbal forms in certain contexts signal that the predicate of the clause they occur in continues in some way the preceding discourse. This continuation is typically either temporal sequence or some kind of elaboration. I shall propose explanations as to how the function of the expression of discourse dependency developed historically in the various verb forms in question. It will be shown that although the forms are formally different, they exhibit parallels in the historical processes of their semantic change. The data are based mainly on my studies of the C. Barwar and C. Urmi dialects, with occasional references to other dialects.[1]

2. The *bət-qaṭəl* Form

Dialects in the northern half of the NENA dialect area and in the Mosul plain have a future construction that is derived

1 When referring to NENA dialects the abbreviation C. is used to denote a dialect spoken by a Christian community (e.g. C. Barwar, C. Urmi) and the abbreviation J. is used to refer to a dialect spoken by a Jewish community (e.g. J. Dobe).

 https://doi.org/10.11647/OBP.0209.04

historically from the deontic verb 'to want' and a subordinate complement:[2]

(1) **bāʿē* *d-qāṭel*
want.IPFV.3MS COMP-kill.SBJV.3MS
'He wants to kill.'

The deontic verb has undergone morphological reduction and bonding through grammaticalisation. In the dialect of C. Barwar, for example, the basic form of the construction in slow careful speech is as follows:

(2) C. Barwar
bət-qaṭəl
FUT-kill.SBJV.3MS
'He will kill.'

The verb has been phonetically contracted and the subordinating complementiser has been affixed to the deontic form and devoiced. In some dialects there is no devoicing, e.g. C. Qaraqosh *bəd-qaṭəl*.

The process of grammaticalisation has reduced person distinctions in the deontic verb and the particle *bət* is used before verbs of all persons:[3]

2 For discussions of the future form in NENA, see Fox (2015) and Noorlander (2017).

3 This is cross-linguistically a common feature of future forms derived historically from deontic verbs (Noorlander 2017, 191).

(3) C. Barwar

3ms.	*bət-qaṭəl*
3fs.	*bət-qaṭla*
3pl.	*bət-qaṭli*
2ms.	*bət-qaṭlət*
2fs	*bət-qaṭlət*
2pl.	*bət-qaṭlitu*
1ms.	*bət-qaṭlən*
1fs.	*bət-qaṭlən*
1pl.	*bət-qaṭləx*

In normal fast speech, moreover, the particle undergoes further phonetic reduction, resulting in the following allomorphs:

(4) C. Barwar

b-garəš	'he will pull'
p-šate	'he will drink'
p̂ṱ-azəl	'he will go'
ṱ-azəl	'he will go'
t-yawənnax	'I shall give you (fs)'

The construction can be shifted into the past to express a future in the past by attaching the past-shifting affix *-wa*:

(5) C. Barwar

bət-qaṭəl-wa

FUT-kill.SBJV.3MS-PST

'He would kill.'

2.1. Functions of the *bət-qaṭəl* Form

In the C. Barwar dialect the following functions of the *bət-qaṭəl* form can be identified (Khan 2008, 598–608). These functions are the typical functions of the future construction also in other NENA dialects. They can be classified broadly into functions that involve the expression of future tense (§2.1.1.–§2.1.3.) and those that involve the expression of discourse dependency (§2.1.4.). As will be argued below, the discourse dependency function, which is the main focus of this section, has developed from the future function.

2.1.1. Deontic Future

This function retains the deontic meaning of the source construction.[4] In such cases, it conveys an element of will and expresses various degrees of intention, obligation, request and permission regarding a future action.

When the verb has an agentive 1st singular subject the *bət-qaṭəl* form generally has a sense expressing deontic intention, e.g.

4 Cf. Noorlander (2017, 191–92).

(6)	*b-ṣə̀lyən*ˈ	*b-tápqən*	*bìye.*ˈ
	FUT-descend.SBJV.1MS	FUT-meet.SBJV.1MS	on.him

'I shall go down and shall meet him.' (A4:21)[5]

When the verb has an agentive 1st plural subject, the form often has a cohortative sense ('Let's …'), e.g.

(7)	*bas-ṯ-ázexi*	*ṭalbə́x-la*	*m-báb-a*	*dìya.*ˈ
	but-FUT-go.SBJV.1PL	ask.SBJV.1PL-3FS	from-father-her	of.her

'But let us go and ask her father for her hand.' (A29:38)

The form may express deontic obligation. In such cases the verb generally has an agentive 2nd person subject, e.g.

(8)	*ṯ-azítu*	*qam-do-gə̀ppa*ˈ …	*b-qarìtu:*ˈ
	FUT-go.SBJV.2PL	before-that-cave	FUT-call.SBJV.2PL
	ʾó	*Bə́lbəl Hazàr!*ˈ	
	oh	Bəlbəl Hazar	

'You should go to the cave … You should cry "Oh Bəlbəl Hazar."' (A8:28)

5 References are to texts in vol. 3 of Khan (2008). In the cited examples the sign ˈ marks the end of an intonation group. An acute accent (e.g. *á*) indicates non-nuclear word-stress. A grave accent (e.g. *à*) marks the nuclear stress of the intonation group.

Occasionally the form expresses deontic obligation also in other persons, e.g.

(9)	*ṯ̂-ázəl*	*ṭaləb-la*	*m-be-bába*	*dìya.*|
	FUT-go.3ms	ask.3MS-3FS	from-house-father.her	of.her

'He should go and ask her father's family for her hand.' (A29:39)

2.1.2. Predictive Future

In many cases the construction does not have clear deontic force, but rather expresses a prediction of an eventuality that will happen in the future. This can be regarded as resulting from the grammaticalisation of the deontic construction, parallels to which are found in many languages. The core of this process involves a semantic extension whereby an implicature of the original deontic construction, in particular one with a 3rd person subject, is incorporated into the meaning, e.g. *he wants to go to town* implies that it is likely that he will go (Bybee 2010, 55).

The predictive future function of the *bət-qaṭəl* construction is generally found where the subject of the verb is 3rd person or where it is a non-agentive 1st or 2nd person, e.g.

(10)	*b-nayə̀s-li*|	*ṯ̂-axə̀l-li.*|
	FUT-bite.SBJV.3MS-1MS	FUT-eat.SBJV.3MS-1MS

'He will bite me. He will eat me.' (A1:17)

(11)	*ʾáni*	*b-nεsí-le*	*b-màyəθ*|
	they	FUT-bite.SBJV.3PL-3MS	FUT-die.SBJV.3MS

'They will bite him and he will die' (A10:1)

2.1.3. Conditional Constructions

The *bət-qaṭəl* form is used in the apodosis of conditional sentences. In the majority of cases it expresses an eventuality that is temporally sequential to a hypothetical situation in the future, e.g.

(12) *ʾən-kpìn-ni,*ˈ *ṱ-axlə̀n-ne.*ˈ

if-hunger.PFV-1S FUT-eat.SBJV.1MS-3MS

'If I am hungry, I shall eat it.' (A23:5)

(13) *ʾən-ʾamrə́n-nux* *ʾáp-ʾati* *b-šànət.*ˈ

if-say.SBJV.1MS-2MS also-you FUT-faint.SBJV.2MS

'If I tell you, you will faint.' (A11:2)

In some cases it expresses a future eventuality that follows logically from a given, real situation in the present denoted by the protasis clause, e.g.

(14) *ʾən-íle* *xwarzàyi,*ˈ *ṱ-áθe*

if-COP.3MS nephew.my FUT-come.SBJV.3MS

t-yăðé-la *ʾánna* *mòdi=la.*ˈ

FUT-know.SBJV.3MS-3PL these what=COP.3PL

'If he is my nephew, he will come and he will know what these are.' (A25:49)

One of the most common uses of the 'future in the past' form *bət-qaṭəlwa* is in the apodosis of conditional sentences. Such sentences may refer to a hypothetical condition in the past that was not fulfilled, e.g.

(15) *ʾən-mbaqrə̀t-wa,*| *t-yawə́n-wa-lux* *zùze,*|
if-ask.IPFV.2MS.-PST FUT-give.SBJV.1MS-PST-2MS money

bás *là* *mbuqə́r-rux.*|
but NEG ask.PFV-2MS

'If you had asked, I would have given you money, but you did not ask.'

In some cases the construction may denote a hypothetical condition in the present or future that the speaker assesses to be impossible to fulfil, e.g.

(16) *ʾən-maṣə̀n-wa,*| *ṱ-aθə̀n-wa,*|
if-be.able.SBJV.1MS-PST FUT-come.SBJV.1MS-PST

bás *lè-y-maṣən.*|
but NEG-HAB-be.able.IPFV.1MS

'If I could, I would come, but I cannot.'

2.1.4. Discourse Dependency

In conditional constructions such as those described in §2.1.3., the apodoses with the *bət-qaṭəl* and *bət-qaṭəlwa* forms are dependent syntactically on the preceding protasis. The forms are sometimes used outside of conditional constructions in clauses that are more loosely dependent on the preceding discourse. Various types of discourse dependency are attested. In some cases the forms express events that are temporally sequential to what precedes:

(17) *čɛrxì-wa-la* *máθa*| *xáṣə* *dawɛ̀re.*|...
take.round.IPFV.3PL-PST-3FS village back.of mules

*ʾay-ṯ-*__*aθyà-wa,*__| *ṯ-*__*orà-wa,*__|
she-FUT-come.SBJV.3FS-PST FUT-enter.SBJV.3FS-PST

*ʾu-ṯ-*__*oðá-wa*__ *ṣlìwa,*| *mə̀šxa,*|
and-FUT-make.SBJV.3FS-PST cross oil

gu-tắrət qàṣra.|
in-door.of house

‘They would take her (the bride) round the village on the back of mules. ... (Then) **she would come back, enter (the house) ... and make** (the sign of) the cross in oil on the door of the house.’ (B10:34–35)

(18) *báθər ʾéða gòṛa*| ... *ʾìθena*| *ʾéðət sulàqa.*|
after festival big there.is festival.of ascension

xàrθa| *ṯ-*__*áθe*__ *xá-ʾeða xréna zòra,*|
afterwards FUT-come.SBJV.3MS one-festival other small

y-amrí-le ʾéðət musàrde.|
HAB-say.IPFV.3PL-3MS festival.of musarde

‘After the Great Festival ... the festival of Ascension takes place. ... **Afterwards comes** a small festival, which is called *musarde*.’ (B6:5–8)

(19) *la-θéle rēš-ṣàwma?*| __*b-šaqlə́x-wa*__ *kúlla*
NEG-come.PFV.3MS head.of-fast? FUT-take.SBJV.1PL-PST all

ʾamànən,| *kùlla* __*b-šaqlə́x-wa-la*__| *dɛ́rəx-wa*
vessels.our all FUT-take.SBJV.1PL-PST-3PL put.SBJV.1PL-PST

qə̀ṭma mxallə̀x-wa-la.|
ash wash.SBJV.1PL-PST-3PL

‘When the beginning of the (Lent) fast came, **we would take** all our vessels, **we would take them** all to put ash on them to clean them.’ (B16:7)

In some cases the *bət-qaṭəl* and *bət-qaṭəl* forms do not express temporal sequentiality but only some kind of relevance to a preceding clause, typically elaboration:

(20)

báwθə	*Ninwàye*|	*ʾáp-ʾay*	*ʾìtwa.*|
petition.of	Ninevites	also-it.3FS	there.was

ṣɛmì-la.|	***ṱ-ámri***	*díge=u*	*kθàye*|
fast.IPFV.3PL-3PL	FUT-say.SBJV.3PL	cocks=and	chickens

ʾáp	*ʾan-zóre*	*xtàye.*|
also	those-small	lower

'The Rogation of the Ninevites was also observed (in our community). They would fast during it. **They would say** "The cocks and the chickens, and also the small lowly creatures (should observe the fast)."' (B16:15)

(21)

qam-ṣàwma|	*ʾíθ*	*xošébə*	*bnàθa.*|
before-fast	there.is	Sunday.of	girls

bnáθa	*kúlla*	***p̂ṱ-azí-wa***	*bɛ̀θa,*|
girls	all	FUT-go.SBJV.3PL-PST	home

b-šaqlí-wa	*ʾixála*	*mən-dáwwa*	*dáwwa*
FUT-take.SBJV.3PL-PST	food	from-this.OBL	this.OBL

dàwwa,|	***ṱ-azí-wa***	*gu-xa-ṭùra,*|
this.OBL	FUT-go.SBJV.3PL-PST	in-a-mountain

ṱ-atwì-wa,|	***ṱ-axlì-wa,***|	***b-šatì-wa.***|
FUT-come.SBJV.3PL-PST	FUT-eat.SBJV.3PL-PST	FUT-drink.SBJV-PST

'Before the fast (of Lent) was Girls' Sunday. All the girls **went** home, **took** food from here and from there, then **went** to the mountains, they **sat**, **ate** and **drank**.' (B16:18)

In (20) the clause introduced by the *bət-qaṭəl* form *ṯ̂-ámri* constitutes an elaboration of the preceding statement that people would hold a fast, which could be paraphrased 'with regard to this fasting they say ....'.

In (21) the clause containing the first *bət-qaṭəlwa* verb, *p̂ṯ̂-azíwa*, opens a section of discourse that elaborates on the preceding general statement that the festival of Girls' Sunday took place. The dependency expressed by the verbal forms bind them semantically to what precedes signalling that the descriptions of the specific events in the clauses are intended to be understood as components of the festival.

When the *bət-qaṭəl* and *bət-qaṭəlwa* forms have this discourse dependency function, they generally express habitual events, as is the case in the examples above. The construction is sporadically used in narratives where they refer to specific events that are dependent on, and typically sequential to, what precedes, e.g.

(22)

ʾə́rbe	*máxe*	*l-ġðàðe,*|	***ṯ̂-ázi***
sheep	strike.SBJV.3MS	to-each.other	FUT-go.SBJV.3PL

xa-fàtra|	*ʾal-salíqə*	*zòrna.*|	*máxe*	*zórna*
a-while	on-tune.of	pipe	strike.SBJV.3MS	pipe

xa-salíqa	*xèna,*|	*ʾə́rbe*	***b-dὲri,***|	*b-ganèy.*|
one-tune	other	sheep	FUT-return.SBJV.3PL	by-themselves

'He gathered the sheep together and they went off for a while according to the tune of the pipe. He played another tune on the pipe and the sheep returned by themselves.' (A25:27)

(23)

b-lέle	*qímla*	*šárya*	*bănúda*	*dìya,*|
at-night	rise.PFV.3FS	untie.SBJV.3FS	bands.her	of.her

*ṱ-àza,*ˈ	*pθíxla*	*tắra*	*qðìla.*ˈ
FUT-go.SBJV.3FS	open.PFV.3FS	door	key

'At night she got up, untied her bands, then went and opened the door with a key.' (A18:3)

2.2. Analysis

2.2.1. From Apodosis to Discourse Dependent

When used in the first three functions described above, viz. deontic future, predictive future and apodosis of conditionals (§2.1.1–2.1.3.), the *bət-qaṭəl(wa)* form expresses future tense. There is a crucial difference, however, between the deontic future and predictive future, on the one hand, and conditional constructions, on the other, with regard to the reference point of the future tense. Following the temporal analysis proposed by Reichenbach (1947), we should be careful to distinguish event time (E), speech time (S) and the temporal reference time (R). The original system of Reichenbach has undergone various modifications in more recent research, but the 'neo-Reichenbachian' approaches still distinguish these three components of analysis. The reference time (R), sometimes referred to as the 'evaluation time' (Hatav 2012), is the contextual temporal anchor to which the future verb form relates. One may say that the future form is temporally 'bound' to this anchor (Hatav 2012). In the case of the deontic future and predictive future functions, the reference time overlaps with speech time, i.e. the contextual temporal anchor is the speech situation. For the *bət-qaṭəl(wa)* form in the apodosis of conditional constructions, however, the reference time is that of the eventuality expressed in the protasis clause. In such cases the *bət-qaṭəl(wa)* form expresses an eventuality that is posterior to this reference time but this reference time does not necessarily overlap with speech time.

According to the original Reichenbachian system of representation, the analysis of these functions of the *bət-qaṭəl(wa)* form would be as follows (where a comma indicates temporal overlap and a dash — indicates temporal separation):

bət-qaṭəl

Deontic future: R,S—E

The event time is posterior to the reference time and the reference time overlaps with speech time.

Predictive future: R,S—E

The event time is posterior to the reference time and the reference time overlaps with speech time.

Apodosis: S—R—E or S,R—E

The reference time is that of the eventuality of the protasis and this may be posterior to speech time, e.g. (12—13) above, or overlap with it, e.g. (14) above. The event time is posterior to the reference time.

bət-qaṭəlwa

Apodosis: R—E—S or R,S—E

These two analyses correspond to (15) and (16) respectively. In both cases the reference time is that of the eventuality of the protasis and the event is posterior to this. The speech time varies according to whether the construction expresses a hypothetical condition in the past or in the present.

According to some Neo-Reichenbach approaches (e.g. Johnson 1981; Dinsmore 1982; Verkuyl 2012), rather than consisting of a single triple system, the analysis should consist of two pairs of components, namely S and R, on the one hand, and E and R, on the one hand. The relationship between S and R would correspond to tense, whereas the relationship between E and R would be one of posteriority or anteriority independent of tense. The analyses, therefore, would be:

Table 1: Analysis of *bət-qaṭəl* and *bət-qaṭəl-wa*

bət-qaṭəl			***bət-qaṭəlwa***		
Deontic future:	R—E	R,S			
Predictive future:	R—E	R,S			
Apodosis:	R—E	R—S	Apodosis:	R—E	R—S
	R—E	R,S		R—E	R,S

As can be seen, according to this temporal analysis all of these three future constructions share the common feature of R—E, i.e. the event time is posterior to the reference time.[6] What this Reichenbachian temporal analysis does not show, however, is that the reference time in the three constructions has different locations. In the deontic and predictive future constructions the reference time is internal, i.e. it coincides with the utterance of the clause. The reference time of the verb of the apodosis, however, is external to the clause and is located in the preceding protasis clause. This distinction is referred to by Hatav (2012) as local versus long distance semantic binding of tenses.

As for the aspect of the *bət-qaṭəl(wa)* form, in the examples cited above for its functions of deontic future, predictive future and apodosis of a condition the verb denotes a specific temporally bounded event and so is perfective. The form in these constructions may also denote iterative events (Khan 2008, 599, 606), e.g.

6 In some NENA dialects the *bət-qaṭəl* form is used in performative expressions, e.g. Qaraqosh (Khan 2002, 315): *ʾána bəd-qárən šə́mmux Tòma*ˈ 'I (hereby) call your name Toma'. This can be analysed as a deontic expression with reference time overlapping with event time: R,E.

(24) *kút-yom* *ṯ-áθi* *làxxa.*ˡ
every-day FUT-come.SBJV.3PL here

'They will come here every day.'

(25) *ʾən-maṣə́n-wa* *t-yawə́n-wa-lux* *zúze*
if-be.able.SBJV.1MS-PST COMP-give.SBJV.1MS-PST-2MS money

*kùt-yum,*ˡ *t-yawə̀n-wa-lux,*ˡ *bás*
every-day FUT-give.SBJV.1MS-PST-2MS but

*le-y-maṣə̀n-wa.*ˡ
NEG-IND-be.able.1MS-PST

'If I had been able, I would have given you money every day, but I could not.'

It is important to distinguish iterativity from habituality (Dahl 1985, 97; Bertinetto and Lenci 2012). Verbs expressing iterativity assert the occurrence of the event on multiple occasions, typically specified by an adverbial ('He visited us three times', 'He visited us every day'). Such predicates are perfective and express repeated temporally bounded events, i.e. events that are viewed as a whole typically from a reference time that is external to it (G. Carlson 2012, 835). Verbs expressing habituality present an event as a characterizing property of an individual, which occurs on the majority of occasions during a particular time interval (*He usually visits us every week*). Unlike iterative predications, habitual predications are not completely 'lawlike' (Dahl 1985, 97) and are contingent on circumstances (*He usually visits us every week, but he did not come last week because he was ill*). A habitual predicate is imperfective in aspect since it includes the reference time within it and is viewed from within (G. Carlson 2012, 835).

The *bət-qaṭəl* and *bət-qaṭəlwa* forms in deontic future, predictive future and apodosis constructions may express iterative predicates but not habitual predicates.

When expressing the deontic future, predictive future or the apodosis of a conditional the *bət-qaṭəl* and *bət-qaṭəlwa* forms are modal. Their modality is either root modality or epistemic modality. Root modality qualifies the subject of the clause indicating that some factor is inherent in the subject (e.g. ability, volition) or is operative upon the subject (e.g. obligation, circumstances) that influences the occurrence of the event. Epistemic modality involves the speaker's assessment of the truth value of the propositional content of the sentence as possible, probable or certain. The various types of modality inherent in the three aforementioned functions can be identified follows:

Table 2: Root and Epistemic Modality

Root modality		
volition of subject	(deontic future)	*ṱ-azən* 'I will go'
obligation on subject	(deontic future)	*ṱ-azət* 'you will go'
circumstantial	(conditional circumstances operative upon subject)	*ʾən ʾaθət, ṱ-azəl* 'if you come, he will go' (conditioned by circumstances)
Epistemic modality	predictive future	*ṱ-azəl* 'he will go'

Turning now to the discourse dependency function of *bət-qaṭəl(wa)*, this has a close family relationship to the apodosis function in conditional constructions. Indeed, I shall argue that it developed historically by a process of extension of conditional constructions. The *bət-qaṭəl(wa)* form in discourse dependency constructions exhibits long distance semantic binding, as is the case with the verbs in apodoses. The reference point precedes the event in the discourse, but, unlike in apodoses, this is not a temporal relationship. Rather the *bət-qaṭəl(wa)* verb is bound to a topical reference point that has been invoked by the preceding discourse. It depends on this and continues it in some way.

This phenomenon can be represented in the dependency framework of mental spaces proposed by Fauconnier (1994) and Dinsmore (1991). According to this model, knowledge can be represented in a network of mental spaces. These spaces are constructed by the listener, interpreting grammatical or lexical cues. Spaces contain information belonging to distinct times, locations or realities. 'Space builders' are cues that construct new mental spaces. Dependent verbs such as the *bət-qaṭəl(wa)* form express events that belong to a current, already constructed mental space.

The differences from the conditional construction, therefore, involve (i) the change of the temporal reference point to a topical reference point and (ii) the dependency on preceding discourse rather than on a preceding syntactically subordinate clause. This can be explained using a model of linguistic change through schematisation of constructions (e.g. Fillmore, Kay and O'Connor 1988; Goldberg 1995; 2006; Langacker 1987; Bybee 2010). This involves extensions of components of constructions by a process of substitutions of items with a family resemblance, thereby making the slots of the components more schematic, i.e. abstract. Another feature of the extension of constructions is their incorporation of pragmatic associations and implicatures into their meaning (Bybee 2010, 48). An example of this process of extension of constructions that is often cited (e.g. Bybee 2015, 124; 2010, 55) is the development of future constructions consisting of movement verbs, e.g. English *he is going to eat.* This originated as a construction that expressed real physical movement of an animate agentive subject, but it became schematised as SUBJECT + BE + *going to* + VERB, whereby any subject or verb could fill the subject or infinitive slots. Moreover, when used in the third person, although it originally expressed an intention, it implied that the predicate would be carried out. This implicature became conventionalised in the construction and so its meaning was extended to include prediction, e.g. *The branch is going to fall.*

The temporal reference point of the *bət-qaṭəl(wa)* apodosis that was in the preceding clause was schematised to being a more abstract cognitive reference point, referring to the general situation rather than specifically to a point in time. The *bət-qaṭəl(wa)* predication, therefore, is cognitively but not temporally bound to this preceding point. It is linked to it through discourse coherence analogous to a topic—comment relationship, or, to use Fauconnier's model, it is a continuation of the mental space of the preceding discourse. This does not mean that the topical situation itself may not have a reference time, but rather the *bət-qaṭəl(wa)* form no longer expresses temporal posteriority to this reference time but rather communicative posteriority to the more abstract topical situation, i.e. topical reference point—comment. One of the consequences of this is that the *bət-qaṭəl(wa)* may express discourse dependency on a non-propositional topic constituent without a temporal reference time, as is the case in (28) below.

The process of extending the location of the reference point of the *bət-qaṭəl(wa)* form from specifically the subordinate protasis clause to a broader component of preceding discourse that establishes a topic can also be identified as schematisation. This may have been facilitated by the fact that protasis clauses can in some contexts be used pragmatically as strategies for introducing a topical frame for what follows (Khan 2008, 1005). This pragmatic usage would then have been conventionalised (see Bybee 2010, 48 and the discussion above), e.g.

(26)	*fa-ʾən-maṭiní-wa-le*	*ʾíθwa*	*xàwla.*ˡ
	and-if-load.IPFV.3PL-PST-3MS	there.was	rope

'If they loaded it (the mule), there was a rope (= As for when they loaded it ...).' (B5:128)

The preceding topic-establishing discourse may be propositional, as in (17, 19–23), or it may be a non-propositional constituent such as an adverbial, as in (18) (repeated here as (27)), or a noun phrase (28—the example is from the C. Mawana dialect):

(27)

*xàrθa*ˡ	***ṯ̂-áθe***	*xá-ˀeða*	*xréna*	*zòra.*ˡ
afterwards	FUT-come.SBJV.3MS	one-festival	other	small

‘Afterwards, comes a small festival.’ (B6:5–8)

(28) C. Mawana (fieldnotes)

ɟózə	*barȕzə,*ˡ	*hădə́*	*ˀắt*	*b-⁺răp̂ə́t-wa-lə*
walnuts	dry	now	you	FUT-throw.SBJV.2MS-PST-3MS

ɟózux	*ˀàtxa.*ˡ
walnut.your	thus

‘As for (the game) dry walnuts, you would throw your walnut like this.’

Conditional clauses and topics are coded identically in a number of unrelated languages. This reflects the fact that their semantic analysis is very similar (Haiman 1978; Ebert, Ebert, and Hinterwimmer 2014). This would have facilitated the proposed development of the *bət-qaṭəl*.

2.2.2. Sequentiality and Habituality

It was noted above that when the *bət-qaṭəl(wa)* form expresses discourse dependency, the eventuality it presents is sometimes temporally sequential to what precedes but other times is an elaboration without temporal sequentiality. This can be understood as arising from the fact that its reference point in the preceding discourse is not temporal but rather topical. The fact that it is often used to express temporally sequential events is, therefore, an epiphenomenon arising from the fact that events expressed in successive clauses are typically temporally sequential. The construction, however, does not express temporal sequentiality directly.

When the *bət-qaṭəl(wa)* form is used to express discourse dependency, it most frequently expresses the imperfective aspect of habituality. It is very commonly used in expository discourse describing customs. As we have seen, the *bət-qaṭəl(wa)* form does not express habituality in its other functions of future and apodosis constructions. Why does the discourse dependent *bət-qaṭəl(wa)* form most commonly have habitual meaning?

Since the discourse dependent *bət-qaṭəl(wa)* does not have a future meaning, we must assume that it has acquired a reference time that coincides with the eventuality that it denotes. The development can be represented as follows, where T = Topic:

Table 3: Sequentiality and Discourse Dependency of *bət-qaṭəl(wa)*

Apodosis	**Discourse Dependency**
R—E	T—R,E

A chain of *bət-qaṭəl(wa)* forms that comment on a topical situation would share the same topical reference point. This can be represented thus:

T_1—R_1,E_1, + T_1—R_2,E_2 + T_1—R_3,E_3 + T_1—R_4,E_4

This can be regarded as the resumption of the topic by a form of anaphora, analogously to the way topical referents are resumed by anaphoric pronouns.

These anaphoric topics are variables that are bound by and dependent on the antecedent topic, just as anaphoric pronouns are variables bound by an antecedent topic. This anaphoric binding of the topic can be regarded as a type of modality, so the construction is modal, just as a *bət-qaṭəl(wa)* form in an apodosis is modal. Indeed according to some approaches, the binding of anaphoric pronouns to antecedents is also a type of modality (Roberts 1987; 1989).

It is noteworthy that the *bət-qaṭəl* form in C. Barwar is not used in generic predicates such as (29).

(29) *tálga xwàra y-áwe.*ˈ

snow white HAB.be.3MS

'Snow is white.'

This is because such generic predicates are typically independent of discourse context and do not comment on a preceding topical situation.[7]

The normal habitual meaning of the discourse dependent *bət-qaṭəl* form most likely arises from a retention of the contingent semantics of a conditional apodosis. As remarked, habitual predications are not completely 'lawlike' (Dahl 1985, 97) and are contingent on circumstances.

As we have seen, the *bət-qaṭəl(wa)* form is attested occasionally in narratives (22–23). Following the analysis that has just been proposed, we may say that they have the communicative function of expressing a comment on a previously mentioned situation, which has been set up as a topic. This analysis is appropriate for (22) (repeated below as (30)), since it consists of two situations that are set up in contrastive opposition. Contrastive oppositions are typically expressed by contrasting topics. The topical situations can be glossed by 'when'–clauses:

(30) *ˀə́rbe máxe l-ġðàðe,*ˈ ***ṯ-ázi***

sheep strike.SBJV.3MS to-each.other FUT-go.SBJV.3PL

7 There are interesting parallels here with English habitual constructions containing the auxiliary *would*. It has been observed that such habituals have a similar dependency on situations or 'mental spaces' established in the context, e.g. Carlson and Spejewski (1997) and Boneh and Doron (2013), who refer to this as 'modal subordination'. A habitual sentence *used to*, on the other hand, has no such dependency, e.g. *My grandmother used to make delicious apple pies. She would go to the orchard to pick the apples herself* (adapted from Carlson and Spejewski 1997, 102). These authors do not discuss the history of the construction.

xa-fàtra|	*ʾal-salíqə*	*zòrna.*|	*máxe*	*zórna*
a-while	on-tune.of	pipe	strike.SBJV.3MS	pipe

xa-salíqa	*xèna,*|	*ʾə́rbe*	***b-dὲri,***|	*b-ganèy.*|
one-tune	other	sheep	FUT-return.SBJV.3PL	by-themselves

‘(When) he had gathered the sheep together, they went off for a while according to the tune of the pipe. (When, on the other hand,) he had played another tune on the pipe, the sheep returned by themselves.’ (A25:27)

Example (23) (repeated below as (31)) can be given a similar analysis of topical situation—comment, with the topical situation glossed by a ‘when’–clause:

(31)	*b-lέ́le*	*qímla*	*šárya*	*bănúda*	*dìya,*|
	at-night	rise.PFV.3FS	untie.SBJV.3FS	bands.her	of.her

	ṱ-àza,|	*pθíxla*	*tắra*	*qðìla.*|
	FUT-go.SBJV.3FS	open.PFV.3FS	door	key

‘(When) at night she had got up and untied her bands, she went and opened the door with a key.’ (A18:3)

These constructions in narrative contain what can be termed an ‘episodic topic’ with the status of an adverbial expression that sets the spatio-temporal frame for what follows. They appear to be used to mark boundaries in the discourse. In (30), as remarked, the two episodic topics set up two episodes in contrastive opposition. In (31) the episodic topic marks the onset of a new section of narrative.

In some NENA dialects the discourse dependent form with the original future particle *bət/bəd* has developed further and can be used as an actual present without first presenting a situation as its topic. This was the case in the now extinct Jewish dialect of Dobe (on the north bank of the Zab river). In this dialect, for example, the form *bd-ez* (FUT-go.SBJV.3MS) can be used as

(i) a deontic or predictive future: 'he will go'

(ii) a habitual dependent on a specified situation, such as an adverbial in (32):

(32)	*kud*	*bqatta*	*bd-ez*	*ʾəl-ʾăra*
	every	morning	FUT-go.SBJV.3MS	to-land

'Every morning he goes to the (cultivated) land.'

(iii) actual present: *bd-ez* 'he is going (now before our eyes)'.[8]

This extension of the construction to the actual present can be explained as having arisen by a process similar to Greenberg's (1978) 'cycle of definiteness', whereby anaphoric pronouns develop into non-anaphoric definite articles. The anaphoric topical component of the dependent *bət-qaṭəl* construction has come to be used where the speaker assumes the hearer can identify the situation that is being referred to without explicitly presenting an antecedent topical situation in the preceding discourse. It appears that the speaker assumes that the hearer can identify the speech situation as the situation that is being talked about, i.e. it expresses situational immediacy.

8 The data on the Dobe dialect were gathered in field work in 1999 in the Moshav Menuḥa, Israel. The usage of the *bd-* particle was identified in recorded texts and elicited sentences.

3. Past Forms with the Prefix *qam-*

3.1. Attested Constructions

In many NENA dialects, a perfective past tense is expressed by combining the prefixed particle *qam-*, or variant forms of this, with the subjunctive verb form *qaṭəl*. The variant forms of the prefix attested across the dialects arise from a range of phonetic reductions, e.g. *qəm* (C. Barwar, etc.: vowel centralisation), *kəm* (C. Qaraqosh, etc.: vowel centralisation and fronting of the uvular), *qa* (C. Koy Sanjak: elision), *tam, ta* (C. Sulemaniyya and C. Sanandaj: fronting of the uvular and elision). In the documented dialects this construction is restricted to verbs with pronominal suffixes expressing the direct or indirect object. It is used predominantly to express past perfective events in narrative (33–34) or the occurrence of a punctual event in the recent past in conversational discourse (35). In the examples the particle is given the gloss QAM:

C. Barwar (Khan 2008, 609–11)

(33)	*qəm-mparqí-li*	*m-gu-ʾiθàθux.*ˈ
	QAM-save.SBJV.3PL-1S	from-in-your.hands

‘They saved me from your hands.’ (B17:15)

(34)	*qəm-hawí-la*	*xáčča*	*ʾixàla*ˈ
	QAM-give.SBJV.3PL-3PL	some	food

‘They gave them some food.’ (A8:12)

(35)	*ʾáti*	*qəm-xalṣàt-li*ˈ	*mən-dáwwa*	*mòθa.*ˈ
	your	QAM-save.SBJV.3FS-1S	from-this	death

‘You have saved me from death.’ (A14:35)

Various hypotheses have been proposed for the historical origin of this verbal construction.[9] Pennacchietti (1997) argued that it developed from a construction consisting of the verb *qayəm* 'he gets up' followed by the subjunctive, e.g. *qayəm qaṭəl-le*. He found support for this in the grammar of Rhétoré (1912, 225–26), who states that such a construction could be used in the sense of 'aussitôt il le tua' ('he immediately killed him'), i.e. the event happened immediately after the event mentioned before it. Rhétoré, who unfortunately does not specify in which dialect(s) he found this construction, states that its original meaning was 'se levant, il le tue' ('getting up, he kills him'), i.e. a sequence of events in the present.[10] Pennacchietti, however, proposes that it originated as a construction expressing the immediate future 'he will immediately kill him', comparing constructions such as *qemən ʾazən* 'I shall immediately go', which are found in various NENA dialects. He draws attention to the fact that several languages use a construction that originated as the expression of the immediate future to narrate a sequence of events in the past, e.g. Catalan[11] (36) and late medieval French (14th-16th century) (37):

(36) Catalan

vaig cantar
I.go to.sing

'I sang'

9 See Fassberg (2015) who surveys the various proposals.

10 Eleanor Coghill in an unpublished paper given at the 23rd International Conference on *Historical Linguistics*, San Antonio, Texas, 2017, argued in favour of this view.

11 For further discussion of the Catalan construction see, for example, Jacobs (2011).

(37) Late medieval French

et	*comme*	*elle*	*faisoit*	*ce*	*partage,*
and	when	she	was.making	this	division

son	*mari*	*va*	*revenir*	*à*	*l'ostel*
her	husband	goes	to return	at	the.hostel

'While she was making this division, her husband returned home.'

The second verb in the original construction *qayəm qaṭəl-le* would, therefore, have been a subjunctive in a purpose clause 'he gets up in order to kill him' rather than an indicative present, as suggested by Rhétoré's translation 'se levant, il le tue'.

Here I would like to present some additional data that strengthen Pennacchietti's hypothesis.

In some NENA dialects a subordinating particle regularly occurs before initial /ʾ/ verbs after the *qam* in the *qam-qaṭəlle* construction, e.g.

(38) C. Meze (field notes):

qam-d-axəl-le

QAM-COMP-eat.SBJV.3MS-3MS

'He ate it'

This reflects the fact that the verb after the *qam* was originally a subordinate subjunctive. Some isolated cases of the subordinating particle are found before initial /ʾ/ verbs in C. Barwar, (Khan 2008, 609), e.g.

(39) C. Barwar

qəm-ṯ-amə́r-ra

QAM-COMP-say.SBJV.3MS-3FS

'He said to her.' (A4:4)

The crucial missing link in the evidence, however, is provided by the dialects from the north-western sector of NENA. In some dialects in this region, such as the dialects in the area of the Cudi mountain and Billin, the initial inflected verb in immediate future constructions such as *qemən ʾazən* has become grammaticalised to *qam* without person inflection. Most of my data come from the Harbole dialect (Cudi), e.g.

Harbole (field notes)[12]

(40) *qam-ʾàzən.ˈ*

QAM-go.SBJV.1MS

'I am about to go/I am going to go right now.'

This immediate future construction can be used with both intransitive and transitives verbs. An example with a transitive verb is (41):

(41) *qam-ʾaxlə̀n-ne.ˈ*

QAM-eat.SBJV.1MS-3MS

'I am about to eat it/I am going to eat it immediately.'

---

12 Most of the material from the Harbole dialect that I present below was gathered from consultations with Professor Efrem Yildiz (University of Salamanca), who is a native speaker of the dialect. I would like to express here my gratitude to him for his help.

The future construction may be given a past reference time ('was about to') by adding the past shifting suffix *-wa*, e.g.

(42) *qam-ʾaxlə̀n-wa.*ˈ
QAM-eat.SBJV.1MS-PST
'I was about to eat.'

This can be used in initial position in a discourse such as the following:

(43)	*qam-ʾaxlə́n-wa*	*ʾixàla,*ˈ	*bás*	*là*	*bréla*
	QAM-eat.SBJV.1MS-PST	food	but	NEG	be.possible.PFV-3FS

*mə́nni.*ˈ
from.me

'I was about to eat food but I have not been able to.'

The construction is also used in narrative discourse in the Harbole dialect to express an event that occurred immediately after the event mentioned in the preceding clause. According to speakers, an event expressed by the construction in this context is typically unexpected and surprising, i.e. it has a mirative function. The immediate future form is used with or without the past shifting *-wa* suffix, i.e. *qam-ʾaxlən* or *qam-ʾaxlənwa*, e.g.

(44)	*plə̀ṭli,*ˈ	*ʾu-qam-xazə́n-na*	*bàxti.*ˈ
	go.out.PFV.1S	and-QAM-see.SBJV.1MS-3FS	my.wife

'I went out and I (suddenly, unexpectedly) saw my wife'

(45)

ʾána	*bitáya*	*làxxa,ˈ*	*qam-xazə́n-wa*
I	come.PROG.	here	QAM-see.SBJV.1MS-PST

xa	*ʾárya*	*b-ùrxa.ˈ*
one	lion	on-road

'When I was coming here, I saw (unexpectedly) a lion on the road.'

As can seen in (45), the lexical verb of the construction does not have to have a pronominal object suffix, as is the case in most other NENA dialects. Indeed the verb can be intransitive, e.g.

(46)

ʾána	*ʾu-xáwri*	*plə̀ṭlanˈ*
I	and-my.friend	go.out.PFV.1PL

ʾu-qam-màyət	*xáwri.ˈ*
and-QAM-die.SBJV.3MS	my.friend

'I and a friend went out and (suddenly unexpectedly) my friend died.'

(47)

m-bátər	*plə́ṭlan*	*ʾána*	*ʾu-xàwri,ˈ*
from-after	go.out.PFV.1PL	I	and-my.friend

qam-nápəl	*go-šaqìta.ˈ*
QAM-fall.SBJV.3MS	in-canal

'After I and my friend went out, he (suddenly unexpectedly) fell into the canal.'

A further variant of the construction is the substitution of the *qaṭəl* form by the *qṭəlle* form after the *qam* in past narratives, e.g.

(48)	*ʾána*	*ʾu-xáwri*	*plə̀ṭlan*ˈ	*ʾu-qam-mə̀tle*
	I	and-my.friend	go.out.PFV.1PL	and.QAM-die.PFV.3MS
	*xáwri.*ˈ			
	my.friend			

'I and a friend went out and my friend died.'

Speakers judge constructions such as *qam-mətle* in (48) to express an unexpected and surprising event, but to be in the less immediate past than *qam-mayət* (46).

3.2. Analysis

In this section I should like to propose an explanation as to how the immediate future constructions with *qam* came to be used to express past events in narrative.

An example such as (44) above is likely to have originated in a juxtaposition of the immediate future construction with the previously mentioned situation, which meant 'I went out and I was about to see my wife'. The reference time of the immediate future, therefore, coincided with the reference time of the first event. This can be represented as follows, with the index on R indicating the coincidence of reference time:

R_1,E *I went outside*

R_1–E *I was about to see my wife*

This was a strategy for expressing the immediate succession of the events. The preparatory onset phase of the second event overlaps with the first event. The events are connected together cognitively in the same mental space. It was also a strategy for giving prominence to the second event by anticipating it before it had occurred in the narration of events.

An immediate future construction such as *qam-ʾazən* 'I am about to go' would have been a deontic future, but as with other future constructions, when used with a third person, i.e. *qam-ʾazəl* 'he is about to go', there is an implicature that the event will happen, and so the construction comes to function also as a predictive future, presenting the event as a certainty. When combined with a past event, as in (44), the certainty of the future occurrence shifts to the assertion of the occurrence of the event in close succession to the preceding event. This comes about by the *qam*-construction acquiring a reference time that coincides with its event:

R_1,E_1	*I went out*
R_1—R_2,E_2	*I saw my wife* (R_2) *after going out* (R_1)

The original reference time of the *qam*-construction is retained (R_1) and this expresses a sequential or continuative meaning, i.e. the event took place at reference time R_2 in relation to reference time R_1. The past tense of *qam-xazənna* is not expressed morphologically. The form can be assumed to have had a 'relative tense' that was determined by being bound to the R_1 of the past verb *pləṭli*. This past verb was marked morphologically as past, i.e. its reference time was before speech time (R_1—S).[13]

When the construction developed the meaning of immediate sequence, this marked type of sequence was associated with the implicature of mirativity (surprise), and also with salience and, in turn, with the recent past. Speakers of the Harbole dialect report that the construction has these associations.

The *qam*-constructions in examples such as (45), with a preceding imperfective circumstantial expression ('When I was coming here') and (47) with a posterior temporal adverbial clause ('After I and my friend went out') cannot be so easily analysed as having the temporal structure R_1—R_2,E with two reference times,

13 For the possibility of a verb having two reference points see Comrie (1985, 128).

one anterior to the other. This is because from a temporal point of view the eventuality in the *qam*-clause is overlapping with, rather than sequential to, what is expressed by the circumstantial construction and the 'after' adverbial clause. It appears that the first reference point is no longer temporal but rather has become a cognitive topical anchor, similar to the process described in §2.2. in the development of the discourse dependency *bət-qaṭəl(wa)* form. This can be represented as T—R,E, where T = the episodic topical situation that acts as the spatio-temporal frame for what follows:

When I was coming here (topical frame)—*I saw a lion.*

After I and my friend went out (topical frame)—*he fell into the canal.*

Note that in (45) the past shifting suffix -*wa* is added to the *qam*-construction (*qam-xazənwa*), indicating that it has its own tense marking, i.e. its tense is absolute and it is not bound as a relative tense to the tense of a preceding verb. This is likely to be because it is preceded by a tenseless expression (*ʾana bitaya* 'I coming').

The *qam*-construction is not obligatory in constructions of the type illustrated in the preceding examples. Contrast the following:

(49) *xəzyali* vs. *qam-xazənna*

a. *ʾána bitáya làxxa, xəzyá-li bàxti b-úrxa.ˈ*
I come.PROG here see.PFV.3FS-1S my.wife on.road
'While I was coming here, I saw my wife on the road.'

b. *ʾána bitáya làxxa,ˈ qam-xazə́n-na bàxti b-úrxa.ˈ*
I come.PROG here QAM-see.SBJV.1MS-3FS my.wife on.road
'While I was coming here, I saw my wife on the road.'

(50) *štelan* vs. *qam-šatuxwa*

a.	*ˀáxni*	*bəplàxa,ˈ*	*štélan*	*čày.ˈ*
	we	work.PROG	drink.PFV.1PL	tea

‘Whilst we were working, we drank tea.’

b.	*ˀáxni*	*bəplàxa,ˈ*	*qam-šatúx-wa*	*sàḥma.ˈ*
	we	work.PROG	QAM-drink.SBJV.1PL-PST	poison

‘Whilst we were working, we drank poison.’

The (a) sentences of (49) and (50) with the past perfective *qṭəlle* form are matter-of-fact descriptions of events. The (b) sentences present the events as surprising and unexpected.

As has been remarked, a hybrid construction exists, in which the *qaṭəl* form in the *qam*-construction is substituted by the *qṭəlle* form ((48) repeated below as (51)). This still has a different pragmatic association from a corresponding construction with *qṭəlle* without the preceding *qam-* (52):

(51)	*ˀána*	*ˀu-xáwri*	*plə̀ṭlanˈ*	*ˀu-qam-mə̀tle*
	I	and-my.friend	go.out.PFV.1PL	and.QAM-die.PFV.3MS
	xáwri.ˈ			
	my.friend			

‘I and a friend went out and my friend died.’

(52)	*ˀána*	*ˀu-xáwri*	*plə̀ṭlanˈ*	*ˀu-mə̀tle*
	I	and-my.friend	go.out.PFV.1PL	and-die.PFV.3MS
	xáwri.ˈ			
	my.friend			

‘I and a friend went out and my friend died.’

According to my consultant for the dialect, (51) implies a causal connection between the going out and the death whereas there is no such implicature in (52). This could arise from the fact that the *qam-qṭəlle* construction, like the *qam*-construction with the *qaṭəl* form, expresses immediate succession and close cohesion in the same mental space, an implicature of which could be causal connection.

In Harbole, as we have seen, the *qam*-construction with the *qaṭəl* form can be used in narrative in both transitive and intransitive clauses. There is no obvious feature of behaviour of the construction in this dialect that could explain why it became restricted to transitive verbs with pronominal objects in most of NENA. This specific distribution in other dialects appears to have been a strategy to avoid using internal pronominal objects in the *qṭəlle* form, especially 1st and 2nd person objects.[14] In such dialects the *qam*-construction became a general past perfective form substituting for *qṭəlle* where the verb would have had pronominal objects. One can compare this to, for example, to the *vaig cantar* construction in Catalan (see (36)), which became a general past perfective form. This development of the *qam*-construction would doubtless have been facilitated by the fact that already in Harbole the temporal reference point of the construction in the preceding clause came to be analysed as a topical reference point in some contexts (i.e. R_1—R_2,E became T—R,E). As with the *bət-qaṭəl(wa)* form, this would have facilitated the use of a series of *qam*-constructions with the same spatio-temporal topical frame in narratives.

The generalised *qam*-construction did, however, retain some of the features of its embryonic form seen in the Harbole dialect. Firstly, when it takes 3rd person pronominal objects in narrative, these are anaphoric to the preceding discourse so the verb is sequential to or at least continuative of what precedes, as it is in Harbole. Secondly, speakers of some dialects report that in conversational discourse where the expression of a pronominal

14 See the studies of expression of pronominal objects in Pennacchietti (1994), Coghill (2016), Khan (2017), Noorlander (2018).

object is possible in both a *qṭəlle* or *qam*-construction, the *qam*-construction refers specifically to the recent past whereas the *qṭəlle* form does not have this restriction, e.g. *qam-xazən-a* (QAM-see.SBJV.1MS-3FS) 'I have just seen her' vs *xəzy-a-li* (see.PST-3FS-1S) 'I saw her' (not necessarily recently) (Shaqlawa dialect, field notes). This is reflected by the fact that the particle *na*, which is used in the Shaqlawa dialect to express immediacy, is more frequently used with the form *qam-xazəna* than with *xəzyali*.[15]

4. Narrative Subjunctive

4.1. Attested Constructions

In NENA dialects the bare present stem *qaṭəl* functions as a subjunctive. This is used in a variety of irrealis contexts, including jussive main clauses, irrealis subordinate clauses and conditional clauses. An example of a subjunctive clause in a subordinate purpose clause from the C. Barwar dialect is given in (53):

(53)	*ṣə̀lyɛ=le*ˈ	*ta-t-ʾázəl*	*ʾùrxa.*ˈ
	go.PTCP=COP.3MS	to-COMP-go.SBJV.3MS	road

'He went down in order to set off on the road.' (A15:5)

15 The verb *q-y-m* 'to rise' is used in various other types of constructions, the discussion of which is beyond the scope of this paper. For example, a past form of the verb *q-y-m* is used in NENA dialects in a serial construction with another past verb to express the onset of an activity at a discourse boundary, e.g. C. Barwar *qímla wídla tàgbir*ˈ (rise.PST.3PL make.PST.3PL plan) 'They made a plan.' (Khan 2008, 937–38). The preverbal particle *qam-* is used in the dialect of J. Bəjil to express the progressive, e.g. *qam-patəxle* 'he is opening it' (Mutzafi 2002) (I thank Paul Noorlander for drawing my attention to this reference). This is likely to have had a different semantic development from the construction with *qam-* that is discussed in this paper.

The indicative present, such as the progressive and habitual, are typically expressed by innovative forms, such as the following in the C. Barwar dialect:

Indicative habitual

ʾi-qaṭəl:

(54)	*kút-yum*	*y-áxəl*	*làxma.*[1]
	every-day	HAB-eat.IPFV.3MS	bread

‘Every day he eats bread.’

Progressive

hole qṭala (deictic copula + progressive stem) or *qṭalɛ=le* (progressive stem + enclitic copula). The progressive stem is derived historically from the infinitive:

(55)

a.	*hole*	*zala*
	DEIC.COP.3MS	go.PROG

‘He is going.’

b.	*zalɛ=le*
	go.PROG=COP.3MS

‘He is going.’

In the C. Barwar dialect the *qaṭəl* subjunctive form is often used in narratives as a perfective sequential form. It typically continues an event or events that are expressed by a narrative past form (*qṭille* or *qṭilɛle*), e.g.

(56) *ʾáp ʾaw-lɛ́le xéna qìmla,*| *sáʾət ṭḷáθa*
also that-night other rise.PFV.3FS hour.of three

b-lɛ̀le,| ***šárya*** *bănúda dìya,*| *ʾu-**ʾáza***
at-night untie.SBJV.3FS bands.her of.her and-go.SBJV.3FS

ʾáxla *xá-brona xéna ʾu-**dɛ̀ṛa,***|
eat.SBJV.3FS one-son other and-return.SBJV.3FS

dàmxa.| ***páθxa*** *tằra,*| ***dámxa***
sleep.SBJV.3FS open.SBJV.3FS door sleep.SBJV.3FS

gu-dudìya.|
in-cradle

'Also the next night she got up, at three o'clock in the morning, **untied** her bands, **went** and **ate** another child, then **returned** and **went to sleep**. She **opened** the door and **went to sleep** in the cradle.' (A18:5–6)

(57) *šqílə=l-le xmàra*| *ʾu-tàwra.*|
take.PTCP.=COP.3MS-3MS ass and-ox

ʾu-zìlɛ=le.| *šúryɛ=le zràya.*|
and-go.PTCP=COP.3MS begin.PTCP=COP.3MS cultivate.PROG

šúry=ɛle zráya hàl-ʾaṣərta.| *ʾaṣə́rta*
begin.PTCP=COP.3MS cultivate.PROG until-evening evening

ʾáθe *l-bɛ̀θa.*| ***mànyəx,***| ***ʾázəl*** ***sàxe***|
come.SBJV.3MS to-house rest.SBJV.3MS go.SBJV.3MS swim.SBJV.3MS

*ʾu-**ʾàwər.***|
and-enter.SBJV.3MS

'He took the ass and the ox and went off. He began cultivating. He began cultivating (and continued) until evening. In the evening he **came** home. He **rested**, **went** and **bathed** and **entered** (the house).' (A21:12)

Sporadically the *qaṭəl* form is used as a sequential habitual:

(58)

*ʾu-**máxa***	*xa-mə́šxa*	*gu-be-ʾéne*	*dìye*ˈ
and-put.SBJV.3PL	one-oil	in-place.of-eyes.his	of.him

ʾoðí-le	*rúšma*	*ʾax-ṣlìwa.*ˈ
do.SBJV.3PL-3MS	sing	like-cross

'And they put some oil on his forehead and make the sign of the cross.' (B6:36)

The use of the bare *qaṭəl* form in narratives looks *prima facie* like the active participles that are commonly found in narratives in earlier types of Aramaic, such as Biblical Aramaic, e.g.

(59) קָרֵ֤א מַלְכָּא֙ בְּחַ֔יִל ... עָנֵ֨ה מַלְכָּ֜א וְאָמַ֣ר׀ לְחַכִּימֵ֣י בָבֶ֗ל

qɔ:ʀ̣é:	malkɔ́:	ba-ḥá:yil	**ʿɔ:né:**	malkɔ́:
call.PTCP.MS	king	with-force	answer.PTCP.MS	king

vɔ-ʾ**ɔ:má:aʀ̣**	la-ḥakki:mé:	vɔ:vɛ́:ɛl
and-say.PTCP.MS	to-sages.of	Babylon

'The king **cries aloud** … The king **answers** and **says** to the wise men of Babylon.' (Dan. 5:7)

This is, however, a false analogy, since the Barwar *qaṭəl* form, although derived historically from the active participle of earlier Aramaic, now has a subjunctive function. A closer analogy to the use of active participles in earlier Aramaic narratives is the occasional use of the progressive form inflected by a copula (*qṭalɛ=le*) or sometimes without a copula (*qṭala*) in C. Barwar narratives, e.g.

(60) *yómə ṯ̈làθa*ˡ ***márɛ = le*** *xóne díye*
day.of three say.PROG = COP.3MS brother.his of.him

mára *ṯ̂-ázəx ṣ̀ɛda.*ˡ *ʾánna* ***plàṭɛ = la,***ˡ
say.PROG FUT-go.SBJV.1PL hunt they go.out.PROG = COP.3PL

kúlla ***zála*** *ṣ̀ɛda.*ˡ
all go.PROG hunt

'On the third day his brother says .. **he says** "Let's go hunting." **They go out, they all go** hunting.' (A13:7)

In some NENA dialects the progressive construction is, indeed, the verb form that is most commonly used in narratives. This is the case, for example, in the C. Urmi dialect:

(61) C. Urmi (Khan 2016, vol. 2, 186–87)

⁺bar-dáha ***bərràxšə = lə*** *cəs-màlca.*ˡ
after-OBL.this go.PROG = COP.3MS at-king

⁺bəṯ̂lábə = lə *⁺paxàlta mə́nnu.*ˡ
ask.PROG = COP.3MS forgiveness from.him

'After that **he goes** to the king. **He asks** for forgiveness from him.' (A 3:54)

4.2. Analysis

I should like to argue here that the narrative *qaṭəl* form is indeed a modal subjunctive, which has been extended from its use in subordinate clauses, in particular purpose clauses. In C. Barwar, purpose clauses are introduced by a particle, typically a directional preposition such as *ta* 'to' as in (62), or are asyndetic without an introductory particle (63) (Khan 2008, 582–83, 667, 995–95):

(62)

ṣə̀lyɛ=le|	*ta-t-ʾázəl*	*ʾù̀rxa.*|
go.down.PTCP=COP.3MS	to-COMP-go.SBJV.3MS	way

'He went down **to go** on the road.' (A15:5)

(63)

ʾána	*θíθ=ən*	*mpalṭán-nux*
I	come.PTCP=COP.1FS	bring.out.SBJV.1FS-2MS

m-gu-sə̀jən.|
from-in-prison

'I have come to bring you out of the prison.' (A26:82)

Purpose clause constructions are also used to express the final outcome or result of a preceding action, whereby the speaker presents the chain of events from the viewpoint of this outcome (Khan 2008, 995), e.g.

(64)

ṣlàya,|	*ṣálya*	*šátya*	*mìya,*|
go.down.PROG	go.down.SBJV.3FS	drink.SBJV.3FS	water

ta-t-qàlba	*xá-bena*	*xéna.*|
to-COMP-return.SBJV.3FS	a-time	other

'She went down to drink water and then finally returned again.' (A33:8)

Such result clauses appear to have developed from the common implicature of purpose clauses that the event took place, especially after verbs of movement, e.g. *I went to buy some bread* has the implicature that I did in fact buy bread (Schmidtke-Bode

2009, 178). This conventionalisation of an implicature as the expression of a real event that is reflected in result clauses is likely to have been the pathway of development also of dependent narrative *qaṭəl* forms. This may be represented as follows:

(65)

a.	**Main clause**	**Purpose clause**
	R_1,E	R_1—E
b.	**Main clause**	**Result clause**
	R_1,E	R_1—R_2,E
c.	**Main clause**	**Narrative sequential**
	R_1,E	R_1—R_2,E

This analysis is similar to that of the development of the *qam*-construction forms discussed above. In the purpose clause construction the subjunctive verb is irrealis and takes as its reference time that of the main clause (represented by the repeated R_1 in (65a)). The event time of the purpose clause, therefore, is posterior to its reference time and so the predicate is analogous to a future construction such as the immediate future *qam*-construction. In (65b) and (65c) the subjunctive clause has been reanalysed as a real asserted event. This involves the acquisition of a reference time coinciding with the event (R_2). It can be assumed that the clause retains the R_1 reference time, to which it is posterior. This reflects its reanalysis as a real asserted event that is sequential to what precedes.

As remarked, in the C. Urmi dialect the normal narrative verb form is the progressive. The narrative subjunctive is, however, sporadically used in this dialect. It is significant that in the attested examples in my text corpus it occurs predominantly after verbs of movement:

(66) C. Urmi (Khan 2016, vol. 2, 122)

mə́jjət=da	*ʾá*	*náša*	*xə̀šlə*ˡ	*ɟášə̭k*
indeed=also	this	man	go.PFV.3MS	see.SBJV.3MS

ʾó	*bétu*	*súra*	*víyyə=va*	*xá*	*yácca*
that	his.house	small	become.PTCP=COP.PST.3MS	a	big

máx	*bə́tət*	*màlcə*	*víyyə=va.*ˡ
like	house.of	kings	become.PTCP=COP.PST.3MS

'Indeed the man went off and **saw** that his small house had become huge, it had become like the house of kings.' (A 54:5)

Cross-linguistically purpose clauses are very commonly preceded by verbs of movement (Schmidtke-Bode 2009, 98) and this is also the case in NENA dialects, see (60)–(61) from C. Barwar. An example from C. Urmi is (67), where the purpose clause is asyndetic:

(67) C. Urmi (Khan 2016, vol. 2, 122)

xə́šla	*báxta*	*⁺tárra*	*patxà-lə*ˡ
go.PFV.3FS	woman	door	open.SBJV.3FS-3MS

'The woman went to open the door.' (A 18:2)

This can be taken as evidence, therefore, that the sequential narrative subjunctive had its origin in subordinate purpose clauses.

The subjunctive *qaṭəl* form in purpose clauses is neutral as to aspect and can be used in habitual contexts, e.g.

(68) C. Barwar

kut-béna	*béna*	*ˀáxni*	*y-ázəx*	***ˀaxlə́x***
every-time	time	we	HAB-go.IPFV.1PL	eat.SBJV.1PL

*kəs-xòni.*ˈ
with-my.brother

'From time to time we go to eat with my brother.'

This could explain the sporadic use of *qaṭəl* as a habitual sequential (see (58)).

According to (65) the narrative subjunctive, which developed from subordinate clauses, retained the temporal structure of result clauses, i.e.

Main clause	**Narrative sequential**
R_1,E	R_1—R_2,E

The 'main clause' in this model of its development would be a clause in the preceding discourse. As can be seen in the examples (56) and (57) the narrative subjunctive can be used in chains of clauses. This could be represented thus:

$R_1—R_2,E_2 + R_2—R_3,E_3 + R_3—R_4,E_4 + R_4—R_5,E_5$

Each subjunctive form would take as its anterior reference time the reference time of the previous verb.

Alternatively, it could be proposed that by a further development the anterior reference time in the structure R_1—R_2,E has become schematised to a cognitive topical reference point analogously to the analysis we have proposed for the development of the *bət-qaṭəl* and *qam-qaṭəl* forms, i.e. T(opic)—R,E. This, therefore, would not be a temporal point in the preceding discourse but rather a topical frame, which in narrative would be typically a spatio-temporal frame. The chain of narrative subjunctives would all cohere together in the same 'mental space' and be linked to this spatio-temporal frame. This is clear in (57), in which the chain of narrative subjunctives begins after the adverbial *ʾaṣərta* 'in the evening', which sets the spatio-temporal frame. The clauses would anaphorically resume this topical frame, thus:

$$T_1\text{—}R_1,E_1 + T_1\text{—}R_2,E_2 + T_1\text{—}R_3,E_3 + T_1\text{—}R_4,E_4 + T_1\text{—}R_5,E_5$$

It has been remarked that the progressive form is occasionally used in C. Barwar as a narrative form and that this is the normal narrative form in C. Urmi. It is relevant to note that the progressive form can also express purpose, similarly to a subjunctive clause, e.g.

(69) C. Barwar (Khan 2008, 732)

*ṣə̀lyɛ=le*ˈ	***mzabònə=l-le.***ˈ
go.down.PTCP=COP.3MS	sell.PROG=COP.3MS-3MS

'He went down to sell it.' (A22:2)

(70) C. Urmi (Khan 2016, vol. 2, 191)

bərrə̀xšə=lə	***máya***	*xá*	*dána*	*bàxta.*ˈ
go.PROG=COP.3MS	bring.PROG	one	unit	woman

'He goes to bring a woman.' (A 1:37)

This usage possibly originated in the use of the progressive in circumstantial constructions such as the following

(71) C. Barwar (Khan 2008, 727)

xzɛ́gən	*xònəx*ˈ	*ʾu-Mắmo*	*ṱ-íla*
see.IMP.FS	your.FS.brother	and-Mămo	REL-COP.3PL

tíwe	***mṭawóle***	*b-šətrənjàne.*ˈ
sit.PTCP.PL	play.PROG	at-chess

'See your brother and Mămo who are sitting playing chess.' (A26:64)

(72) C. Urmi (Khan 2016, vol. 2, 190)

ʾana	*ɟəddàlu*ˈ	*⁺házər*	*vid-è=vən,*ˈ
I	its.threads	ready	make.PTCP-3PL=COP.1MS

partúlə	*⁺ʾal-⁺ʾuydàlə.*ˈ
twist.PROG	on-each.other

'I have prepared its threads, twisting (them) together.' (A 3:74)

The sequential narrative use of the progressive may, therefore, have also developed through the pathway of a purpose clause.

5. Conclusions

In this paper I have discussed various verbal forms in NENA dialects that express dependency on the preceding discourse beyond the syntactic confines of a sentence. These include the *bət-qaṭəl(wa)* form, the *qam-qaṭəl* form and the narrative subjunctive form. These can be used to express continuity of the preceding discourse, which can be interpreted as temporal sequence or elaboration according to the context. The proposed historical development of the three verbal forms with these functions share several common features. In all cases the verbs originally expressed some kind of future or, to be more precise, an event time that was posterior to its reference time. From the perspective of this reference time they expressed contingent events that were modally dependent on a preceding eventuality.

Parallels to such discourse dependent verbal forms have been documented in a variety of other languages. Numerous languages of Africa have special verbal forms for the expression of continuity in discourse. These are used, for example, for the chaining of clauses in narratives and descriptions of habitual procedures.[16] This continuity may be temporal sequence or elaboration. Such forms are often identical to forms that express modal subordination in subordinate clauses and so have been referred to as narrative subjunctives (R. Carlson 1992; Seidel 2015, 180). In some African languages the consecutive forms can be used independently of preceding discourse as a future or modal form denoting an unrealised action (e.g. Seidel 2015, 186). Historical reconstructions of Oceanic languages have revealed connections between narrative continuity devices and future verbal forms (Lichtenberk 2014).

Within Semitic one can find some parallels to what has been described in this paper. Owens (2018) argues persuasively that the preverbal particle *b-* that is found in a variety of Arabic dialects originates in the deontic verb *baġa* 'to want' (cognate with Aramaic *baʿe*). What is of interest is that although it has retained its deontic or modal sense in some dialects of the Gulf, in some dialects it has developed into an indicative (e.g. Levant). The missing link, Owens claims, is its use in Nigerian Arabic to express what he calls 'propositional adjacency', which corresponds to what I have been calling here discourse dependency. The situation in the J. Dobe dialect, where the *bət-qaṭəl* form can be used as an indicative, would represent the same advanced stage of development as indicative *b-* in Levant Arabic.

The indicative preverbal particle *ka-* in Moroccan Arabic appears to have its origin in the modal use of the auxiliary verb *kān* in conditional clauses (Corriente 1977, 140–41; Stewart 1998, 111–12; Hanitsch 2019, 256–58). This also, therefore, may

16 Verbal forms of this type in numerous African languages are discussed in the papers of the volume edited by Payne and Shirtz (2015). See also Palmer (1986, 204–07), Longacre (1990) and Persohn (2017, §7.1).

have followed a similar pathway of development as Neo-Aramaic *bət-qaṭəl*.

Tsukanova (2008) has identified the use of dependent subjunctive forms containing the modal auxiliary *čān* in Gulf Arabic as a continuative form in narratives.

The Neo-Aramaic discourse dependent *bət-qaṭəl* and the narrative subjunctive exhibit close parallels also with continuative verbal forms in Biblical Hebrew.[17]

Finally, in addition to cross-linguistic typological parallels one should also take into account the factor of language contact. It is noteworthy, for example, that the NENA dialects that exhibit the *bət-qaṭəl* future forms are/were mainly in the region of Northern Kurdish (Kurmanji). The NENA dialects in the region of Central Kurdish (Sorani) do not generally exhibit a specific future marker. This distribution corresponds to the presence of a dedicated future verbal prefix in Northern Kurdish and the absence of such a prefix in Central Kurdish. What is of particular interest is that in Northern Kurdish verbs with the future particle are sometimes used as discourse dependency habitual forms just like the *bət-qaṭəl(wa)* form in Neo-Aramaic (Haig 2018, 292).

References

Bertinetto, Pier Marco, and Alessandro Lenci. 2012. 'Habituality, Pluractionality, and Imperfectivity'. In *The Oxford Handbook of Tense and Aspect*, edited by Robert I. Binnick, 852–80. Oxford: Oxford University Press.

Boneh, Nora, and Edit Doron. 2013. 'Hab and Gen in the Expression of Habituality'. In *Genericity*, edited by Alda Mari, Claire Beyssade, and Fabio Del Prete, 176–91. Oxford: Oxford University Press.

Bybee, Joan L. 2010. *Language Usage and Cognition*. Cambridge: Cambridge University Press.

———. 2015. *Language Change*. Cambridge: Cambridge University Press.

17 These parallels with the Biblical Hebrew verbal system are discussed in Khan (2021 to appear).

Carlson, Gregory. 2012. 'Habitual and Generic Aspect'. In *The Oxford Handbook of Tense and Aspect*, edited by Robert I. Binnick, 828–51. Oxford: Oxford University Press.

Carlson, Gregory N., and Beverly Spejewski. 1997. 'Generic Passages'. *Natural Language Semantics* 5: 101–65.

Carlson, Robert. 1992. 'Narrative, Subjunctive, and Finiteness'. *Journal of African Languages and Linguistics* 13: 59–85.

Coghill, Eleanor. 2016. *The Rise and Fall of Ergativity in Aramaic: Cycles of Alignment Change*. Oxford Studies in Diachronic and Historical Linguistics 21. Oxford: Oxford University Press.

Comrie, Bernard. 1985. *Tense*. Cambridge University Press.

Corriente, Federico. 1977. *A Grammatical Sketch of the Spanish Arabic Dialect Bundle*. Madrid: Instituto Hispano-Árabe De Cultura.

Dahl, Östen. 1985. *Tense and Aspect Systems*. Oxford-New York: Blackwell.

Dinsmore, John. 1982. 'The Semantic Nature of Reichenbach's Tense System'. *Glossa* 16: 216– 239.

———. 1991. *Partitioned Representations. A Study in Mental Representation, Language Understand and Linguistic Structure*. Dordrecht: Kluwer.

Ebert, Christian, Cornelia Ebert, and Stefan Hinterwimmer. 2014. 'A Unified Analysis of Conditionals as Topics'. *Linguistics and Philosophy* 37: 353–408.

Fassberg, Steven. 2015. 'The Origin of the Periphrastic Preterite Kəm/Qam-Qāṭəlle in North-Eastern Neo-Aramaic'. In *Neo-Aramaic and Its Linguistic Context*, edited by Geoffrey Khan and Lidia Napiorkowska, 172–86. Piscataway, NJ: Gorgias Press.

Fauconnier, Gilles. 1994. *Mental Spaces: Aspects of Meaning Construction in Natural Language*. Cambridge: Cambridge University Press.

Fillmore, Charles J., Paul Kay, and Mary C. O'Connor. 1988. 'Regularity and Idiomaticity in Grammatical Constructions'. *Language* 64: 501–38.

Fox, Samuel E. 2015. 'The History of the Future'. In *Neo-Aramaic in Its Linguistic Context*, edited by Geoffrey Khan and Lidia Napiorkowska, 162–71. Piscataway, NJ: Gorgias Press.

Goldberg, Adele E. 1995. *Constructions: A Construction Grammar Approach to Argument Structure*. Chicago: University of Chicago Press.

———. 2006. *Constructions at Work: The Nature of Generalization in Language.* Oxford: Oxford University Press.

Greenberg, Joseph. 1978. 'How Does a Language Acquire Gender Markers?' In *Universals of Human Language*, edited by Joseph Greenberg, 3:47–82. Stanford: Stanford University Press.

Haig, Geoffrey. 2018. 'The Iranian Languages of Northern Iraq'. In *The Languages and Linguistics of Western Asia: An Areal Perspective*, edited by Geoffrey Haig and Geoffrey Khan, 267–304. The World of Linguistics 6. Berlin: De Gruyter Mouton.

Haiman, John. 1978. 'Conditionals Are Topics'. *Language* 54: 564–89.

Hanitsch, Melanie. 2019. *Verbalmodifikatoren in den Arabischen Dialekten: Untersuchungen zur Evolution von Aspektsystemen.* Porta Linguarum Orientalium. Neue Serie 27. Wiesbaden: Harrassowitz.

Hatav, Galia. 2012. 'Bound Tenses'. In *The Oxford Handbook of Tense and Aspect*, edited by Robert I. Binnick, 611–37. Oxford: Oxford University Press.

Jacobs, Bart. 2011. 'Present and Historical Perspectives Onthe Catalan Go-Past'. *Zeitschrift für Katalanistik* 24: 227–25.

Johnson, Marion R. 1981. 'A Unified Temporal Theory of Tense and Aspect'. In *Syntax and Semantics, 14: Tense and Aspect*, edited by Philip J. Tedeschi and Annie Zaenen, 145–75. New York: Academic Press.

Khan, Geoffrey. 2002. *The Neo-Aramaic Dialect of Qaraqosh.* Studies in Semitic Languages and Linguistics 36. Boston, MA: Brill.

———. 2008. *The Neo-Aramaic Dialect of Barwar.* 3 vols. Leiden: Brill.

———. 2016. *The Neo-Aramaic Dialect of the Assyrian Christians of Urmi.* 4 vols. Studies in Semitic Languages and Linguistics 86. Leiden-Boston: Brill.

———. 2017. 'Ergativity in Neo-Aramaic'. In *Oxford Handbook of Ergativity*, edited by Jessica Coon, Diane Massam, and Lisa Travis, 873–99. Oxford: Oxford University Press.

———. 2021 (to appear). 'The Coding of Discourse Dependency in Biblical Hebrew Consecutive *Weqaṭal* and *Wayyiqṭol*'. In *New Perspectives in Biblical and Rabbinic Hebrew*, edited by Aaron D. Hornkohl and Geoffrey Khan. Cambridge Semitic Languages and Cultures. Cambridge: University of Cambridge & Open Book Publishers.

Langacker, Ronald. 1987. *Foundations of Cognitive Grammar: Theoretical Prerequisites*. Vol. 1. Stanford: Stanford University Press.

Lichtenberk, Frantisek. 2014. 'Sequentiality-Futurity Links'. *Oceanic Linguistics,* 53: 61–91.

Longacre, Robert E. 1990. *Storyline Concerns and Word Order Typology in East and West Africa*. Studies in African Linguistics Supplement 10. Los Angeles: University of California.

Mutzafi, Hezy. 2002. 'Barzani Jewish Neo-Aramaic and Its Dialects'. *Mediterranean Language Review* 14: 41–70.

Noorlander, Paul. 2017. 'The Proximative and Its Correlatives in North Eastern Neo-Aramaic'. In *Prospective and Proximative in Turkic, Iranian and Beyond,* edited by Agnes Korn and Irina Nevskaya, 188–210. Wiesbaden: Reichert Verlag.

———. 2018. 'Alignment in Eastern Neo-Aramaic Languages from a Typological Perspective'. Ph.D. Thesis, Leiden: University of Leiden.

Owens, Jonathan. 2018. 'Dialects (Speech Communities), the Apparent Past, and Grammaticalization: Towards an Understanding of the History of Arabic'. In *Arabic Historical Dialectology*, edited by Clive Holes, 206–56. Oxford Studies in Diachronic and Historical Linguistics 30. Oxford: Oxford University Press.

Palmer, Frank R. 1986. *Mood and Modality*. Cambridge: Cambridge University Press.

Payne, Doris L., and Shahar Shirtz, eds. 2015. *Beyond Aspect: The Expression of Discourse Functions in African Languages*. Typological Studies in Language 109. Amsterdam-Philadelphia: John Benjamins.

Pennacchietti, Fabrizio. 1994. 'Il Preterito Neoaramaico Con Pronome Oggetto'. *Zeitschrift der Deutschen Morgenländischen Gesellschaft* 144: 259–83.

———. 1997. 'On the Etymology of the Neo-Aramaic Particle Qam/Kim-'. *Massorot* 9–11: 475–82.

Persohn, Bastian. 2017. *The Verb in Nyakyusa: A Focus on Tense, Aspect and Modality*. Berlin: Language Science Press.

Reichenbach, Hans. 1947. *Elements of Symbolic Logic*. New York: Macmillan.

Rhétoré, P. Jacques. 1912. *Grammaire de la Langue Soureth ou Chaldéen Vulgaire*. Mossoul: Imprimerie des Peres Dominicains.

Roberts, Craige. 1987. 'Modal Subordination, Anaphora, and Distributivity'. Ph.D. Thesis, Amherst, N.Y: University of Massachusetts, Amherst.

———. 1989. 'Modal Subordination and Pronominal Anaphora in Discourse'. *Linguistics and Philosophy* 12: 683–721.

Schmidtke-Bode, Karsten. 2009. *A Typology of Purpose Clauses*. Amsterdam-Philadelphia: Benjamins.

Seidel, Frank. 2015. 'Rethinking Narrative Tenses Based on Data from Nalu (Atlantic) and Yeyi (Bantu)'. In *Beyond Aspect: The Expression of Discourse Functions in African Languages*, edited by Doris L. Payne and Shahar Shirtz, 177–217. Typological Studies in Language 109. Amsterdam-Philadelphia: John Benjamins.

Stewart, Devin J. 1998. 'Clitic Reduction in the Formation of Modal Prefixes in the Post-Classical Arabic Dialects and Classical Arabic Sa-/Sawfa'. *Arabica* 45: 104–28.

Tsukanova, Vera. 2008. 'Discourse Functions of the Verb in the Dialect of Sedentary Kuwaitis'. In *Between the Atlantic and Indian Oceans. Studies on Contemporary Arabic Dialects. Proceedings of the 7th AIDA Conference, Held in Vienna from 5–9 September 2006*, edited by Stephan Procházka and Veronika Ritt-Benmimoun, 447–55. Münster-Vienna: LIT-Verlag.

Verkuyl, Henk J. 2012. 'Compositionality'. In *The Oxford Handbook of Tense and Aspect*, edited by Robert I. Binnick, 563–85. Oxford: Oxford University Press.

CONDITIONAL PATTERNS IN THE JEWISH NEO-ARAMAIC DIALECT OF ZAKHO

Eran Cohen

A full picture of the conditional subsystem within a grammatical system is hard to come by and the issue is often given very limited space in grammatical descriptions. The case of the Christian dialect of Barwar (Khan 2008) is exceptional, since a relatively large chapter is devoted to conditional constructions (ibid., 1004–25). In this paper I intend to study conditionals in the Jewish dialect of Zakho (henceforth JZ) as well as discuss some general issues that come up during this investigation.

Although not always clearly stated, conditionals belong semantically to the domain of modality. This is sometimes overlooked because conditionals are traditionally classified, in grammatical descriptions, with other clause types such as different adverbial or subordinate clauses. This notwithstanding, they are a syntactic expression of modality, very similar semantically to other expressions which reflect different degrees of certainty, as the particle *perhaps*.

The objectives of this paper are: first, to explain the place of conditional constructions within epistemic modality; second, to provide a survey of conditional expressions in JZ; third, to discuss the relationships of the conditionals with other clause-types (concessive, temporal, relative); and fourth, to show the effect of the combination of conditional expressions and other epistemic expressions.

https://doi.org/10.11647/OBP.0209.05

1. Modality in General

Although linguistic modality has been defined with respect to several parameters (e.g., subjectivity, or 'speaker's attitude'). The following definition summarises the conclusion of a paper that attempts a definition of modality (Narrog 2005), viz. that only the parameter of factuality is actually useful in distinguishing between what is modal and what is not:

> Modality is a linguistic category referring to the factual status of a state of affairs. The expression of a state of affairs is modalized if it is marked for being undetermined with respect to its factual status, i.e. is neither positively nor negatively factual. (ibid., 184)

Modality is subdivided in different ways, but it is enough, in this framework, to keep the old division between deontic and epistemic modality.

1.1. Deontic Modality

Deontic modality is the type of modality covering will and obligation in non-factual utterances. The **imperative form** is *the* deontic expression par excellence. It always has this function, expressing different levels of the speaker's will.

1.2. Epistemic Modality

The definitions for epistemic modality are less complicated and seem to cover the domain quite well. Nuyts (2006, 6, emphasis mine), for example, offers the following definition:

> The core definition of this category is relatively noncontroversial: it concerns an indication of the estimation, typically, but not necessarily, by the speaker, of **the chances that the state of affairs expressed in the clause applies in the world**. In other words, **it expresses the degree of probability of the state of affairs.**

1.3. The Epistemic Scale

Ordinary conditionals are constructions that denote epistemic modality. As such, they reflect various points on the **epistemic scale**, representing different degrees of reality ascribed to the situation or event. As Akatsuka (1985, 636–37) points out:

> The two conceptual domains, realis and irrealis, do not stand in clear-cut opposition, but rather are on a continuum, in terms of the speaker's subjective evaluation of the ontological reality of a given situation. In conditionals, the S_1 of *if* S_1 can express the speaker's attitude at any point within the irrealis division of the scale. In short, this epistemic scale reflects the speaker's evaluation of S_1's realizability, ranging in value from zero (i.e. counterfactuals) to one (i.e. realis)

The definition is given higher resolution some twenty years later by Nuyts (2006,6):

> As in deontic modality, this dimension can be construed as a scale—from absolute certainty via probability to fairly neutral possibility that the state of affairs is real. Moreover, if one assumes that the category also involves polarity, the scale even continues further on to the negative side, via improbability of the state of affairs to absolute certainty that it is not real.

The dimension of polarity (as presented in Taylor 1996) includes anything on the scale between affirmative and negative, namely, it is very similar conceptually.

Conditional expressions are semantically analogous to epistemic particles such as *perhaps,* or similar epistemic expressions like 'he must be home now.' They are all found on that same scale, which stretches between real and unreal, or between affirmative and negative. Dancygier (1998, 72, 82) explains that *if* marks the protasis clause as **unassertable** and consequently the apodosis is **unassertable** as well, both may be regarded as assumptions.[1]

1 For a similar view, see Palmer (1986, 189): 'Conditional sentences are unlike all others in that both the subordinate clause (the protasis) and the main clause (the apodosis) are non-factual. Neither indicates that an

In other words, **neither the protasis nor the apodosis are a statement of fact**. This issue seems important given the generally held view that a conditional protasis is analogous to various adverbial clauses and, accordingly, the conditional apodosis is equivalent to the main clause in these adverbial clauses. Note, however, that, unlike the latter, the apodosis of ordinary conditionals cannot exist without its protasis, otherwise it would not be conditioned.

Illustration 1 of the modal paradigm shows where conditionals are located with regard to other expressions of modality:

Illustration 1: The modal paradigm (Cohen 2012a, 174)

1 indicative
2 epistemic
conditional (the entire scale) ordinary conditionals hypothetical conditionals counter-factual conditionals
judgements interrogative
3 deontic

The modality conveyed by ordinary conditionals is in fact one type of epistemic modality, and, therefore, fully comparable with other expressions of likelihood—*probably*, *perhaps*, *surely*, etc.

The scale relating to conditional structures, which also has to do with degrees of likelihood, is also represented in Illustration 2, where it is presented as a round scale in which both extremes

event has occurred (or is occurring or will occur); the sentence merely indicates the dependence of the truth of one proposition upon the truth of another.'

virtually meet. This is because an expression of unreal conditional is very close to a negative factual statement.

Illustration 2: The hypotheticality scale within conditionals (Cohen 2012a, 174)

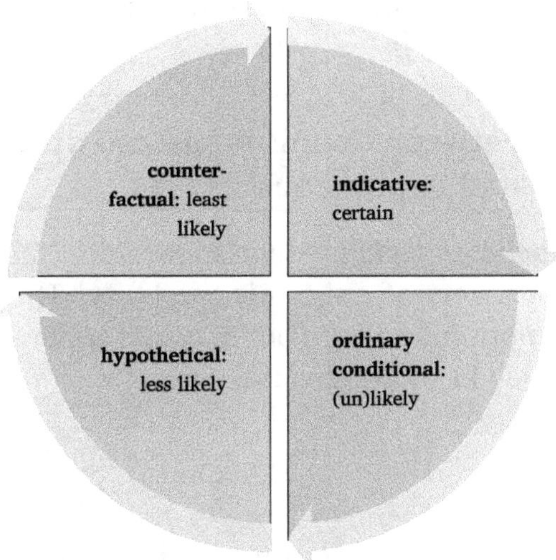

1.4. Technical Information

The following table serves as a legend for the different verbal forms in JZ:

Table 1: Legend for verbal forms

Simple verbal forms		+ Backshift	Function
šqəl-le	preterite 1 (trans. and intr.)	*šqəl-wa-le*	plupreterite
qam-šāqəl-le	preterite 2 (trans. only)	*qam-šāqəl-wa-le*	plupreterite
k-šāqəl	general present	*k-šāqəl-wa*	past imperfective
p-šāqəl	future	*p-šāqəl-wa*	counterfactual
šāqəl	subjunctive	*šāqəl-wa*	'past' subjunctive

The suffix *-wa* (glossed B) termed 'backshift' moves the predication back—mostly in time (when suffixed to present and past-denoting forms), but occasionally in modality, as happens with future-denoting forms and sometimes with subjunctive forms. The former denote counter-factuality, the latter has subtle functions and occasionally is an agreement to a past-denoting matrix verb.

1.5. Relation between Conditionals and other Epistemic Particles and Expressions

The particle *balki* ~ *balkin* ~ *balkət* meaning 'maybe/perhaps' is one of the carriers of epistemic modality. The link between a conditional notion and 'maybe' may not seem natural at first glance. Example (1) shows this link:

(1)

a.

baxta,	*hakan*	*hoyā-wa*	*smәxta,*
woman	if	SBJV.be.3FS-B	pregnant
g-oz-ī-wā-la	*tre',*		
PRS-do-3PL-B- DAT.3FS	two		
xa'	*ta=brōna*	*xa'*	*ta=brāta;*
one	to=boy	one	to=girl

b.

balkin	*hāwē-la*	*brōna*	*gәbe*
maybe	SBJV.be.3MS- 3FS	boy	need.3MS
hāwe	*ta=brōna*	*xa'.*	
SBJV.be.3MS	to=boy	one	

c.

hakan	*hāwē-la*	*brāta*	*xa'*	*ta=brāta*
if	SBJV.be.3MS-DAT.3FS	girl	one	to=girl

‘**If** a woman was pregnant, they used to make her two [chickens for the ritual of *kappara*], one for a boy, one for a girl.

If (lit. **perhaps)** she had a boy,**it was necessary** to have one for a boy.

If she had a girl, (then) one for a girl.’ (SAG 3.)2

The initial condition is generic or habitual (see §3). The specifications (whether it is a boy or a girl) are in privative relations and hence similar to a real condition. Note that whereas in the first specification *balkin* ‘maybe’ is used, in the second the particle used is *hakan* ‘if.’ The co-occurrence of conditional and *balki* is further discussed under §4.

2. A survey of Conditional Expressions in Jewish Zakho

2.1. Apodosis

Conditional structures are in general complex modal expressions, that is, **the likelihood of one state of affairs to take place is contingent upon the realisation chances of the other**. They are an expression of likelihood, a point on the epistemic scale and **this likelihood relates to the entire structure**. The semantic essence of an ordinary condition is illustrated in (2):

(2)	*xōr-i,*	*ʾāna*	*bə-msafr-ēna*	*əl=xa=bāžer,*
	friend-1S	NOM.1S	FUT-travel-1MS	to=INDEF=city
	ū=pāre	*dīd-i*	*šuttāwe*	*kəs-lox*
	CONN=money	POSS-1S	SBJV.be.3MS	with-2MS

ənkān	*dʾər-ri*	*bə-yāw-ə́t-tū-li…*		
if	return.PST-1S	FUT-give-2MS-3PL-DAT.1MS		
ū=ʾənkan	*la*	*dʾər-ri*	*pāre*	*šuttāwe*
CONN=if	NEG	return.PST-1S	money	SBJV.be.3PL
tā-lox				
to-2MS				

'My friend, I intend to travel to some city,

so let my money be with you.

If I return, you will give it (back) to me…

but if I do not return, let the money be for you.' (286)

There are two directive syntagms, i.e., two expressions of will in the example: 'let my money be with you' and 'let the money be for you.' However, it is easy to see that their semantic status is different. While the former is **merely an expression of the speaker's will**, the latter is more of **a permissive nature** and, in addition, it is **conditioned by external circumstances**. That is, it depends on whether the speaker returns or not.

2.2. Conditional Forms and Values

There are two types of conditional form: patterns with an introductory particle and paratactic patterns. It is important to state that they are only partially related and the paratactic pattern is probably not derived from the other type.

"Form' refers to what the pattern consists of, namely, if one starts with the pattern headed by an introductory particle, one needs to specify the introductory particle as well as the forms occurring in the protasis and in the apodosis.

Several **introductory particles** occur in free variation, all consisting of the core element *kan* (< Arab. *kān* 'he was'), often with some addition: *ənkan, hakan, (i)zakan, īskan,* without any apparent difference.

The forms commonly occurring in the protasis of ordinary conditionals are the subjunctive *šāqəl* and the preterite forms *šqəlle* and *qam-šāqəlle*. There are no temporal differences between the forms:

(3)	*ənkān*	***yāqer***	*xōla*	*yāʾ-ən*
	if	SBJV.be.heavy.3MS	rope	SBJV.know-1MS

	baxt-i	*ṣāx=ī-la...*
	wife-1S	alive=COP-3FS

	ū=ʾənkan	***la***	***yqər-re***	*xola*
	CONN=if	NEG	be.heavy.PST-3MS	rope

	x̱ō	*yāʾ-ən*	***ʾənnu***	*mət-la*
	then	SBJV.know-1MS	COMP	die.PST-3FS

‘If the rope **grows heavy**, then I will know my wife is alive...

But if the rope **does not grow heavy**, then I will know that she died.’ (26)

This is the essential profile of *kan* protases. The important point is that the forms *šqəlle* and *qam-šāqəlle*, although referring to the past in other constructions, do not do so here. In fact, they do not point at any time in particular, because temporal opposition does not exist in the protasis. The majority of conditional cases are predictive and consequently refer to the future (see (2)).

The conditional expression may occur in a subordinate environment, namely, the protasis may be associated with a subordinate apodosis (e.g. (11)).

The relationship of conditional clauses to modality is apparent from several angles. One of these is the relationship obtaining between a full protasis and a minimal or elliptic negative protasis following a directive or other expressions of obligation such as:

(4)

hakān	***lá***	*hōya*	*⁺ḥāzər*	*b-ās-ət*
if	NEG	SBJV.be.3FS	ready	FUT-come-2MS

əḷ=qəṭḷa
to=death

'**If it is not ready**, you will be killed.' (730–31)

(5)

ū=g-əbe	*hōya*	*mulḥam-ta*	*ū= ⁺ḥāzər*
CONN=PRS-need.3MS	SBJV.be.3FS	soldered-FS	CONN=ready

hakān	***lā,***	*b-ās-ən*	***l=qəṭḷa***
if	NEG	FUT-come-1MS	to=death

'and it (=the king's ring) must be soldered and ready. **If not**, I will be killed.' (729)

The lexical content of the protasis could either be expressed explicitly inside it (example[4], 'if it is not ready…') or, alternatively, be expressed outside it, as a command or obligation followed by an 'empty' protasis containing merely an indication of the possibility that something may not happen (example [5], the 'if not' strategy).

Present forms are rare in the protasis and refer to a persistent state of affairs. The apodosis is basically made up of either future *pšāqəl* or subjunctive *(šud) šāqəl* ~ imperative *šqōl*. That is, the normal opposition between the forms is **modal**, rather than aspectual or temporal. Rare present-like forms occur here with the present copula (e.g. *īle* 'He is'), the predicative possessor (e.g. *ətle* 'He has') and the non-verbal expression of ability (*ībe* 'He is able').

2.3. Conditional Types

The predominant conditional type is the **ordinary condition**, which answers to the definition given above in §2.1.

Another type is the **speech-act conditional**, where the apodosis is not conditioned, but rather reflects a fact:

(6)

yā	*brōn-i*	*kan*	*g-əb-ət*	*qaṭl-ət-ti*	*čū=sēpa*
VOC	son-1S	if	PRS-wish-2MS	SBJV.kill-2MS-1S	no=sword

*láq-qāṭe*ʾ	*qzāl-i*	*ġēr*	*sēpa*	*dīd-i*
NEG.NPST-cut.3MS	neck-1S	except	sword	POSS-1S

d=məlʾḗl	*mənn-i*
NMLS=above	from-1S

'O my son, if you want to kill me, (you should know that) no sword will cut my neck except my sword which (is) above me.' (417)

The factual apodosis substantially weakens the modality of these examples. The protasis merely serves as the background or explanation of the utterance in the apodosis. In example (6) it is an unconditioned fact that the sword of the giant woman (who is the speaker) is the only sword that would kill her. The protasis merely specifies in what circumstances it is important.

A **concessive conditional** is yet another type where the apodosis is factual:

(7)

kan	***zamr-ət***	***hīl***	***mʾāb-ət***
if	SBJV.sing-2MS	till	SBJV.die-2MS

lag-napq-ən	*xá-gar*	*xet*	*mən*	*dūk-i*
NEG.NPST-exit-1MS	one-time	another	from	place-1S

'(Even) if you sing until you die, I will not come out of my place once more.' 457

The snake (who is the source of the utterance) is more or less making a vow not to move from his place for the man's sake. This vow is unconditioned, not being contingent upon the protasis. Despite this difference, concessive conditionals still share a pattern with ordinary conditionals, as is shown below, §2.4.

In **inferential conditionals**, the protasis is the premise from which the conclusion in the apodosis is drawn, as illustrated in example . The particle *xō~xū* is used here to signal this inferential relationship.

2.4. Paratactic Conditional or Concessive Conditional Pattern

This pattern is a sequence whose basic functional value is **conditional** or **concessive conditional** (see Cohen 2007). Unlike the protasis with *kan*, this type of protasis only occurs with the subjunctive form *šāqəl:*[2]

(8) *āna* ***lá=mēs-ət-ti*** *xā=sūse,*

NOM.1S NEG=SBJV.bring-2MS-DAT.1S INDEF-horse

lák-ēs-ən *bəd=ʾaql-i*

NEG.NPST-come-1MS by=foot-1S

2 The subjunctive form in the first part occasionaly denotes temporality. For instance:

āwa ***ṭāweʾ*** *b-ẓabḥ-an-ne*

NOM.3MS SBJV.fall.asleep-3MS FUT-slaughter-1FS-3MS

'(when) he falls asleep, I shall slaughter him' (MA 12.2)

'As for me, **should you not bring me a horse**, I will not go by foot.' (218)

(9)

b-ya-n-nox[3]	*qōl*	*ṭlahá*	*yōme.*	***hama***
FUT-give-1S-DAT.2MS	condition	three	days	PTCL

la = šār-ə́tū-la	*ʾē = sāfīna*	*mən = go = palgū́s*
NEG = SBJV.release-2PL-3FS	DEF = boat	from = in = mid

baḥḥar,	*ʾāna*	***b-dār-ən***	*sēpa*	*go = huzāye.*
sea	NOM.1S	FUT-put-1MS	sword	in = Jews

'I give you a respite of three days. **Should you not free this ship from mid-sea**, I will put the Jews to the sword.' (MA 15.5–6)

These examples are representative of the construction in question in form and in content. Example (8)–(9) contain a subjunctive form that cannot be interpreted as a negative imperative (which is a common function of the 2nd person subjunctive). The only way it could be interpreted is as a conditional protasis 'should you not....' The negative form *lak-šāqəl* in the apodosis is the negative of both the forms *k-šāqəl* and *p-šāqəl* (and is thus glossed NEG.NPST).

The relationship with the pattern marked by *kan* is exemplified in the following pair of examples. The character is asked by strangers whether he is a believer or a heretic:

(10)

ʾamr-ən-nu	*kāfər*
SBJV.say-1MS-DAT.3PL	infidel

3 The full form is *b-yāw-ən-nox*.

ṣad-li *ʾāni* *amin* *hāwe* *ū=b-qaṭl-ī-li*

fear-1S NOM.3PL believer SBJV.be.3PL CONN=FUT-kill-3PL-1S

'**Should I tell them** 'infidel',

I fear they may be believers and **will kill me.**' 381

(11) *kan* *ʾamr-ən-nu* *ʾamin*

if SBJV.say-1MS-DAT.3PL infidel

ṣad-li *hāwe* *ʾāni* *kāfer* *wu=ham*

fear-1S SBJV.be.3PL NOM.3PL infidel CONN=also

b-qaṭl-ī-li

FUT-kill-3PL-1S

'**If I tell them** 'believer',

I fear they may be infidels and **will** also **kill me.**'381–82

Recall that the protasis with *kan* may consist of a preterite form as well, while in the paratactic pattern only the subjunctive form *šāqəl* is attested. Examples (10) and (11), however, have the same value here. Note that the conditional state of affairs in both examples is a expressed by a complement clause of *ṣadli* 'I am afraid.'

Whereas the pattern with *kan* is essentially conditional, the paratactic pattern may be either conditional or concessive-conditional (table 2). The two values are differentiated based upon a particle, which occasionally precedes them: *hama*. The particle *hama* is otherwise a focus particle meaning 'just.' Here it has an entirely different function—it identifies the pattern *#šāqəl—p-šāqəl#* as conditional, that is, when *hama* precedes the pattern (i.e., *#hama šāqəl—p-šāqəl*), it marks it as a conditional.

On the other hand, when the particle šud precedes *šāqəl*, the pattern is positively identified as a concessive conditional.

(Otherwise šud identifies the subjunctive form as syntactically independent.) The details of the pattern of the paratactic conditional are as follows:

Table 2: Conditional Patterns

Conditional		**Protasis**	**Apodosis**
paratactic	*(hama)*	± subjunctive: *šāqəl*	± future: (*p-šāqəl*~*lak-šāqəl*)
			± subjunctive: *šāqəl*
conditional particle	*kan*	± subjunctive: *šāqəl*	± future: (*p-šāqəl*~*lak-šāqəl*)
		± preterite: *qam-šāqəl-le, šqəlle*	± subjunctive: *šāqəl*; present: *k-šāqəl*

Note that the order protasis—apodosis is strictly kept with the paratactic pattern but not with the construction with the conditional particle. Another point is that in view of the obvious differences between both patterns, the paratactic pattern does not seem to have been derived from the pattern with an explicit conditional marker.

2.5. Counter-factual Conditional Patterns

Counter-factual expressions are located at the far end of the modal scale, very close in fact to the point of negative factuality (see Illustration 2). They cover events (or states) that did (or will) not happen, but which are still not reported as factual but rather through some modal filter:

(12)	*bale*	***kan***	***yāʾ-ən-wa***	*ʾāhat*	*g-əb-at-ti*
	but	if	SBJV.know-1MS-B	NOM.2FS	PRS-want-2FS-1S

	lák-ēs-ən-wa	*gō=bēs-ax*	*d=maxṭ-ən*
	NEG.NPST-come-1MS-B	in=house-2FS	CONJ=CAUS.sin-1MS

gyān-i
REFL-1S

'but **if I had known** (that) you wanted me,

I would not have come into your house, to lead myself to sin.' (783)

A virtually similar clause is 'I didn't know and therefore I came.' This latter clause is, however, factual and does not impart the regrets and wishes of the speaker implied in the counterfactual expression in example (12). The opposite order, apodosis—protasis, is also attested:

(13) *mani* *k-īʾe* *mā́* ***sē-la*** *l=ʾurx-ət*
who PRS-know.3MS what come.PST-3FS to=way-CST

dáw=jwanqa *dīd-i* *ū=mā* ***b-asyā-wa***
DEF=youngster POSS-1S CONN=what FUT-come.3FS-B

b=rēš-i ***kan*** ***lá-hōy-an-wa*** ***tfəq-ta***
in=head-1S if NEG-SBJV.be-1FS-B meet.PTCP-FS

bəd=danya=ṭḷāha
in=DEM=three

'Who knows what happened to that youth of mine and what **would have happened** to me **if I had not met** these three.' (870)

In (13) two apodoses are conjoined in a complement clause of not-knowing (which is often very similar to the expression of an indirect question). One is factual ('what happened') and the other is a counterfactual conditional ('what would have happened if...'). The latter conveys an alternative universe.

The pattern of the counterfactual conditional, which is common in NENA, is presented in Table 3:

Table 3: Counterfactual Conditional Pattern

	Protasis	Apodosis
kan	±*šāqəl-wa*	±*p-šāqəl-wa*~*lak-šāqəl-wa*
	(backshifted subjunctive)	(backshifted future)

The form *p-šāqəl-wa* is used in general to express counterfactuality, also outside the domain of conditionals—for instance, in circumstantial expressions (see Cohen 2015, 269–70).

Unlike ordinary condition, the protasis of counterfactual conditionals may interchange with a simpler expression:

(14)	*āna*	*lák-iʾē-n*	*ʾēkắ=la*	*gēhənnām.*
	NOM.1S	NEG.NPST- know-1MS	where=COP.3FS	hell
	<u>*laxwa*</u>	***b-āz-ən-wa***	*ʾap-āna*	
	otherwise	FUT-go-1MS-B	FOC-NOM.1S	
	mēs-ə́n-wā-li	*mən=tāma*	*pāre*	
	SBJV.bring-1MS-B-DAT.1S	from=there	money	

'I do not know where hell is. <u>Otherwise</u> I too **would have gone** there to bring money.' (529)

(15)	<u>*p=qətl-i*</u>	***lág-b-ə́n-wa***	*bary-ā-wa*
	in=death-1S	NEG.NPST-wish-1MS-B	SBJV.happen-3FS-B

mā́-d *brē-la*

what-CST happen.PST-3FS

'(even in exchange) for my death, **I would not have wanted** what happened to happen.' (903)

Such 'adverbial' substitutes (underlined) are hinted at by the form of the apodosis. The form *p-šāqəl-wa* is a rare form outside the counterfactual apodosis. JZ has the following paradigm for the counterfactual protasis:

Table 4: The Counterfactual Protasis Paradigm

Protasis	Gloss	Apodosis
kan šāqəl-wa	'if he had taken'	*p-šāqəl-wa* 'he would have taken'
laxwa	'otherwise'	
pqəṭli	'(even) for my death'	

The ultimate significance of this interchangeability is that, unlike the protasis of the ordinary conditional, deemed as sui generis, the counterfactual protasis is comparable with smaller entities (as are, for instance, many subordinate clauses).

More common is the **asyndetic counterfactual** conditional pattern:

(16) *yā* *ʾīlāha,* *šxēra uxudēra* *ū=ʾṓha =nāša*

VOC God by god's benevolence CONN=DEF=man

fāhəm-wa *šaqəl-wa* *xá=ṭarpa…*

SBJV.understand.3MS-B SBJV.take.3MS-B INDEF=leaf

*ū=**māwə́š-wā-le*** *ū=xarāye* ***dāyə́q-wā-le…***

CONN=SBJV.dry.3MS-B-3MS CONN=then SBJV.ground.3MS-B-3MS

ū = ***bāzə́r-wā-le***	*ʾəl* = *axon-e*
CONN = SBJV.sprinkle.3MS-B-3MS	to = brother-3MS

u = *ʾaxōn-e*	***bə-qāyəm-wa***
CONN = brother-3MS	FUT-stand.up.3MS-B

'Oh God, by God's benevolence, **had** this man **understood**, **taken** a leaf ... and **dried** it, and then **ground** it... and **sprinkled** it over his brother, his brother **would have stood up**.' (278–79)

The expression *šxēra uxudēra* does not seem to be part of the construction. Note that it is actually connected by *ū* to the conditional pattern. The pattern in this case consists of five clauses in the protasis and one in the apodosis.

3. Relationships of the Conditionals with other Clause-Types

In §2.3 above, several types of conditionals were explained and exemplified. In certain cases one finds a structure similar to a conditional pattern, but the function is different. For instance, conditional-like dependencies sometimes occur within a descriptive narrative passage:

(17)	*baxta,*	***hakan***	***hoyā-wa***	*sməxta,*
	woman	if	SBJV.be.3FS-B	pregnant

g-oz-ī-wā-la	*tre*ʾ,
PRS-do-3PL-B-DAT.3FS	two

'**If a woman was** pregnant, **they used to make her** two [chickens for the ritual of *kappara*].'SAG 3.2

Example (17) is a conditional-like structure. It is, however, different. It is clear that the structure shows neither modality, nor counterfactuality, but only an **interdependency** between two states of affairs, which are in fact two factual, regularly recurring states or events. What makes this clear is the form *kšāqəlwa* in the apodosis (whereas in the standard counterfactual conditional pattern one would expect a *šāqəlwa—pšāqəlwa* sequence, as in Table 5, with the backshifted future**).**

The next example is similar; although it does have the right apodosis form (*pšāqəlwa*), the so called protasis is introduced by *dammət* 'when':

(18) *...ū=dammət sanq-ī-wa l=xá-məndi*
CONN=when SBJV.need-3PL-B to=some-thing

b-āz-ī-wa *xakma mənn-u l=xá=gundəke*
FUT-go.3PL-B some of-3PL to=INDEF=village

*u=m-**mēsē-wa*** *mā-d d-ī-lu lāzəm*
CONN=FUT-bring.3PL-B what-CST ATTR-COP-3PL[4] need.3MS

.'..and whenever they would need something, some of them **would go** to a village and **bring** whatever was needed.' (947)

Note that conditionals are not typical of narrative. They are common in dialogue, and possibly also in narratorial comments,

4 The form *dīlu* 'they are' (as well as any other copulas which are prefixed by *d-*, i.e., *dīwın* vs. *wın* 'I am') are copula forms that occur after any element in the construct state (glossed CST). It is for this reason that they are referred to as attributes (which is the basic function of the second part of a genitive construction) and are glossed accordingly (ATTR). See Cohen (2010, 90–93) and (2012b, 119–21).

but not in the stream of events. Another similar example is worth considering:

(19) *ṓha=šēx ... k-ī'ē-wa bəd=ṣurr-ət nāše.*
DEM=sheikh PRS-know.3MS-B IN=secret-CST people

xa hāwē-wa náṣax, k-ī'ē-wa
INDEF.PRON SBJV.be.3MS-B sick PRS-know.3MS-B

ənkan māyes u='ənkan bə-ṭāreṣ
whether SBJV.die.3MS CONN=whether FUT-recover.3MS

ū=xa=baxta dīd hōyāwa sməxta
CONN=INDEF=woman REL SBJV.be.3FS-B pregnant

k-ī'ē-wa 'ənkan brōna=le u='ənkan
PRS-know.3MS-B whether boy=COP.3MS CONN=whether

brāta=la.
girl=COP.3FS

This sheikh ..., he used to know the secrets of people. Someone (who) was sick, he would know whether he would die or recover. And a woman who was pregnant, he would know whether it is a boy or a girl.' (226–27)

All three examples (17)-(19) refer to generic a state of affairs. Note that in these cases conditional, temporal and relative clauses converge and are almost interchangeable in this context.

Table 5: The Structure of Narrative Conditionals

Example	Protasis		Apodosis	Formal type	Type
(12), (13)	*(ha)kan*	*šāqəlwa*	*pšāqəlwa*	conditional	counterfactual conditional patterns
(16)	*šāqəlwa*		*pšāqəlwa*		
	hakan	*šāqəlwa*	*kšāqəlwa*	conditional	generic
	dammət	*šāqəlwa*	*pšāqəlwa*	temporal	
	(dīd)	*šāqəlwa*	*kšāqəlwa*	relative	

Where conditional, temporal and relative forms functionally converge, the result is a **non-modal, generic dependency**. This genericity goes hand in hand with character description—not an individual occurrence, but rather a permanent feature, as in example (19), describing the sheikh.

4. The Combination of Conditional Expressions and Epistemic Expressions

Lastly, in the following example two similar expressions of possibility—conditional and the expression of epistemic possibility—co-occur:

(19) *⁺mōrəm-le ʾṓ=⁺pālavan ū=məttū-le*

lift.PST-3MS DEF=athlete CONN=put.PST-3MS

xa=rašōma əl=dṓ=jwanqa čukun xzē-le

INDEF=blow on=DEF=youngster since see.PST-3MS

d=lēba čū=fayda ***kan*** *ʾāwa*

COMP=NEG.EXIST no=use if NOM.3MS

lá-mamreʾ-le	***balki***	*ʾō=xət*	*qāṭəl-le*
NEG-SBJV.hurt.3MS-3MS	maybe	DEF=other	SBJV.kill.3MS-3MS

'The athlete lifted (his hand) and delivered a blow on the youngster because he saw that it was no use: **If** he does not hurt him, **perhaps** the other one may kill him.' (768)

The explanation for this is that these expressions do not have the same function. The particle *balki* has its own function in the example. The conditional particle possibly signals two things: first, that both events or states of affairs are merely possible; and second, the relationship between them:

> The only assertion that is made in a conditional construction is **about the relation between the protasis and the apodosis** (Dancygier 1998, 72, emphasis mine)

This assertion is best felt when its existence is shaken by a modal particle which has the entire construction in its scope or by a question. The modal particle in our case refers specifically **to the relation between the protasis and the apodosis**, namely, it shakes the dependency between the protasis and the apodosis, expressing doubt about this relationship.

5. Conclusions

This paper provides a description, classification and discussion of the various conditional phenomena in the Jewish Neo-Aramaic dialect of Zakho.

1. The different conditional types are explained and exemplified:
    - Ordinary conditionals, which denote different degrees of epistemic modality (these constitute the bulk of the examples);

- Inferential conditionals, where the conclusion in the apodosis is drawn from the premise expressed in the protasis. The inferential relationship is marked by the particle *xō~xū*.
- Speech-act conditionals, which rather than expressions of modality, are in fact a structure where the protasis serves as the background for the utterance in the (non-conditioned) apodosis.
- Concessive-conditionals ('even if…'), where the protasis expresses epistemic modality, but the apodosis, on the other hand, is not conditioned.

2. Two patterns expressing ordinary conditionals are presented; one with a conditional particle at the head of the protasis, and another where no conditional particle is involved (which we termed paratactic) are presented. Each pattern is formulated based on the forms which appear in the protasis and the apodosis. They are different in their semantic scope—the paratactic pattern can express either a conditional or a concessive conditional.
3. Counterfactual conditional patterns are similarly characterised. In addition, a special trait of this conditional type is discussed, namely the fact that a couple of expressions can take the place of the counterfactual protasis without changing the function of the entire pattern.
4. A special function of similar constructions termed 'narrative conditionals' is examined and compared with counterfactuals. Their function is explained vis-à-vis other clause types. It is concluded that they are generic expressions.
5. Finally, the co-occurrence of ordinary conditionals, which express epistemic modality, with seemingly synonymous epistemic particles (e.g., 'perhaps') is analysed and the different functions of each are distinguished functionally.

References

Akatsuka, Noriko. 1985. 'Conditionals and the Epistemic Scale'. *Language* 61: 625–39.

Cohen, Eran. 2007. 'Zakho Neo-Aramaic and Old Babylonian Akkadian: The (Concessive-)Conditional Pattern'. In *Studies in Semitic and General Linguistics in Honor of Gideon Goldenberg*, edited by Tali Bar and Eran Cohen, 159–77. Alter Orient und Altes Testament 334. Münster: Ugarit.

———. 2010. 'Marking Nucleus and Attribute in North-Eastern Neo-Aramaic'. In *Proceeding of the VIII Afro-Asiatic Congress* (September 2008, Naples), *Studi Maghrebini* (Nuova Serie), VI: 79–94.

———. 2012a. *Conditional Structures in Mesopotamian Old Babylonian*. Languages of the Ancient Near East 4. Winona Lake: Eisenbrauns.

———. 2012b. *The Syntax of Neo-Aramaic: The Jewish Dialect of Zakho*. Gorgias Neo-Aramaic Studies 13. Piscataway: Gorgias.

———. 2015. 'Circumstantial Clause Combining in the Jewish Neo-Aramaic Dialect of Zakho'. In *Clause Combining in Semitic: The Circumstantial Clause and Beyond*, edited by Bo Isaksson and Maria Persson, 271–93. Abhandlungen für die Kunde des Morgenlandes. Harrassowitz: Wiesbaden.

Dancygier, Barbara. 1998. *Conditionals and Prediction*. Cambridge: Cambridge University Press.

Khan, Geoffrey. 2008. *The Neo-Aramaic Dialect of Barwar*. Handbook of Oriental Studies I-96. Leiden: Brill.

Narrog, Heiko. 2005. 'On Defining Modality Again.' *Language Sciences* 27 (2): 165–92.

Nuyts, Jan. 2006. 'Modality: Overview and Linguistic Issues'. In *The Expression of Modality*, edited by William Frawley, 1–26. Berlin: Walter de Gruyter.

Palmer, Frank. 1986. *Mood and Modality*. Cambridge: Cambridge University Press.

Taylor, John. 1997. 'Conditionals and Polarity'. In *On Conditionals Again*, edited by Angeliki Athanasiadou and René Dirven, 289–306. Amsterdam: Benjamins.

Corpus

[bare numbers] = Polotsky, Hans J. 1944–1947. Unpublished Zakho Texts. Jerusalem.

MA= Meehan, Charles and Jaqueline Alon. 1979. 'The Boy Whose Tunic Stuck to Him: A Folktale in the Jewish Neo-Aramaic Dialect of Zakho (Iraqi Kurdistan)'. *Israel Oriental Studies* 9: 174–203.

SAG= Sabar, Yona. 2007. 'Agonies of Childbearing and Child Rearing in Iraqi Kurdistan: A Narrative in Jewish Neo-Aramaic and its English Translation'. In *Studies in Semitic and General Linguistics in Honor of Gideon Goldenberg*, edited by Tali Bar and Eran Cohen, 107–45. Alter Orient und Altes Testament 334. Münster: Ugarit.

LANGUAGE CONTACT AND ṬUROYO: THE CASE OF THE CIRCUMSTANTIAL CLAUSE

Michael Waltisberg

Introduction

When one studies language contact, especially between closely related languages such as Aramaic and Arabic, grammatical replication, as opposed to, for instance, phonological borrowing, remains problematic.[1] The term 'grammatical replication' describes constructions that are reproduced by linguistic means in the borrowing language. Mithun (2012, 15) correctly states:

> Speakers replicate categories and patterns with native material. Without the substance, the process can be difficult to detect.

A case in point, which clearly illustrates this problem, is the circumstantial clause in Ṭuroyo. As I argued in an article published a few years ago, this can be ascribed to Arabic interference (Waltisberg 2013).[2] This conclusion was not necessarily premature or rash, but I did not discuss the whole spectrum of the problem and all the relevant data. The current article resumes the earlier discussion and summarises the relevant linguistic facts, arriving at a slightly different conclusion.

1 For introductory literature see, for example, Weinreich (1953); Hickey (2010); Epps et al. (2013).

2 Kurdish seems to be irrelevant to the argument (see Bedir Khan and Lescot 1986 and Chyet 1995).

 https://doi.org/10.11647/OBP.0209.06

1. Ṭuroyo

The circumstantial clause in Ṭuroyo (see Waltisberg 2016, 316ff.) is either asyndetic, i.e. without a conjunction, or syndetic, i.e. with the conjunction *w-* 'and'. It may occur before or after the matrix clause. It usually indicates concomitant states and actions or refers to the narrative background. There is no discernible distinction between the two syntactic options, as the following examples show.

A preposed asyndetic circumstantial clause:[3]

(1)

ăḥna	***naʿime,***	*koṯe*	*l-bol-i,*
we	children	it.is.coming	to-mind-my

b-i-qriṯo	*ĭzzawăyna*	*qŭṭliwăyna*	*ăd-debure*
in-the-village	we.used.to.go	we.used.to.kill	the-wasps

'**When we were children**, it occurs to me, we used to go and kill the wasps in the village.' (R2 456.1)

Here the circumstantial clause is formed with the pronoun *ăḥna* 'we' and the noun *naʿime* 'little ones, children'. There is no copular element.

A circumstantial clause may also occur within matrix clauses:

(2)

mĭḷḷa …	*gdoṯe*	*zlam,*	***hăt***	***damixo,***
she.said	he.will.come	man	you	sleeping

gqoṭĭʿ	*qărʿ-ŭx*
he.will.cut.off	head-your

3 The transcription of Ṭuroyo used in this paper follows Jastrow (1997) and consistently indicates lax vowels (mostly in closed syllables) with a breve diacritic.

'She said: a man will come, (and) **while you are asleep**, he will cut your head off.' (R3 354.47)

Morphosyntactically, syndetic circumstantial clauses are almost identical. They simply introduce the clause with the conjunction *w-*:

(3) *măṣrĭn-ne* ***w-ʿăyn-i*** ***măṣre*** *măwfăqqă-lli*
they.shackle-them and-eyes-my bound they.led.out-me

m-u-băyt-awo
from-the-house-that

'They shackled (my hands). **With my eyes covered**, they led me out of that house.' (Talay 2004, 76.127)

The next example has the same semantics as (2) above, but is joined to what precedes syndetically:

(4) *w-kfĭxle* *b-feme* *d-Kăyalo*
and-he.poured.it in-mouth of-Kăyalo

w-hiye ***damixo***
and-he sleeping

'and he poured (the grease) into Kăyalo's mouth, **while he was asleep.**' (R2 574.153)

All the examples cited so far have a non-verbal predicate. It is not entirely certain whether circumstantial clauses with a verbal predicate exist, as such constructions largely overlap with coordinated clauses. Some examples, however, may be interpreted as a circumstantial clause. The present tense form *koroqĭḏ* 'he dances' in example (5) below serves as the predicate of the circumstantial clause:

(5)	*disane*	*bdele*	*moḥe*	*ʿal*	*i-ʿărban-ayo*
	again	he.began	he.beats	upon	the-timbrel-that

	diḏe	***w-u-măymun***	***koroqĭḏ***
	of.his	and-the-monkey	he.is.dancing

'He began to beat his timbrel again, **while the monkey was dancing.**' (Jastrow 1968, 46.54)

The following syntactic features of the circumstantial clause in Ṭuroyo emerge from these examples:

(6) Features of the circumstantial clause:

a. It is syndetic or asyndetic (with or without the conjunction *w-* 'and').

b. A subject pronoun (or noun) stands at the head of the clause and the predicate immediately follows.

c. There is no copula, but examples with verbal predicates (in the present tense) possibly occur.

We may thus come to the preliminary conclusion that the circumstantial clause in Ṭuroyo is a perfect replica of the Arabic circumstantial clause (cf., for example, Reckendorf 1921, 447ff.; Brustad 2000, 339ff.; Procházka 2002, 159).

Despite the morphosyntactic and semantic similarities, however, there are some problems with this conclusion:

(7) Arguments against Arabic interference:

a. Some dialects of Anatolian Arabic use a copula in non-verbal clauses, even in circumstantial clauses.

b. In older Aramaic, especially in Syriac, circumstantial clauses also occur with the conjunction *w-* 'and'; this is, however, rare, as they mostly involve the conjunction *kaḏ* (Nöldeke 1898, 261 = 1904, 272).

c. In Barwar Neo-Aramaic, there are similar clauses which, according to Khan (2008, 22, 849ff.), cannot be assigned to Arabic interference.

Anatolian Arabic

The situation in Anatolian Arabic is significant. The copula of the third person singular masculine and feminine has the following paradigm in the dialect of Hasköy (Kurdish Dêrxas, Muş province, eastern Turkey):

(8) *ism-i* *Mḥamma-**wa***
name-my Mḥamma-it.is

'My name **is** Mḥamma.' (Talay 2001, 77ff.)

(9) *Aḷmānya* *bōš* *kwīse* *mī-**ya***
Germany very good not-it.is

'Germany **is** not that good.' (ib.)

A copula may also be used in circumstantial clauses, for example in the Mḥallami dialect of Kinderib (Mardin province, south-eastern Turkey), as shown in the two following examples, which contain the 3fs (-*ye*) and the 3ms (-*we*) copulas respectively:

(10)

ṭalaʿu	*dáwrəya*	***w-əd-dənye***	***b-əl-layl-ye***
they.went.out	patrol	and-the-world	in-the-night-it.is

'**During the night**, they went out on patrol.' (Jastrow 2003, 458.3)

(11)

hal-səwwēqīn …	***w-hūwe***	***qāyəm-we***	*baqa*
the-ploughmen	and-he	standing-he.is	INCHOATIVE

yətfarrağūn

they.look.on

'The ploughmen began to look on, **while he was standing** (there).' (Jastrow 2003, 462.31)

If the variety of vernacular Arabic that is the contact language of Ṭuroyo uses a copula, even in circumstantial clauses, the borrowing of this construction from Arabic into Ṭuroyo would be less likely. This is because Ṭuroyo, as we have seen, never uses a copula in non-verbal circumstantial clauses.

There are, however, also circumstantial clauses without the copula in Kinderib, as the following asyndetic example shows:

(12)

yḥəṭṭū-hu	*ṛāṣ-u*	*fə*	*l-ġarb*	*w-sāqāt-u*
they.put-it	head-his	in	the-west	and-feet-his

lə	*ṣawb*	*əš-šarq*	***hūwe***	***ʿa***	***n-naʿš***
to	direction.of	the-east	he	on	the-bier

'They put the head (of the body) to the West, and his feet in the direction of the East, **while he was lying on the bier.**' (Jastrow 2003, 108.40)

There are further instances of circumstantial clauses without copulas in the Mḥallami dialect, such as the following example from Sasse (1971):

(13) *l-yăwm* *tətroḥin* *trăyr* *rəḥki* *neyme*
today you.leave you.see yourself sleeping

ʿa *lə-zbale* ***w-čăntət-ki*** ***tăḥt*** ***ras-ki***
on the-dunghill and-bag-your under head-your

'(When) you leave today, you will see yourself sleeping on top of the dunghill, **with your bag under your head.**' (Sasse 1971, 290.5)

Circumstantial clauses without copulas are attested also in some other varieties of Anatolian Arabic, such as the dialect of Āzəx (Şırnak province, SE Turkey):

(14) *məsku* *l-ḥabl* ***w-hūwe*** ***qāyəm*** ***qədda***
they.took the-rope and-he standing in.front.of

s-səğara
the-tree

'They took the rope, **while he was standing in front of the tree.**' (Wittrich 2001, 160)

Compare this example with the semantically very similar clause in (11) above. The main difference is the use of the copula in Kinderib and its absence in Āzəx.

The evidence from Anatolian Arabic, therefore, does not necessarily contradict the assumption of Arabic influence on the Ṭuroyo circumstantial clause.

3. Other Aramaic Varieties

The situation in older varieties of Aramaic is also important for this issue, for the syntax of the Ṭuroyo circumstantial clause may be the continuation of earlier linguistic usage. Syriac, as stated above, rarely uses the conjunction *w-* ‘and’ in circumstantial clauses, which are normally introduced by *kaḏ*. The following example is from the *Julian Romance* (probably 6th century C.E.), transcribed according to the eastern Syriac tradition:

(15)	*w-lå*	*eṯmṣiw*	*la-mšåwzåḇu-ennon*	*men*
	and-not	they.were.able	to-save-them	from

yaqdånå	*d-nurå*	*aykannå d-*	*paṣy-an*
immolation	of-fire	as	he.saved-me

Mšiḥå	*w-šåwzḇ-an*	*men*	*yaqdånå*
Christ	and-he.delivered-me	from	immolation

d-nur-åḵ	***w-ʿayn-ayk***	***ḥåzyån***
of-fire-your	and-eyes-your	seeing

‘They could not save them from the fiery immolation, as Christ saved and delivered me from your fiery immolation, **while you were looking on**.’ (Hoffmann 1880, 52.11 = Sokoloff 2017, 111.10)[4]

The interpretation of such clauses may sometimes be somewhat problematic. In the following example, taken from the story about Mar Maʾin, the clause in question, despite its morphosyntactic similarities, may not actually be a circumstantial clause, but rather a sequential clause with a participle in durative function:

4 Sokoloff’s text erroneously gives <ʾykʾ> for *aykannå*.

(16)

håydẹn	*npaq*	*nåšå*	*hålẹn*	*l-ṭurå*
then	they.went.out	people	these	to-mountain

w-hennon	***meṯkarkin***	***b-ẹ***	*w-ʿal*
and-they	moving.about	in-it	and-they.entered

l-håy	*mʿarṯå*	*w-eškḥu-y*
into-that	cave	and-they.found-him

'Then these men left for the mountains, **and they were walking about**, went into that cave and found him.' (Brock 2008, 31.-14)

Despite its rather rare occurrence, this older Aramaic usage may have continued in Ṭuroyo.

Similar clauses can be found in other modern Aramaic varieties such as those of North-Eastern Neo-Aramaic (NENA). These are mostly asyndetic, as, for instance, in the Christian dialect of Barwar. Khan (2008, 22, 849ff.) rejects Arabic interference for this variety, presumably on the grounds of a predominantly Kurdish environment. Therefore, these clauses must be an independent development. An asyndetic example reads as follows:

(17)

yazíwa	*zràʾaˈ*	*yazíwa*	*xzàdaˈ*
they.used.to.go	cultivating	they.used.to.go	harvesting

yazíwa	*mɛθóye*	*mə́ndi*	*ta-bɛ̀θaˈ*
they.used.to.go	bringing	something	for-house

ʾáni	***ṣìme.ˈ***
they	fasting

'They would go to cultivate (the fields), go to harvest, go and bring things for the house, **while they were fasting**.' (Khan 2008, 851)

The syntax of the clause *ʾáni ṣìme* is the same as in the Ṭuroyo examples (1) and (2) above, i.e. *ăḥna naʿime* and *hăt damixo* respectively. It is not entirely certain what such parallels, apparently independent from each other, mean for the syntax of modern Aramaic in general, as they could well be due to tendencies toward paratactic structures in spoken language (cf. the short remark in Givón 2001, 218).

4. Conclusion

From the evidence presented in this paper, some questions arise:

a. Is the circumstantial clause in Ṭuroyo an independent development, as presumably it is in NENA, i.e. Christian Barwar?
b. Can the Ṭuroyo circumstantial clause still be interpreted as the result of Arabic interference, despite the existence of copular circumstantial clauses in Anatolian Arabic (primarily Kinderib)?
c. How does the evidence of older Aramaic, i.e. Syriac, which rarely uses the conjunction *w-* 'and' in such clauses, fit into this picture?
d. Can the Ṭuroyo circumstantial clause be explained by a so-called trigger effect 'releasing or accelerating developments which mature independently' (Weinreich 1953, 25)?

This leads to the following tentative conclusion. The model of Arabic syntax played a part in the Ṭuroyo circumstantial clause, if only in the sense of reinforcing developments already nascent in Ṭuroyo; see the evidence from Syriac and NENA cited earlier. Clues for Arabic interference in the circumstantial clause of Ṭuroyo may be found in the following syntactic features:

a. Ṭuroyo uses the conjunction *w-* 'and' regularly and without exception. Despite the Syriac evidence, this regular feature seems to be dependent on an Arabic prototype.

b. Ṭuroyo never has a copula in circumstantial clauses, as is the case in most dialects of Anatolian Arabic (see Mḥallamī and Āzəx). There is no apparent reason why Ṭuroyo by itself should not use its own copula in such a conspicuous construction.

c. In addition, the occurrence of a verbal predicate (present tense) in a circumstantial clause may be due to Arabic influence, but this remains uncertain.

On the whole, therefore, the circumstantial clause in Ṭuroyo is a perfect example of the complex interaction between several internal and external factors in the development of linguistic features. The exact degree of influence of each of these factors is difficult, if not impossible, to determine.

References

Bedir Khan, Emir Djeladet and Roger Lescot. 1986. *Kurdische Grammatik. Kurmanci-Dialekt.* Disputationes Linguarum Et Cultuum Orbis K 1—Disputationes Linguae Et Cultus Kurdica 1. Bonn: Kurdisches Institut.

Brock, Sebastian P. 2008. *The History of the Holy Mar Ma'in. With a Guide to the Persian Martyr Acts.* Persian Martyr Acts in Syriac 1. Piscataway, NJ: Gorgias.

Brustad, Kristen E. 2000. *The Syntax of Spoken Arabic. A Comparative Study of Moroccan, Egyptian, Syrian, and Kuwaiti Dialects.* Washington, D.C.: Georgetown University Press.

Chyet, Michael L. 1995. 'Neo-Aramaic and Kurdish. An Interdisciplinary Consideration of their Influence on each other'. *Israel Oriental Studies* 15: 219–52.

Epps, Patience et al. 2013. 'Introduction: Contact Among Genetically Related Languages'. *Journal of Language Contact* 6: 209–19.

Givón, Talmy. 2001. *Syntax. An Introduction.* Volume II. Amsterdam: John Benjamins.

Hickey, Raymond (ed.). 2010. *The Handbook of Language Contact.* Malden: Wiley-Blackwell.

Hoffmann, J. Georg E. 1880. *Iulianos der Abtruennige. Syrische Erzählungen.* Leiden: Brill.

Jastrow, Otto. 1968. 'Ein Märchen im neuaramäischen Dialekt von Mīḏin (Ṭūr ʿAbdīn)'. *Zeitschrift der deutschen morgenländischen Gesellschaft* 118: 29–61.

———. 1997. 'The Neo-Aramaic Languages.' In *The Semitic Languages*, edited by Robert Hetzron. London: Routledge, 334–77.

———. 2003. *Arabische Texte aus Kinderib.* Semitica Viva 30. Wiesbaden: Harrassowitz.

Khan, Geoffrey. 2008. *The Neo-Aramaic Dialect of Barwar.* 3 vols. Handbuch der Orientalistik 96. Leiden: Brill.

Mithun, Marianne. 2012. 'Morphologies in Contact: Form, Meaning, and Use in the Grammar of Reference'. In *Morphologies in Contact*, edited by Martine Vanhove, Thomas Stolz, Aina Urdze and Hitomi Otsuka. Studia Typologica 10. Berlin: Akademie, 15–36.

Nöldeke, Theodor. 1898. *Kurzgefasste syrische Grammatik.* Anhang: Die handschriftlichen Ergänzungen in dem Handexemplar Theodor Nöldekes und Register der Belegstellen bearbeitet von Anton Schall. 1966. Darmstadt: Wissenschaftliche Buchgesellschaft.

———. 1904. *Compendious Syriac Grammar.* Translated (with the sanction of the author) from the second and improved German edition by James A. Crichton. London: Williams & Norgate.

Procházka, Stephan. 2002. *Die arabischen Dialekte der Čukurova (Südtürkei).* Semitica Viva 27. Wiesbaden: Harrassowitz.

R2,3 = Ritter, Hellmut. 1969–1971. *Ṭūrōyo. Die Volkssprache der syrischen Christen des Ṭūr ʿAbdîn. A: Texte.* Vol. II, III. Wiesbaden: Steiner (Kommission).

Reckendorf, Hermann. 1921. *Arabische Syntax.* Zweite, unveränderte Auflage. Reprint 1977. Heidelberg: Winter.

Sasse, Hans-Jürgen. 1971. *Linguistische Analyse des arabischen Dialekts der Mḥallamīye in der Provinz Mardin (Südosttürkei).* PhD thesis. Munich: University of Munich.

Sokoloff, Michael. 2017. *The Julian Romance. A New English Translation. Revised Edition.* Texts from Christian Late Antiquity 49. Piscataway, NJ: Gorgias.

Talay, Shabo. 2001. 'Der arabische Dialekt von Hasköy (Dēr-Khāṣ) Ostanatolien. Teil I: Grammatikalische Skizze'. *Zeitschrift für arabische Linguistik* 40: 71–89.

——— (ed.). 2004. *Lebendig begraben. Die Entführung des syrisch-orthodoxen Priesters Melki Tok von Midən in der Südosttürkei. Einführung, Aramäischer Text (Turoyo), Übersetzung und Glossar.* Studien zur Orientalischen Kirchengeschichte 29. Münster: Lit.

Waltisberg, Michael. 2013. 'Ṭuroyo und Arabisch'. In Nicht nur mit Engelszungen. *Beiträge zur semitischen Dialektologie. Festschrift für Werner Arnold zum 60. Geburtstag,* edited by Renaud Kuty et al. Wiesbaden: Harrassowitz, 353–64.

———. 2016. *Syntax des Ṭuroyo.* Semitica Viva 55. Wiesbaden: Harrassowitz.

Weinreich, Uriel. 1953. *Languages in Contact. French, German and Romansh in Twentieth-century Switzerland.* 2nd printing 1963. The Hague: Mouton.

Wittrich, Michaela. 2001. *Der arabische Dialekt von Āzəx.* Semitica Viva 25. Wiesbaden: Harrassowitz.

THE MORPHOSYNTACTIC CONSERVATISM OF WESTERN NEO-ARAMAIC DESPITE CONTACT WITH SYRIAN ARABIC

Ivri Bunis

1. Introduction

This paper is a historical-comparative study of basic tense, aspect and mood (TAM) distinctions in two closely related languages: Western Neo-Aramaic and Syrian Arabic. It compares their shared cognate verbal paradigms, shows the overlap and differences in their grammatical functions and discusses the independent parallel developments such as the innovation of new verbal constructions. It will demonstrate that the Western Neo-Aramaic conservatism and resilience to contact-induced change in its verbal system is striking in light of its prolonged and close contact with Syrian Arabic and the morphological similarities between the Western Neo-Aramaic and Syrian Arabic verbal paradigms—factors which have been found to facilitate contact-induced change in other bilingual situations.

Two of the four cases of divergence that are presented in this article also stand out in that they involve embedded structures, specifically, modal and phasal complement clauses and conditional protases. Western Neo-Aramaic preserves more complex patterns of subordination with these structures than is found in Syrian Arabic, which is the dominant language in the Western Neo-Aramaic speech region. This appears to go against Matras's suggestion (2009, 244 and see also ibid., 248–50) that such embedded structures are prone to contact-induced

 https://doi.org/10.11647/OBP.0209.07

convergence with the linguistic patterns of the model or donor language.

Of the two branches of Aramaic that are known to us from the Late Aramaic stage (3rd–6th centuries CE), namely Western and Eastern Aramaic, the sole surviving heirs to the varieties that were part of the western branch are the three Neo-Aramaic dialects spoken in the Qalamun mountains in Syria, around 60 kilometres North-East of Damascus. Unlike the majority of the eastern Neo-Aramaic dialects, which have been in contact mostly with non-Semitic languages, possessing very different morphologies from their own, Western Neo-Aramaic has developed in contact with Arabic. Both Aramaic and Arabic belong to Central Semitic. The genetic relation between the two language groups entails a large degree of morphological similarity. Western Neo-Aramaic especially stands out in the extreme closeness of its verbal morphology to that of Syrian Arabic. The morphological affinity between Western Neo-Aramaic and Syrian Arabic in general, particularly in their verbal morphology, provides an opportunity to examine a case of prolonged contact between closely related languages, in this instance likely spanning over a millennium.

Syrian Arabic is the dominant language in the Western Neo-Aramaic speech region and all Western Neo-Aramaic speakers have been bilingual for several generations at the very least (Correll 1978, 136). Evidence for the long history of contact between Western Neo-Aramaic and Syrian Arabic is found in the extensive influence of Syrian Arabic on Western Neo-Aramaic in the areas of lexicon (Arnold and Behnstedt 1991, 61) and morphology and syntax (Correll 1978, 135–53).

One central feature of the verbal morphology of the Western Neo-Aramaic dialects that brings it very close to Syrian Arabic verbal morphology is the retention of both of the earlier Central Semitic finite verbal paradigms, namely the suffix conjugation (i.e. *qtal*) and the prefix conjugation (i.e. *yiqtol*). These conjugations exist alongside the imperative and the two participial paradigms, i.e. the so-called active participle and the so-called passive or resultative participle. Western Neo-Aramaic contrasts in this feature with nearly all of the eastern varieties of Neo-Aramaic, in which the two finite paradigms have fallen out of use and the verbal system is based on the historical active and resultative participles. Only Neo-Mandaic has preserved one of the finite paradigms, namely the *qtal* conjugation (Häberl 2009, 178ff.).

The participial forms of Western Neo-Aramaic have undergone some development. Notably, they have acquired prefixal person inflection (Arnold 1990b, 75, 77), which parallels suffixal person marking in eastern varieties of Neo-Aramaic. However, apart from this development, which has also affected adjectives, and some other changes to inflectional morphemes expressing person, number and gender, Western Neo-Aramaic verbs preserve the morphology of Late Western Aramaic, which in turn constitutes the general verbal morphology of Central Semitic.

The retention of the two finite verbal paradigms has special significance for the issue of language contact between Western Neo-Aramaic and Syrian Arabic. Syrian Arabic too has suffix and prefix conjugations, an active participle, a passive/resultative participle and an imperative paradigm. The morphology of the Western Neo-Aramaic suffix and prefix conjugations and the active participle very closely parallels that of Syrian Arabic.

For the discussion of language contact, I adopt here the terms 'matter replication' and 'pattern replication' employed by Matras (2009, 234–35) to refer respectively to borrowings of concrete forms of words or morphs as opposed to the replication of more abstract patterns. Matras (ibid., 240–43) presents a model for pattern replication based on 'pivot-matching', whereby speakers identify pivotal features of a pattern in the model language, and match them 'to the inventory of context-appropriate forms' and 'their formation and combination rules' (ibid., 243). The result is the replication of the model pattern using inherited linguistic material.

Much of the study of language contact is devoted to understanding which elements of language tend to be replicated as borrowed linguistic matter, as linguistic patterns or the combination of both. Various hierarchies have been suggested concerning the propensity of various elements to be taken over in the replica language through matter or pattern replication (Matras 2009, 153–65, 243–45).

Since the focus of the present article is the function of verbal paradigms of Western Neo-Aramaic, in relation to cognate Syrian Arabic verbal paradigms, the most relevant type of linguistic change in this context would be pattern replication. The occurrence of pattern replication is explained in various ways, with a prominent role given to bilingualism. As noted, Aramaic/Syrian Arabic bilingualism has existed among Western Neo-Aramaic speakers for an extended period of time. In this context, a suggested motivation for pattern replication is to maximise the efficiency of speech production in a bilingual situation, by allowing patterns to converge (Matras 2009, 235). Furthermore, prolonged bilingualism is believed to result in the levelling of structures through 'orientation toward a prestigious outsider language', which may be accompanied in the case of diglossia by 'a considerable influx of loanwords' (ibid., 237). Loss of categories through language contact has also been reported (ibid., 258). The dominance of Syrian Arabic in the Western Neo-Aramaic speech-region is very much reflected in such an influx of Arabic loanwords and the replacement of many original Aramaic lexemes. On the other hand, as this article aims to show, the morphosyntax of the expression of TAM reflects a large measure of stability, in that the levelling of structures and loss of categories has not occurred.

Studies of language contact that specifically touch on morphology suggest that the morphological similarities between the Syrian Arabic and Western Neo-Aramaic verbal systems could have had the potential to facilitate the replication of the Syrian Arabic patterns by cognate, similar-sounding forms in Western Neo-Aramaic. Firstly, replication involving derivational and even inflectional morphology is attested even between languages with very different morphologies (Matras 2009, 258–65). Noorlander (2014) has applied Matras's model to the eastern varieties of Neo-Aramaic. He has found many examples of morphosyntactic replication among varieties of Eastern Neo-Aramaic that were induced by their contact with Kurdish, an Indo-European language, despite its very different morphology. Khan (2020) has drawn attention to the fact that contact between North-Eastern Neo-Aramaic dialects and Iranian languages can result in partial convergence based on the matching of particular details between the languages without replicating full grammatical systems. Moreover, the morphological and phonological similarities that exist between Western Neo-Aramaic and Syrian Arabic cognate verbal forms are known from other contact situations to have served as pivotal features facilitating pattern replication (Matras 2009, 245–46).

The potential for pattern replication and its lack of realisation in the case of Western Neo-Aramaic and Syrian Arabic is the main concern of this article, to which I apply Matras's model. In this case, the close similarities in sound and morphology between cognate Western Neo-Aramaic and Syrian Arabic verbal forms would be the potential pivotal features that could have facilitated pattern replication.

When compared with many of the contact situations that have been studied by contact linguists, the degree of sound-similarity between the cognate verbal forms of Syrian Arabic and Western Neo-Aramaic, which I address later on in this article, stands out. An important additional factor is that some of the cognate and similar-sounding forms already had parallel functions in both languages as a result of parallel development in both languages or shared retention. Lastly, I aim to show that speakers of Western Neo-Aramaic have recognised the morphological closeness between Western Neo-Aramaic and Syrian Arabic verbal forms.

We would have expected that these factors, coupled with the prolonged contact between the two languages, and the dominance of Syrian Arabic, would have facilitated and prompted the replication of Syrian Arabic morphosyntactic patterns within Western Neo-Aramaic.

Correll (1978, 142–53) has devoted attention to the question of the Syrian Arabic influence on Western Neo-Aramaic verbal syntax, on the basis of the texts that he had at his disposal. Correll generally finds much Syrian Arabic influence on the function of the Western Neo-Aramaic verb, though he often qualifies this influence, noting somewhat obscurely that 'with all of the recognised impact of the donor language [i.e. Arabic], it is hardly possible to speak of explicit Arabisation' (Correll 1978, 148).[1] Notably, Correll (ibid., 153) proposes that the contact with Arabic might have been a conservative force, responsible for the preservation of the two finite verbal paradigms in Western Neo-Aramaic. Arabic, Correll suggests, hindered the inherent tendencies of the precursors of Western Neo-Aramaic, which might have led to the loss of the earlier finite verbal paradigms as happened in the eastern varieties of Aramaic. In the relevant sections of the present article, some of Correll's remarks will be considered in greater detail.

The opinions Correll expresses on this issue seem to be somewhat contradictory (1978, 142–45). With respect to the *qtal* and *yiqtol* paradigms in Western Neo-Aramaic, he states that their functions are very close to those of the cognate Syrian Arabic forms, making Syrian Arabic influence on their function likely. And yet, he reasons, their functions are too close to those found in older Aramaic to establish Syrian Arabic influence with certainty. Nevertheless, Correll strongly believes that the Western Neo-Aramaic active participle has converged in its functions with Syrian Arabic *b-* + *yiqtol*, stating in this regard

> There can be no doubt that this is a case of direct and meticulous replication of the circumstances in Arabic (Correll 1978, 144–45).[2]

Arnold (2007, 189) notes that *qtal* and *yiqtol* in Western Neo-Aramaic 'are used to express preterite tense and subjunctive exactly as in the Arabic dialects of Syria'.

The present article aims to show that despite the factors of prolonged contact of Western Neo-Aramaic with Syrian Arabic

---

1 '... von ausdrücklicher Arabisierung kann also, bei aller zugestandenen Einwirkung von seiten der Adstratsprache, schwerlich gesprochen werden' (my translation).

2 'Es kann wohl nicht der geringste Zweifel daran bestehen, daß man es hier mit einer geradezu minuziösen Nachbildung der Gegebenheiten im Arabischen zu tun hat' (my translation), and see also Correll's comment, p. 144, n. 272.

and the close morphological affinity between the two languages, Western Neo-Aramaic preserves a significant degree of difference from Syrian Arabic in its verbal morphosyntax.

The examination presented here is contrastive. In order to appreciate the significance of the functional divergences presented in Section 4, between cognate and similar-sounding verb forms in Western Neo-Aramaic and Syrian Arabic, these divergences are contrasted with other contexts in which Syrian Arabic influence on Western Neo-Aramaic is significant (Sections 2–3), and Western Neo-Aramaic and Syrian Arabic show parallel functions of their cognate verbal forms (Section 3). It is within this wider context, which, I suggest, includes a recognition on the part of the speakers of the correspondences between Western Neo-Aramaic and Syrian Arabic, that the existence of such divergences is striking.

The investigation offered in this article consists of three sections. In Section 2, I illustrate the close and extensive contact that has existed between Western Neo-Aramaic and Syrian Arabic by reviewing facets of lexical, morphological and syntactic influences of Syrian Arabic outside of the verbal system. In Section 3, I present shared features of the Western Neo-Aramaic and Syrian Arabic verbal forms, due to independent development, shared retention or convergence. This section serves as a background, against which, the functional divergences, presented in Section 4, between the cognate Syrian Arabic and Western Neo-Aramaic verbal paradigms, can be fully understood.

2. Syrian Arabic Influence on Western Neo-Aramaic: Loanwords and Multiword Expressions, and their Syntactic Context

To appreciate the divergences that are the focus of this paper, the duration of the contact between Western Neo-Aramaic and Syrian Arabic and the ways that this contact has impacted on Western Neo-Aramaic need to be understood.

Throughout this article, the linguistic examples are transcribed as they appear in the respective publications.

With regard to the duration of contact, Arnold (2002, 6–7) has pointed out two phonological features of Syrian Arabic loanwords that reflect prolonged contact between Western Neo-Aramaic and Syrian Arabic.

Some Arabic loanwords in Western Neo-Aramaic, such as *rkʿ* 'return' in the fourth stem, contain the consonant /k/ where contemporary Syrian Arabic has /ǧ/ or /ž/ (cf. *ržʿ* 'return'). In words of Aramaic stock, /k/ most often originates from the voiced velar stop **g*, e.g. *felka* < **pelgā* 'half' (Spitaler 1938, 17).

Other Arabic loanwords in Western Neo-Aramaic reflect spirantisation of *bgdkpt* consonants, e.g. *xōf* <Arabic *kāfi* 'enough'.

Arnold convincingly suggests that the first category of loanwords was borrowed into the precursors of Western Neo-Aramaic before the voiced velar stop /g/ in Syrian Arabic shifted to /ǧ/ and subsequently in many of the Syrian Arabic dialects to /ž/. Later borrowings from Syrian Arabic contain /ž/, e.g. *čōžra* 'merchant' < Syrian Arabic *tāžer*. Following Spitaler (1938, 21), Arnold suggests that the second category goes back to the time when the twofold pronunciation of the *bgdkpt* consonants in Aramaic, as either stops or fricatives, was still allophonic. The two realisations are no longer allophonic in contemporary Western Neo-Aramaic, but have developed into discrete phonemes. Thus [k] and [x], which were originally allophones of /k/ constitute minimal pairs in *xafna* 'hunger' versus *kafna* 'burial shroud' < Arabic *kafan* (Arnold 1990b, 14). The initial /k/ in the Arabic loanword *kafna* in contrast to the initial /x/ in *xōf* < Arabic *kāfi* also presumably signifies that the former was borrowed into Western Neo-Aramaic at a later period than *kāfi*.

The influence of contact with Syrian Arabic on the lexicon of all three Western Neo-Aramaic dialects is massive. It includes the replacement of many Aramaic lexemes with Arabic lexemes (1).

(1) Maʕlūla

aḥḥaḏ ***ifqer*** *w-aḥḥaḏ* ***iġən***

'one **poor** man and one **rich** man' (Arnold 1991, 12:1)

Most Syrian Arabic loanwords, including the forms *ifqer* < Arabic *faqīr* and *iġən* < Arabic *ġanī* in example (1), reflect integration into Western Neo-Aramaic morphology, which is also an indication of the long duration of contact.

Material replication of Syrian Arabic lexicon is not limited in Western Neo-Aramaic to content words but includes many function words as well. Just to illustrate, these include adverbs such as *baḥar* 'much, very' < Arabic *baḥar* 'sea', *bnawb* 'completely' < Syrian Arabic *bnawb* with the same meaning, subordinators such as *ḥetta* 'in order that' and the reciprocal pronoun *baʿḏ̣* < Arabic *baʿḍ*. In Matras's view, since contact-induced linguistic change originates in the discourse of bilingual speakers, discourse markers are particularly prone to be materially replicated (Matras 2009, 98–100, 144–45). A significant portion of the replicated Syrian Arabic function words in Western Neo-Aramaic includes discourse markers, such as *ṭayyeb* 'OK, good', *bass* 'but', *yaʿni* 'I mean'. All of these originate in identical Syrian Arabic forms with the same meanings.

The ordinal numbers in Western Neo-Aramaic have been completely replaced by Syrian Arabic forms: *awwal*,[3] *ṯēn(i)*, *ṯēleṯ*, etc. (Arnold 1990b, 403). In this regard, Western Neo-Aramaic is extreme. There is much documentation in the world's languages for the borrowing of 'first' and 'second' but not of higher ordinals (Matras 2009, 202–03), which may point to a special propensity of lower ordinals to undergo contact-induced material replication. This holds for a number of Aramaic dialects as well. The Arabic form *ʾawwal* 'first' was taken over by varieties of Palestinian Aramaic already in the Middle Ages (Fassberg 2010,

3 Following Arnold's practice, an initial glottal stop is not indicated in the transcription of Western Neo-Aramaic.

92, n. 102). A number of North-Eastern Neo-Aramaic dialects have borrowed either *ʾawwal*[3] by itself (Garbell 1965, 56–7; Khan 2008, 186–87; Fassberg 2010, 92), or together with forms for 'second' (Khan 1999, 181; Khan 2004, 206; Khan 2009, 213). Likewise in some dialects of Ṭūrōyo, 'first' and 'second' have been replaced by Arabic forms and the Arabic ordinal for 'third' (*tēlǝṯ*) is occasionally used alongside a native Aramaic form (Ritter 1990, 47). In the Mīdin dialect of this group 'second' and 'third' are borrowed from Arabic, whereas *qamoyo*, the older Aramaic form for 'first' is preserved and used adjectivally (Jastrow 1985, 245). By contrast Western Neo-Aramaic has replaced all ordinals from 'one' to 'ten' with Arabic forms. Aramaic cardinal numbers, though, have been retained in Western Neo-Aramaic. In Trans-Zab Jewish varieties of North-Eastern Neo-Aramaic, we find a combination of matter and pattern replication with all ordinal numbers. In these varieties, ordinals are formed on the basis of native Aramaic cardinal numbers, which are suffixed with *-mīn*. The suffix *-mīn* has been materially replicated from Kurdish, and Kurdish is also the model for the pattern CARDINAL + suffix (Noorlander 2014, 215).

The influence of Syrian Arabic is not limited to the material replication of lexical items, but includes replication of derivational morphemes and pattern replication. Two clear examples of this are the Arabic elative pattern *aqtal*, and the seventh and eighth Arabic verbal stems. For Matras (2009, 209–10), a requirement for recognising morphological borrowing is 'backwards diffusion', i.e., 'replication of borrowed morphs in connection with pre-existing, inherited lexicon'. The elative *aqtal* pattern is used not only with Arabic loanwords, such as *aqwa* 'stronger', from the Arabic root *qwy*, but with Aramaic roots as well, as in *awrab* 'greater, older' from *rbb*.[4]

Syntactic influence of Syrian Arabic is evident with the ordinal numbers and the elative, on top of the lexical and morphological influence that those two categories reflect. When these categories

4 The seventh and eighth Arabic derived stems are discussed in Section 3 below (see further Correll 1978, 25–6, 141).

function as modifiers, Western Neo-Aramaic (2a-c) replicates the syntactic pattern in which they appear in Syrian Arabic (3a-c). The pattern consists of a noun phrase structure in which the modifier, in an uninflected masculine singular form, precedes the head noun, an unusual word order elsewhere in Western Neo-Aramaic, but one that is well known in Arabic (Grotzfeld 1965, 71, 93–4).

(2) Western Neo-Aramaic (Maʕlūla)

a. *awwal yōma*

'first day' (Arnold 1991, 72:23)

b. *ṯēn lēlya*

'second night' (Arnold 1991, 34:178)

c. *awrab aḥḥaḏ*

'oldest one', literally 'greater one' (Arnold 1991, 136:2)

(3) Syrian Arabic (ʿAyn et-Tīne)

a. *awwal xarūf*

'first ram' (Behnstedt 2000, 360:14)

b. *ṯēni lēle*

'second night' (Behnstedt 2000, 364:44)

c. *aktar šī*

'mostly', literally 'most thing' (Arnold 1987, 1:1)

Multiword expressions constitute a category with which matter replication also inherently involves syntactic structures, which fall into the category of patterns (Matras 2009, 240–43).

Numerous Syrian Arabic expressions such as (4) have been borrowed into Western Neo-Aramaic. I adduce this example to illustrate how the structural affinity between the two languages has enabled such expressions to be adopted almost as they appear in the model language. In (4), the dimension of syntax also indicates how speakers of Western Neo-Aramaic are able to match forms in Syrian Arabic with non-cognate forms with parallel function in Western Neo-Aramaic.

In (4), the Arabic expression *qaṭaʿ-∅ əl-ʾamal* '[he] lost hope' (4a), literally '[he] cut the hope' is mirrored by a very close expression in Western Neo-Aramaic (4b). The noun *ʾamal* 'hope' has been borrowed and integrated into Western Neo-Aramaic morphology in the form *aml-a*, whereby it has acquired the Western Neo-Aramaic nominal suffix *-a*. The root *qṭʿ* 'cut' is found historically both in Arabic and in Aramaic, but its use in Western Neo-Aramaic in this phrase in collocation with *aml-a* doubtless originates in the Syrian Arabic expression.

(4)

a. Syrian Arabic

lā	*tə-qṭaʿ-∅*	*əl-ʾamal*
not	2-cut.IMP-MS	DEF-hope

'Don't give up hope.' (Stowasser 1964, 118b)

b. Neo-Aramaic (Maʿlūla)

qaṭʿ-ul-l	*aml-a*
cut.QTL-3MPL-DOM	hope-NPSFX

'They lost hope.' (Arnold 1991, 14:39)

Thus, beyond the borrowing of the Syrian Arabic lexical item *ʾamal* and its morphological integration into Western Neo-Aramaic, the replica phrase exemplifies how Western Neo-Aramaic makes use of its own morphosyntax to replicate the pattern of the model expression in the donor language. In Syrian Arabic, the noun *ʾamal* appears in the phrase in its definite form, marked as such by the definite article *əl-*, a nominal prefix. No fully analogous definite article in the form of a nominal prefix is found in Western Neo-Aramaic, though other means are found for marking noun phrases as definite, one of which is the verbal suffix *-l*, which differentially marks the definite direct object nominal. In (4b) this morpheme appears in the replicated pattern with the verbal form *qaṭʿ-ul-l*, marking its direct object *aml-a* as definite.

The Western Neo-Aramaic pattern in (4b) fully corresponds to the Syrian Arabic pattern, even in the definiteness of the noun *aml-a*. Western Neo-Aramaic, however, has not replicated the matter that is used to express the noun's definiteness in the model language, but uses a native component belonging to a different category to replicate the Syrian Arabic pattern. Pivot-matching on the basis of phonological similarity might have played a role in the replication of the Syrian Arabic definite article *əl-* by means the Western Neo-Aramaic verbal suffix *-l*.

3. Shared Features of the Western Neo-Aramaic and Syrian Arabic Verbal Systems due to Shared Retention, Convergence or Parallel Development

To appreciate the significance of the divergences between Western Neo-Aramaic and Syrian Arabic that are the focus of this paper, Section 2 above serves as a general background. Its purpose is to illustrate that Western Neo-Aramaic has extensively borrowed Syrian Arabic lexicon and morphology, and has replicated Syrian Arabic morphosyntactic patterns associated with those borrowings, either by means of the borrowed forms themselves, or through its own linguistic matter.

The divergences in the verbal system, which are presented in section 4 below, are striking not only against this general background of extensive impact of Syrian Arabic, but especially in light of similarities both in matter and in pattern, or in form and in function, between the verbal systems of the two language groups.

The scope of the present article does not permit a close examination of all of the functions of the Western Neo-Aramaic and Syrian Arabic verbal paradigms, but I present here a comparison of some major functions of the shared cognate paradigms (i) *qatal* (Syrian Arabic) and *qtal* (Western Neo-Aramaic), (ii) *yiqtol*, (iii) *qātel* (Syrian Arabic) and *qōtel* (Western Neo-Aramaic) and (iv) of the Western Neo-Aramaic *qtīl/qattīl* paradigm of the resultative participle.

3.1 Background to the Divergences in the Verbal System: Cognate Inflectional Morphology

As noted in the introduction, due to the shared origins of the two languages, the inherited verbal morphology of Western Neo-Aramaic very closely parallels that of Syrian Arabic. Table 1 outlines the parallel Tense–Aspect–Mood (TAM) inflectional paradigms of the Syrian Arabic and Western Neo-Aramaic verbal systems, as they are reflected in the first or basic stem.

Table 1: The TAM Paradigms of the Syrian Arabic and Western Neo-Aramaic Verbs

Paradigm	**Arabic** (*ktb* 'write')	**Aramaic** (*fṯḥ* 'open', *ḏmx* 'sleep')
qatal/qtal	*katab*	*ifṯaḥ* (< earlier Aramaic **pṯaḥ*)
yiqtol	*yəktob*	*yifṯuḥ*
imperative	*ktōb*	*fṯōḥ*
qātel/qōtel[5]	*kāteb*	*ḏōmex* (< earlier Aramaic **dāmex*)
resultative participle	*maktūb*	*iḏmex* (< earlier Aramaic **dmīx* (i.e. **qtīl*)) *šammeʿ* < **šammīʿ* (**qattīl*, Arnold 1990b, 76)

Adapted from Arnold and Behnstedt (1993, 12, 55) and Grotzfeld (1965, 108).

5 Historically, the active participle.

One of the central features of the Western Neo-Aramaic verbal morphology is the retention of the suffix and prefix conjugations unlike other Neo-Aramaic dialects. Syrian Arabic and Western Neo-Aramaic share these two paradigms, to which I shall refer as *qatal* (Syrian Arabic) or *qtal* (Western Neo-Aramaic) and *yiqtol* respectively. They also share the *qātel* (Syrian Arabic) or *qōtel* (Western Neo-Aramaic) paradigm, which goes back historically to the active participle, as well as the imperative paradigm. Thus, in the morphology of the TAM paradigms, the two languages reflect complete parallelism. The exception is the resultative participles: these show divergent forms.

The Person–Number–Gender (PNG) inflectional morphology of the verbal system, too, is largely parallel, but not completely identical, in the two languages, as exemplified in Table 2 (taken from Arnold and Behnstedt 1993, 55) with respect to the *qatal/qtal* paradigm of the verb *ḍḥk* 'laugh' in the first stem, which has been borrowed into Western Neo-Aramaic from Syrian Arabic. The Western Neo-Aramaic column contains the forms that are found in the dialect of Maˁlūla.

Table 2: Verbal Inflection of the *Qatal/Qtal* Paradigm, First Stem

	Arabic	**Aramaic (Maˁlūla)**
3MS	*ḍaḥak-∅*	*iḍḥek-∅*
3FS	*ḍaḥak-it*	*ḍiḥk-aṯ*
3PL	*ḍaḥak-u*	*iḍḥek-∅*
2MS	*ḍaḥak-t*	*ḍiḥk-ič*
2FS	*ḍaḥak-ti*	*ḍiḥk-iš*
2MPL	*ḍaḥak-tu*	*ḍiḥk-ičxun*
2FPL	*ḍaḥak-tu*	*ḍiḥk-ičxen*
1S	*ḍaḥak-t*	*ḍiḥk-iṯ*
1PL	*ḍaḥak-na*	*ḍiḥk-innaḥ*

ḍḥk 'laugh'

As Table 2 indicates, the two language groups share the same general inflectional scheme, which in the case of the *qatal/qtal* paradigm consists of verbal suffixes. Through their verbal inflection, the two languages express the same categories of PNG, with the exception of three significant differences. In the Neo-Aramaic dialects of Maʿlūla and Ǧubbʿadīn, gender distinction is preserved between the 2mpl. and 2fpl. forms, whereas in Syrian Arabic this distinction has been levelled out. Syrian Arabic also does not formally distinguish between 1s. and 2ms., whereas these are distinct in Western Neo-Aramaic. Conversely, Syrian Arabic maintains number distinction between 3ms. and 3pl., whereas these are expressed by identical forms in Western Neo-Aramaic.

The cross-linguistically rare case of the replication of inflectional morphology from Syrian Arabic has not been found in Western Neo-Aramaic. A possible example, though, of pattern replication with respect to Syrian Arabic inflectional paradigms occurs in the Western Neo-Aramaic dialect of Baxʿa. In this dialect, as in Syrian Arabic, gender distinction has been lost in plural verb forms through the generalisation of historical mpl. forms. Thus, in the *qtal* conjugation of the dialect of Baxʿa, the 2pl. suffix for both genders is *-iċxun*, whereas the other two Western Neo-Aramaic dialects maintain separate forms (see Table 2). Arnold and Behnstedt (1993, 56) plausibly attribute the development in the Western Neo-Aramaic dialect of Baxʿa to the influence of the Syrian Arabic of the nearby villages.

3.2. Background to the Divergences in the Verbal System: Borrowing of Verbal Derivational Morphology

One area in which there is clear influence of Syrian Arabic on the Western Neo-Aramaic verbal system is in the replication of Arabic derivational morphology, i.e. of derived stems which are not found in earlier Aramaic. Replication of verbal derivational morphology is apparently quite uncommon cross-linguistically (Matras 2009, 211). The forms of these stems have been borrowed extensively into Western Neo-Aramaic, notwithstanding the typical Western Neo-Aramaic sound changes, as shown in Table 3, which contains the 3MS forms of the *qatal/qtal* conjugation (Arnold and Behnstedt 1993, 58).

Table 3: The Syrian Arabic Derived Stems in Western Neo-Aramaic

Arabic stem	Arabic form	Aramaic form	Gloss
III	*šāraṭ*	*šōreṭ*	'bet'
VI	*trāfaq*	*črōfeq*	'join'
VII	*nfağar*	*inᵊfžar*	'explode'
VIII	*ftaham*	*ifᵊčham*	'be understood'
X	*staqbal*	*sčaqbel*	'accept'

Matter and pattern replication coincide in the borrowing of the derived stems.

Firstly, the borrowing of the Syrian Arabic derived stems is not merely part of the lexical influence of Syrian Arabic on Western Neo-Aramaic, but clearly constitutes morphological borrowing. The borrowed derived stems show 'backwards diffusion', namely, the 'replication of borrowed morphs in connection with pre-existing, inherited lexicon' (Matras 2009, 209–10). In other words, the borrowed Arabic stems are widely used with existing Aramaic roots.

Secondly, the Syrian Arabic VII and VIII passive stems, i.e. *nfaʿal* and *ftaʿal*, borrowed into Western Neo-Aramaic as *inᵊfʿal* and *ifᵊčʿal* respectively, additionally reflect pattern replication (Arnold and Behnstedt 1993, 58–9). These borrowed stems have replaced the older Aramaic *ʾetpʿel* passive stem, which has been retained in Western Neo-Aramaic through one verbal lexeme (see Arnold 1990b, 62, 126–28). Active verbs of the first stem, whether Arabic or Aramaic in origin, are passivised through Arabic stem VII: *ifṭaḥ* '[he] opened' > *inᵊfṭaḥ* '[he] was opened', unless their first radical is /n/, in which case they are passivised through the Arabic eighth stem, as with *inxas* '[he] slaughtered' > *inᵊčxas* '[he] was slaughtered', from the originally Aramaic root *nxs*. The same morphophonemic rule operates in Syrian Arabic. Thus, the Syrian Arabic pattern has been replicated in Western Neo-Aramaic both with respect to the use of Arabic stems VII and VIII as the passive counterparts of stem I, as well as in terms of the morphophonemic rule that governs the selection of each of these stems.

Coghill (2015, 83–107) has compared the borrowing of Arabic derived stems in Western Neo-Aramaic and in dialects of Eastern Neo-Aramaic. She has found that of all of the Neo-Aramaic dialects, Western Neo-Aramaic has borrowed the largest number of Arabic stems. Likewise, Western Neo-Aramaic shows the greatest degree of integration of derived stems; of all of the Neo-Aramaic dialects that she examined, only the replicated Arabic seventh and eighth stems in Western Neo-Aramaic show use with native Aramaic verbal roots. As factors in the acceptance of Arabic derived stems, she suggests duration and intensity of contact and the specific repertoire of inherited derived stems. I would suggest, in addition to those factors, that the close morphological similarities that existed between Arabic and Western Neo-Aramaic, but not other Neo-Aramaic dialects, in the inflection of the TAM paradigms (Table 1) as well as in the inflection for PNG (Table 2) facilitated the borrowing and integration of Syrian Arabic derived stems in Western Neo-Aramaic.

As we have seen, the clear formal parallelism that is reflected in the verbal morphologies of Syrian Arabic and Western Neo-Aramaic correlates with Syrian Arabic influence on both Western Neo-Aramaic verbal inflection and derivational morphology, in the form of pattern replication as well as matter replication, especially in the case of the seventh and eighth Arabic stems. This would suggest a recognition of the parallelism between the morphologies of the Western Neo-Aramaic and Syrian Arabic verbs at some level on the part of the speakers of Western Neo-Aramaic.

3.3. Background to the Divergences in the Verbal System: Shared Functions and Morphosyntactic Contexts of Cognate Syrian Arabic and Western Neo-Aramaic Verbal Paradigms

Table 1 presents the cognate TAM paradigms of Syrian Arabic and Western Neo-Aramaic. Pattern replication appears to be common in many languages with respect to TAM (Matras 2009, 236, 248–49), yet in this category significant divergences are found between the two languages, as shown in Section 4 below.

The divergences in the uses of the verb forms are striking in light of the functions and morphosyntactic patterns in which the Western Neo-Aramaic *qtal* and *yiqtol* conjugations parallel cognate and similar-sounding *qatal* and *yiqtol* conjugations of Syrian Arabic. These are covered in this section. In the examples below I use the following glosses for the verbal paradigms: QTL: *qtal* (Western Neo-Aramaic)/*qatal* (Syrian Arabic), YQTL: *yiqtol* (Western Neo-Aramaic and Syrian Arabic), QĀTL: *qātel* (Syrian Arabic historical active participle), QŌTL: *qōtel* (Western Neo-Aramaic historical active participle), and QTĪL: *qtīl/qattīl* (Western Neo-Aramaic historical resultative participle).

The shared functions of Western Neo-Aramaic *qtal* and *yiqtol* and cognate *qatal* and *yiqtol* of Syrian Arabic are likely to be the outcome of independent development in each language or possibly shared retention in the case of *qatal/qtal*, and not language contact.

To these shared functions, however, contact between Western Neo-Aramaic and Syrian Arabic has added very extensive matter replication of Syrian Arabic content and function words, and multiword expressions (§2). This has resulted in numerous contexts in which Western Neo-Aramaic corresponds to Syrian Arabic at two levels: (i) At the level of the verbal form, its *qtal* and *yiqtol* forms match cognate *qatal* and *yiqtol* of Syrian Arabic in both function and sound; (ii) At the level of the construction, replicated elements, such as lexical items loaned from Arabic, match forms in Syrian Arabic, in meaning (in the case of calques), or in both meaning and sound (in the case of materially replicated lexical borrowings).

These contexts created a potential for bilingual speakers of Western Neo-Aramaic and Syrian Arabic to match Syrian Arabic forms with cognate, similar-sounding Western Neo-Aramaic forms (i.e. pivot-matching), by way of analogy, in other contexts where these cognate forms did not function as in Syrian Arabic. This type of contact-induced analogical levelling is known cross-linguistically (Matras 2009, 237). In Section 4, we shall see that despite this potential, such analogical pattern replication did not occur.

The *qatal* conjugation (Syrian Arabic) and *qtal* conjugation (Western Neo-Aramaic) express the general past tense in both languages. This shared function exists in Late Aramaic and Classical Arabic, and is either a parallel innovation or even a feature of Central Semitic to which both languages belong. In example (5a), taken from the Syrian Arabic dialect of ʿAyn et-Tīne, an Arabic-speaking village situated about three and a half kilometres to the south of Maʿlūla, the *qatal* form *žāb* 'he brought' is past relative to the moment of speaking reflected in the initial clause beginning with *badd-i* 'I wish'. Similarly in (5b) from the Western Neo-Aramaic dialect of Baxʿa, the *qtal* form *ććaffq-iṯ* 'I agreed' is past relative to the moment of speaking, which is reflected in the preceding verb *amar-∅* 'he said' and the direct speech that follows it.

(5)

a. Syrian Arabic (ʿAyn et-Tīne)

badd-i	*∅-ḥki-l-kun*	*ʾiṣṣa*
desire-1s	1s-tell.YQTL-to-2PL	story
ʿan	*Žiḥi…*	*marṛa*
about	Žiḥi…	once
žāb-∅	*əʾrūn*	
bring.QTL**-3**MS	horn.PL	

'I wish to tell you a story about Žiḥi … once he brought horns.' (Behnstedt 2000, 360:1, 3)

b. Neo-Aramaic (Baxʿa)

amar-∅…	*ōṯ*	*aḥḥaḏ*	*sʿūḏay-∅*
say.QTL-3	EXIST	one	saudi-MS
ććaffq-iṯ	*ʿemm-i*		
agree.QTL-1s	with-3MS		

'He said: "… there is a Saudi with whom I agreed…"' (Arnold 1989, 198:16)

The *yiqtol* conjugation is found in both languages in many parallel contexts. In main clauses it functions as a modal form, expressing irrealis (i.e. non-indicative) moods. This modal function is a parallel innovation in both languages. *Yiqtol* already developed into an irrealis mood in the documented Late Western Aramaic dialects. As in many other dialects of Spoken Arabic, though, in Syrian Arabic *yiqtol* can also appear with a number of preverbal particles that express TAM categories such as indicative and progressive (see §4.1.). Therefore, bare *yiqtol* is transcribed in the examples as *∅-yiqtol*, and glossed as MOD, i.e. modal.

A context shared by both languages in which *yiqtol* expresses deontic modality is formulas of blessings (6a, c) and curses (6b, d). This modal function of *yiqtol* already appears in Late Aramaic. In Middle Arabic as well, *yiqtol* is commonly found in this use, in contrast to Classical Arabic, which mostly employs the suffix conjugation *qatala*, the precursor of later Arabic *qatal*, in such formulas (Blau 2002, 45).

(6)

a. Syrian Arabic (ʿAyn et-Tīne)

al̤l̤a	*∅-y-xallī-∅-l-ak*	*abū-k*
God	MOD-3M-leave.YQTL-S-for-you.MS	father.CST-2MS

'May God preserve your father.' (Arnold 1987, 368:80)

b. Syrian Arabic (ʿAyn et-Tīne)

ʾal-ū-l-u	*∅-yi-xrib-∅*	*bēt-ak*
say.QTL-3PL-to-him	MOD-3M-destroy.YQTL-S	house.CST-2MS

'They said to him: "May [God] destroy your house."' (Behnstedt 2000, 368:101)

c. Neo-Aramaic (Maʿlūla)

y-ṭawwlel-∅-l	*ʿomr-ax*	*Alō*
3M-lengthen.YQTL-S-DOM	life.CST-2MS	God

'May God lengthen your life.' (Arnold 1991, 24:47)

d. Neo-Aramaic (Baxʿa)

amr-il-l-un	*alō*	*y-ḥurpel-∅-l*
say.QTL-1s-to-them	come.IMP-2FS	eat.IMP-2S

payṯ-ay-xun
house-PL.CST-2PL

'I said to them: "May God destroy your houses."' (Arnold 1989, 204:83)

Many of the blessing and curse formulas in Western Neo-Aramaic, including (6c, d) replicate multiword expressions in Syrian Arabic, similarly to example (4b) above. This is detailed in the following paragraphs. As with (4b), the replication is mostly at the level of the lexicon and lexical semantics, whereas the morphosyntax is that of Western Neo-Aramaic. For instance, in both (6c) and (6d) the definiteness of the direct object nominal is expressed through the verbal suffix *-l*. Nonetheless, these replicated expressions largely match the model Syrian Arabic expressions in sound and function, both at the level of the replicated lexical elements and of the cognate *yiqtol* forms.

In (6c) from Maʿlūla, both the verbal lexeme *ṭwl* (stem II) 'lengthen' and the noun *ʿomr-a* 'life' are material replications of Syrian Arabic *ṭwl* (stem II) 'lengthen' and the noun *ʿomr* 'life'.

The curse in Neo-Aramaic example (6d) is noteworthy in that, unlike (6c) or (4b), it does not materially replicate the parallel Syrian Arabic expression, which appears in (6b), but matches it with cognate, similar-sounding forms. Most conspicuous is the matching of the Syrian Arabic verbal root *xrb* (6b) in the first stem with the cognate Western Neo-Aramaic verbal root *ḥrb* 'destroy', also in the first stem. The first radical of the Aramaic root /ḥ/, matches /x/ in Syrian Arabic, even though /ḥ/ and /x/ are discrete phonemes in Western Neo-Aramaic. The expression itself is not necessarily a replication of Arabic. At the very least, the root *ḥrb* 'destroy', as well as the collocation *ḥrb* + *byt* 'house' occur in a variety of earlier Aramaic dialects, such as Christian

Palestinian Aramaic, a dialect of Late Western Aramaic: *šbyq l-kwn* ***byt-kn ḥrb*** 'your **house** is left to you **desolate**' (Matthew 23:38).

In the Neo-Aramaic story in which (6d) appears, the curse formula appears in direct speech, in a conversation between a Neo-Aramaic speaker and a group of Syrian Arabs, which no doubt took place in Syrian Arabic. This would indicate that for the narrator, the curse in (6d) actually represents the common Syrian Arabic curse in (6b). The use of a very similarly sounding formula, however, in which Arabic *xrb* is matched with Aramaic *ḥrb*, again points to the recognition on the part of bilingual speakers of Western Neo-Aramaic and Arabic of the parallelisms in sound and structure between the two languages. A similar case of matching of similar-sounding, though not identical, cognate verbal roots between Aramaic and Arabic occurs below, example (10).

The overlapping use of the *yiqtol* conjugation in the two languages is also very obvious in specific constructions, shared by both languages, in which *yiqtol* consistently appears in embedded clauses. Here too, Western Neo-Aramaic is matched with Syrian Arabic at two levels. The cognate *yiqtol* forms match in sound and modal function, and the constructions more generally overlap in their functions, lexical components and morphosyntax.

For example, in both languages, *yiqtol* is the embedded verb form in the modal complement of verbs of ability. Also this use is found in earlier varieties of Aramaic and Arabic. It is likely to be an independent innovation in both languages and not the direct result of contact between Syrian Arabic and Western Neo-Aramaic. On the other hand, ability is expressed in both languages by the same matrix verbal lexeme, which Western Neo-Aramaic has replicated from Syrian Arabic. In Syrian Arabic, the verb *qdr* and its variant *ġdr* 'be able' is the most common matrix verb of ability, as seen in (7a), from the village of Ğrēğir, located around thirty kilometres North-East of Maʿlūla. This lexeme has been borrowed into Western Neo-Aramaic as *qtr*, in the forth stem *aqtar* 'be able' and is also widely used (7b).

(7)

a. Syrian Arabic (Ǧrēǧir)

ma	***ġidr-u***	*∅-**y-saww-u***	*f-ī*	*šī*
not	**able.**QTL-3PL	MOD-3M-**do.**YQTL-PL	in-him	thing

'**They were** not **able to do** anything with him.' (Behnstedt 2000, 354:13, and see also Cowell 1964, 348 [17])

b. Neo-Aramaic (Maʕlūla)

lōfaš	*∅-**maqətr-a***	***č-iḏeʕ***
not	**3-able.**QŌTL-FS	3FS-**know.**YQTL

'**She is** not **able to know.**' (Arnold 1991, 8:7)

Other specific constructions that are shared by both languages make use of the Arabic pseudo-verb *badd-* 'desire', which has been replicated in the Western Neo-Aramaic dialects of Maʕlūla and Baxʕa as *batt-*. In both languages, these forms appear with pronominal suffixes and a modal complement. The basic function of Syrian Arabic *badd-* (8a) and the replicated form *batt-* (8b) is to express volition. The Western Neo-Aramaic dialect of Ǧubbʕadīn uses the native Aramaic form *bēl-* (8c) in place of *badd-/batt-*. Like *badd-*, *bēl-* appears with possessive suffixes and a modal complement and expresses volition. Correll (1978, 219) posits that the form *bēl-* developed from *bʕē*, the resultative participle of *bʕy* 'desire' + the preposition *l-* 'to'.

(8)

a. Syrian Arabic (ʿAyn et-Tīne)

badd-i	*∅-∅-**ḥki-l-kun***	*ʾiṣṣa*
desire-1s	MOD-**1s-tell.**YQTL-**to-you.**PL	story

'**I wish to tell** you a story.' (Behnstedt 2000, 360:1)

b. Neo-Aramaic (Baxʿa)

amər-laḥ-l-i	***batt-aḥ***	***n-zē-ḥ***
say.QTL-1PL-to-him	**desire-**1PL	**1-go.**YQTL-1PL
ʿa	*sʿudōyṯa*	
to	Saudi.Arabia	

'We said to him: "**We wish to go** to Saudi Arabia."' (Arnold 1989, 198:6)

c. Neo-Aramaic (Ǧubbʿadīn)

b-aḥ	***n-aḥəč***	*ext*
desire-1PL	**1-tell.**YQTL	how
∅-ṭōqn-an	*ḥaml-ōṯa*	
3-become.QŌTL-FPL	flood-FPL	

'**We wish to tell** [you] how floods occur.' (Arnold 1989, 198:6)

The same construction of pseudo-verb with pronominal suffix and modal complement in *yiqtol* has been expanded to express purpose. Again, this shared function is expressed in Syrian Arabic through *badd-* (9a), in the Western Neo-Aramaic dialects of Maʿlūla and Baxʿa through the Arabic loanword *batt-* (9b), and in the dialect of Ǧubbʿadīn, by means of the native Aramaic *bēl-* (9c). Such purpose clauses are often embedded by motion verbs.

(9)

a. Syrian Arabic (ʿAyn et-Tīne)

iž-u	*hadōli*	***badd-un***
come.QTL-3PL	these	**desire**-3MPL

∅-yi-ʾətl-ū
MOD-3M-**beat.**YQTL-PL.**him**

'These [men] came **in order to beat him.'** (Behnstedt 2000, 362:25)

b. Neo-Aramaic (Maʿlula)

ṯō-l-un	***batt-ayy***	***y-xuṭb-un-na***
come.QTL-to-3MPL	**desire**-3MPL	3M-**betroth.**YQTL-PL-**her**

'They came in order to betroth her.' (Arnold 1991, 26:74)

c. Neo-Aramaic (Ǧubbʿadīn)

∅-qōym-a	*∅-ṯy-ō-l-a*	*hō*
3-rise.QŌTL-FS	3-come.QŌTL-FS-to-her	this.FS
ḥarīmča…	***bēl-a***	***č-laṭṭaʿen-ne***
woman…	**desire**-3FS	3FS-**form.**YQTL-**it**

'The woman comes … in order to form it.' (Arnold, 1990a, 22, 3:5)

A precursor to *bēl-*, based on the resultative participle of *bʿy*, is not found in Late Western Aramaic as a matrix predicate taking a volitional clause. Rather, Late Western Aramaic employs active forms, including the active participle of *bʿy* for this purpose. Considering this, as well as the similarity between of the morphosyntax of *bēl-* and Arabic *badd-*, it is not unlikely that *bēl-* replicates the morphosyntactic pattern of Arabic *badd-*.

4. The Divergences between Western Neo-Aramaic and Syrian Arabic Cognate Verb Forms

The previous sections provide the background to this section, which is the main focus of the article. This section shows how despite the potential for Syrian Arabic verbal forms to be functionally matched with cognate Western Neo-Aramaic verbal forms, with respect to the expression of TAM, Western Neo-Aramaic preserves the independent functions of its verbal forms.

It was shown in the previous sections that a combination of factors created the potential for matching: (i) Similarity in morphology and sound between cognate verbal forms; (ii) Functions of the suffix conjugation (Arabic *qatal* and Aramaic *qtal*), and prefix cojugation (Aramaic and Arabic *yiqtol*) that were already shared between the two languages as a result of independent parallel development; (iii) the fact that Western Neo-Aramaic reflects a very large degree of material replication of Syrian Arabic lexicon, pattern replication of Syrian Arabic words and multiword expressions (calques) and the combination of both. As a result numerous contexts arose in which Syrian Arabic is matched with Western Neo-Aramaic, both at the level of the verbal form and at the level of the syntactic construction or multiword expressions.

4.1. Parallel Functions Performed by Non-cognate Forms

This sub-section presents the first type of divergence between Syrian Arabic and Western Neo-Aramaic verbal morphosyntax. Here, Western Neo-Aramaic and Syrian Arabic share a verbal function but do not mark it with a shared historically cognate verbal paradigm. Western Neo-Aramaic employs a different verbal paradigm, even though it has inherited a paradigm that is cognate and similarly-sounding to the Syrian Arabic paradigm. This contrasts with examples (5–9), in which the shared historical descent and the sound-similarity of the *qatal/qtal* and *yiqtol* paradigms correlates with parallel functions in the two languages.

The first example is the non-past indicative. Syrian Arabic and Western Neo-Aramaic each possess such a form, with parallel usages, one of which is to express the general or simple present. The form is *b-yiqtol* (10a) in Syrian Arabic, consisting of the preverb *b-* and the *yiqtol* paradigm. The *∅-yiqtol* paradigm, i.e. the form without the preverb, is used in the irrealis mood and modal complements (examples [6–9]). In the glosses, I mark this preverbal particle *b-* as IND. In Western Neo-Aramaic, however, the same function of non-past indicative is expressed by the *qōtel* paradigm, which is cognate with the Syrian Arabic *qātel* paradigm. Both are historically the active participle.

(10)

a. Syrian Arabic (ʿAyn et-Tīne)

lə-ḥʾūl	*ʿan-na*	***b-i-samm-ū-ha***
DEF-field.PL	at-us	IND-**3-call.**YQTL-PL-**her**
miṯl	*əl-ḥwekīr*	
like	DEF-ḥwekīr	

'**They call our** fields "ḥwekīr" = our fields are called "ḥwekīr."' (Arnold 1987, 1:7)

b. Neo-Aramaic (Maʿlūla)

šužžōtča	***∅-mšammy-il-l-a***
šužžōtča	**3-call.**QŌTL-MP-**to-her**

'**They call it** "šužžōtča" = it is called "šužžōtča."' (Arnold 1991, 264:40)

Examples (10a) and (10b) are very similar to examples (6–9) in that Western Neo-Aramaic (10b) parallels a Syrian Arabic construction (10a). But whereas in (6–9) both languages employ *yiqtol* within the parallel constructions, here Western Neo-Aramaic employs *qōtel* where where Arabic employs *b-yiqtol*.

The Aramaic expression in (10b) relates to the Arabic expression in (10a) very similarly to the way Aramaic (6d) relates to Arabic (6a) above. There the Syrian Arabic verbal root *xrb* is matched in Western Neo-Aramaic with cognate *ḥrb* within a shared expression, both appearing in the first stem. Here, Syrian Arabic *smy* 'call' (10a) is paralleled by the cognate Aramaic root *šmy* 'call' (10b), both in the second stem, also within a shared expression. Both verbs appear in the 3MPL form, which constitutes a shared impersonal construction. In both languages the verbal root is derived from the noun for 'name', which is *ʾism* in Arabic and *ušm-a* in Western Neo-Aramaic. As with *ḥrb* in (6d), the derived verbal root *šmy* 'call' in (10b) is documented in earlier Aramaic, as is its use in the second stem as in (10b). Therefore, this parallel derivation of *smy* and *šmy* from the respective nouns *ʾism* and *ušm-a* 'name' in both languages is not likely to be the result of language contact. Still, the selection of this expression or preference for it in Western Neo-Aramaic might well have been influenced by the existence of a similar expression in Syrian Arabic. This adds to the general impression that bilingual speakers of Western Neo-Aramaic and Syrian Arabic recognise the parallelisms between the two languages.

It should be noted that Western Neo-Aramaic shares a preverbal particle *ʿam(mal)-* with Syrian Arabic, which marks progressive, continuous and habitual aspects (Correll 1978, 61–2; Grotzfeld 1965, 84, 87). The specific uses of this shared particle in both languages are beyond the scope of this article, and warrant a separate study, which I aim to undertake in a future publication. Nonetheless, in Syrian Arabic this preverbal particle appears with either the *∅-yiqtol* or *b-yiqtol* paradigms. In the Syrian Arabic texts published by Arnold (1987) and Behnstedt (2000) from the Qalamun region, where Western Neo-Aramaic is spoken, *ʿam(mal)-* is most commonly found with *∅-yiqtol*. In Western Neo-Aramaic it appears with the *qōtel* paradigm and not with the *yiqtol* paradigm.

Another verbal function where the two languages diverge is the expression of perfect aspect. The perfect is an innovation in both Western Neo-Aramaic and Syrian Arabic but the two languages use distinct verbal forms. The paradigm that expresses perfect aspect in Syrian Arabic, illustrated in (11a, b) is *qātel*, an innovation that is widespread in Spoken Arabic, also outside of the Levant (Brustad 2000, 182–84). This is historically the active participle of which the reflexes in Western Neo-Aramaic, namely *qōtel*, express the general present. In Western Neo-Aramaic, however, the perfect is not expressed by cognate *qōtel*, but by means of the *qtīl/qattīl* paradigm, the Aramaic resultative participle. Judging from the testimony of documented forms of Late Aramaic, this innovation crystalised in Western Neo-Aramaic after the Late Aramaic period. The morphological patterns *qtīl/qattīl*, which are used in the first stem, have been inherited from earlier Aramaic. In (11c), the pattern *qtīl* is reflected in the historically transparent form *ṭmir-* of the first stem. In the other stems, the older Aramaic forms of the resultative participles with initial *m-* such as **mqattal*, **maqtal* for the second and fourth stems respectively, have not been preserved, in contrast to some of the Eastern Neo-Aramaic dialects (e.g. Khan 1999, 94; Fassberg 2010, 96). They have been replaced with innovative forms, created by analogy with the pattern *qtīl* of the first stem. In (11d) this is exemplified by the form *hirreb-*, reflecting the innovative pattern *qittīl* of the second stem. Two features have been expanded from *qtīl* of the first stem to the rest of the stems, namely, the lack of initial *m-*, and the vowel *ī*, which in *hirreb-* is realised as *e* (see Spitaler 1938, 211, §187l; Arnold 1990b, 82, 252).

(11)

a. Syrian Arabic (ʿAyn et-Tīne)

tʿažžab-u	*hadōli*	***žayy-īn***
wonder.QTL-PL	those	**come.**QĀTL-MPL
yi-ʾətl-u	*žiḥi*	
3-beat.YQTL-PL	Žiḥi	

'Those who **had come** to beat Žiḥi wondered.'
(Behnstedt 2000, 362:31)

b. Syrian Arabic (ʿAyn et-Tīne)

ʾal-l-ha	*iži-t*	*il-ʾarmbi*
say.QTL-to-3FS	come.QTL-3FS	DEF-rabbit.FS
ma	***mwaṣṣī-∅-ha***	*ʾabəl*
REL	**ask.QĀTL-MS-her**	before
yōm		
day		

'He said to her [=his wife]: "Did the rabbit come?"' [in other words,] what he had asked of her [=his wife] the day before.' (Behnstedt 2000, 368:79)

c. Neo-Aramaic (Maʿlūla)

eččṭ-il	*malka*	*nša-čč-il*
wife-CS	king	forget.QTL-3FS-DOM
santūqa	*ti*	***∅-ṭmir-∅-lē-la***
box	REL	**3-bury.QTĪL-MS-DO-for.her**
beʿl-a		
husband-her		

'The wife of the king forgot the box that her husband **had buried** for her.' (Arnold 1991, 20:12)

d. Neo-Aramaic (Baxʿa)

ḥmi-nnaḥ	*bikāp*	*urdunōy-∅*
see.QTL-1PL	pickup.MS	Jordanian-MS
up-p-a	*šaġġil-ō*	*surōy-in*
EXIST-in-her	worker-MPL	Syrian-MPL
∅-hirreb-∅-l-un		
3-smuggle.QTĪL-MS-**to**-3MPl		

'We saw a Jordanian pickup truck, in which there are [=were] Syrian workers which he [=our driver] had smuggled.' (Arnold 1989, 202:75)

Examples (10–11) reflect two TAM functions that are shared between Syrian Arabic and Western Neo-Aramaic, namely, the expression of the general present and the expression of the perfect aspect. In (10) the Syrian Arabic expression even appears to be matched in Western Neo-Aramaic by elements such as a cognate verbal root and stem, and identical impersonal construction. What is noteworthy here, however, is that there is no matching between Arabic and Aramaic morphological forms, as was the case with *qatal/qtal* and with *yiqtol*, whose patterns of use and morphological forms were matched in the two languages (see §3.3.).

In the construction in (10) there would have been a potential to match in the same way the element *yiqtol* in Syrian Arabic *b-yiqtol* with the cognate and similar-sounding form *yiqtol* in Western Neo-Aramaic. On the basis of the many shared contexts where cognate and similar-sounding *yiqtol* forms in Aramaic and Arabic are matched in their function (§3.3.), the bilingual speakers of Western Neo-Aramaic and Syrian Arabic could have reanalised Aramaic *yiqtol* as *∅-yiqtol*, replicating the Syrian Arabic pattern of verbal morphology that characterises its *yiqtol* paradigm. Subsequently, preverbal prefixes could have been replicated in Aramaic, such as the Syrian Arabic preverbal particle *b*, to express the indicative. We have seen that matter replication of an Arabic preverbal particle is already attested in Western Neo-Aramaic with *ʿam(mal)-*. Despite this potential, however, Western Neo-Aramaic uses a non-matching morphological form for expressing the general present.

Similar potential would have existed to match Syrian Arabic *qātel* with the cognate and similar-sounding Western Neo-Aramaic Neo-Aramaic *qōtel* to express the perfect. Nonetheless, a non-matching morphological form is used in Western Neo-Aramaic.

4.2. Divergences in Verbal Function in which Western Neo-Aramaic Marks Distinctions Absent from Syrian Arabic

In this section I present the most striking category of divergences between the Western Neo-Aramaic verbal paradigms and those of Syrian Arabic with respect to the expression of TAM, when we consider the general background presented in Sections 2–3, especially 3.3. The two divergences are revealed by examining two syntactic constructions in Syrian Arabic and Western Neo-Aramaic and comparing the verbal forms used in them in each language.

The constructions in question are both embedded clauses, namely, phasal complements of the matrix verb 'begin' and protases of counterfactual conditions. We shall see that Western Neo-Aramaic preserves a more complex pattern of embedding than Syrian Arabic with respect to these constructions. This fact is in itself noteworthy. As pointed out in the introduction, the preservation of independent morphosyntactic patterns with these constructions appears to go against Matras's suggestion (2009, 244 and see also ibid., 248–50) that such embedded constructions are typically among the first in the replica language to converge with the patterns of the model language.

The special significance of these divergences, however, is that in these two respective constructions Syrian Arabic *yiqtol* is matched in Western Neo-Aramaic by *qōtel*, and Syrian Arabic *qatal* is matched by Western Neo-Aramaic *yiqtol*. By contrast, in

Section 3.3. we saw various other contexts in which Syrian Arabic *qatal* and *yiqtol* are matched in their function with cognate and similar-sounding Western Neo-Aramaic *qtal* and *yiqtol*. Those contexts where cognate *qatal/qtal* and cognate *yiqtol* have the same function in both languages would have created a potential for the levelling of the Western Neo-Aramaic grammatical distinction by analogy with Syrian Arabic. Despite this potential, levelling has not occurred.

The first syntactic construction is that of phasal complements of the matrix verb 'begin'. In Syrian Arabic, the morphosyntax of modal and phasal complements are similar. The complement is in the ∅-*yiqtol* form (Grotzfeld 1965, 90, §e1). By contrast, Western Neo-Aramaic clearly differentiates between modal (e.g. denoting ability and volition) and phasal complements. Like Syrian Arabic, modal complements follow the matrix verb in *yiqtol* form, but unlike Syrian Arabic, phasal complements take *qōtel* forms.

This is striking given that the Aramaic matrix verbs of phasal complements are likely to be calques of those found in Syrian Arabic. One such verb that takes phasal complements in Western Neo-Aramaic is *ṯqn*, which Arnold and Behnstedt (1993, 64) identify as a calque of Syrian Arabic *ṣār*. In Syrian Arabic, *ṣār* 'become' is a very common inchoative verbal lexeme, which most commonly takes complements in ∅-*yiqtol* (12a, b). The verb *ṯqn* in Western Neo-Aramaic likewise signifies 'become' and is used in the sense of 'begin' with a complement clause. In contrast to Syrian Arabic *ṣār*, Aramaic *ṯqn* takes a complement in *qōtel* (12c, d).

(12)

a. Syrian Arabic (Ǧrēǧir)

w-ṣōr-∅	***∅-y-karkir-∅***	*hal-mayy*
and-become.QTL-3MS	MOD-3M-**trickle.**YQTL-S	the-water
min	*ǧism-u*	
from	body-his	

'And the water began to flow from his body.' (Behnstedt 2000, 356:36)

b. Syrian Arabic (ʿAyn et-Tīne)

ṣār-u	***∅-y-daʿws-u***	*ʿl-ē*
become.QTL-3PL	MOD-3M-**trample.**YQTL-PL	on-him

‘They began to trample upon it [=the grave].’ (Behnstedt 2000, 370:133)

c. Neo-Aramaic (Maʿlūla)

ṯiqn-aṯ	***∅-marqy-a***
become.QTL-3FS	**3-harass.**QŌTL-FS

‘She began to harass.’ (Arnold 1991, 60:73)

d. Neo-Aramaic (Baxʿa)

ṯiqn-iṯ	***ni-mqalleb-∅***	*b-ā*
become.QTL-1S	**1-turn.**QŌTL-MS	in-her

‘I began to turn it.’ (Arnold 1989, 202:55)

Two other very similar verbal lexemes that are used in the two languages as matrix verbs of phasal complements are Syrian Arabic *qʿd* and Western Neo-Aramaic *qʿy* in the first stem, both meaning ‘sit’. Again despite their close semantics, as in the case of *ṣār* and *ṯqn*, Syrian Arabic *qʿd* embeds a ∅-*yiqtol* form (13a), whereas Western Neo-Aramaic *qʿy* embeds a *qōtel* form (13b).

(13)

a. Syrian Arabic (ʿAyn et-Tīne)

iž-u	***ʾaʿd-u***	***∅-yi-sʾal-ū***
come.QTL-3PL	**sit.**QTL-3PL	MOD-3M-**ask.**YQTL-PL.**him**

‘They came and began to ask him.’ (Behnstedt 2000, 360:7)

b. Neo-Aramaic (Maʕlūla)

qʕō-l-e	***∅-mnažžar-∅***
sit.QTL-to-3MS	**3-work.wood.QŌTL-MS**

'He began to work wood.' (Arnold 1991, 30:125)

The Western Neo-Aramaic morphosyntax reflected in the phasal complements in (12–13), although divergent from that of the parallel Syrian Arabic constructions, is identical to that found in Late Western Aramaic. All three Late Western Aramaic dialects, Samaritan, Christian Palestinian and Jewish Palestinian reflect a parallel distinction to that found in Western Neo-Aramaic between matrix verbs of volition and ability, which commonly embed modal complement clauses with *yiqtol*, and the matrix verb *šry* 'begin' of the second stem, which embeds an active participle (Bunis, forthcoming). This morphosyntactic distinction appears to have been preserved in Western Neo-Aramaic.

The final example that will be presented here is the use of divergent verb forms in Syrian Arabic and Western Neo-Aramaic, in verbal protases of counterfactual conditionals. In this example, Syrian Arabic employs *qatal* or *b-yiqtol*, whereas Western Neo-Aramaic employs *yiqtol* or *qtīl/qattīl* forms. This contrasts with many other contexts (examples [5–9]) in which the two Syrian Arabic finite paradigms *qatal* and *yiqtol* are functionally matched with cognate and similar-sounding Western Neo-Aramaic *qtal* and *yiqtol* and Western Neo-Aramaic *qtīl/qattīl* (the resultative participle) functionally corresponds to Syrian Arabic *qātel* (historically the active participle).

Both Syrian Arabic and Western Neo-Aramaic distinguish between predictive conditions, and those that are highly hypothetical or counterfactual. With regard to the structure of the protasis, however, this distinction is expressed somewhat differently in Syrian Arabic and in Western Neo-Aramaic.

In Syrian Arabic, the distinction between predictive conditions and hypothetical conditions is expressed by the conditional conjunction that introduces the protasis. Predictive protases follow the conjunction *ʾiza, ʾiḏa* (14a, b) whereas highly hypothetical or counterfactual protases are introduced either by *law, lu* or *law la, lu la* (14c) (see Cowell 1964, 331–7; Grotzfeld 1965, 106–7). In both types of conditionals, and in all time references, *qatal* is commonly used, as can be seen in (14a, c). According to Grotzfeld (1965, 106), *qatal* freely interchanges with *b-yiqtol* in conditionals, with all time references. Bruweleit (2015, 161–3), on the other hand, reports that in the closely related Lebanese Arabic dialect of Beirut, *qatal* is used in the protasis in all time references, whereas *b-yiqtol* is only used in conditionals with present or future time reference.

I adduce here examples (14a, b) from the dialect of ʿAyn et-Tīne, which show the interchange of *qatal* and *b-yiqtol* in predictive protases with future time reference introduced by *ʾiḏa*. Example (14c) of a counterfactual condition is taken from a text included in Grotzfeld's grammar of Damascene Arabic. According to the textual context, its time reference is past. The main point here is that neither *∅-yiqtol* nor *qātel* forms are used in any type of protasis in Syrian Arabic, whether predictive, hypothetical or counterfactual. This contradicts Correll's comment that Syrian Arabic is 'not limited, in the protasis of hypothetical sentences, to any specific form, and can also employ the *y*-imperfect [i.e., the *∅-yiqtol* form] here' (1978, 144).[6]

6 '...in der Protasis hypothetischer Sätze ja an keine bestimmte Form gebunden ist und unter anderem hier auch das *y*-Imperfekt zur Anwendung bringen darf' (my translation). Correll (1978, 144, note 267) bases this statement on Bloch (1965, 20–21), but in my view Bloch's examples there are not relevant for Correll's claim.

(14) Syrian Arabic

a. ʿAyn et-Tīne

ʾiḏa	***ʾiža-w***	*b-ti-bʿat-ī-hun*
if	**come.**QTL-3PL	IND-2-send.YQTL-FS-MPL
laʿind-i	*ʿa-l-barrīye*	
to-1S	to-DEF-field	

'If they come, you will send them to me, to the field.' (Behnstedt 2000, 366:68)

b. ʿAyn et-Tīne

iḏa	***b-ti-nzil-∅***
if	IND-**2-go.down.**YQTL-MS
ʿa-ssaʾi	*bi-t-laʾī-∅-ha*
to-irrigated.fields	IND-2-find.YQTL-MS-her
miṯəl	*əžnāyin*
like	gardens

'If you go down to the irrigated fields you will find that they are like gardens.' (Arnold 1987, 1:5)

c. Damascene

lula	***ma***	***rakad-ti***
if	**not**	**run.**QTL-2FS
w	***ʾəl-tī-li***	*mama*
and	**say.**QTL-2FS-**to.me**	mama
ma	*b-a-ʿrf-ek*	*ʾənno*
not	IND-1S-know.YQTL-2FS	that
ʾənti	*bənt-i*	
you.FS	daugther-my	

'If you had not run and said to me "Mama", I wouldn't have known that you are my daughter.' (Grotzfeld 1965, 107)[7]

It should be noted with regard to the verbal forms in the protases in examples (14a, b), that in the published texts the forms are transcribed as ∅*-yiqtol* forms, i.e. *tibʿatīhun* (14a) and *tinzil, tlaʾīha* (14b). I have listened, however, to the recordings of the texts on the Semitisches Tonarchiv website of the University of Heidelberg and have been able clearly to discern the preverb *b-* with all three forms, as I have transcribed in the examples.[8]

In Western Neo-Aramaic, the distinction between predictive and hypothetical or counterfactual conditions is manifested in

7 For the full context see Grotzfeld (1965, 131), third paragraph from the top of the page. In the text on page 131, the conjunction is *lu la*, which I have copied in (14c), whereas the form that appears in the analysis on page 107 is *lu*.

8 The recordings are found respectively at https://heidicon.ub.uni-heidelberg.de/eas/partitions/3/0/316000/316723/ce062ce58090716df9e7b3b019b76a1eae1a2090/audio/mpeg/behnstedt_sprachatlas_s360.mp3 and https://heidicon.ub.uni-heidelberg.de/eas/partitions/3/0/316000/316712/ead2e3bc00501a076568a3b7a0bbe5bab5018f28/audio/mpeg/arnold_aynittine_01.mp3 (both accessed 23 April 2020).

the structure of the protasis in an additional way. Besides the use of different conditional conjunctions, as in Syrian Arabic, to introduce protases of the two conditional sub-types, the distinction between predictive and hypothetical or counterfactual conditions is also expressed through the use of different verb forms within the protasis.

In the most recent texts of Western Neo-Aramaic, namely, those recorded by Arnold, the conjunctions *lōb* (15b), the Arabic loanword *iḏa* (15a) and *lab* are used in the dialects of Maʿlūla, Baxʿa and Ǧubbʿadīn respectively for predictive conditions, while *yīb, yīb, ib/lib* are used respectively in the three dialects for hypothetical and counterfactual conditions (Arnold 1990b, 398–9). Arnold notes in addition, that the Arabic loanword *law* is also used with the latter type of conditions. Another form is found in his texts but not presented in his grammar, namely, *lōla* (15c, d). With respect to the verb form within verbal protases, either *qtal* or *qōtel* is employed with predictive conditionals (15a, b respectively), but with hypothetical or counterfactual conditionals, either *yiqtol* or the resultative participle *qtīl/qattīl* is used (15c, d respectively).

(15) Neo-Aramaic

a. Baxʿa

iḏa	***aḥək-∅***	*mett*
if	**say.**QTL-3MS	something

n-qaṭel-∅-l-i
1-beat.PART-MS-to-3MS

'If he says anything I will kill him.' (Arnold 1989, 206–208:134)

b. Maʿlūla

lōb	***ču***	***č-mayṯē-∅-l***
if	**not**	**2-bring.QŌTL-MS-DEF**
žwōba …	*bann-∅*	*n-quṭ^{əʿ}-l-ēx*
answer…	desire-1MS	1-cut.YQTL-to-2MS
rayš-ax		
head-2MS		

‘If you do not bring the answer … I will cut off your head.’ (Arnold 1991, 142:29)

c. Maʿlūla

lō-la	***n-arəxp-enxun***	*w*
if-not	**1-give.ride.YQTL-2MPL**	and
n-ayṯ-∅-enxun	*la*	*nafḏ-ičxun*
1-bring.YQTL-2MPL	not	arrive.QTL-2MPL

‘If I had not given you a ride and brought you here, you would not have arrived.’ (Arnold 1991, 40)

d. Maʿlūla

lō-la	***∅-ʿayyīz-∅-l-a***	*la*
if-not	**3-need.QTĪL-MS-to-3FS**	not
šaql-∅-a		
take.QTL-3MS-3FS		

‘If he had not needed it, he would not have taken it.’ (Arnold 1991, 80:6)

This distribution of verbal forms was also found in the earlier texts analysed by Correll. The divergence from the Syrian Arabic pattern prompted Correll to suggest that the occurrence of *qtal* forms, in conformity with Arabic, solely in protases of predictive conditions, and their absence from protases of counterfactual conditions was due to insufficient examples of the latter type (Correll 1978, 123–5). Arnold's texts show that this suggestion is not correct. They clearly demonstrate that counterfactual protases in Western Neo-Aramaic consistently differ in their verbal forms from the forms in the corresponding Syrian Arabic constructions.

It is unknown when *yiqtol* and *qtīl/qattīl* began to be used in counterfactual protases in the precursor to Western Neo-Aramaic. This use, however, might well have developed after the Late Aramaic stage (i.e. after the 6th century CE). In Late Western Aramaic, the morphosyntax of counterfactual protases actually resembles that of modern Syrian Arabic and not Western Neo-Aramaic. Counterfactual protases with past time reference contain *qtal* and not *yiqtol* forms. The development of *qtīl/qattīl* into a perfect aspect is also not yet documented in Late Western Aramaic.

On the other hand, the use of *qtal* in Western Neo-Aramaic predictive protases is likely to be an inheritance from older Aramaic, as it is documented in Late Aramaic. This use of *qtal* is another morphosyntactic context, in addition to expressing the general past tense ([5] above), where Syrian Arabic *qatal* is paralleled by cognate and similar-sounding Western Neo-Aramaic *qtal*. Despite these contexts, which could have facilitated the levelling of the Western Neo-Aramaic distinction between predictive protases with *qtal* (or *qōtel*) and counterfactual protases with *yiqtol* and *qtīl/qattīl* by analogy to Syrian Arabic, this levelling has not occurred.

5. Summary and Discussion

This comparative study has demonstrated that despite the prolonged and extensive language contact between two closely related Semitic languages, Western Neo-Aramaic and Syrian Arabic diverge in the way their cognate verbal constructions express TAM. Contact with Arabic has resulted in considerable matter and pattern replication in many Western Neo-Aramaic constructions. In the verbal system, however, contact has not lead to change.

First of all, both languages share features of morphology and phonology due to their common origins, and perhaps relatively conservative nature. Western Neo-Aramaic, which is the most conservative among the Neo-Aramaic dialects, is particularly close to Syrian Arabic in its verbal morphology. The two language groups share four cognate verbal paradigms, namely, *qatal/qtal* (suffix conjugation), *yiqtol* (prefix conjugation) and *qātel/qōtel* (active participle) and the imperative. The PNG inflection in each of these paradigms strongly parallel each other in the two language groups.

Whereas the verbal paradigms of both languages are very close in morphology, they show important differences in their functions. Despite prolonged and close contact with Arabic, Western Neo-Aramaic has not replicated the functions of the cognate Syrian Arabic verbal forms, but has preserved the independent functions of its verbal forms. Such conservatism is significant given their use alongside Syrian Arabic in a largely bilingual setting.

The divergent functions in themselves require no explanation. Arabic and Aramaic innovated independently, whereby their historically cognate paradigms took on different functions. Indeed, many of the distinct functions of the Western Neo-Aramaic verbal forms are already documented in Late Western Aramaic and are likely to have existed in the precursor of Western Neo-Aramaic before it came into intensive contact with Arabic.

The lack of convergence, however, is highly significant, given that there would have been potential for contact-induced change. Specifically, with Western Neo-Aramaic being a minority language, spoken within a largely Arabic-speaking population, we might have expected that the Western Neo-Aramaic verbal paradigms would replicate the patterns of use of the cognate Syrian Arabic paradigms, and take on their functions, but this did not take place.

The phonological and morphological similarities in verbal morphology did facilitate the borrowing of Syrian Arabic derived stems into Western Neo-Aramaic. Such correspondences could potentially have facilitated full convergence in pattern but they did not. Table 4 presents a summary of the comparison of the uses of the Western Neo-Aramaic and Syrian Arabic verbal paradigms for marking TAM, discussed in this article. The constructions that diverge are in bold.

Table 4: Correspondences in the Functions of Syrian Arabic and Western Neo-Aramaic Verbal Paradigms within Parallel Morphosyntactic Contexts

<table>
<tr><th>Functional Context</th><th>Arabic</th><th>Aramaic</th></tr>
<tr><td>General past time
Predictive protases</td><td rowspan="2">qatal</td><td>qtal</td></tr>
<tr><td>Past time counterfactual protases</td><td rowspan="2">qtīl/qattīl (yiqtol)</td></tr>
<tr><td>Perfect aspect</td><td>qātel</td></tr>
<tr><td>Irrealis mood (main clause)
Modal complements</td><td rowspan="2">yiqtol</td><td>yiqtol</td></tr>
<tr><td>Complement of ‘begin’</td><td rowspan="2">qōtel</td></tr>
<tr><td>General present
Predictive protases</td><td>b-yiqtol</td></tr>
</table>

Table 4 indicates four different functional contexts that are shared by Western Neo-Aramaic and Syrian Arabic (in bold), in which the two languages employ non-cognate and non-similar-sounding verbal forms. The significance of these divergences is illuminated by the wider context in which the verbal forms occur in the two languages.

The two most striking contexts of divergent verbal function are phasal complements and counterfactual protases with past time reference. The preservation of these two distinctions in Western Neo-Aramaic through its verbal paradigms is significant in that modal and phasal complement clauses and conditional protases are both embedded structures, which goes against the expectations of Matras's functional-communicative model. The fact that Western Neo-Aramaic preserves more complex patterns of subordination with these structures than is found in Syrian Arabic goes against Matras's suggestion that

> The pressure to converge the inventory of constructions in the repertoire [might be expected] to begin with those that organise complex propositions. We would expect the structure of complement clauses, adverbial clauses, and relative clauses and embeddings as well as the structure of coordination to be targeted first in the process of convergence (Matras 2009, 244 and see also ibid., 248–50).

Western Neo-Aramaic distinguishes between phasal complements in *qōtel* and modal complements, which use *yiqtol*. This distinction has been inherited from Late Western Aramaic. Its preservation, however, is significant in light of the fact that Syrian Arabic uses *yiqtol* for both functions and also given that both languages use *yiqtol* for deontic modality in main clauses. Thus, various morphosyntactic contexts existed, as detailed in Subsection 3.3. and summarised in Table 4, in which both Syrian Arabic and Western Neo-Aramaic employed cognate and similar-sounding *yiqtol*, without a connection to language contact. Language contact, however, added to the similarities in that within these contexts, Western Neo-Aramaic borrowed much Syrian Arabic lexicon (matter replication), or replicated its lexical semantics (pattern replication). This is exemplified in this article with the matter replication of ability verbs *qdr* (Syrian Arabic) as *qtr* (Western Neo-Aramaic), the volitional pseudo-verbs *badd-* (Syrian Arabic) as *batt-* (Western Neo-Aramaic) 'desire', and in various formulas of blessings and curses. The numerous contexts where Syrian Arabic and Western Neo-Aramaic were matched both at the level of the verbal paradigm, i.e. in their use of cognate *yiqtol*, and more widely at the levels of morphosyntax and lexicosyntax would have created the potential for Western Neo-Aramaic to level the inherited distinction between phasal and modal complements, by analogy with Syrian Arabic and use *yiqtol* for both functions. Despite this potential, Western Neo-Aramaic preserves this distinction.

With respect to conditional clauses, similarly, Western Neo-Aramaic distinguishes by means of the embedded verbal paradigm between counterfactual protases with past time reference and predictive protases. The former employs *yiqtol* or *qtīl/qattīl* whereas predictive protases use *qtal* or *qōtel.* This distinction is due to independent innovation in Western Neo-Aramaic, but again, its preservation is significant in light of contact with Syrian Arabic. In Syrian Arabic these two types of conditional protases are not distinguished by means of the verbal paradigm in the same way. *Qatal* is used in both. *B-yiqtol* is also used in predictive protases for present and future time refences. Thus, here too, when considering the wider context of contact between Western Neo-Aramaic and Syrian Arabic, there were constructions in which both languages use cognate and similar-sounding forms, that could have facilitated analogical levelling in Western Neo-Aramaic. Both languages employ *qatal/ qtal* in predictive protases, and to express the general past tense. As discussed in the previous paragraph, the *yiqtol* form used in counterfactual protases in Western Neo-Aramaic is matched with Syrian Arabic *yiqtol* in numerous other shared constructions. These numerous contexts could have created the potential for bilingual speakers of Western Neo-Aramaic and Syrian Arabic to level the Western Neo-Aramaic grammatical distinction between predictive and counterfactual protases, by analogy with Syrian Arabic. Nonetheless, Western Neo-Aramaic preserves this distinction.

Two other cases of divergence concern the expression of the general present and the perfect aspect. The two languages share both of these TAM categories, yet each language expresses it by means of a distinct verbal construction. To express the general present, Syrian Arabic uses *b-yiqtol.* Aramaic, on the other hand, employs *qōtel* (< **qātel*), historically the active participle, and cognate with Syrian Arabic *qātel.* The use of the active participle **qātel-* to express the general present is a common Aramaic innovation, inherited from pre-modern Aramaic. Nonetheless, the wide range of contexts in which Western Neo-Aramaic *yiqtol* parallels Syrian Arabic *yiqtol,* as outlined in the previous paragraphs, could have facilitated analogical replication of Syrian Arabic *b-yiqtol,* on the basis of the cognate *yiqtol* paradigm of Western Neo-Aramaic. The material replication of a Syrian Arabic preverbal particle (such as *b*-) is already documented in Western Neo-Aramaic for *ʿam*(*mal*)-, which, together with *qōtel*, expresses continuous and progressive aspects.

Lastly, the two languages innovated independently in the expression of the perfect aspect. Syrian Arabic expresses the perfect aspect by means of *qātel* (the active participle cognate with Aramaic *qōtel*) but Western Neo-Aramaic by means of *qtīl/qattīl* (the historically resultative participle).

To conclude, the data we examined reflect a recurrent theme: Western Neo-Aramaic preserves the independent morphosyntax of its TAM system despite factors that could have facilitated analogical levelling and reanalysis of its paradigms in conformity with the cognate paradigms of Syrian Arabic. These factors include:

(i) close morphological and phonetic similarity between the Western Neo-Aramaic and Syrian Arabic verbal systems;

(ii) shared inheritance and/or parallel development of the TAM functions of the *qatal/qtal* and *yiqtol* paradigms in the two languages;

(iii) a large degree of replication of Syrian Arabic lexical matter and lexical semantics, which created numerous contexts of shared constructions in which both languages employ common Central Semitic *qatal/qtal* or *yiqtol*;

(iv) indications that bilingual speakers of Western Neo-Aramaic and Syrian Arabic have recognised the structural parallelism between the two languages.

Glossing Abbreviations not in the Leipzig Glossing List

IND	Syrian Arabic preverbal particle *b-*.
DM	Discourse marker.
MOD	Modal.
QĀTL	Syrian Arabic *qātel* paradigm (historical active participle).
QŌTL	Western Neo-Aramaic *qōtel* paradigm (historical active participle).
QTĪL	Western Neo-Aramaic historical resultative participle.
QTL	*qatal* and *qtal* suffix conjugations in Syrian Arabic and Western Neo-Aramaic respectively.
YQTL	*yiqtol* prefix conjugation in Syrian Arabic and Western Neo-Aramaic

References

Arnold, Werner. 1987. 'Text I aus ʿĒn iṭ-Ṭīne: Aus der Landwirschaft'. Text and translation published on the website of the Semitisches Tonarchiv (http://semarch.ub.uni-heidelberg.de/).

———. 1989. *Das Neuwestaramäische*. Vol. 1, *Texte aus Baxʿa*. Semitica Viva 4/I. Wiesbaden: Harrassowitz.

———. 1990a. *Das Neuwestaramäische*. Vol. 2, *Texte aus Ǧubbʿadīn*. Semitica Viva 4/II. Wiesbaden: Harrassowitz.

———. 1990b. *Das Neuwestaramäische*. Vol. 5, *Grammatik*. Semitica Viva 4/V. Wiesbaden: Harrassowitz.

———. 1991. *Das Neuwestaramäische*. Vol. 4, *Orale Literatur aus Maʿlūla*. Semitica Viva 4/IV. Wiesbaden: Harrassowitz.

———. 2002. 'Zur Geschichte der arabischen Lehnwörter im Neuwestaramäischen'. In *Neue Beiträge zur Semitistik: erstes Arbeitstreffen der Arbeitsgemeinschaft Semitistik in der Deutschen Morgenländischen Gesellschaft vom 11. bis 13. September 2000 an der Friedrich-Schiller-Universität Jena*, edited by Norbert Nebes, 5–11. Jenaer Beiträge zum Vorderen Orient 5. Wiesbaden: Harrassowitz.

———. 2007. 'Arabic grammatical borrowing in Western Neo-Aramaic'. In *Grammatical Borrowing in Cross-Linguistic Perspective*, edited by Yaron Matras and Jeanette Sakel. 185–95. Empirical Approaches to Language Typology 38. Berlin: Mouton de Gruyter.

Arnold, Werner and Peter Behnstedt. 1993. *Arabisch-Aramäische Sprachbeziehungen im Qalamūn (Syrien)*. Semitica Viva 8. Wiesbaden: Harrassowitz.

Behnstedt, Peter. 2000. *Sprachatlas von Syrien*. Vol. 2, *Volkskundliche Texte*. Semitica Viva 17/II. Wiesbaden: Harrassowitz.

Blau, Joshua. 2002. *A Handbook of Early Middle Arabic*. The Max Schloessinger Memorial Series: Monographs 6. Jerusalem: The Max Schloessinger Memorial Foundation.

Bloch, Ariel. 1965. *Die Hypotaxe im Damaszenisch-Arabischen: Mit Vergleich zur Hypotaxe im Klassisch-Arabischen*. Abhandlungen für die Kunde des Morgenlandes XXXV, 4. Wiesbaden: Steiner.

Bruweleit, Stefan. 2015. *Aspect, Tense and Action in the Arabic Dialect of Beirut*. Studies in Semitic Languages and Linguistics 79. Leiden: Brill.

Brustad, Kristen E. 2000. *The Syntax of Spoken Arabic: A Comparative Study of Moroccan, Egyptian, Syrian, and Kuwaiti Dialects*. Washington D.C.: Georgetown University Press.

Coghill, Eleanor. 2015. 'Borrowing of Verbal Derivational Morphology between Semitic Languages: the Case of Arabic Verb Derivations in Neo-Aramaic'. In *Borrowed Morphology*, edited by Francesco Gardani, Peter Arkadiev and Nino Amiridze, 83–107. Language Contact and Bilingualism 8. Berlin: Mouton de Gruyter.

Correll, Christoph. 1978. *Untersuchungen zur Syntax der neuwestaramäischen Dialekte des Antilibanon (Maˁlūla, Baḫˁa, Gubb ˁAdīn) mit besonderer Berücksichtigung der Auswirkungen arabischen Adstrateinflusses*. Abhandlungen für die Kunde des Morgenlandes XLIV, 4. Wiesbaden: Steiner.

Cowell, Mark W. 1964. *A Reference Grammar of Syrian Arabic (Based on the Dialect of Damascus)*. Arabic Series: Number 7. Washington, D. C.: Georgetown University Press.

Fassberg, Steven E. 2010. *The Jewish Neo-Aramaic Dialect of Challa*. Studies in Semitic Languages and Linguistics 54. Leiden: Brill.

Garbell, Irene. 1965. *The Jewish Neo-Aramaic Dialect of Persian Azerbaijan: Linguistic Analysis and Folkloristic Texts*. Janua Linguarum Studia Memoriae Nicolai Van Wijk Dedicata: Series Practica III. London: Mouton.

Grotzfeld, Heinz. 1965. *Syrisch-Arabische Grammatik (Dialekt von Damaskus)*. Porta Linguarum Orientalium: Neue Serie VIII. Wiesbaden: Harrassowitz.

Häberl, Charles. 2009. *The Neo-Mandaic Dialect of Khorramshahr*. PhD Diss., Rutgers.

Jastrow, Otto. 1985. *Laut- und Formenlehre des neuaramäischen Dialekts von Mīdin im Ṭūr ʿAbdīn*. 3rd Expanded Edition. Wiesbaden: Harrassowitz.

Khan, Geoffrey. 1999. *A Grammar of Neo-Aramaic: The Dialect of the Jews of Arbel*. Handbook of Oriental Studies 47. Leiden: Brill.

——— 2004. *The Jewish Neo-Aramaic Dialect of Sulemaniyya and Ḥalabja*. Studies in Semitic Languages and Linguistics XLIV. Leiden: Brill.

——— 2008. *The Jewish Neo-Aramaic Dialect of Urmi*. Gorgias Neo-Aramaic Studies 2. Piscataway, NJ: Gorgias.

——— 2009. *The Jewish Neo-Aramaic Dialect of Sanandaj*. Gorgias Neo-Aramaic Studies 10. Piscataway, NJ: Gorgias.

———. 2020. 'Contact and Change in Neo-Aramaic Dialects'. In *Historical Linguistics 2017*, edited by Bridget Drinka, 391–411. Amsterdam: Benjamins.

Matras, Yaron. 2009. *Language Contact*. Cambridge: Cambridge University Press.

Noorlander, Paul M. 2014. 'Diversity in Convergence: Kurdish and Aramaic Variation Entangled'. *Journal of Kurdish Studies* 2 (2): 201–224.

Ritter, Helmut. 1990. *Ṭūrōyo: Die Volkssprache der syrischen Christen des Ṭūr ʿAbdîn*. Vol. C, *Grammatik*. Schriften der Wissenschaftlichen Gesellschaft an der Johann-Wolfgang-Goethe-Universität Frankfurt am Main: Geisteswissenschafltliche Reihe; Nr. 6. Stuttgart: Franz Steiner.

Spitaler, Anton. 1938. *Grammatik des neuaramäischen Dialekts von Maʿlūla (Antilibanon)*. Abhandlungen für die Kunde des Morgenlandes XXIII, 1. Leipzig: Deutsche Morgenländische Gesellschaft.

Stowasser, Karl and Moukhtar Ani. 1964. *A Dictionary of Syrian Arabic: English-Arabic*. Arabic Series: Number 5. Washington, D.C.: Georgetown University Press.

ON THE *AFEL* STEM IN WESTERN NEO-ARAMAIC

Steven E. Fassberg

1. Introduction

The historical reconstruction of Aramaic from its earliest attestations to the modern-day dialects can, at times, be difficult. For example, how far back was the dialectal split between the eastern and western branches of Aramaic?[1] The reconstruction at other times, however, can be relatively straightforward. For instance, a basically linear development is discernible in the Aramaic of Syria-Palestine. One begins with the Middle Aramaic attested in the Dead Sea Scrolls, moves on to the Late Aramaic corpora of Jewish Palestinian, Christian Palestinian and Samaritan Aramaic, and concludes with Western Neo-Aramaic.[2]

The study of Western Neo-Aramaic began in 1863 with the publication by Jules Ferrette (1863) of transcriptions of a text and vocabulary items from Maʿlula. Since then, the dialect of Maʿlula has been fortunate that outstanding Semitists have turned their attention to it. The greatest of Semitists, Theodor Nöldeke, commented on Ferrette's material already in 1867, and contributed more insights in an article from 1917–1918

1 The split is fully evident in Late Aramaic (as delineated in Joseph A. Fitzmyer's 1979 classification of the Aramaic periods), but there are indications of a dialectal divide already in Old Aramaic inscriptions. See Greenfield (1968, 1978); and most recently Fales and Grassi (2016). Margaretha Folmer (1995) has shown dialectal differences in the Official Aramaic corpus, which preceded Late Aramaic.

2 Abraham Tal (1979, 1980, 1983) has demonstrated this in a series of articles dealing with different Western Aramaic grammatical phenomena.

 https://doi.org/10.11647/OBP.0209.08

following Gotthelf Bergsträsser's publication of the texts (1915) collected by Eugen Prym and Albert Socin. Many scholars have investigated Western Neo-Aramaic, but three in particular have shaped the field: Bergsträsser with the publication of texts (1915; 1919–1920), a glossary (1921), and a short grammatical description (1928, 80–9), Anton Spitaler with a grammar (1938) and texts (1957), and especially Werner Arnold with an unparalleled wealth of oral texts (1989; 1990_1; 1991_1; 1991_2) as well as a synchronic grammar (1990_2), which includes not only Maᶜlula, but also the two other Western Neo-Aramaic dialects spoken in the nearby villages of Baxᶜa and Jubbᶜadin. Moreover, Arnold has recently published a comprehensive dictionary of the three villages (2019). To date the comparative notes in Spitaler's grammar remain the fullest historical treatment of Maᶜlula. Since the publication of that grammar, however, thanks to the intensive investigation into the literary dialects of Late Western Aramaic and the rich material from Maᶜlula, Baxᶜa, and Jubbᶜadin that Arnold has presented, scholars now have the wherewithal to investigate further the links between older Western Aramaic and Western Neo-Aramaic. A detailed diachronic description of the development of Western Late Aramaic into Western Neo-Aramaic remains a desideratum.

2. Afel

In general, the verbal system of Western Neo-Aramaic has diverged less from earlier Aramaic than have the verbal systems of other varieties of Neo-Aramaic. The morphosyntax of Maᶜlula, Baxᶜa, and Jubbᶜadin is, on the whole, easily derived from older Western Neo-Aramaic forms,[3] though it shares innovations paralleled in other non-Western varieties of Neo-Aramaic, for

3 Yet, there are some noteworthy changes from older Aramaic that are attested in Western Neo-Aramaic, e.g., the prefixing of pronominal morphemes to the old active participle and the penetration of the *qattīl* nominal pattern into the verbal system.

example, the tendency of native Aramaic reflexive-passive *t*-stems to disappear, leaving behind only lexical traces.

I wish to focus on one phenomenon of the verbal system that Spitaler noted in his grammar (1938, §120c) but did not attempt to explain: the presence in Maʕlula of *Afel* verbs that in older Aramaic are inflected in *Peal*, and in Arabic in the 1st form. Spitaler collected a number of such verbs, some of which are frequent in the language. He cited four Aramaic roots: *nḏr* 'praise', *rhṭ* 'run' *xwy* 'burn', *ykl* (*ʾaukel*) 'overpower'. The list of borrowings from Arabic is significantly longer: *ʕṣy* 'be stubborn', *ʕzm* 'invite', *bdw* 'begin', *dʕw* 'curse', *ḍll* 'remain', *dwy* 'echo', *ḍžž* 'rumble, roar', *fzz* 'jump up', *ġḍb* 'be angry', *ġrq* 'fall asleep', *ġyb* 'be absent', *hwn* 'be light', *ḥky* 'speak', *ḥll* 'settle', *ḥqq* 'be right', *ḥrf* 'answer', *ḥss* 'notice', *ksb* 'earn', *ndm* 'regret', *nṭṭ* 'leap, spring up', *qdr* 'be able', *ṣʕd* 'rise, ascend', *ṣbr* 'wait', *ṣḥw* 'guard against', *tʕb* 'become tired', *tmm* 'remain', *wṣf* 'prescribe', *xṣṣ* 'concern, affect', *zʕl* 'be angry', *ẓhr* 'show oneself'. Spitaler commented that most of the verbs are intransitive. I think this fact is significant, as I shall try to show below.

Spitaler (1938, §121) wrote of the tendency in Maʕlula for weak verbs to shift from one verbal category to another. This phenomenon is also true for earlier periods of Aramaic. Spitaler mentioned I-ʾ verbs influencing medial II-*w/y* verbs, and geminates influencing I-*n*. Of relevance to the discussion is the *Afel*-looking participle *mōmar* 'saying' from the root *ʾmr*, whose creation Spitaler (1938, §121, §162b) attributed to a similarity with the II-*w/y Afel* verbal forms and an imperfect analogy of the type

ōqem (*Afel* 'he raised') : *mōqem* (*Afel* 'he raises') ::

ʾōmar (*Peal* 'he says') : X

X = *mōmar*.[4]

Another germane example given by Spitaler (1938, §171b) is the *Afel* verb *appi* 'he gave', which is commonly derived from the

4 The vowel *a* is a reflex of the older Aramaic rule **i > a /_ guttural.*

root *yhb* 'gave' (Bergsträsser, 1928, 84). According to Bergsträsser, a shift such as 3fs **yahbat* > **yabbat* led to an analogy of the type

xassat ('she covered'; III-*y* root) : *appat* ('she gave') ::

xassi ('he covered') : X

X= *appi*.[5]

In his brief discussion, Spitaler did not include as examples of the shift from *Peal* to *Afel* the preterite *Peal* II-w/y *áqam* 'he arose' and *ámet* 'he died', but I believe that the initial vowels in these forms show an incipient move to *Afel*, like *mōmar* and *appi* mentioned above, and thus are relevant to the discussion at hand.

3. Explanation of the Phenomenon

Why is there a movement of older Aramaic *Peal* verbs and Arabic 1st stem verbs to *Afel* in Maʿlula? Is it the result of contact with another language? Is it an internal semantic development in Maʿlula, or can its origins be reconstructed back to an earlier period of Aramaic?

3.1. Contact with Arabic?

Because of the considerable influence of Arabic on Maʿlula and the widescale absorption of Arabic verbs into the vocabulary of Maʿlula, one might be tempted to seek the origins of the phenomenon in the centuries of contact that existed between Aramaic and Arabic in Syria. The mutual influences of the two languages have been described by Arnold and Behnstedt (1993). The authors noted that the Aramaic *Afel* is extremely productive in Western Neo-Aramaic, but that the Arabic 4th stem has mostly disappeared from the spoken Arabic of the Qalamūn area, and those 4th form verbs that have survived reflect the influence of literary Arabic, e.g., *aslam/yislem* 'convert to Islam' (Arnold and

5 As if from the root **npy* (Bergsträsser 1928, 84). Spitaler noted that speakers could interpret the form as the *Pael* of a root **ʾpy*.

Behnstedt 1993, 57–58). In his description of the Damascene dialect, Heinz Grotzfeld (1965, 27) gave more examples of literary 4th stem forms that appear in the vernacular: *ʾazhar* 'bloom', *ʾaḥka* 'speak', *ʾaznab* 'sin', *ʾamkan* 'be able', *ʾaṣbaḥ* 'become', *ʾaxṭa* 'sin'. Arnold and Behnstedt pointed out that sometimes the Aramaic *Afel* verbs of Arabic etymology are derived not only from 4th form verbs, but also from 1st form verbs and from nouns:

Arabic		Aramaic
ʿutma 'darkness'	>	*ʿačem* 'become dark'
ġiriq fi nnawm 'fall asleep'	>	*ʿaġreḳ* 'fall asleep'
ʿazam 'invite'	>	*aʿzem* 'invite'
bada 'begin'	>	*abət* 'begin'
ḍall 'remain'	>	*ōḍel* 'remain'

The merger of the 4th and 1st forms in many Neo-Arabic dialects has been attributed to phonetic factors—the aphaeresis of the initial *alif* in the Perfect (*ʾafʿala* > *fʿal*) and Imperative *ʾafʿil* > *fʿel* as well as the conditioned neutralisation of *u* and *i*, which led to blurring of the distinction between the Imperfect of both forms: *yufʿil* > *yəfʿel*.[6] A confusion of 1st and 4th forms is known already in Middle Arabic texts, where it is especially common in geminates and other weak verbs.[7] In the light of the movement from the 4th form to the 1st form in the Neo-Arabic of the region, it is clear that the Aramaic phenomenon in Maʿlula of the shift of *Peal* to *Afel* cannot be attributed to Arabic influence.

---

6 Nöldeke (1904, 36); Blau (1966, §51.2, n. 44); Fischer and Jastrow (1980, 46). In the Damascene dialect, the meaning of the 4th form, on the other hand, is taken over by verbs in the 2nd form (Grotzfeld 1965, 27).

7 Nöldeke (1904, 36); Blau (1966, §51.2); Hopkins (1984, §72).

3.2. Shift of *Peal* to *Afel* in Western Neo-Aramaic

A tendency of *Peal* verbs to shift to *Afel* appears to be unknown in the dialects of NENA, Central Neo-Aramaic, and Mandaic,[8] but does occur in all three Western Neo-Aramaic dialects. Because we possess more oral texts from Maʿlula than from Baxʿa or Jubbʿadin, it is not surprising that there are more examples from Maʿlula than from the other two dialects.

Is the movement from *Peal* to *Afel* an internal semantic development in Maʿlula? In different Semitic languages the C-stem is sometimes intransitive with an ingressive nuance, i.e., entering into a state or condition, e.g., Hebrew הֶאֱדִים 'become red', הִלְבִּין 'become white', Syriac ܐܓܪܒ 'become leprous', ܐܢܗܪ 'begin to shine' and Arabic *ʾaqbala* 'approach', *ʾaslama* 'become a Muslim'.[9] A weakening of ingressivity seems to have led on occasion to a blurring of the difference between verbs that occur in both the G and C stems, and this can be detected, for instance, in Syriac ܗܦܟ and ܐܬܗܦܟ'turn around', and ܟܬܒ and ܐܟܬܒ 'write'.[10] The Hebrew of the Second Temple period—Late Biblical Hebrew, the Hebrew of the Dead Sea Scrolls, and Rabbinic Hebrew—also testifies to the merger of *Qal* and *Hifil*. Some transitive and intransitive *Qal* verbs move to *Hifil*, e.g.,

בָּזָה 'despise' > הִבְזָה,
גָּדֵל 'grow' > הִגְדִּיל,
לָעַג 'mock' > הִלְעִיג.[11]

In the case of a weak verb like יָשִׂים 'he will place', the morphological ambiguity—it can be parsed as *Qal* or *Hifil*—led

8 Other shifts of stems are attested. For example, in Jewish Koy Sanjak (Mutzafi 2004, 75–77) some older *Pael* verbs have integrated into the Koy Sanjak *Peal*, while others have integrated into *Afel*; in Jewish Urmi (Khan 2008, 65–67) older *Pael* stem verbs have merged with *Peal* or with *Afel*; in Jewish Sanandaj (Khan 2009, 65–67) *Pael* has on the whole merged with *Peal*; in Bohtan (Fox 2009, 31–36) *Pael* includes some verbs from older *Peal*.

9 Wright (1896, §45); Leemhuis (1977, 38–42).

10 Duval (1881, §198). ܐܟܬܒ also retains its causative meaning 'dictate'.

11 Moreshet (1976).

to a reinterpretation of the Classical Biblical Hebrew *Qal* in Late Biblical Hebrew as a *Hifil* and the subsequent creation of a passive *Hufal.* Yet, despite the semantic overlapping of G and C in some Semitic languages, I wonder if more is at play in Maᶜlula, and a look at earlier Western Aramaic may provide the key.

3.3. Shift of *Peal* to *Afel* in Earlier Western Aramaic

I propose that the origin of the shift to *Afel* lies in the Late Western Aramaic dialects of Jewish Palestinian, Christian Palestinian, and Samaritan Aramaic. The latter two dialects evidence a general retraction of stress, which led to an increase in prosthetic vowels.[12] Earlier Aramaic corpora have sporadic anaptyctic vowels before consonantal clusters involving sibilants and dentals, however, the helping vowel is not related to a retraction of stress, e.g., Biblical Aramaic אֶדְרָע 'arm', אִשְׁתִּיו 'they drank', Syriac ܐܶܫܟܰܚ 'he found'. In the three dialects of Late Aramaic from Syria-Palestine the number of examples with prosthetic vowels grows considerably. In Christian Palestinian and Samaritan Aramaic the prosthetic vowel sometimes occurs before the word-initial cluster and other times breaks up the cluster:[13]

(1) Jewish Palestinian:

אַדְמָה 'the blood', אִישְׁתָּה 'six', אַרְתַּכָּה 'wagon', אשקק 'lane', אידמיך 'he slept, he died', איזמר 'he pruned', אנהרין 'they (f.) shone'

12 Stress may have shifted back also in Jewish Palestinian Aramaic, but there is no direct evidence for this.

13 Historically, the insertion of a medial vowel in these two dialects is not the preservation of the original full vowel, but rather a secondary lengthening of a reduced vowel (*shewa mobile*). See Bar-Asher (1977, 421–482); Müller-Kessler (1991, §3.1.3.2); Ben-Ḥayyim (2000, §8.9); Tal (2013, §2.3.26). The examples listed here are taken from Bar-Asher (1977); Tal (2000); Sokoloff (2014); Sokoloff (2017).

(2) Christian Palestinian:

ܐܕܡܐ 'the blood', ܐܙܒܢ 'time', ܐܫܡܝܢ/ܫܘܡܝܢ 'heavens', ܐܫܘܩ 'lane', ܐܬܡܘܪܝܢ 'dates', ܡܪܝܡ 'he raises', ܢܫܪ 'we shall sing'

(3) Samaritan:

אדמה 'the blood', *azbån* 'time', אסתב 'winter', אשתה 'six', שומים 'heavens', *åbådåt* 'she made', *anbåqu* 'they (m.) left', *anbåqi* 'they (f.) left'

The creation of prosthetic vowels in *Peal* stems was probably more extensive in Late Aramaic speech than in the written texts that have survived. The assimilation of the *t* of *t*-stems in verbs in these dialects (e.g., Jewish Palestinian' אשתכח > אשכח 'he was found'; Fassberg 2012, 30) may also have been interpreted by speakers as *Peal* intransitive forms with prosthesis. From the vocalisation of Jewish Palestinian, the Samaritan oral tradition, and the use of *matres lectionis* in Christian Palestinian Aramaic, one sees that there were three prosthetic vowels *i*, *ə*, and *a*; the first two appeared more frequently before sibilants.

I would like to suggest that it was the retraction of stress and the subsequent creation of initial epenthetic vowels, a phenomenon that began in Late Western Aramaic, which led in Western Neo-Aramaic to the reinterpretation of *Peal* verbs as *Afel* forms. Maʿlula and Jubbʿadin preserve verbs of the **qatila* type, i.e., intransitive verbs that have a reflex of *e* in the base of the verb in the perfect: *iḏmex* 'he slept', *išmeʿ* 'he heard', *isleq* 'he ascended'.[14] The retraction of the stress and the creation of a prosthetic vowel may have led speakers to associate *Peal* intransitive verbs of the shape *Vqtel* with *Afel* preterite forms. I surmise that this process began with intransitive verbs and then was extended to transitive

14 In Baxʿa speakers have tended to shift **qatila* verbs into the pattern of **qatala*: *idmax* (but still *išmeʿ*). See Arnold (1990_2, §3.1.1).

verbs of the *iqtal* type. I think that indirect corroboration for this reconstruction can be found in the fact that many of the verbs which show up in *Afel* in Maʿlula are indeed intransitive, as noted by Spitaler. Additional pressure for the reinterpretation of *Peal* forms as *Afel* would have come from the II-*w/y* *Peal* verbs in which the retraction of stress created *Afel*-looking forms, e.g.

áqam 'he/they arose' vs. older Aramaic *qām*

ámet 'he died' vs. older *mīṯ*

Although Arabic dialects of the region cannot be responsible for this development, it is curious that the creation of prosthetic vowels before word-initial consonantal clusters in **qatila* verbs can be found in an Arabic dialect in Syria. As pointed out to me by Simon Hopkins, Palmyrene Arabic shows the curious form *ʾönzel* 'he descended', which developed from *nazila* > *nizil* > *ʾönzel.*[15] Unfortunately, Aramaic inscriptions from the same area but from a much earlier period and written in Palmyrene Aramaic give no written indication of prosthesis and a retraction of stress.

4. Conclusion

The shift of *Peal* verbs to *Afel* in Western Neo-Aramaic dialects may have begun in an earlier period of Western Aramaic, probably Late Western Aramaic, in which there was a widespread retraction of stress and subsequent creation of prosthetic vowels that resolved word-initial consonantal clusters. This situation might have led in Proto-Western Neo-Aramaic to the reinterpretation of *Peal Vqtel* (< **qatila*) forms as *Afel* forms. This reanalysis would have been reinforced by the overlap between *Peal* and *Afel* verbs in expressing state and condition. *Peal* and *Afel* did not merge completely in Maʿlula, but a trend, which may have begun much earlier in Western Aramaic, increased significantly in Western Neo-Aramaic.

15 Cantineau (1934, 121). Cf. *katab* 'he wrote' (< **qatala*).

References

Arnold, Werner. 1989. *Das Neuwestaramäische. 1: Texte aus Baxʿa*. Semitic Viva 4.1. Wiesbaden: Harrassowitz.

———. 1990_1. *Das Neuwestaramäische. 2: Texte aus Ǧubbʿadin*. Semitic Viva 4.2. Wiesbaden: Harrassowitz.

———. 1990_2. *Das Neuwestaramäische. 5: Grammatik*. Semitic Viva 4.5. Wiesbaden: Harrassowitz.

———. 1991_1. *Das Neuwestaramäische. 3: Volkskundliche Texte aus Maʕlūla*. Semitic Viva 4.3. Wiesbaden: Harrassowitz.

———. 1991_2. *Das Neuwestaramäische. 4: Orale Literatur aus Maʕlūla*. Semitic Viva 4.4. Wiesbaden: Harrassowitz.

———. 2019. *Das Neuwestaramäische. Teil VI: Wörterbuch: Neuwestaramäisch–Deutsch*. Semitic Viva 4.6. Wiesbaden: Harrassowitz.

Arnold, Werner and Behnstedt, Peter. 1993. *Arabisch-Aramäische Sprachbeziehungen im Qalamūn (Syrien)*. Semitica Viva 8. Wiesbaden: Harrassowitz.

Bar-Asher, Moshe. 1977. מחקרים בסורית של ארץ ישראל: מקורותיה, מסורותיה ובעיות נבחרות בדקדוקה [*Palestinian Syriac Studies: Source-Texts, Traditions and Grammatical Problems*]. Jerusalem: n.p.

Ben-Ḥayyim, Ze’ev. 2000. *A Grammar of Samaritan Hebrew Based on the Recitation of the Law in Comparison with the Tiberian and Other Jewish Traditions*. Jerusalem/Winona Lake, IN: Magnes Press/Eisenbrauns.

Bergsträsser, Gotthelf. 1915. *Neuaramäische Märchen und andere Texte aus Maʕlūla hauptsächlich aus der Sammlung E. Prym’s und A. Socin’s*. Abhandlungen für die Kunde des Morgenlandes 13.2. Leipzig: Deutsche Morgenländische Gesellschaft.

———. 1919–1920. ‘Neue Texte im aramäischen Dialekt von Maʻlūla’. *Zeitschrift für Assyriologie* 32 (1919): 103–163; 33 (1920): 68–69.

———. 1921. *Glossar des neuaramäischen Dialekts von Maʕlūla*. Abhandlungen für die Kunde des Morgenlandes 15.4. Leipzig: Deutsche Morgenländische Gesellschaft.

———. 1928. *Einführung in die semitischen Sprachen: Sprachproben und grammatische Skizzen*. München: Max Hueber.

———. 1933. *Phonogramme im neuaramäischen Dialekt von Malula: Satzdruck und Satzmelodie*. Munich: Verlag der Bayerischen Akademie der Wissenschaften.

Blau, Joshua. 1966. *A Grammar of Christian Arabic Based Mainly on South-Palestinian Texts from the First Millennium*. 3 vols. Corpus Scriptorum Christianorum Orientalium 27–29. Louvain: Secrétariat du CorpusSCO.

———. 2002. *A Handbook of Early Middle Arabic*. Jerusalem: Max Schloessinger Memorial Foundation, Hebrew University of Jerusalem.

Cantineau, Jean. 1934. *Le dialecte arabe de Palmyre. Tome 1: Grammaire*. Beyrouth: Institute français de Damas.

Duval, Rubens. 1881. *Traité de grammaire syriaque*. Paris: F. Vieweg.

Fales, Frederick Mario and Grassi, Giulia Francesca. 2016. *L'aramaico antico: Storia grammatica, testi commentati* con un'appendice paleografica di Ezio Attardo. Fonti et Testi: Raccolta di Archeologia e Storia dell'arte. Udine: Forum.

Fassberg, Steven E. 2012. 't-Stem Verbs without Metathesis in Aramaic and Hebrew Documents from the Judean Desert'. In *Language and Nature: Papers Presented to John Huehnergard on the Occasion of His 60th Birthday*, edited by Rebecca Hasselbach and Na'ama Pat-El, 27–37. Chicago: Oriental Institute of the University of Chicago.

Ferrette, Jules. 1863. 'On a Syriac Language, Still Spoken in the Antilebanon'. *Journal of the Royal Asiatic Society of Great Britain and Ireland* 20: 431–436.

Fischer, Wolfdietrich and Jastrow, Otto. 1980. *Handbuch der arabischen Dialekte*. Porta Linguarum Orientalium Neue Serie 16. Wiesbaden: Harrassowitz.

Fitzmyer, Joseph A. 1979. 'The Phases of the Aramaic Language'. *A Wandering Aramean: Collected Aramaic Essays*, 57–84. Society of Biblical Literature Monograph Series 25. Chico, CA: Scholars Press.

Folmer, Margaretha L. 1995. *The Aramaic Language in the Achaemenid Period: A Study in Linguistic Variation*. Orientalia Lovaniensa Analecta 68. Louvain: Peeters.

Fox, Samuel Ethan. 2009. *The Neo-Aramaic Dialect of Bohtan*. Gorgias Neo-Aramaic Studies 9. Piscataway, NJ: Gorgias Press.

Greenfield, Jonas C. 1968. קווים דיאלקטיים בארמית הקדומה ['Dialect Traits in Early Aramaic'], *Lĕšonénu* 32: 359–368.

———. 1978. 'The Dialects of Early Aramaic'. *Journal of Near Eastern Studies* 37: 93–99.

Grotzfeld, Heinz. 1965. *Syrisch-Arabische Grammatik*, Wiesbaden: Harrassowitz.

Hopkins, Simon. 1984. *Studies in the Grammar of Early Arabic Based upon Papyri Datable to before 300 A.H./912 A.D.* London Oriental Series 37. Oxford: Oxford University Press.

Khan, Geoffrey. 2008. *The Jewish Neo-Aramaic Dialect of Urmi*. Gorgias Neo-Aramaic Studies 2. Piscataway, NJ: Gorgias Press.

———. 2009. *The Jewish Neo-Aramaic Dialect of Sanandaj*. Gorgias Neo-Aramaic Studies 10. Piscataway, NJ: Gorgias Press.

Leemhuis, Frederik. 1977. *The* D *and* H *Stems in Koranic Arabic: A Comparative Study of the Function and Meaning of the faʿʿala and ʾaf ʿala Forms in Koranic Usage*. Leiden: Brill.

Moreshet, Menachem. 1976. הפעיל ללא הבדל מן הקל בלשון חז"ל ['The Hifʿil in Mishnaic Hebrew as Equivalent to the Qal']. *Bar-Ilan Annual* 13: 249–281.

Müller-Kessler, Christa. 1991. *Grammatik des christlich-palästinisch-Aramäischen, Teil 1: Schriftlehre, Lautlehre, Formenlehre*. Texte und Studien zur Orientalistik 6. Hildesheim: Georg Olms.

Mutzafi, Hezy. 2004. *The Jewish Neo-Aramaic Dialect of Koy Sanjaq (Iraqi Kurdistan)*. Semitica Viva 32. Wiesbaden: Harrassowitz.

Nöldeke, Theodor. 1867. 'Beiträge zur Kenntnis aramäischer Dialekte I'. *Zeitschrift der Deutschen Morgenländischen Gesellschaft* 21: 183–200.

———. 1904. *Neue Beiträge zur semitischen Sprachwissenschaft*. Strassburg: Karl J. Trübner.

———. 1917–1918. 'Texte im aramäischen Dialekt von Maʿlūla'. *Zeitschrift für Assyriologie* 31: 203–230.

Sokoloff, Michael. 2014. *A Dictionary of Christian Palestinian Aramaic*. Orientalia Lovaniensia Analecta 234. Leuven: Peeters.

———. 2017. *A Dictionary of Jewish Palestinian Aramaic of the Byzantine Period*. 3rd revised and expanded edition. Ramat-Gan: Bar-Ilan University Press.

Spitaler, Anton. 1938. *Grammatik des neuaramäischen Dialekts von Maʿlūla*. Abhandlungen für die Kunde des Morgenlandes 23.1. Leipzig: Deutsche Morgenländische Gesellschaft.

Tal, Abraham. 1979. רבדים בארמית היהודית של ארץ-ישראל: הנו"ן המוספת כאמת מידה ['Layers in Jewish Palestinian Aramaic: The Appended *Nun* as a Criterion']. *Lěšonénu* 43: 165–84.

———. 1980. בירורים בארמית של ארץ-ישראל: כינויי הרמז ['Investigations in Palestinian Aramaic: The Demonstrative Pronouns']. *Lěšonénu* 44: 43–65.

———. 1983. המקור לצורותיו ברובדי הארמית היהודית בארץ-ישראל ['The Infinitive and Its Forms in the Layers of Jewish Palestinian Aramaic']. In מחקרי לשון מוגשים לזאב בן-חיים בהגיעו לשיבה [*Hebrew Language Studies Presented to Professor Zeev Ben-Ḥayyim*], edited by Moshe Bar-Asher et al., 201–218. Jerusalem: Magnes Press.

———. 2000. *A Dictionary of Samaritan Aramaic*. Handbuch der Orientalistik 50. Leiden: Brill.

———. 2013. *Samaritan Aramaic*. Lehrbücher orientalischer Sprachen 3.2. Münster: Ugarit-Verlag.

Wright, William. 1896. *A Grammar of the Arabic Language*. Vol. 1. 3rd edition revised by W. Roberston Smith and M. J. de Goeje. Cambridge: Cambridge University Press.

THE RE-EMERGENCE OF THE GENITIVE IN NORTH-EASTERN NEO-ARAMAIC[1]

Ariel Gutman

1. Introduction

A commonplace claim in historical linguistics is that languages change in cycles: morpho-syntactic markers appear to make a given construction clearer, then disappear when they are felt redundant, and then re-appear again in different guise. Maybe the best known case of such a linguistic cycle is the cyclic reappearance of pre- and post-verbal negation markers in various languages, a phenomenon that has been termed 'Jespersen's cycle' by Dahl (1979) following the earlier work of Jespersen (1917).

Yet in core morphological domains of language, such as case morphology, it is difficult to come across documented cases of cyclic change, most probably due to the long time spans in which core morphology changes. Aramaic, however, with its almost 3,000 years of documented history, provides one such case study, that I shall examine in this paper.

Based on the evidence from Akkadian and Classical Arabic, it is generally assumed that proto-Semitic exhibited a three-way case system, distinguishing nominative, accusative and genitive

1 Acknowledgements: I would like to thank my doctoral supervisors for their support and much appreciated feedback. First and foremost Eleanor Coghill, who was a truly exceptional *doktormutter*, as well as Frans Plank and Eran Cohen, and initially also Pollet Samvelian. The research was funded for one year (2011–2012) by a doctoral grant awarded by the École Normale Supérieure (Paris) and subsequently (2012–16) by the *Deutsche Forschungsgemeinschaft* as part of the project 'Neo-Aramaic morphosyntax in its areal-linguistic context' led by Eleanor Coghill.

 https://doi.org/10.11647/OBP.0209.09

cases. Yet Aramaic, from its earliest attested stages, shows no case system. The fact that Aramaic used to have a case system in its pre-historical stage, however, can be deduced from the Aramaic Samʾal inscriptions from the 8th century BCE, where masculine plural nouns conserve an archaic distinction between nominative and oblique cases (Dion 1978, 117).

The main cycle of change I shall describe here, based on my PhD thesis (Gutman 2016; Gutman 2018), is the re-emergence of the genitive case (and thus case-marking in general) in North-Eastern Neo-Aramaic after about 2,500 years of absence of case marking. This cyclic change is accompanied by other cyclic morphological changes, that will be examined as well.

1.1. Terminology

I shall use here the term attributive construction to denote constructions in which a head nominal (the primary) is qualified semantically and syntactically by another nominal (the secondary). The prototypical attributive construction in Semitic languages is the annexation construction, also known as the construct state construction, in which the head noun is marked by a special morphological form called the construct state.

From a dependency grammar point of view, we may say that the attributive construction exhibits an attributive relation between the primary and the secondary (see Goldenberg 1987). From a morpho-syntactic point of view, however, this relation can be marked by different means. The different markers can be classifed on the following two dimensions, following the work of Plank (1995, 38ff.):

- Two loci of marking: primary and secondary.
- Two types of marking: relational (pure morpho-syntactic marking) and pronominal (marking that has a nominal referent).

This yields four principal marker types, that are presented in Table 1 together with the corresponding gloss label, that will be used in the examples below.

Table 1: Four AC marker-types

	Primary	**Secondary**
Relational	Construct state (CST)	Genitive case (GEN)
Pronominal	Possessive (POSS)	Linker (LNK)

I reserve the notion of case to denote morphological marking of the dependent, i.e. the secondary. Hence, in the context of attributive constructions, the notion of genitive case is reserved for relational marking of the secondary, while the parallel marking of the primary is considered to pertain to the domain of *state marking*. The *construct state* is a morphological marking of a noun that indicates that it has a complement (i.e. it is a primary of an attributive construction), while a noun that is not thus marked is said to be in the *free state*. For an analysis of the category of state as a valid cross-linguistic category reflecting the *syntactic valency* of nouns see Gutman (2018, 32) as well as Creissels (2009, 74).

Pronominal markers are defined as markers that have referential power, substituting for a noun phrase, and thus can themselves serve as primaries or secondaries.

To clarify these terms, we can consider the following Turkish textbook example:

(1) *oda-nın kapı-sı*

room-GEN door-POSS.3

'the door of the room' (Turkish, Göksel and Kerslake 2005: 183)

The suffix *-sı* marks the primary *kapı* 'door'. It is a pronominal marker, since the expression *kapısı* can stand by itself meaning 'its door'. The suffix *-nın*, on the other hand, is a pure relational marker of the secondary *oda* 'room' (though it also conveys the semantic value of definiteness), and therefore it is an example of genitive case.

1.2. Methodology

The aim of this paper is to investigate and explain language-change processes observed in NENA dialects. The claims made here are based on a detailed study of several different NENA dialects, of which text samples have been arranged in an extensive database, as described in Gutman (2016; 2018, 13ff.).[2] As this paper gives, however, a "bird-eye's view" of the processes involved, the best examples from different dialects will be presented in order to justify the different claims. I invite the interested reader to refer to Gutman (2016, especially §10.4; 2018, especially 320ff.) for a more detailed description.

Throughout the paper, I shall assume that a process of language change can ideally be attributed either to influence of some contact language, or be language-internally motivated. Of course, in most cases it is probable that both motivations exist to some extent.

As NENA is spoken in the same area as Kurdish dialects, both of the Sorani and Kurmanji types, I shall concentrate on these dialects as the main contact languages. As the point of departure of the changes in NENA, I shall take Syriac, a Classical Aramaic dialect spoken between the 2nd and 7th centuries (at least) as the backdrop for these changes, serving as an approximate 'Proto-NENA' (disregarding the question whether the NENA dialects stem in fact from a unique proto-language). Syriac was spoken in the same area as NENA is spoken, and many structural features of NENA can be traced back to Syriac constructions. Thanks to the extensive ancient literature that has survived in Syriac (due to its important role in the propagation of Eastern Christianity), it is a very well described and documented ancient dialect of Aramaic.

2. Attributive Constructions in Syriac

In Syriac we find three principal attributive constructions. The expression 'house of a/the king', for example, can be expressed in the following three ways:

---

2 The database can be found online as part of Gutman (2016).

(i) The *construct state construction* (=CSC), restricted mostly to idioms and fixed expressions. In this construction the primary noun is marked by the construct state:

(2) *bēṯ* *malkā*
house.CST king

The construct state can be in general identified as lacking the emphatic-state suffix *-ā*, which in Syriac marks free-standing nouns, such as the secondary *malkā* 'king' in (2). In older strata of Aramaic, this suffix marked definiteness, yet in Syriac it lost this function, and became instead a formal exponent of free-state nouns. Consequently, the construct-state form can be regarded as derived by *apocope* from the free-state noun.

(ii) The *analytic linker construction* (=ALC), which is the most productive and frequent of the three. In this construction the primary is left unmarked (in the free state), but instead a proclitic *d-* particle, a linker, intervenes between the two nouns:

(3) *bayta* *d=* *malkā*
house LNK= king

(iii) The *double annexation construction* (=DAC); in contrast to the former two constructions, this construction implies definite reading ('house of the king'). As the above construction, it is marked by the proclitic *d-*, but in addition to that the primary noun is marked by a possessive suffix co-referent with the secondary:

(4) *bayt-ēh* *d=* *malkā*
house-POSS.3 LNK= king

Some authors have treated the *d-* proclitic as being a genitive case marker (see for example Doron and Meir 2013 or Bulakh 2009 regarding a similar Geʿez particle), yet, as Goldenberg (1995, 3–6) notes, since it is a pronominal element, it is distinct from a genitive case marker. Its pronominal nature is clear in examples where it completely assumes the role of the primary, in the absence of an explicit nominal primary:

(5)	*habaw*	*hākēl*	***d=***	*qesar*	*l=*	*qesar*
	give.IMP.PL	then	LNK=	Caesar	to=	Caesar
	w=	***d=***	*alāhā*	*l=*	*alāhā*	
	and=	LNK=	God	to=	God	

‘Give then **that which** is of Caesar to Caesar and **that which** is of God to God.’ (Peshitta, Matthew 22:21; Muraoka 1997, 71)

In Syriac, therefore, as in all Aramaic varieties of antiquity, there is no genitive marker.

3. Emergence of a Genitive Case in NENA

Following Cohen (2010), I have showed in Gutman (2016) and Gutman (2018, chapter 4) that the Syriac *d-* linker diversified into 3 different markers in NENA dialects:

1. A modern *d-* linker, with possible variations of its form
2. A neo-construct state suffix *-əd*
3. A genitive prefix *d-*

In what follows, I shall concentrate on the development of the two latter markers, and especially the genitive marker.

3.1. Stage I: Emergence of the Neo-CSC in NENA

Following Mengozzi (2005), one can trace the Neo-CSC of NENA dialects, in which the construct state noun is marked by an *-əd* suffix, back to the Syriac DAC, exemplified here by the expression *bayt-ēh d=malkā*. Judging by the evidence from the NENA manuscripts from the 17th century, the transformation process can be broken down into the following steps:

1. The possessive suffix *-ēh*, which in Syriac can inflect, becomes morphologically fossilised and attenuates phonetically to a schwa *-ə*.
2. The proclitic linker *d-* encliticises to the primary, resulting in a sequence *-ə=d*.
3. The resulting unit is reanalysed as a unitary construct state suffix.

As a result the NENA Neo-CSC emerges with the form *baytəd malka*.

The above is a description of the 'mechanics' of the change process. What, however, motivates it? One can postulate three motivating forces:

- A universal tendency of functional elements to become enclitics and subsequently suffixes (Lahiri and Plank 2010: 395).
- An areal preference for head-marked constructions (cf. Cohen 2015). See, however, Gutman (2017) and Gutman (2016, §10.3; 2018, 307) for a negative evaluation of the possibility that this is a direct pattern replication of the Kurmanji *ezafe* construction.
- The cognitive force of linguistic economy (cf. Slobin 1977, 186): a single-marked construction is simpler than a double-marked construction.

3.2. Stage II: Hopping of the *d-* segment back to the secondary

The process continues further. Judging by dialectal evidence, we see that the *d-* segment, now part of the CSC suffix, is phonologically not stable:

1. In environments where the secondary has an initial vowel (or a glottal stop), the final *-d* has a tendency to re-syllabify with the secondary: **ṣadr-əd awwa susa* 'chest of this horse' > *ṣadr-ə d-awwa susa* (Barwar, Khan 2008b, 397)
2. A final schwa following an open syllable is not stable, with the result that it is sometimes elided: *yal-əd axona* 'children of my brother' > **yal-ə -d=axona* > *yal -d=axona* (Qaraqosh, Khan 2002: 208)
3. Alternatively, to save the schwa, the [d] may geminate: **paqart-əd ane ḥawāwīn* 'neck of these animals' > **paqartə d=áne ḥawāwīn* > *paqart-əd d=ane ḥawāwīn* (Qaraqosh, Khan 2002: 208)

Note that in all the examples above, the primary noun is distinct from the corresponding free-state forms (*ṣadra, yala, paqarta*), thus the resulting constructions are different from the ALC, which still exists in the NENA systems.

3.3. Stage III: Reanalysis of the *d-* segment as a genitive prefix

The aforementioned stage is purely phonological, yet the crucial step happens due to a reanalysis of the added phonological material: when the *d-* segment is doubled, the *d-* prefix can be reanalysed as a genitive prefix.

(6) *pumm-əd d-aw nāša*
mouth-CST GEN-DEF.MS man
'the mouth of the man' (Jewish Zakho, Cohen 2012, 107 (76))

This happens indeed with a select class of vowel-initial demonstratives and determiners, as shown by Cohen (2010). A partial selection of these elements is shown in Table 2.

Table 2: Case inflected definite determiners in Jewish Zakho (Cohen 2010, 88)

Case		**Determiner**	
		aw	MS
−GEN	*ʾ-*	*ay*	FS
+GEN	*d-*	*an*	PL

Following this reanalysis, the *d-* marked genitive forms appear in environments where the original phonological motivation is no longer present, but where genitive-case marking is expected, such as NPs following prepositions, or on phrase-internal demonstratives:

(7) *mən d-ay xzēna*
from GEN-DEF treasure
'from the treasure' (Jewish Zakho, Cohen 2012, 108 (77))

(8) *gnay-ət tawra d-o= goṛa*
fault-CST ox GEN-DEF.MS= big.MS
'the fault of the big ox' (Barwar, Khan 2008b, 517 [D2:19])

Yet the introduction of a genitive prefix is highly surprising, not only because it re-introduces a case system into Aramaic, absent for about 2,500 years, but also because it goes against the aforementioned universal tendency of suffixation. So a natural question is: What were the motivations for this re-analysis?

Several potential answers can be given. First, we note that the high frequency of vowel-initial demonstratives or determiners acting as secondaries (or the first elements thereof), makes the morphological re-analysis of the phonological realignment plausible.

A partial internal explanation, suggested by Khan (2009a, 71), may be the analogy of the *d-* marked demonstratives with independent genitive pronouns, which also start with a [d] segment such as Barwar *bεθa diy-a* 'her house'. Yet such an analogy would explain only the genitive form of independent demonstratives, and not of determiners.

It seems, however, that the main driving force of this grammatical change lies in language contact, and more specifically in an analogy with the Kurdish Kurmanji demonstrative system.

As shown in Table 3, the Kurmanji demonstratives exhibit two cases: a nominative and an oblique case. It may be no coincidence that the nominative, as in Aramaic, is vowel-initial, while the oblique is consonant-initial.

Table 3: Kurmanji near-deixis demonstratives

	NOM	OBL
MS		*vî*
FS	*ev*	*vê*
PL		*van*

It should be noted that the various contexts where the genitive-marked NENA demonstratives appear (i.e. marking attributive NPs or complements of prepositions) fit the usage of the Kurmanji oblique demonstratives. Thus, the emergence of a NENA genitive-prefix may result from a *pattern replication* process, in the sense of Matras and Sakel (2007), of the Kurmanji system. Indeed, the geographical distribution of the NENA genitive prefix corroborates this hypothesis, since the prefix is present mainly in NENA dialects that are in direct contact with Kurmanji dialects.

Yet, as Cohen (2010, 90) notes, there is a difficulty with this idea, since the NENA genitive prefix, in contrast to the Kurmanji oblique case, does not mark complements of verbs. Does this difficulty refute the pattern-replication hypothesis? Not necessarily. It is quite possible that while replicating the Kurmanji pattern the NENA speakers did not generalise the occurrence of the *d-* segment outside its initial domain of appearance, but rather restricted its reanalysis to the attributive domain. The occurrence of the genitive prefix after prepositions is natural in this respect, as the construct-state suffix can appear on certain prepositions, as in the following example:

(9) *mənn-ət bela*
from-CST house
'from the house' (Jewish Urmi, Khan 2008a, 196)

3.4. Stage III: Reanalysis of the *d-* segment as an oblique prefix

Interestingly, at least in one dialect, namely the peripheral dialect of Jewish Sanandaj, the *d-* prefix has completely replicated the Kurmanji pattern, as it is used not only as a marker of adnominal complements of nouns and prepositions, but also as a marker of verbal objects (preceding the verb as is the case in Kurdish), as the following three examples show:

(10) *bela d-o*
house OBL-3S
'his house' (Jewish Sanandaj, Khan 2009b, 200)

(11) *reša d-o*
on OBL-3S
'on it' (Jewish Sanandaj, Khan 2009b, 224)

(12) *d-o grəš-le*
OBL-3MS pulled-A.3MS
'He pulled him.' (Jewish Sanandaj, Khan 2009b, 159)

In these three examples the form *d-o* is used as an independent pronoun, but it can also be used as a case-marked determiner of an NP. It is also worth noting that except these uses of the *d-* prefix (which are in fact optional), there are no other reflexes of the Classical Aramaic *d-* linker in this dialect.

Khan (2009b, 158) explains the usage of the *d-* prefix as a verbal-complement marker, as being a sub-case of the prepositional-complement marker, since it can also appear after the accusative preposition *həl*:

(13) *həl= d-o grəš-le*
ACC= OBL-3MS pulled-A.3MS
'He pulled him.' (Jewish Sanandaj, Khan 2009b, 158)

Thus, Khan (2009b, 158) explains example (12) as resulting from the simple omission of the preposition *həl*. Yet, given the above outlined development path of the case-marking *d-* prefix in NENA dialects, it is plausible to analyse this development as the final step of replication of the Kurmanji pattern, in which the *d-* prefix assumes completely the role of an oblique case-marker. Interestingly, this happens in the dialect of Jewish Sanandaj, which is not in direct contact with Kurmanji (the Kurdish spoken in Sanandaj is of the Sorani type, in which there is no case-marking). As the origin of the pattern replication must be in the

Kurmanji-speaking area, this seems to be an indication that the speakers of Jewish Sanandaj came originally from that area.

4. Renaissance of the Apocopate Construct State

The reanalysis of the *d-* prefix as a genitive marker has led in some dialects to the reanalysis of the apocopate primary form as a new construct state formation. In the following example, the form *brāt* can be contrasted with the free-state form *brāta* 'daughter', effectively being a construct-state form:

(14) *brāt* *d-ay* *baxta*
daughter.CST GEN-DEF.FS woman
'the daughter of the woman' (Jewish Zakho, Cohen 2012, 110)

It is worthwhile noting that the new apocopate construct state is formally similar to the historical construct state, as both are formed by apocopation, yet as some irregular forms show, it is distinct from it. For example, the Syriac construct state of the noun *brāta* is *bat*.

Once the new form has been reanalysed as a new kind of construct-state marking (on a par with the neo-construct-state suffix *-əd* marking), it spreads to contexts where no *d-* prefix is found:

(15) *ʾaqlās* *xa* *mənn-u*
feet.PL.CST one from-3PL
'the feet of one of them' (Jewish Zakho, Cohen 2012, 115)

This development marks again a closure of a cycle. In the earliest strata of Aramaic the apocopate construct state was the standard way of marking the attributive relation. Later, in Syriac it lost its expressive power and became confined mostly to idioms, yet in NENA it re-emerges as a standard way of marking the attributive relation, alongside other morpho-synactic means.

5. Conclusions

In this paper I have drawn attention to the existence of two important cycles of morpho-syntactic change in the nominal domain in the long history of Aramaic:

1. The disappearance of the case system of the earliest strata of Aramaic followed by the re-emergence of case marking (genitive or oblique) in NENA dialects, about 2,500 years later.
2. The decline of the apocopate construct state in Syriac, followed by the development of suffixed neo-construct-state marking in NENA dialects, which in turn led to the emergence of a neo-apocopate construct-state marking in some dialects.

These cycles are accompanied by a phonological cycle, in which a proclitic element (the *d-* linker) becomes a suffix (in the construct state suffix) and then shifts back to being a prefix (as a genitive case-marker). Yet a key observation is that phonological re-arrangements (cliticisation, resyllabification) cannot by themselves cause a morpho-syntactic change of the linguistic system. Rather, they must be followed by a process of reanalysis of the phonological material in order for them to have a lasting effect.

From the point of view of the marking quantity of the attributive constructions, we can observe another abstract cycle. The double annexation construction of Syriac, in which the primary is marked by a possessive suffix and the secondary by a pronominal linker, transforms into a single-marked construction (the suffixed construct-state construction of NENA), which in turn transforms back in some environments and dialects to another double-marked construction, in which the primary is marked by the construct-state (either apocopate or suffixed) and the secondary is marked by the genitive case. Intriguingly, we see that while the original double construction used pronominal markers on both loci, the modern double construction uses relational markers on both sites.

The history of Aramaic permits us to corroborate the old idea that languages do indeed change in cycles, yet we see that these cycles do not constitute exact repetition. The fluctuations in marking-quantity corroborate the idea that two opposing forces shape language: economy, on one hand, and clarity, on the other hand. In slightly different terms, this idea has been neatly summarised by Slobin (1977, 192):

> The first two charges—clarity and processibility—strive toward segementalisation. The other two charges—temporal compactness and expressiveness—strive toward synthesis, however. As a result, Language constantly fluctuates between the poles of analyticity and syntheticity, since none of the charges can be ignored.

The details of the various processes should, in principle, be attributed to specific motivations, either language-internal motivations or, as is often the case, to language-contact. Yet even in the most pristine 'laboratory' conditions of language change, which Aramaic with its richly documented history approaches, not all details of change can be accounted for. This is since the various forces operating on the development of a language are ultimately mediated by the creativity of its speakers.

References

Bulakh, Maria. 2009. 'Nota Genitivi *za-* in Epigraphic Geez'. *Journal of Semitic Studies* 54 (2): 393–419.

Cohen, Eran. 2010. 'Marking nucleus and attribute in North-Eastern Neo-Aramaic'. In *Proceeding of the VIII Afro-Asiatic Congress (September 2008, Naples)*, 79–94. Studi Maghrebini (Nuova Serie) 7.

———. 2012. *The Syntax of Neo-Aramaic: The Jewish Dialect of Zakho.* Gorgias Neo-Aramaic Studies 13. Piscataway, NJ: Gorgias Press.

———. 2015. 'Head-Marking in Neo-Aramaic Genitive Constructions and the *ezafe* Construction in Kurdish'. In *Semitic Languages in Contact*, edited by Aaron M. Butts. Studies in Semitic Languages and Linguistics 82. Leiden: Brill, pp. 114–25.

Creissels, Denis. 2009. 'Construct Forms of Nouns in African Languages'. In *Proceedings of a Conference on Language Documentation and Linguistic Theory 2*, edited by Peter K. Austin, Oliver Bond, Monik Charette, David Nathan, and Peter Sells, 73–82. London: SOAS.

Dahl, Östen. 1979. 'Typology of Sentence Negation'. *Linguistics* 17 (1-2): 79–106.

Dion, Paul-E. 1978. 'The Language Spoken in Ancient Samʾal'. *Journal of Near Eastern Studies* 37 (2): 115–18.

Doron, Edit and Irit Meir. 2013. 'Construct State: Modern Hebrew'. In *Encyclopedia of Hebrew Language and Linguistics*, edited by edited by Geoffrey Khan, Shmuel Bolozky, Steven E. Fassberg, Gary A. Rendsburg, Aaron D. Rubin, Ora R. Schwarzwald, and Tamar Zewi, 1: 581–89. Leiden-Boston: Brill, 2013.

Göksel, Aslı and Celia Kerslake. 2005. *Turkish: A Comprehensive Grammar*. Comprehensive Grammars. London: Routledge.

Goldenberg, Gideon. 1987. 'יחסים תחביריים וטיפולוגיה בלשונות שמיות' [Syntactic Relations and Typology in Semitic Languages]. In עיונים בעקבות מפעלו של פולוצקי: דברים שנאמרו בערב לכבוד יעקב פולוצקי בהגיעו לגבורות [Following Polotsky's Teachings: Lectures in honour of H. J. Polotsky on the occasion of his eightieth birthday]. Delivered at the Israel Academy of Sciences and Humanities in a meeting held on the 21st of January 1986, 7–18. Jerusalem: Israel Academy of Sciences and Humanities. Translated into English by Shmuel Bar in Gideon Goldenberg. 1998. *Studies in Semitic Linguistics: Selected Writings*. Jerusalem: Magnes Press, 138–47.

———. 1995. 'Attribution in Semitic Languages'. *Langues Orientales Anciennes: Philologie et Linguistique* 5–6: 1–20. Reprinted in Gideon Goldenberg. 1998. *Studies in Semitic Linguistics: Selected Writings*, 46–65. Jerusalem: Magnes Press.

———. 1998. *Studies in Semitic Linguistics: Selected Writings*. Jerusalem: Magnes Press.

Gutman, Ariel. 2016. 'Attributive Constructions in North-Eastern Neo-Aramaic: Areal, Typological and Historical Perspectives'. Doctoral thesis, University of Konstanz. URL: http://nbn-resolving.de/urn:nbn:de:bsz:352-0-352520.

———. 2017. 'Can Pattern Replication be Easily Established? The Case of the Neo- Aramaic Neo-Construct'. 18e Rencontres Jeunes Chercheurs en Sciences du Langage, June 2015, Paris, France. In: *Actes des 18e Rencontres Jeunes Chercheurs en Sciences du Langage*. URL: https://hal-univ-paris3.archives-ouvertes.fr/hal-01495125.

———. 2018. *Attributive Constructions in North-Eastern Neo-Aramaic*. Language Science Press. URL: http://langsci-press.org/catalog/book/123.

Jespersen, Otto. 1917. *Negation in English and Other Languages*. København: A. F. Høst.

Khan, Geoffrey. 2002. *The Neo-Aramaic Dialect of Qaraqosh*. Studies in Semitic Languages and Linguistics 36. Leiden: Brill.

———. 2008a. *The Jewish Neo-Aramaic Dialect of Urmi*. Gorgias Neo-Aramaic Studies 2. Piscataway, NJ: Gorgias Press.

———. 2008b. *The Neo-Aramaic Dialect of Barwar*. 3 vols. Handbook of Oriental Studies I-96. Leiden: Brill.

———. 2009a. 'The Genitive and Relative Clauses in the North-Eastern Neo-Aramaic Dialects'. In *Relative Clauses and Genitive Constructions in Semitic*, edited by Janet C.E. Watson and Jan Restö, 69–87. *Journal of Semitic Studies* Supplement 25. Oxford: Oxford University Press.

———. 2009b. *The Jewish Neo-Aramaic Dialect of Sanandaj*. Gorgias Neo-Aramaic Studies 10. Piscataway, NJ: Gorgias Press.

Lahiri, Aditi and Frans Plank. 2010. 'Phonological Phrasing in Germanic: The Judgement of History, Confirmed through Experiment'. *Transactions of the Philological Society* 108 (3): 370–98.

Matras, Yaron and Jeanette Sakel. 2007. 'Investigating the Mechanisms of Pattern replication in Language Convergence'. *Studies in Language* 31 (4): 829–65.

Mengozzi, Alessandro. 2005. 'Extended Prepositions in Neo-Aramaic, Kurdish and Italian'. In *Studi Afroasiatici (Afro-Asiatic Studies): XI Incontro Italiano di Linguistica Camitosemitica (11th Italian Meeting of Afro-Asiatic Linguistics)*, edited by Alessandro Mengozzi, 371–90. Materiali linguistici 52. Milano: FrancoAngeli.

Muraoka, Takamitsu. 1997. *Classical Syriac: A Basic Grammar with a Chrestomathy*. Porta Linguarum Orientalium—Neue Serie 19. Wiesbaden: Harrassowitz Verlag.

Plank, Frans. 1995. '(Re-)Introducing Suffixaufnahme'. In *Double Case: Agreement by Suffixaufnahme*, edited by Frans Plank, 3–110. New York: Oxford University Press.

Slobin, Dan I. 1977. 'Language Change in Childhood and in History'. In *Language Learning and Thought*, edited by John Macnamara, 185–214. Perspectives in Neurolinguistics and Psycholinguistics. New York: Academic Press.

MODELLING VARIATION IN THE NEO-ARAMAIC DIALECT OF AZRAN WITH ARTICULATORY PHONOLOGY

Lidia Napiorkowska

1. Introduction

Linguistic theories, as perhaps theories in general, are neat and helpful constructs, but they represent a state well beyond the basic data analysis. This is true, for example, of the traditional binary classification of sounds into phonemes and allophones. Whereas this division allows us to organise the material in a transparent way, it requires compromises and simplifications to a smaller or larger extent (cf. Lyons 1971, 68; Jung and Himmelmann 2011, 204). The tension between the theory and the description of the empirical data results in the need to find a balance between presenting the material in a coherent way and presenting it in a faithful way. This issue is familiar to any field linguist who faces the challenge of transcribing audio material. In practical terms, the dilemma consists in deciding how much of the rich repertoire of each speaker should be represented, typically what is identified as phonemic, and how much should be left out, typically what is identified as allophonic variation? The question is even more complex when the data come from a linguistic community that has a background of dialect mixing. The North-Eastern Neo-Aramaic (NENA) dialect of Azran dealt with in the present paper is a case in point. I wish to propose a way to deal with the aforementioned challenge by suggesting an alternative way of analysing phonetic empirical data,

 https://doi.org/10.11647/OBP.0209.10

employing not the traditional units of phonemes, but rather gestures involved in speech production.[1]

2. The Dialect and the Data

Azran is a NENA dialect whose speakers now live in the town of Diyana in northern Iraqi Kurdistan. Azran was a village in the Turkish area of Gardi in the vicinity of Shemizdin. I was not able to identify its precise location. The Azran speakers regard themselves as belonging to the Gargarnaye tribe, which includes also the speakers of other dialects, such as Hawdiyan. The dialect of Azran is close to the Christian Diyana-Zariwaw (CDZ) variety described by Napiorkowska (2015a; 2015b). They, however, exhibit distinct features and so should be classified as separate varieties. The Azran examples presented below are based on the author's own fieldwork (Napiorkowska 2015c).

It needs to be borne in mind that the Azran community, as is the case with many other Neo-Aramaic communities, has experienced displacement and migration. This combined with the factor of language contact, mainly with Kurmanji Kurdish, has resulted in a substantial degree of linguistic variation. Both a 'horizontal' and a 'vertical' variation can be identified. The horizontal variation arises from contact with other languages and NENA varieties. The vertical variation, on the other hand, has arisen from different degrees of linguistic change across different generations and groups of speakers. Variation is a conspicuous phenomenon in Azran, which needs to be accommodated in the description of the dialect if it is to reflect the linguistic reality.

1 The data on this variety were gathered during the project 'The Documentation of the Neo-Aramaic Cluster of Gargarnaye', IPF 0203 funded by the Endangered Languages Documentation Programme, SOAS, and carried out at the University of Cambridge.

3. Transcription Challenges

A commonly adopted transcription practice, following from the two-way distinction mentioned in §1, is to represent phonemic contrasts and exclude phonetic features that are identified as allophonic. For instance, in the Azran word 'scattered (fs.)' [bʊr.ˈbəs.tʰa] from *barbuze* 'to scatter', the devoicing of */z/* to [s] occurs under the influence of */t/* as a predictable process; consequently, the word is transcribed as *burbəzta.* Many properties of speech, however, are not easily sifted out in the same way, since they do not occur regularly. In this paper, I shall consider the cases of phonological fronting, and to a smaller extent also phonological emphasis, whose distribution is far from regular in Azran.

Consider the word *ṱəḷḷa* < **ṭəllā* [ˈtˤə̠lˤ.lˤa] 'shade', where the former emphatic, i.e. pharyngealised, **ṭ* developed into an unaspirated */ṱ/*, influencing also the neighbouring segments.[2] Historical emphasis is, however, very different in the case of words like *ṱinten* realised as [ˈtən.t͡sʰən] 'I have become pregnant (f.)' < **ṭ-ʾ-n* 'to carry'. Here there is lack of aspiration in the segment in the onset of the first syllable, reflecting historical emphasis, but heavy aspiration in the second */t/*, resulting in an affricate. The affrication in this word is conditioned by a process that is different from the loss of historical emphasis. Should such a process that has led to the emergence of an affricate be represented, or is the marking of the lack of emphasis sufficient in the transcription? Furthermore, a word such as 'stone, rock' **kēpā* > *čipa* involves a range of interchangeable realisations, i.e. [ˈkʲiːpʰa]~ [ˈt͡ʃʰiːpʰa]~[ˈt͡sʰiːpʰa], which do not seem to be conditioned variants. They all represent the word 'stone' for the Azran speakers, the latter being considered a hallmark of the dialect.[3] The different realisations of the same word are

2 For the discussion of phonological emphasis in the dialects of Diyana see Napiorkowska (2015a) where it is argued that the lack of aspiration in /ṱ/ in CDZ is a reflex of the former emphasis in *ṭ. This is also the case in Christian Urmi (Khan 2016).

3 The Azran speakers are apparently often teased about their rendition of the historical velar stops.

perceptible to the speakers. How should then the word 'stone' be represented in the transcription? One way would be to treat the alveolar affricate [t͡s^{h}] as an allophone of a postalveolar phoneme, which can be represented /*č*/, based on its diachronic derivation. Then, however, the perceived reality of Azran would be compromised. Could we perhaps find grounds for regarding [t͡s^{h}] as a separate phoneme, which could be represented /*c*/?

The examples above illustrate the transcription challenges based on linear approaches where phonemes are strung one after another and transitions between units are largely ignored. These transitions, however, produce phonetic output that do not necessarily match the phonological representation. In order to diminish this gap between phonology and phonetics let us consider a dynamic model that combines the two.

4. Articulatory Phonology

Articulatory Phonology (ArtP) is a model of phonological description developed mainly by Browman and Goldstein in a series of articles (*inter alia* 1986; 1989; 1991; 1992). The fundamental assumption of ArtP is the organisation of speech into gestures, i.e. degrees of constriction in particular locations within the vocal tract. These are the velum (VEL), tongue body (TB), tongue tip (TT), lips (LIPS) and glottis (GLO). Each gesture is specified for the location and degree of constriction. In addition, it has an inherent duration. ArtP is a non-linear model since it construes speech as overlapping spatio-temporal events. According to this model, the Azran word *čipa* 'stone' could be represented as displayed in Illustration 1.

The leftmost boxes represent the major gestural actors (called 'vocal trajectories') and the values within the boxes specify the constriction location and degree (closure, critical, narrow, middle or wide). The closure (clo) gesture is mainly associated with the TT, TB and LIPS and the production of stops, whereas the gesture critical (crit) is responsible for creating friction. Vowels and approximants are determined by the middle (mid), narrow or wide gestures.

Illustration 1: Articulatory Phonology Model

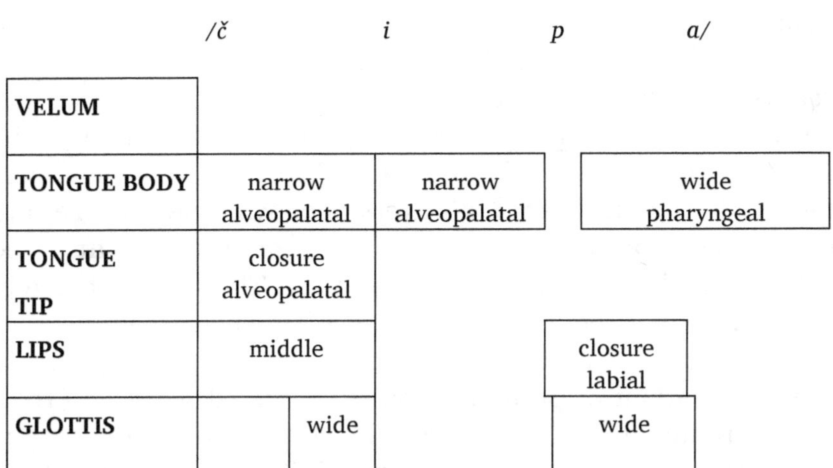

Finally, the glottis and the velum may be defined as wide open for the productions of devoicing and nasals, respectively.

The size of each box represents the duration of gesture with respect to a particular sound.[4] The temporal parameter of ArtP predicts that the retiming of a specific gesture results in the overlapping or disjoining of gestures.

This retiming, in turn, gives rise to processes, such as, for example, fronting of the place of articulation.[5] Another important implication of the spatio-temporal parameter of ArtP is that the magnitude of each gesture may be increased or reduced, depending on the phonetic, but also pragmatic factors, and due to individual conditioning of the speaker. ArtP is, thus, a model which has ample room for accommodating variation and changes in progress, such as those encountered in Azran.

---

4 In this article it is represented in a purely impressionistic manner, rather than based on gesture duration measurement.

5 Some cases of partial or total overlapping of gestures are no different from the well-known process of assimilation. Here, however, the focus is on the mechanics of the processes and their immediate outcomes, for which assimilation is only a label.

5. ArtP and the NENA Data

Using the set of grids (called 'scores' in ArtP) we can visualise the way in which the shift in Azran from the form *kipa* (< **kēpā*) to *čipa* is likely to have occurred. It is here assumed that first the narrow alveopalatal gesture responsible for the production of the vowel /*i*/ was retimed, i.e. produced before the completion of the previous gesture, and so it overlapped with the velar gesture of the tongue body constriction in /*k*/. As a result, a shift of the velar /*k*/ to the alveopalatal /*č*/ took place. This is represented in (1a) and (1b), where the relevant areas have been shaded.

Building on this assumption it may be postulated that in the third variant of pronunciation encountered in Azran (1c) a further retiming of /*i*/ influences the constriction of the tongue body responsible for the production of /*č*/. The narrow vocalic gesture spreads from the alveopalate to the alveolar ridge and so the closure is advanced to the alveolar region.[6] The result is realised as an affricate /*c*/ [t͡sʰ]. Note also the spreading of lips associated with this pronunciation.

(1) Palatalisation and advancement to alveolar ridge with vowel opening

čipa 'stone' < **kēpā*

(1a) [ˈkʲiːpʰa] [7]

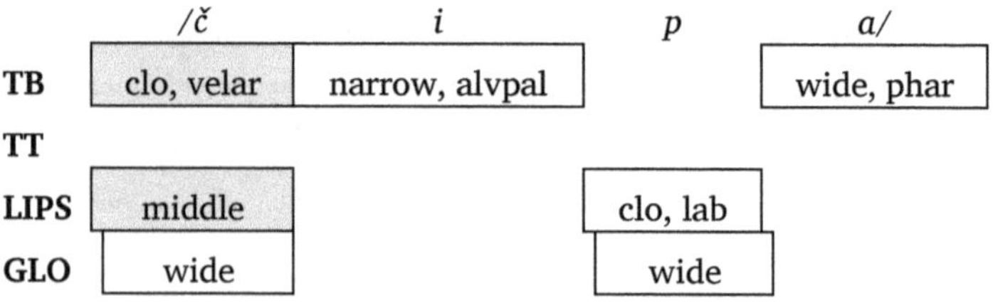

6 Cf. the characterisation of the alveopalatal sounds by Ladefoged as those produced with the blade of the tongue 'always close to the back part of the alveolar ridge (…), made farther in the mouth' than the alveolars (Ladefoged 2006, 12).

7 Within the scores the following abbreviations were used: alv for alveolar, alvpal for alveopalatal, pal for palatal, phar for pharyngeal, lab for labial

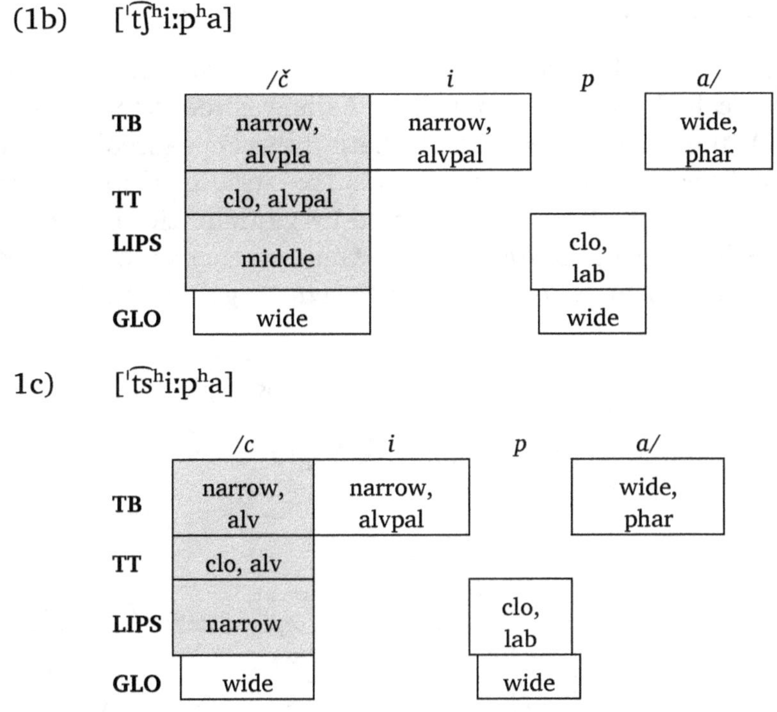

(Within the ArtP framework, the variation of /k~ č~ c/> [kʲ > t͡ʃʰ> t͡sʰ] in *kēpā> kipa> čipa> cipa 'stone' is easily handled as a spectrum of articulations triggered by the anticipation of the alveopalatal vowel gesture. Moreover, such a representation bypasses the stage of categorical phonemic vs. allophonic division between /k~ č~ c/. I have, therefore, decided to represent [t͡sʰ] with a separate symbol /c/. It is not claimed that /c/ constitutes a separate phoneme in its canonical sense; rather, introducing /c/ represents a significant perceived auditory feature of Azran. In other words, differentiating between /č/ and /c/ in transcription does not mark a transgression of boundaries between phonemes, but rather mirrors the linguistic reality of the dialect with such internal variation.

---

and uvu-phar for uvular-pharyngeal.

6. Further Examples

The ArtP model may further be employed to represent the feature called emphasis spread. In Azran, as mentioned above (§3.0.), the reflex of earlier emphatic (pharyngealised) **ṭ* is a non-pharyngealised unaspirated /ṱ/. The gesture of tongue tip closure for /ṱ/ is, thus, accompanied by glottalic closure. If this gesture is retimed, the following relevant segments are rendered unaspirated, such as /p̆/ in *ṱəp̆ṛa* < **ṭəprā* 'fingernail' in (2):

(2) Emphasis spread or retiming of closed glottis gesture

ṱəp̆ṛa 'fingernail' [ˈtəp.rˤa] < **ṭəprā*

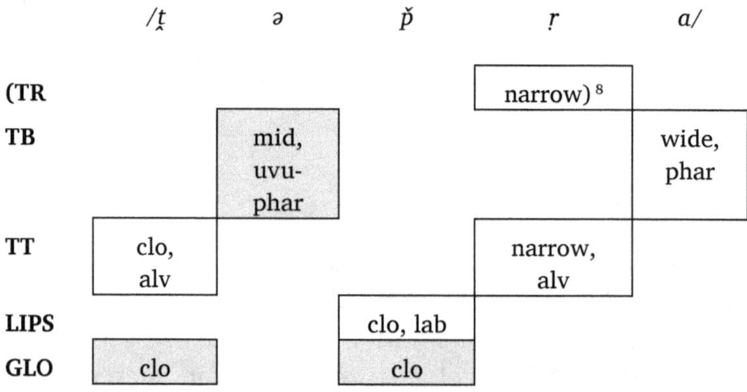

The gesture of the closed glottis appears here as almost a continuum, pertaining to the relevant segments. The approach of ArtP has, therefore, an advantage over a linear approach, where we would have two segments specified each for the feature of nonaspiration.

8 The ArtP model is yet to develop a unified way of representing the tongue root gestures. Here, the TR narrow gesture is equivalent to the [+RTR] feature and stands for the articulatory setting generally assumed in NENA for the production of the emphatic consonants, i.e. the constriction of the upper pharynx (cf. Khan 2013, 112).

The next example (3) is similar to (1), but involves the voiced counterpart. It is likewise assumed that the retiming of */i/* is responsible for the shift from the alveopalatal */j/* [d͡ʒ] to alveolar [d͡z]. Consequently, [d͡z] is represented by a separate symbol */ɟ/*.

The final example (4) illustrates not the strictly temporal, but rather the gradable parameter of gesture magnitude. Here, the first segment is the unaspirated reflex of the earlier emphatic **ṭ*, whereas the final consonant */t/* is the aspirated stop of the feminine suffix. In (4a), */ṱ/* is still pronounced with some emphasis, i.e. constriction of the pharynx and retraction of the tongue root. It is, thus, sufficiently different from the pronunciation of the aspirated */t/* where no tongue root gesture is involved. In (4b), by contrast, where the only reflex of the earlier emphasis is the lack of aspiration, there is a need to magnify the difference between */ṱ/* and */t/*. As a result, the shift of the tongue tip from closure in */t/* in (4a) to a critical position in (4b) renders the affricate [t͡sʰ], whereby the contrast between the two consonants in question is maximised.

(3) Advancement to alveolar ridge with vowel opening

jiya 'tired' (ms.) < *g-h-y*

(3a) [ˈd͡ʒɪːja]

	/j	*i*	*y*	*a/*
TB	narrow, alvpal	narrow, alvpal	narrow, pal	wide, phar
TT	clo, alvpal			
LA	mid	narrow		
GLO	clo			

(3b) 

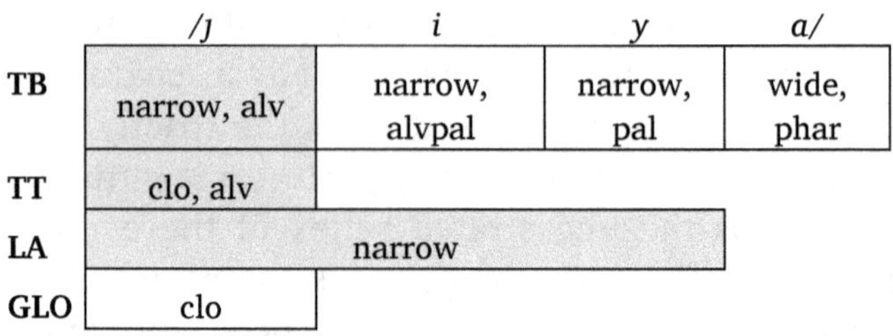

(4) The maximisation of glottalic gesture contrast

ṱinta 'pregnant'

(4a) [ˈtˤə̠n.tʰa][9]

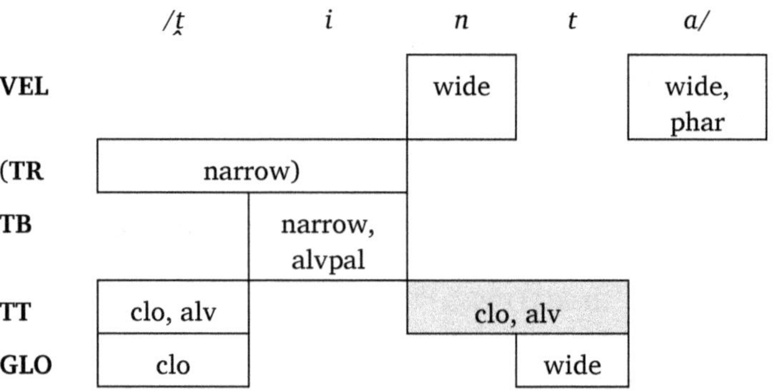

(4b) [tən.t͡sʰa]

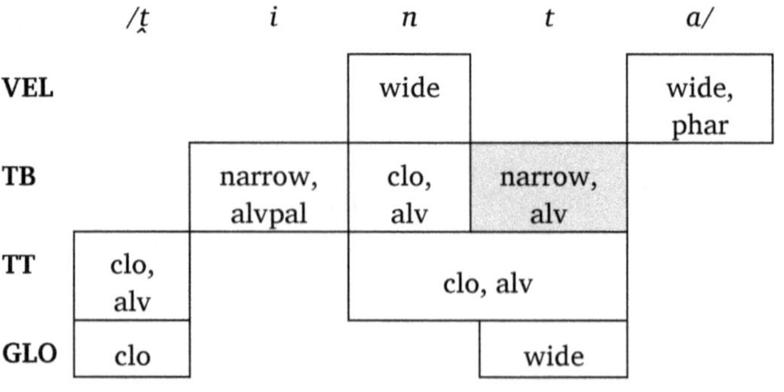

9 The spread of nasality was ignored in this example.

7. ArtP and Language Contact

The palatalisation of the velar stops, presented in the Azran examples in (1) and (3), is not unique to this dialect (see also Christian Urmi in Khan 2016) and appears to be an areal feature of the Eastern Anatolian and Caucasian *Sprachbünde*. The NENA dialects have undoubtedly been heavily influenced by the surrounding varieties, mainly Kurmanji Kurdish, in which palatalisation is well attested (Kapeliuk 2011, 737). Nonetheless, it should be borne in mind that external influence is rarely the sole factor responsible for linguistic change. Rather, it is coupled with an internal potential of the language to accommodate the influence. In the light of ArtP, we may observe how the shift */k/> /č ~ c/* emerges as an innovation independently of external influence. Furthermore, similar developments of the velar stops are typologically wide-spread, for example, among the Bantu varieties (Hyman and Moxley 1996) where no external motivation for change has been postulated. Among internal factors one could also include sociolinguistics and the rather low prestige of Azran compared to other NENA varieties, such as the Iraqi koine. According to Trudgill (2011), the non-standard or isolated varieties tend to employ more casual and careless speech, which results in reduction processes in pronunciation and grammar. The speakers of Azran indeed constitute a rather small and tightly-knit community. This would be expected to licence a less careful pronunciation, leading to a phonological shift.

It is not claimed here that the fronting and palatalisation in Azran, or indeed in NENA, is totally unconnected with the similar processes in Kurdish. Rather, it is suggested that there is a need to recognise both the external and the internal motivations for a change. Acknowledging equally the role that the input from the inside and outside play in shaping the language is a more satisfactory approach to the study of sound change. In the case of the palatalisation and affricativisation in Azran, we may say that the mechanism of gesture retiming is a development that is reinforced by language contact rather than primarily conditioned by it.

8. Conclusions

ArtP is a model enabling us to observe how the reorganisation of gestures results in allophonic variation ranges, which pass seamlessly across boundaries delimited by phonemes in linear approaches (ex. 1, 2 and 3). It is, therefore, an efficient means of capturing variation. Moreover, it handles well some cases of the so-called 'mixed-words', i.e. former emphatic words containing front segments (example 4), which are otherwise problematic within the approach of vowel harmony and autosegmental phonology. Lastly, giving credit to the internal mechanism of sound shift together with language contact allows us to identify the multiple causation of linguistic change with greater precision.

Returning to the initial question of tension between theory and empirical data in the creation of transcriptions, it must be admitted that ArtP is impractical for documentation purposes. Some critics have judged it to be inconclusive or in many respects inadequate (e.g. McMahon, Foulkes and Tollfree 1994; Clements 1992). Nevertheless, it is here argued that ArtP is highly valuable as a model for the interface between phonology and phonetics. Including a few selected ArtP scores in a phonological description of a language would help to justify the transcription convention that is adopted in the documentation, such as introducing /c/ and /ɟ/ here. In practical terms, ArtP allows us to achieve a deeper understanding of what it is that we are trying to represent through a highly conventionalised transcription system.

Abbreviations

alv	alveolar
alvpal	alveopalatal,
ArtP	Articulatory Phonology
clo	closure
crit	critical
GLO	glottis

lab	labial
pal	palatal,
phar	pharyngeal
TB	tongue body
TT	tongue tip
uvu-phar	uvular-pharyngeal
VEL	velum

References

Ball, Martin, Nicole Müller and Ben Rutter. 2010. *Phonology for Communication Disorders*. New York: Psychology Press.

Beltzung, Jean-Marc, Céderic Patin and George N. Clements. 2015. 'The feature [ATR]'. In *Features in Phonology and Phonetics: Posthumous Writings by Nick Clements and Coauthors*, edited by Annie Rialland et al., 217–246. Berlin: Mouton de Gruyter, 2015.

Browman, Catherine P. and Louis Goldstein. 1986. 'Towards an Articulatory Phonology'. *Phonology Yearbook* 3: 219–252.

———. 1989. 'Articulatory Gestures as Phonological Units'. *Phonology* 6: 201–251.

———. 1991. 'Tiers in Articulatory Phonology, with some Implications for Casual Speech.' In *Papers in Laboratory Phonology I: Between the Grammar and the Physics of Speech*, edited by Mary E. Beckman and John Kingston, 341–376. Cambridge: Cambridge University Press.

———. 1992. 'Articulatory Phonology: An Overview'. *Phonetica* 49: 155–180.

Bybee, Joan L. 2001. *Phonology and Language Use*. Cambridge: Cambridge University Press.

Clements, George N. 1992. 'Phonological Primes: Features or Gestures?' *Phonetica* 49: 181–193.

Goldstein, Louis. 2014. *English Gestures Dictionary*. [online] http://sail.usc.edu/~lgoldste/ArtPhon/.

Haig, Geoffrey, Nicole Nau, Stefan Schnell and Claudia Wegener. 2011. 'Introduction: Documenting Endangered Languages before, during and after DoBeS Programme'. In *Documenting Endangered Languages*, edited by Geoffrey Haig et. al., 1–14. Berlin: Mouton de Gruyter.

Haine, Bernd and Tania Kutewa. 2005. *Language Contact and Grammatical Change.* Cambridge: Cambridge University Press.

Halle, Morris, Bert Vaux and Andrew Wolfe. 2000. 'On Feature Spreading and the Representation of Place of Articulation'. *Linguistic Inquiry* 31 (3): 387–444.

Hyman, Larry M. and Jeri Moxley. 1996. 'The Morpheme in Phonological Change: Velar Palatalization in Bantu'. *Diachronica* 13 (2): 259–282.

Jung, Dagmar and Nikolaus P. Himmelmann. 2011. 'Retelling the Data: Working on Transcription'. In *Documenting Endangered Languages*, edited by Geoffrey Haig et al., 200–220. Berlin: Mouton de Gruyter.

Kapeliuk, Olga. 2011. 'Language Contact between Neo-Aramaic Dialects and Iranian'. In *The Semitic Languages: An International Handbook*, edited by Stefan Weninger et al., 738–747. Mouton: De Gruyter.

Khan, Geoffrey. 2013. 'Phonological Emphasis in North-Eastern Neo-Aramaic'. In *Base articulatoire arièrre: Backing and Backness*, edited by Jean Léo Léonard and Samia Naïm, 111–132. Munich: Lincoln Europa.

———. 2016. *The Neo-Aramaic Dialect of the Assyrian Christians of Urmi.* Vol.1. Leiden: Brill.

Ladefoged, Peter. 2006. *A Course in Phonetics*, 5th ed. Boston: Wadsworth.

Lyons, John. 1971. *Introduction to Theoretical Linguistics*. Cambridge: Cambridge University Press.

McMahon, April, Paul Foulkes and Laura Tollfree. 1994. 'Gestural Representation and Lexical Phonology'. *Phonology* 11: 277–316.

Mowrey, Richard and William Pagliuca. 1995. 'The Reductive Character of Articulatory Evolution'. *Rivista di Linguistica* 7 (1): 37–124.

Napiorkowska, Lidia. 2015a. *A Grammar of the Christian Neo-Aramaic Dialect of Diyana-Zariwaw*. Leiden: Brill.

———. 2015b. 'A Diachronic Perspective on Emphasis in Christian Diyana-Zariwaw'. In *Neo-Aramaic in its Linguistic Context*, edited by Geoffrey Khan and Lidia Napiorkowska, 130–144. Piscataway, New Jersey: Gorgias Press.

———. 2015c. *The Documentation of the Neo-Aramaic Dialect Cluster of Gargarnaye*, 2013–2015 ELDP Project. [online] http://elar.soas.ac.uk/deposit/0291.

Trudgill, Peter. 2011. *Sociolinguistic Typology: Social Determinants of Linguistic Complexity*. Oxford: Oxford University Press.

Walther, Markus and Bernd J. Kroeger. 1994. 'Coupling Phonology and Phonetics in a Constraint-Based Model'. [online] https://archive.org/details/arxiv-cmp-lg9412007.

Zeroual, Chakir and George N. Clements. 2015. 'The Feature [Pharyngeal]'. In *Features in Phonology and Phonetics: Posthumous Writings by Nick Clements and Coauthors*, edited by Annie Rialland et al., 247–276. Berlin: Mouton de Gruyter.

ON THE ORIGIN OF SOME PLANT NAMES IN ṢŪRAYT/ṬŪRŌYO IN ṬŪR ʿABDĪN

Aziz Tezel

1. ʿArkūwo and Ḥaršaf

One of the most important wild plants in Ṭūr ʿAbdīn is termed *ʿarkūwo*. This is 'a thorny plant, whose root and stem are edible, when cooked'. It closely resembles 'cardoon'. The word *ʿarkūwo* occurs in the village dialects of Ṣūrayt/Ṭūrōyo, while the largest Ṣūrayt/Ṭūrōyo dialect, namely the dialect of Mədyad̲, uses the term *ḥaršaf* for the same plant. In the Spring, this plant is highly sought after, especially during the long fasting before Easter. In the region, the term *ʿarkūwo* corresponds to Persian *kangar*, which is also the word used in Turkish and the Kurdish dialect that is spoken in Ṭūr ʿAbdīn. Some Arabic sources render the Persian *kangar* by a Greek loanword *qulqās*,[1] which is translated by Lane as 'the root of a certain plant, which is eaten cooked and used medicinally'.[2] This word of Greek origin is found also in Jewish Aramaic and Syriac (see below §2). Syriac sources refer to the Persian *kangar*. The word also constitutes the base of the Syriac *kangarzad* 'the juice' or 'the gum' of the artichoke', which in Syriac is explained as *dūʿtā d̲-laġnā* (more on this below §2).[3] The Arabic dialects in and around Ṭūr ʿAbdīn use the word *ḥaršaf* to denote the same plant. The aforementioned Ṣūrayt/Ṭūrōyo term *ḥaršaf* is, therefore, a borrowing in the dialect of Mədyad̲. The Arabic *ḥaršaf* also occurs in literary Arabic. The Persian *kangar*, the Greek loanword *qulqās* and Arabic *ḥaršaf* are

1 *al-Munjid* (1975, 701a).

2 Lane (2003, 2560b).

3 *Thesaurus* (1981, col. 1764).

 https://doi.org/10.11647/OBP.0209.11

important words for my further discussion of the word *ʿarkūwo* and of another Ṣūrayt/Ṭūrōyo word, namely *qalqo*, to which I shall return.

Concerning the origin of Ṣūrayt/Ṭūrōyo *ʿarkūwo*, it should be noted first of all that, unlike the foreign word *ḥaršaf*, it ends in the native ending *-o*. This suggests that we are dealing with an inherited word. It is likely to have its origin in the Syriac word with the form *ʿakkūḇā* 'cynara cardunculus', which can be best translated 'cardoon'. This is to be compared to Jewish Aramaic *ʿakkōḇīṯā* 'a thistle sting' and Arabic *ʿakkūb* 'globe-thistle'.[4] For some reason, this important meaning of the Syriac word is lacking in Payne Smith's *Dictionary*, where the Syriac *ʿakkūḇā* is defined as 'a pock-mark; a wart'.[5] In the *Thesaurus Syriacus*, on which Payne Smith's *Dictionary* is founded, however, we note that the Syriac word *ʿakkūḇā* is equated with Arabic *ḥaršaf* and *ʿakkūb* and Persian *kangar*. Payne Smith significantly gives the Syriac synonym *laġnā* defined as 'cynara scolymus, a kind of artichoke'.[6] This *laġnā* seems to be the source of NENA (= North-Eastern Neo-Aramaic) *laġna* 'a thorny plant eaten when young, root and stem', according to Maclean, who is alone in indicating the form *laġna*.[7] Other sources of NENA have *lagna*, with *g*.[8] In my investigation of NENA I could not find any reflex of the Syriac *ʿakkūḇā*. Judging by the meaning of the NENA *laġna* or *lagna*, it denotes the same plant as that of Ṣūrayt/Ṭūrōyo *ʿarkūwo*. It seems that Ṣūrayt/Ṭūrōyo has preserved the reflex of the Syriac *ʿakkūḇā*, while the NENA dialects have retained its synonym *laġnā* (or *lagna*). The latter is also found in Jewish Babylonian Aramaic, although only in the plural *laġnē*.

Turning to the Ṣūrayt/Ṭūrōyo *ʿarkūwo*, the *r* in this word can be explained either as a result of contiguous regressive

4 For the etymological comparison, see Brockelmann (1982, 523b).

5 J. Payne Smith (1903, 412a).

6 For *Thesaurus*, see (1981, col. 2872); for Payne Smith, see (1903, 235b).

7 Maclean (1901, 145b).

8 For example, see *lagna* in the Barwar dialect of NENA, Khan (2008, 1318) and for *lagnə* (pl.), *lagənṯa* (sing.) in the Qaraqosh dialect of NENA, see Khan (2002, 736a).

dissimilation, i.e. **kk* > *rk*, or as a case of epenthesis. The former requires that the change took place when the old gemination was still alive in Ṣūrayt/Ṭūrōyo. If the *r* is the result of epenthesis, it might have arisen by analogy with Ṣūrayt/Ṭūrōyo *ʿarqūwo* 'heel', with which *ʿarkūwo* bears close similarities in its phonological shape and form, although their semantic fields are very different.

The next question that arises is how we can be sure that the Ṣūrayt/Ṭūrōyo *ʿarkūwo* is a reflex of the Syriac *ʿakkūḇā* and not a borrowing from Arabic *ʿakkūb*. The historical phonology of the word gives us the answer we need, since the historical **b* has shifted to *w* as in inherited words, in accordance with the development of the *bgdkpt* consonants in Syriac. If it occurs in foreign words, the sound shift in question must have been taken place in Syriac, for example, Ṣūrayt/Ṭūrōyo *malḥōwo* 'a winnowing-fork', via Syriac *malḥāḇā*, from Arabic *milḥāb*. Direct borrowings from Arabic into Ṣūrayt/Ṭūrōyo do not, as a rule, undergo such a sound shift. We can, therefore, confidently propose that the Ṣūrayt/Ṭūrōyo *ʿarkūwo* is derived from Syriac *ʿakkūḇā*, more precisely, from its Western Syriac form. Is it possible that a borrowing process took place between Syriac *ʿakkūḇā* and Arabic *ʿakkūb*? The question cannot be answered with certainty. If, however, a borrowing process is involved, there are reasons to assume an Arabic borrowing from Syriac. This is because the Arabic *ʿakkūb*, referring to the plant in question, is not a word that is widely used across the Arabic dialects. It seems to be common in Levantine Arabic, concerning which both al-Munjid and Barthélemy state that it is a borrowing from the Syriac *ʿakkūḇā*.[9]

2. Qalqo

When the plant known as *ʿarkūwo* grows old, from an edible stage to an inedible one, it not only changes shape but also name. When it is in this condition, it is called *qalqo* (plural *qalqe*), at least in the dialect of Mīdən and Bsōrīno. It develops beautiful spiky

9 *al-Munjid* (1975, 521c); Barthélemy (1935–1969, 542).

flowers containing its seeds, which resemble small, tiny grains of sand. Its inner seeds are surrounded by a very hard shell, which must be crushed by a stone in order to extract the edible seeds. The origin of this word, unlike that of *ʿarkūwo* and *ḥaršaf*, is not clear. The following observations can be made. Firstly, Syriac possesses a Greek loanword, namely *qalqā* (Western Syriac *qalqō*), from Greek *κάχληξ* 'pebble'. This resembles Ṣūrayt/Ṭūrōyo *qalqo* in form, but its semantic connection is problematic, unless one were to hypothesise that the plant in question in this stage of development was called so because of the resemblance of its seeds to 'pebbles'. Such a semantic development is possible. To be sure, the Ṣūrayt/Ṭūrōyo word *qalqo* in Ritter's *Wörterbuch* is translated 'Kieselstein', referring to its occurrence in the following passage:

> *ʾōno g-saymōno bäblīsōke w-g-māqīmōno ʾū-ʿafro waq-qalqe, ʾī-qyamto g-māqīmalla*
>
> 'Ich werde dann einen Wirbelsturm erregen und Erde und Kiesel aufwirbeln, ihr einen Jüngsten Tag anstellen.'
>
> ('I will then stir up a hurricane and whirl up earth and pebbles, make it a doomsday.')[10]

I strongly suspect, however, that Ritter's translation is based on the Syriac meaning 'pebbles', for the informant (in this case Slēmān Ḥanna Maskōbi, originally from Mīdən), in all probability is referring to the plant in question and not to 'pebbles'. All elderly people in Mīdən know that when *qalqo* becomes dry, it becomes very light and is blown away by whirlwinds. The people of Mīdən, therefore, have coined a figurative phrase *xāyīfō=yo xdū qalqo* 'he is fast like *qalqo*'. Thus, Ritter's translation 'Kieselstein' of the Ṣūrayt/Ṭūrōyo *qalqo* is not correct.

The next noteworthy word is the other aforementioned Greek loanword *qulqās*, whose form in Syriac and Jewish Aramaic is *qōlqās*. The nominal ending *-o* in the word *qalqo*, however, indicates that it has been integrated into the native morphological

10 Ritter (1979, 396; 1969, 626–627).

system, which is likely to have taken place at an earlier period. In fact, in *Supplement to the Thesaurus Syriacus* we find a plural form *qelqē*, exemplified by the phrase *ʾatten qelqē* 'fumigate with colocasia', which, according to this source, is a plural form for the Syriac *qōlqās*.[11] In Brockelmann's *Lexicon*, however, this word is cited with the singular form *qalqā* and is said to be derived from Latin *calx* 'chalk'. Sokoloff, therefore, in his version of Brockelmann's *Lexicon* translates the same phrase *ʾatten qelqē* 'fumigate with chalk',[12] which does not fit contextually. In the context the fumigation with *qelqē* was intended to drive away gnats. It is mentioned together with galbanum in the following Syriac passage:

> *ʾatten ʾaykā ḏ-ḏammiḵ = ʾa(n)t ḥelḇānīṯā w-ḵeḇrīṯā w-ʿārqīn, ʾaw ʾatten qelqē w-ʾāḇdīn*
>
> 'Fumigate the place where thou sleepest with galbanum and sulphur, and they will fly away; or fumigate with colocasia, and they will perish.'[13]

A third possibility is that the Ṣūrayt/Ṭūrōyo *qalqo* reflects an unattested **qalqlo*, which by dissimilation could take the form *qalqo*. Syriac has *qalqīnā* 'a low-growing herb'. Akkadian has a plant name *qulqulliānu*, which refers to an unknown species.[14] Ugaritic has a word with the consonantal skeleton *qlql* 'herb fed to horses', related to Hebrew *qelōqēl* 'miserable food'.[15] Some sources connect these words with Arabic *qilqil*, which in some sources is translated by 'cassia'.[16] In its borrowed form in Persian, the Arabic word *qilqil* is described by Steingass (1977, 985b) as

11 *Margoliouth* (1981, 304b).

12 Brockelmann, (1982, 670b); Sokoloff, (2009, 1375b).

13 For the Syriac text, see Budge (1976, vol. 1, 579), and for the English translation see the same source (1976, vol. 2, 689).

14 For the Syriac *qalqīnā*, see J. Payne Smith (1903, 508a); for Akkadian *qulqulliānu*, see *CAD* (1956-, vol. 13, 301a-b).

15 Gordon (1965, 478b).

16 Koehler and Baumgartner (2001, 1106b-1107a).

'a species of plant producing a grain so hard that it cannot be pounded', which is reminiscent of the Ṣūrayt/Ṭūrōyo *qalqo*. If Ṣūrayt/Ṭūrōyo *qalqo* is derived from Arabic *qilqil*, this form would have to exist in Anatolian Arabic and denote the same plant. I have not yet been able to establish whether Anatolian Arabic has a specific word for *ḥaršaf* when it is growing old. Kurdish in the area uses *kärämber* when Kurdish *kangar* is growing old. Thus, a borrowing from Kurdish is out of the question. Evidence against the hypothesis that the word is borrowed from the neighbouring languages is the native ending *-o*. All borrowed plant names from these languages known to me do not end in *-o*.

Further evidence against the possible borrowing of Ṣūrayt/Ṭūrōyo *qalqo* from a neighbouring language is the fact that the form *qalqa* has been identified by Hezy Mutzafi in the NENA dialect of Mer near Cudi dağı with the meaning of 'the seeds of *lagna*.'[17] As has been remarked, the NENA-*lagna* corresponds in meaning to Ṣūrayt/Ṭūrōyo *ʿarkūwo*. This may be an important indication that the Ṣūrayt/Ṭūrōyo *qalqo* also originally denoted only the seeds of *ʿarkūwo*. The situation in NENA, however, is complicated by the fact that some NENA dialects (the Ṭiyāre dialects) use the form *qaqna* rather than *qalqa* to denote dried *lagna*.[18] It is not clear from the information I have received whether this *qaqna* is also used for the seeds of *lagna*. What is more, in the NENA dialect of Barwar *qaqna* is described as a 'thorny plant'. This is yellow in colour and grows in the mountains. When the sap sets it produces a gum known as *deṯa*, which is softened in water and then chewed.[19] We have seen before that the Persian loanword *kangarzad* 'the juice or the gum of the artichoke' is explained in Syriac as *dūʿtā ḏ-laġnā*. The Barwar *deṯa*, which is a reflex of the earlier *dūʿtā*, denotes the 'gum' of *qaqna* and not of *lagna*.

To sum up the case *qalqo* so far, I find the Syriac plural form *qelqē* in *The Syriac Book of Medicines* to be significant for explaining the Ṣūrayt/Ṭūrōyo *qalqo* (plural *qalqe*). The shift *e*

17 Hezy Mutzafi, personal communication (September 2016).

18 Hezy Mutzafi, personal communication (September 2016).

19 For the Barwar dialect of NENA, see Khan (2008, 1365).

> *a* in a closed syllable is regular in Ṣūrayt/Ṭūrōyo. Thus the change *qelqē* > *qalqe* would not present a problem. Whether this is a plural formation for the Syriac *qōlqās* or a variant plural form of the Syriac *qalqē* 'pebbles' or, as stated by Brockelmann, a borrowing from the Latin *calx*, is a question for further discussion. Notable is the fact that some versions of Bar ʿAlī's *Syro-Arabic Lexicon* have *qelqē* instead of *qalqē* 'pebbles'.[20] NENA *qalqa* is the same word as that of Ṣūrayt/Ṭūrōyo *qalqo*. NENA *qaqna* is probably cognate with *qalqa*.

3. Rašāle, Daḥle and Ḥērafrūfo

The next three words that will be considered are *rašāle* (fem.), *daḥle* (fem.) and *ḥērafrūfo* (masc.). The words *rašāle* and *daḥle* are dialectal words denoting an edible wild plant with a sharp taste, which can be identified as 'cress'. The word *ḥērafrūfo* denotes 'Scandix Ausralis L' (southern chervil), which in some dialects has the form *ḥəfrūfo*. It is, likewise, edible and has a sharp taste, although milder in taste in comparison with *rašāle, daḥle*. Both these are, like *ʿarkūwo*, among those most sought-after plants during the Spring, especially during the long fasting before Easter. The word *rašāle* occurs in the dialect of Mədyaḏ and some village dialects around Mədyaḏ, while *daḥle* occurs in some dialects in the periphery, for example, in the dialect of Mīdən.

Rašāle is a loanword, which ultimately goes back to Arabic *rašād* 'garden peppergrass (Lepidium sativum L)'. This is also the word used to denote this plant in the Kurdish dialect spoken in Ṭūr ʿAbdīn (in the form *rašād* or *rašāl* see below). The Arabic *rašād* has also meanings such as 'integrity of conducts; good sense, maturity', which is a derivative of the Arabic root *rašada* 'to be on the right way'. Given the meaning of the root, one naturally wonders why the plant 'garden peppergrass' was called *rašād* in Arabic. It seems that the meaning relating to this plant originated in Iraqi Arabic. This can be deduced from *Lisān ʾal-ʿarab*, where we read:

20 Bar ʿAlī (1928, 349).

> *war-rašād wa-ḥabbu r-rašādi, nabtun yuqālu lahu ṯ-ṯuffāʾu; qāla ʾabū Manṣūr: ʾahlu l-ʿirāq yaqūlūna lil-ḥurfi ḥabbu r-rašādi, yataṭayyarūna min lafẓi l-ḥurfi li-ʾannahu ḥirmānun fa-yaqūlūna ḥabbu r-rašādi.*[21]
>
> '*Rašād* or the seed of the *rašād* is a plant, which is called *ṯuffāʾ*. ʾAbū Manṣūr said: 'the people of Iraq call the plant known as *ḥurf ḥabbu r-rašād* (the seed of *rašād*). They see an evil omen in the pronunciation of *ḥurf*, because *ḥurf* means 'deprivation, bereavement, ill-fatedness.'

In other words, the plant in question was known to the Arabs either as *ṯuffāʾ* or *ḥurf*. Since *ḥurf* also has meanings with negative connotations, the people of Iraq came to give it the name *rašād*, since *rašād* has, unlike *ḥurf*, positive connotations. If the meaning *rašād* 'garden cress' really originated in Iraqi Arabic, it must have spread from this dialect to the other Arabic dialects in the region, for all major Arabic dialects in the region use the word with this meaning.

Turning to the Ṣūrayt/Ṭūrōyo *rašāle*, as can be seen, it exhibits two differences from the Arabic word *rašād*, namely the shift *d* > *l*, which is unusual in Ṣūrayt/Ṭūrōyo, and the ending *e*. If it reflects a direct borrowing from an Arabic dialect, the Arabic form should be **rašāde* or **rašāda*, with a literary Arabic form *rašādat*^{un}, which I could not find in this meaning. According to the information I have obtained, some Kurdish villages in Ṭūr ʿAbdīn use the form *rašād* and others the form *rašāl*. This suggests that the shift *r* > *l* did not take place in Ṣūrayt/Ṭūrōyo. It took place either in Kurdish or Anatolian Arabic. In any case, if it is a borrowing from Kurdish, the *-e* reflects the Kurdish oblique ending *-e*. The word in the Ṣūrayt/Ṭūrōyo village dialects may have been taken from the dialect of Mədyaḏ or directly from the local Kurdish.

I shall now consider the word *daḥle*, which, like *rašāle*, is a feminine noun ending in *-e*. The ending *-e* in almost all feminine singular nouns in Ṣūrayt/Ṭūrōyo is a foreign element. It reflects

21 *Līsān ʾal-ʿarab* (1955, vol. 3, 177a).

either dialectal Arabic -*e*, which is the reflex of original *a*, or it reflects the Kurdish oblique ending -*e*. In the case of the word *daḥle*, however, the matter is complicated. First it should be pointed out that there seem to be in the language two different words with the form *daḥle*. Some dialects use *daḥle* with the meaning 'a thicket; a fruit orchard with water', while other dialects use *daḥle*, with the meaning 'cress'. With regard to *daḥle* with the meaning of 'a thicket; a fruit orchard', it is relevant to note that in Anatolian Arabic we find *daḥle*, translated into German 'Wald, Waldstück, Gehölz'.[22] The same word occurs in Kurdish, either in the form *deḥl* or *dehl*, with the same or similar meanings. Some Arabic sources also have the form *dahl*, with *h* (thus at least in Dozy).[23] The ultimate origin of this word is probably Arabic *daġl* 'abundance of plants or herbs or trees'. This means that in the case of the Ṣūrayt/Ṭūrōyo *daḥle* 'a thicket; a fruit orchard with water', we are dealing with a borrowing either from Anatolian Arabic *daḥle* or from the Kurdish form *deḥl*.

As for the origin of the Ṣūrayt/Ṭūrōyo *daḥle* 'cress', its ultimate source is Syriac *taḥlā* (plural *taḥlē*); hence also NENA *taxla* 'garden cress', indicated at least for Christian Urmi; however with unknown gender.[24] Most Syriac sources indicate the Syriac *taḥlā* as feminine. As has been suggested, the Ṣūrayt/Ṭūrōyo *daḥle* displays the shift *t* > *d*, which seems to have a considerable time depth, for already in some Syriac sources we find *daḥlā* for the original *taḥlā*. That the *t* in this word is original is also shown by the cognate root of this word in other Semitic languages. Akkadian has *šeḫlātu*, Ugaritic *šḫlt*, Rabbinic Hebrew *šəḥālīm* (plural). The Old Aramaic form of the plural absolute form is also with *š*, namely *šḥlyn*, apparently to be read *šaḥlīn*. The latter corresponds to Jewish Palestinian Aramaic *tḥlyn*, apparently to be read as *taḥlīn*. In Jewish Babylonian Aramaic, the corresponding word is contextually attested only in the plural emphatic form

22 For Anatolian Arabic *daḥle*, see Vocke and Waldner (1982, 151).

23 Dozy (1881, 467a).

24 For Christian Urmi, see Khan (2016, 41).

taḥlē.[25] In Syriac, both the singular form *taḥlā* and the plural *taḥlē* are attested contextually, with the plural form *taḥlē* as the predominant one. The entry in Löw's *Flora* has the Syriac word in the plural form *taḥlē*.[26] The question arises as to whether the *-e* in the Ṣūrayt/Ṭūrōyo *daḥle* reflects the plural morpheme *-e*, which the Ṣūrayt/Ṭūrōyo speakers could have interpreted as the foreign element *-e*. Even if the root of a feminine singular noun ending in *-e* is native, the *-e* is a foreign element, for example, Mədyad *gəddāle* 'braid', formed under the influence of Anatolian Arabic *jəddāle*, i.e. the root *gdl* is native but not the form of the word. A genuine Ṣūrayt/Ṭūrōyo reflex of the Syriac singular form *taḥlā* should thus consistently have the form **taḥlo*, with a plural **taḥle*, and with the shift *t* > *d*, the expected singular form would be **daḥlo*. In Ṣūrayt/Ṭūrōyo there is no sure case of the plural morpheme *-e* occurring on a feminine singular noun. Even words with collective meanings end either in the singular ending *-o* or in the plural ending *-e*, and they are construed syntactically as singulars or plurals respectively. Thus, we say *baqro* 'herd of cattle' *ʾī-baqro* (feminine singular), *bōqo* 'gnats', *ʾī-bōqo* (feminine singular), *qanyōne* 'cattle', *ʾaq-qanyōne* (masculine plural), but never **ʾī-baqre*, **ʾī-bōqe*, **ʾī-qanyōne*. I am aware of the situation in NENA, where some originally plural nouns are interpreted as feminine singular, for example, *kawe* 'a small window', which is interpreted as a reflex of the Syriac plural form *kawwē* (the plural of *kawṯā*), but such an interpretation in Ṣūrayt/Ṭūrōyo is improbable. Thus, if the *-e* in *daḥle* reflects the plural morpheme *-e*, this would mean a unique case in the language. That the Ṣūrayt/Ṭūrōyo *daḥle* is a reflex of the Syriac *taḥla* is also evident from the NENA *taxla*, which has preserved the original form, disregarding the shift *ḥ* > *x*, which is regular in NENA.

The word *ḥērafrūfo* (or *ḥəfrōfo* in some dialects) is of obscure origin. There are three possible ways of reconstructing its background.

25 For a general etymological comparison, see Koehler and Baumgartner (2001, 1462b); for Jewish Palestinian Aramaic *tḥlyn*, see Sokoloff (2002, 579b); for Jewish Babylonian Aramaic *taḥlē*, see Sokoloff (2002, 1200a).

26 Löw (1928, 396).

Firstly, it might be an augmented form of Syriac *ḥūrpā*, explained in Syriac as *ʿesbā (h)w d-lā ʿḏakkīl qṭar qanyā d-šebblē* 'a grass whose stalk has not hardened'. This is related to Jewish Babylonian Aramaic *ḥpwrʾ*,[27] which is tentatively to be read *ḥəp̄ūrā*. As the precise species of this word in Syriac as well as in Jewish Babylonian Aramaic is not clear, it is difficult to be sure about its connection with the Ṣūrayt/Ṭūrōyo *ḥērafrūfo*. An addition problem is the etymology of Syriac *ḥūrpā*, which occurs with three different meanings. These include in addition to the meaning of a type of grass also *ḥūrpā* 'sharpness' or 'a sharp edge' or 'point (of, for example, a sword, nail), and *ḥūrpā* 'a yearling sheep'. *Ḥūrpā* 'sharpness' is a well-known derivative of the root *ḥrp* 'to be sharp', while *ḥūrpā* 'a yearling sheep' has an etymological equivalent in Arabic *ḫarūf* 'a young sheep, lamb, yearling'. Oddly, the etymological dictionaries of Syriac consider the Syriac *ḥūrpā* 'a grass whose stalk has not hardened' to be the same word as *ḥūrpā* 'a yearling sheep',[28] perhaps suggesting that the grass in question is in its early stage of development, as it describes a grass whose stalk has not hardened.

Secondly, I have already mentioned that the word for 'garden cress' was originally termed *ḥurf* in some dialects of Arabic rather than *rašād*. This *ḥurf* in Arabic is considered to be derived from the root *ḥrf*, which in some derivatives has the notion 'sharp; pungent, acrid (the latter of taste)'. This is cognate with Syriac *ḥrp*, which also occurs in Ṣūrayt/Ṭūrōyo, where *ḥarūfo* means 'sharp; pungent' (both of cutting edge and taste). The question is whether the Ṣūrayt/Ṭūrōyo *ḥērafrūfo* is an independent augmentative formation of this *ḥārūfo*.

Thirdly, studies in the neighbouring languages may be of help in identifying this word. A borrowing from the Kurdish used in the area is out of the question for two reasons. The proper Kurdish

27 For the Syriac *ḥūrpā* and its definitions in Syriac, see *Thesaurus* (1981, col. 1379–1380) and for the etymological connection with Jewish Babylonian Aramaic *ḥpwrʾ*, see Sokoloff (2002, 477a).

28 For the Syriac *ḥūrpā* with three different meanings and its comparison with other Semitic languages, see Brockelmann (1982, 258a-b).

word used for this plant in the area is termed *zūčərk*, according to the information I have obtained. The Ṣūrayt/Ṭūrōyo word, moreover, ends in the native ending *-o*. As has been remarked above, all Kurdish borrowings pertaining to the names of flora are non-integrated ones. There remains the possibility that it has its origin in Anatolian Arabic. The word denoting this plant in Anatolian Arabic dialects is, however, so far unknown to me. Before drawing any conclusions, therefore, the name in Anatolian Arabic needs to be established.

4. 'Tree' and 'Thorn Bramble'

In this section I shall consider the words for 'a tree' and for 'a thorn bramble'. The former has a common word, which is termed *dawmo*, while the latter has three etymologically quite different words across the various dialects, namely *ʿəlto, sālənto* and *ṭawʿənto*.

The word *dawmo* is interesting in several respects. It can have the specific meaning of 'oak-tree' in Ṭūr ʿAbdīn, but it is also used with the general meaning 'tree'. The Syriac word for 'tree', *ʾīlānā* has the reflex *ʾīlōno* in Ṣūrayt/Ṭūrōyo. The word *ʾīlōno* is not common in Ṣūrayt/Ṭūrōyo but speakers still know its meaning. All the forests around the villages in Ṭūr ʿAbdīn contain the *dawmo* 'oak-tree' (plural *dawme*). Its fruit is termed in Ṣūrayt/Ṭūrōyo *bālūṭo*, which is a reflex of the Syriac word *ballōṭā*, hence Arabic *ballūṭ*, according to several sources. While in Syriac the word *ballōṭā* denotes both 'the oak-tree' and its fruit 'acorn', in Ṣūrayṭ/Ṭūrōyo the word *bālūṭo* does not denote the 'oak-tree' but only its fruit 'acorn'. The 'oak-tree' is termed either by the word *dawmo* alone or by the phrase *dawmo dū-bālūṭo*. It grows wild. Until fifty years ago, this tree constituted the lifeline in the area. Before modern building techniques were introduced into the area, the timber cut from this tree was used to build ceilings. Its branches were also used as fodder for animals, as also were its fruits, the acorns. Moreover, the wood cut from this tree served as the most important wood fuel during the cold months of the year. During a famine (referred to in Ṣūrayt/Ṭūrōyo by the word *ġāla*, an Arabic loanword) the 'acorns' of this tree were ground into bread flour. The bread baked from this flour served as the most important food for the local people. Nowadays, it is completely forbidden to cut off parts or fell these trees in the forest for the domestic use.

What is the origin of this word *dawmo*? Although it has the native ending *-o*, it is a foreign word in the language, coming from Arabic *dawmat*^{un}, a *nomen unitatis* of the collective *dawm* 'the doom-palm'. The word is also found in English, into which it was introduced via French, from Arabic *dawm*, according to Colin's *Dictionary*. In the Arabic dialects around Ṭūr ʿAbdīn, the word is attested in Qinderib, having both the collective *dawm* and the *nomen unitatis dawme*. According to *al-Munjid*, this tree and its species are growing in Egyptian, Sudan and Saudi Arabia.[29]

As for the words for 'a thorn bramble', among the aforementioned three words, the dialectal word *ʿəlto* (plural *ʿōle*) is readily recognizable. It is a clear reflex of Western Syriac *ʿōltō* (Syriac *ʿāltā*, plural *ʿālē*), a feminine form which has presumably been formed as a *nomen unitatis* from *ʿālā* (or from its pl. *ʿālē*). The form *ʿālā* itself would seem to be a reflex of Syriac *ʿaʾlā*, whose root *ʿʾl* is comparable to that of Hebrew *ṣʾl* in *ṣeʾelīm* and that of Arabic *ḏ̣ʾl* in *ḏ̣aʾl*.[30] The occurrence of the Ṣūrayt/Ṭūrōyo *ʿəlto* (plural *ʿōle*) was until now known only from the dialect of Mīdən, but in my latest research journeys to Ṭūr ʿAbdīn I noted its occurrence also in two other village dialects, namely in the dialect of Bēqusyōno and Zāz. The informants of the dialect of Bēqusyōno stated that for the 'shrub' they say *ʿəlto* (plural *ʿōle*), but for its thorns they say *sālūne* (plural).

This brings us to the other word *sālənto* (plural *sālūne*), which is used in some dialects, among them the dialect of Mədyaḏ. In Syriac, only in the supplement of Augin Manna's *Syro-Arabic Lexicon* could I find a word with the form *selōnā* (Western Syriac: *selūnō*). This is rendered by Arabic *ʾumm ġaylān*, *ʿusaj*, with the

29 For Colin's *Dictionary*, see (1991, 469) under doum or doom-palm; Jastrow (2005, 53b); *al-Munjid* (1975, 230c).

30 Brockelmann (1982, 503a).

same or a similar meaning.[31] The Ṣūrayt/Ṭūrōyo plural form *sālūne* is clearly a reflex of this word, which, oddly, is classified in this source as a foreign word, without giving the etymon of the foreign word in question. The supplement is of very late date and is not written by the author of the lexicon. In any case, I think this word has, one way or another, a historical connection with Syriac *salwā* and Jewish Aramaic *silwā* 'thorn', connected by Koehler and Baumgartner with Hebrew *sallōn*, Arabic *sullāʾ* and Akkadian *ṣ/sillû*, all with the meaning 'thorn'.[32] The Ṣūrayt/Ṭūrōyo *sālənte* could be a backformation from the plural *sālūne*. In favour of such an interpretation is the situation in the dialect of Bēqusyōno, where the tree is called *ʿəlto* (plural *ʿōle*), but its thorns and fruit are termed *sālūne*. There is thus no *sālənto*, according to my informants.

Finally, I shall mention that a group of village dialects, the so-called Rāyīte-dialects, have a word of their own for the 'thorny bramble', namely *ṭawʿənto* (plural *ṭawʿūne*). According to some of my informants, its fruits are termed *ṭawʿūne* because of their being like *ṭawʿūne* (plural) 'small offerings of bread stamped with a symbol of the cross', a diminutive of *ṭawʿe*, the reflex of the Syriac *ṭaḇʿē*, root *ṭbʿ* 'to seal; to sink'. It is difficult to know whether this is a folk-etymology or not. Alternatively it may be proposed that the word has its origin in Syriac *ṭʿūntā* and *ṭʿantā* 'a crop of fruit', root *ṭʿn* 'to bear; to carry'. A reflex of the Syriac word *ṭʿūntā* is found in NENA, e.g. Barwar *ṭunta* 'fruit of a tree'.[33] Such an interpretation would mean that the *w* in the Ṣūrayt/Ṭūrōyo *ṭawʿənto* is secondary; cf. Ṣūrayt/Ṭūrōyo *ʿwōno* 'a sheep', from **ʿōnō*, root *ʿʾn*.

31 Manna (1975, 946a).

32 Koehler and Baumgartner (2001, 756b-757a).

33 Khan (2008, 1427).

References

al-Munjid. 1975. = *al-Munjid fī al-luġa wal-ʾaʿlām*. Beirut: Dār al-mašriq.

Bar ʿAlī's *Syro-Arabic Lexicon*. From *ōlaf* to *mīm* edited by Georg Hoffmann, Kiel 1874. From *nūn* to *taw* edited by Richard H.J Gottheil, Paris 1928.

Barthélemy, Adrien. 1935–1969. *Dictionnaire arabe-français; Dialects de Syrie: Alep, Damas, Liban, Jérusalem*, Paris: Geuthner.

Brockelmann, Carl. 1982. *Lexicon Syriacum*. Editio secunda aucta et emendata. Halis Saxonum (2. unveränderter reprographischer Nachdruck der 2. Auflage, Halle an der Saale 1928: Niemayer, Tübingen): Hildesheim: G. Olms.

Budge, E. A. Wallis. 1976. *The Syriac Book of Medicines: Syrian Anatomy, Pathology and Therapeutics in the Early Middle Ages; with Sections on Astrological and Native Medicine and Recipes by an Anonymous Physician*. Philo Press: Amsterdam.

Dozy, Reinhart. 1881. *Supplément aux dictionnaires arabes*. Brill: Leyde.

Gordon, Cyrus H. 1965. *Ugaritic Textbook*. Pontifical Biblical Institute: Rome.

Ibn Manẓūr, see *Lisān al ʿarab*.

Jastrow, Otto. 2005. *Glossar zu Kinderib*. Wiesbaden: Harrassowitz.

Khan, Geoffrey. 2002. *The Neo-Aramaic Dialect of Qaraqosh*. Brill: Leiden.

———. 2008. *The Neo-Aramaic Dialect of Barwar*. 3 vols. Handbook of Oriental Studies 96. Brill: Leiden.

———. 2016. *The Neo-Aramaic Dialect of the Assyrian Christians of Urmi*. 4 vols. Brill: Leiden.

Koehler, Ludwig and Baumgartner, Walter. 2001. *The Hebrew and Aramaic Lexicon of the Old Testament*: Study Edition, 2 vols. Brill: Leiden.

Lane, Edward William. 2003. *Arabic-English Lexicon*, 8 vols., London 1863–93. Reprinted by the Islamic Texts Society (UK), 2 vols.

Lisān al ʿarab, li-Jamāl ad-Din Muḥammad bin Mukarram ibn Manẓūr. 1955. 15 vols. Dar Sader: Beirut.

Löw, Immanuel. 1881. *Die Flora der Juden*. Verlag von Wilhelm Engelmann: Leipzig.

MacLean, Arthur John. 1901. *A Dictionary of the Dialects of Vernacular Syriac as Spoken by the Eastern Syrians of Kurdistan, North-West Persia, and the Plain of Mosul. With Illustrations from the Dialects of the Jews of Zakhu and Azerbaijan, and of the Western Syrians of Tur 'Abdin and Ma'lula.* Oxford: Clarendon.

Manna, Jacques-Eugene. 1900. *Leksīqōn kaldōyō-ʾarabōyō* - Arabic title: *Qāmūs kaldānī-ʿarabī*- English title: *Chaldean-Arabic Dictionary*. Mosul. [reprinted 1975 with a new appendix by Dr. Raphael J. Bidawid, Chaldean bishop of Beirut. Babel Center Publications: Beirut].

Margoliouth, Payne Jessie. 1927. *Supplement to the Thesaurus Syriacus of* R. Payne Smith, S.T.P. Oxford: Clarendon Press [reprint 1981: Hildesheim-New York: Georg Olms].

Oppenheim, Adolf Leo, Erica Reiner *et al.* (eds.). 1956-. *The Assyrian Dictionary of the University of Chicago*, 21 vols. Chicago, IL.

Payne Smith, Jessie. 1903. *A Compendious Syriac Dictionary*. Oxford: Clarendon.

Payne Smith, Robert. 1981. (ed.), *Thesaurus Syriacus*, I–II. Oxford 1879–1901. Nachdruck der Ausgabe Oxford 1879–1901, Hildesheim, New York: G. Olms.

Ritter, Helmut. *Ṭūrōyo: Die Volkssprache der syrischen Christen des Ṭūr ʿAbdīn*:

———. 1969. *Texte*, Band II, Beirut in Kommission bei Franz Steiner Verlag: Wiesbaden.

———. 1979. *Wörterbuch*. Beirut, in Kommission bei Franz Steiner Verlag: Wiesbaden.

Sokoloff, Michael. 2002. *A Dictionary of Jewish Babylonian Aramaic of the Talmudic and Geonic periods*, Ramat-Gan: Bar Ilan University Press, and Baltimore, MD: Johns Hopkins University Press.

———. 2002. *A Dictionary of Jewish Palestinian Aramaic of the Byzantine Period*, Ramat-Gan: Bar Ilan University Press, and Baltimore, MD: Johns Hopkins University Press.

———. 2009. *A Syriac Lexicon: A Translation from the Latin, Correction, Expansion, and Update of C. Brockelmann's Lexicon Syriacum*, Winona Lake, IN: Eisenbrauns; Piscataway, NJ: Gorgias Press.

Steingass, Francis. 2006. *Persian-English Dictionary*. New Delhi: Manohar Publishers.

Tezel, Aziz. 2003. *Comparative Etymological Studies in the Western Neo-Syriac* (*Ṭūrōyo*) Lexicon. *With Special Reference to Homonyms, Related Words and Borrowings with Cultural Siginification*, Studia Semitica Upsaliensia 18. Elanders Gotab: Stockholm.

Thesaurus, see Payne Smith, R.

Vocke, Sibylle and Waldner, Wolfram. 1982. *Der Wortschatz des anatolischen Arabisch*. Magister-Arbeit, Universität: Erlangen-Nürnberg.

REMARKS ON SELECTED EXPONENTS OF THE 208-SWADESH LIST IN ṬUROYO

Eugene Barsky and Yulia Furman

Introduction

The present paper is a supplement to the 208-Swadesh list for Ṭuroyo published in Barsky, Furman and Loesov (2018).[1] It discusses the following selected exponents of the list that were not included in the original publication: BIRD, HEAD, HUSBAND, MAN (MALE), MAN (HUMAN BEING), SUN, WIFE and WOMAN.

The lexical study is based on fieldwork conducted in Berlin and Gütersloh among the Ṭuroyo-speaking community (August 2016). Another source of our data is the published field corpus of Ṭuroyo, which mainly consists of the texts of H. Ritter (Ritter 1967, 1969 and 1971) and E. Prym and A. Socin (PrS).

The texts from the three Ritter volumes (Ritter 1967, 1969, 1971) will be cited by the number of text and sentence along with the speaker's place of origin, e.g. 61:9, Kfarze. The texts from the Prym-Socin collection, which originate from one Midyat speaker, will be cited by page number and line, e.g. 21/3. The concepts of the Swadesh list will be given in small capitals, e.g. WOMAN, FAT.

1 See the detailed introduction to the work on the Ṭuroyo Swadesh List in Barsky, Furman and Loesov (2018). The 208-Swadesh list is a modified version of the standard 207-Swadesh list (with one additional concept 'to go'), which is a compilation of basic concepts used in comparative and historical linguistics for quantifying the interrelatedness of languages.

 https://doi.org/10.11647/OBP.0209.12

1. Bird

In Ṭuroyo, there are two main lexemes for the notion BIRD: *safruno* (RW 450) and *ṭayro* (RW 531), both in the published corpus and the data from our fieldwork.

Basically, *safruno* means SMALL BIRD, but it can also be used as a generic term for BIRD and as the name of a particular species: SPARROW.

Some of our informants use *safruno* in neutral contexts:

(1) *kito ġắlabe* ***šəklat d-safrune*** *bu=aṯrayḏan*

kito	*ġắlabe*	*šəklat*	*d-safrune*	*b-u=aṯr-ayḏan*
EXIST	many	species	of-birds	in-ART.MS=land-POSSII.1PL

'There are many **bird species** in our land.' (Mzizaḥ)

See also the following examples from the corpus:

(2) *gzobaṭle* ***safruno*** *mede aw ṭayrək mede b-lebe*

g-zobaṭ-le	*safruno*	*mede*	*aw*	*ṭayrək*
PRS-catch.IPFV[2]-3MS-DAT.3MS	bird	some	or	birdie

mede	*b-leb-e*
some	in-heart-POSSI.3MS

'He thinks of **a bird** or a birdie.' (94:436, ʿIwardo)

The passage describes a game in which a participant thinks of a bird name and others are supposed to guess it. Later in the story,

2 This represents the imperfective base also referred to as *infectum*, which, being bare or modified with affixes, appears in various functions (subjunctive, present, future, habitual past etc.).

one of the participants reveals the name of the bird he thought of: *flān safruno-yo* 'This is a certain bird' (94:440, ʿIwardo). It is clear that *safruno* is used here as a general term for BIRD.

In the same text, *safruno* appears in a list of birds inhabiting Ṭur-ʿAbdin and denotes SPARROW:

(3) *af=fərḥoṯe, d-kofayri-ste, hani-ne: (…) **safrune***

af=fərḥoṯe	*d-ko-fayr-i-ste*	*hani-ne*	*safrune*
ART.PL=birds	REL-PRS-fly.IPFV-3PL-too	these-COP.3PL	sparrows

'Flying birds are as follows: (…) **sparrows**.' (94:223, ʿIwardo)

It should be noted that the word *fərḥoṯe* is employed here as a generic term for BIRD, which is not found anywhere else in the searchable corpus. It must be an adapted borrowing from Classical Syriac, which goes back to *pāraḥtā* 'bird' (SL 1236).

On the other hand, *ṭayro* means BIG BIRD, which can also be employed as a general term for BIRD and the name of a particular species: EAGLE. Consider the following examples for the meaning BIRD, both cited by our informants and found in the corpus:

(4) *kit tamo **ṭayro**, bas mən **ṭayro**-yo, lə=kfəraqno u=ğəns d-kətle*

kīt	*tamo*	*ṭayro*	*bas*	*mən*	*ṭayro-yo*
EXIST	there	bird	but	what	bird-COP.3S

lə=k-fəraq-no	*u=ğəns*
NEG=PRS-distinguish.IPFV-1MS	ART.MS=sort

d-	*kət*	*le*
REL	EXIST	DAT.3MS

'There is **a bird** there, but I cannot distinguish what kind of **bird** this is.' (Midyat)

(5) *skandar yaləf b-lišone daḥ=ḥăyewən w* ***daṭ=ṭayre****-stine*

skandar	*yaləf*	*b-lišon-e*	*d-aḥ=ḥăyewən*
PN	learn.PRET.3MS	in-language-EZ	of-ART.PL=animals

w	*d-aṭ=ṭayre-stine*
and	of-ART.PL=birds-too

'Skandar learned the language of animals and **birds**.' (60:10, Kfarze)

Ṭayro may also refer to EAGLE. Some of our informants translated 'Which kind of bird is this one? This is an eagle' as

(6) *mən šəkəl* ***ṭayro/safruno****-yo hano? hano* ***ṭayro****-yo* (Arkaḥ/Mzizaḥ)

mən	*šəkəl*	*ṭayro*	*safruno-yo*	*hano*	*hano*	*ṭayro-yo*
what	kind	bird	bird-COP.3S	this.M	this.M	eagle-COP.3S

'Which kind of bird is this one? This is an eagle.'

It is not clear why Ṭuroyo speakers (i.e. our informants and the informants for the corpus) choose *ṭayro* or *safruno* for denoting BIRD in neutral contexts. Both words can be used in the same situation regardless of the speaker's origin. Nonetheless, *safruno* occurs more frequently in the speech of our informants. In the corpus, occurrences of *ṭayro* and *safruno* with the meaning of BIRD are only sporadic and occur roughly with the same frequency.

A comparable picture can be observed in Soqotri, a Modern South Arabian language, where two terms for BIRD exist: *nóyhər* and *əṣféro*. The former denotes 'a generic small bird' and the latter 'a generic big bird.' These words, however, can also be used synonymously. Furthermore, in the speech of L. Kogan's informants, *nóyhər* denotes a generic bird, while *əṣféro* means a certain bird species, namely SPARROW (Kogan 2015,489). The semantic development of the term *nóyhər* is similar to that of *ṭayro*: *nóyhər* goes back to Proto-West Semitic **našr-* 'eagle'; *ṭayro* goes back to Middle Eastern Aramaic (MEA)[3] *ṭayrā* 'bird, raptor'.

2. Head

According to the data of the published corpus and according to our informants, *qarʿo* (RW 399) is the main word for HEAD in Ṭuroyo, whether of human beings or animals. Contrary to our expectations, *rišo* (RW 443) and *qarʿo* are rarely synonyms. Only one speaker from Midən and one from Bsorino employ *rišo* alongside *qarʿo*. In the corpus, however, a competition between the two words is observed in the texts from Midən, where *qarʿo* and *rišo* occur in the speech of the same speakers with equal frequency:

(7) *grəšle u=sayfo, qṭəʿle* ***qarʿe***

grəš-le *u=sayfo* *qṭəʿ-le*
pull.PRET-3MS ART.MS=sword cut_off.PRET-3MS

qarʿ-e
head-POSSI.3MS

'He unsheathed the sword and cut **his head** off.' (74:159, Midən)

3 The term Middle Aramaic is employed here in accordance with the classification of Klaus Beyer (1984). It includes three Eastern Aramaic varieties (Classical Syriac, Classical Mandaic and Jewish Babylonian Aramaic) and three Western Aramaic idioms (Christian Palestinian Aramaic, Jewish Palestinian Aramaic and Samaritan Aramaic). The term corresponds to Late Aramaic in Fitzmyer's taxonomy (Fitzmyer 1979).

(8) *d-qoyəm ... gqoṭəʿ* ***riše!***

d-qoyəm	*g-qoṭəʿ*
if-stand_up.IPFV.3MS	FUT-cut_off.IPFV.3MS

riš-e
head-POSSI.3MS

'Had he got up, (the emir) would have cut **his head** off!' (74:89, Midən)

(9) *i=kurke gməḥyo ruḥa* ***bayne qarʿe*** *di=kurfayo*

i=kurke	*g-məḥy-o*	*ruḥ-a*
ART.FS= sitting_hen	PRS-throw.IPFV-3FS	REFL-POSSI.3FS

bayne	*qarʿ-e*	*d-i=kurf-ayo*
between	head-EZ	of-ART.FS=snake-that.F

'The sitting hen threw itself directly **on the head** of this snake.' (JL 13.11.9, Midən)

(10) ***riša*** *xud-i=kaffe d-iḏi rabo paṯyo*

riš-a	*xud-i=kaffe*	*d-iḏ-i*	*rab-o*
head-POSSI.3FS	like-ART.FS=palm	of-hand-POSSI.1S	big-MS

paṯy-o
wide-MS

'**Its** (= the snake's) **head** was as big and wide as the palm of my hand.' (JL 13.11.7, Midən).

In published material other than the Midən texts, *qarʿo* occurs much more often than *rišo* as the exponent of HEAD. The word *rišo*, however, is still occasionally used alongside *qarʿo*. The word

may occur in the stories told by the same informant. When *rišo* does appear, what motivates the speaker to use this less frequent variant is unclear to us. Consider the following examples below:

(11) *kul naqqa koḥoyər bi = qaqwoniṯo komər: "ma hawxa-yo?" hiya* ***kohayzo qarʿa*** *w kəmmo: "e!"*

kul	*naqqa*	*ko-ḥoyər*	*b-i = qaqwoniṯo*
every	time	PRS-look.IPFV.3MS	on-ART.FS = partridge

k-omər	*ma*	*hawxa-yo*	*hiya*	*ko-hayz-o*
PRS-say.IPFV.3MS	Q	so-COP.3S	she	PRS-shake.IPFV-3FS

qarʿ-a	*w*	*k-əmm-o*	*e*
head-POSSI.3FS	and	PRS-say.IPFV-3FS	yes

'Each time he looked at the partridge and said: "Is this so?", she **nodded** and said: "It is!" (52:84, ʿIwardo)

(12) *"hawxa-yo lo?"* ***həzla riša:*** *"e!"*

hawxa-yo	*lo*	*həz-la*	*riš-a*	*e*
so-COP.3S	no	shake.PRET-3FS	head-POSSI.3FS	yes

"This is so, is it not?" She **nodded**: "It is!" (52:108, ʿIwardo)

(13) *hedi hedi hazwo* ***qarʿe*** *laq-qəddam w laxalf*

hedi	*hedi*	*haz-wo*	*qarʿ-e*
slowly	slowly	shake.IPFV.3MS-PST	head-POSSI.3MS

laq-qəddam	*w*	*laxalf*
forth	and	back

'He was shaking his **head** slowly back and forth.' (11:231, Midyat)

(14) *harke ḥa, ayko d-maʕle* ***riše****, knəflo ʿayne ʿal ʿito*

harke	*ḥa*	*ayko d*	*maʕle*	*riš-e*
here	one.M	where	lift.IPFV.3MS	head-POSSI.3MS

k-nəfl-o	*ʿayn-e*	*ʿal*	*ʿito*
PRS-fall.IPFV-3FS	eye-POSSI.3MS	on	church

'Here, wherever one lifts his **head**, his eyes fall on a church.' (11:74, Midyat)

It seems that *rišo* made way for *qarʿo* in the sense of HEAD and its usage shifted to the field of derived meanings and set expressions such as the following:

(15) 'top':

saləq ***l-riše du=ṭuro***

saləq	*l-riš-e*	*d-u=ṭuro*
climb.PRET.3MS	to-head-POSSI.3MS	of-ART.MS=mountain

'He climbed **to the top of the mountain**.' (115:89, Midən)

(16) 'tip, point':

mḥalle ***reše du=sayfo*** *b-ʿayne*

mḥa-lle	*reš-e*	*d-u=sayfo*	*b-ʿayn-e*
throw.PRET-3PL	head-EZ	of-ART.MS=sword	into-eye-POSSI.3MS

'They thrusted **the tip of the sword** into his eye.' (70:265, Iḥwo)

(17) 'end':

i=naqqa d-naḥət ***reše du=ḥawlo*** *l-gabe, saləq bu=ḥawlo lalʕəl*

i=naqqa d	*naḥət*	*reš-e*	*d-u= ḥawlo*
when	go_down.PRET.3MS	head-EZ	of-ART.MS=rope

l-gab-e	*saləq*	*b-u=ḥawlo*	*lalʕəl*
to-side-POSSI.3MS	go_up.PRET.3MS	with-ART.MS=rope	up

'As soon as **the end of the rope** was near him, he climbed up the rope.' (69:222, Iḥwo)

(18) 'leader, chief':

qrele ***lu=rišo dax=xodume,*** *d-kətne gabe*

qre-le	*l-u=rišo*	*d-ax=xodume*
call.PRET-3MS	to-ART.MS=head	of-ART.PL=servants

d-kət-ne	*gab-e*
REL-COP-3PL	side-POSSI.3MS

'He called **the head of the servants** that were with him.' (81:55, Midən)

(19) a directional preposition 'towards':

a. *azzé u=faqirawo* ***l-reše*** *du=təğğar*

azzé	*u=faqir-awo*	*l-reš-e*
go.PRET.3MS	ART.MS=poor-that.M	to-head-EZ

d-u=təğğār
of-ART.MS=merchant

'The poor went **to** the merchant.' (108:44, Xarabe Məška)

b. *u=babayḏe … ḥakəm-wa. hule xabro, lat=təxetər kulle. latimi* ***ʿal riše*** *w səmme u=zʿurano ʿamaliye*

u=bab-ayḏe	*ḥakəm-wa*	*hu-le*
ART.MS=father-POSSII.3MS	ruler-COP.PST.3S	give.PRET-3MS

xabro	*l-at=təxetər*	*kul-le*	*latim-i*	*ʿal*
word	to-ART.PL=doctors	all-3PL	gather.PRET-3PL	on

riš-e	*w*	*səm-me*	*u=zʿur-ano*	*ʿamaliye*
head-POSSI.3MS	and	do.PRET-3PL	ART.MS=boy-this.M	surgery

'The father [of this boy] was a ruler. He called all the doctors. They gathered **to him** and performed a surgery on this boy.' (60:244, Kfarze)

(20) in a number of set expressions,[4] e.g.

a. *mi=saye d-aloho, d-**reše d-babayna** w du=šulṭono, mede lo=fayəš bi=arʿo, d-l=axilan*

m-i=saye	*d-aloho*	*d-reš-e*	*d-bab-ayna*
from-ART.FS=shadow	of-god	of-head-EZ	of-father-POSSI.1PL

w	*d-u=šulṭono*	*mede*
and	of-ART.MS=sultan	something

lo=fayəš	*b-i=arʿo*	*d-l=axi-lan*
NEG=remain.PRET.3MS	in-ART.FS=land	REL-NEG=eat.PRET-1PL

'[I swear] by the shadow of God, by **our father's head** and by the sultan's [**head**], nothing is left in the land that we would not have eaten.' (105:47, Sedari)

4 See more in RW 443f.

b. *zux li=briṯayo, mḥay* ***rišo*** *b-emi, babi w tux!*

zux	*l-i=briṯ-ayo*	*mḥay*	*rišo*
go.IMP.MS	to-ART.FS=world-that.F	strike.IMP.S	head

b-em-i	*bab-i*	*w*	*tux*
in-mother-POSSI.1S	father-POSSI.1S	and	come.IMP.MS

'Go to that world, visit (lit. strike **the head** on) my mother and my father and come back!' (58:118, Anḥil)

3. Man (male) and Husband

Both MAN (MALE) and HUSBAND can be rendered by *gawro* (RW 171) and *zlām* (RW 587). Apparently, *gawro* was the main term for both MAN (MALE) and HUSBAND at the time when H. Ritter was collecting his texts. In the speech of our informants, however, *zlām* conveys these meanings, except in the dialects of Midyat and Arkaḥ, where *gawro* is still in use.

In the corpus (1960s) *gawro* is the main term both for MAN (MALE) and HUSBAND, irrespective of the variety.

The core meaning of *zlām* in the published texts is MAN (PERSON), but the word happens to denote MAN (MALE) and HUSBAND in a couple of passages:

(21) *ádyawma ono, d-kətno barṯo, d-kətno ḥurma, hat d-kəttat* ***zlām****, d-kəttat gawro, l-mə gdoṭat l-gabi?*

ádyawma	*ono*	*d-kət-no*	*barṯo*	*d-kət-no*	*ḥurma*
today	I	REL-COP-1S	girl	REL-COP-1S	woman

hat	*d-kəṭṭ-at*	*zlām*	*d-kəṭṭ-at*	*gawro*
you	REL-COP-2S	man	REL-COP-2S	man

l-mə	*gd-oṯ-at*	*l-gab-i*
why	FUT-come.IPFV-2S	to-side-POSSI.1S

'I am a girl, an [unmarried] woman, and you are a **man**, a male, why have you come to me today?' (105:98, Sedari)

(22) *i=naqqa d-huwwe i=bəšra li=emo, li=emo mbašalla u=babo: "ádyawma* ***u=zlamayḏi*** *ǧǧil!"*

i=naqqa d	*huw-we*	*i=bəšra*
when	give.PRET-3PL	ART.FS=good_news

l-i=emo	*l-i=emo*	*mbašal-la*
to-ART.FS=mother	A-ART.FS=mother	report.PRET-3FS

u=babo	*ádyawma*	*u=zlam-ayḏi*
ART.MS=father	today	ART.MS=husband-POSSII.1S

ǧǧil
speak.PRET.3MS

'After they had given the mother the good news, she reported it to her father: "Today **my husband** has begun to speak!" (111:44, Xarabe Məška).

In the searchable corpus, *gawro* HUSBAND has 143 tokens, while *gawro* MAN (MALE) is represented by 37 tokens (the total number of *gawro* tokens including the meanings MAN (MALE), HUSBAND as well as other meanings such as 'a man's man', 'hero', etc. is 306). *Zlām* has 11 entries for HUSBAND and 17 for MAN (MALE), while the total number of *zlām* entries including the aforementioned meanings is 716. This is represented in the Table 1:

Table 1: The meanings of *gawro* and *zlām*

	HUSBAND	MAN	**Total tokens**
gawro	143	37	306
zlām	11	17	716

By contrast, *zlām* is the most frequent word for MAN (MALE) and HUSBAND used by our informants from Midən, Kfarze, Bsorino and Zaz. Midyat and Arkaḥ speakers employ only *gawro*, while a speaker from Mzizaḥ uses both words. Consider the following examples:

(23) ***u=zlamayd̲i*** *taxtor-yo* (Midən) *vs.* ***u=gawrayd̲i*** *doqtor-yo* (Midyat)

u=zlam-ayd̲i	*taxtōr-yo*
ART.MS= husband-POSSII.1S	doctor-COP.3S

u=gawr-ayd̲i	*doqtōr-yo*
ART.MS= husband-POSSII.1S	doctor-COP.3S

'**My husband** is a doctor.'

(24) *l-aloho xləqle* ***zlām (gawro)*** *w pire*

l-aloho	*xləq-le*	*zlām*	*(gawro)*	*w*	*pire*
A-god	create.PRET-3MS	man	man	and	woman

'God created **man** and woman.' (Mzizaḥ)

(25) *ḥamši=****gawre*** *w əšti=niše koʿayši bi=qriṭayd̲an*

ḥamši=gawre	*w*	*əšti=niše*
fifty=men	and	sixty=women

ko-ʿayš-i	*b-i=qriṯ-ayd̠an*
PRS-live.IPFV-3PL	in-ART.FS=village-POSSII.1PL

'Fifty **men** and sixty women live in our village.' (Arkaḥ)

4. Man (Human Being)

The basic exponents of mankind as a HUMAN BEING, regardless of sex, are *ənsān* (RW 252) and *nošo* (RW 369).

In the searchable corpus, the main term is *ənsān*: we have found 80 tokens of *ənsān* meaning HUMAN BEING vs. only nine instances of *nošo* with the same sense.[5] See the following examples:

(26) *uno ḥakimo-no, kul kewo, kul ʿəlle, d-howe lu=**ənsan**, uno kibi manəḥnola*

uno	*ḥakimo-no*	*kul*	*kewo*	*kul*	*ʿəlle*
I	physician-COP.1S	every	illness	every	sickness

d-howe	*l-u=ənsān*	*uno*	*kib-i*
REL-be.IPFV.3MS	to-ART.MS= human	I	can-1S

manəḥ-no-la
cure.IPFV-1MS-3FS.P

'I am a physician, I can cure any **human** illness and sickness.' (24:65, Midyat)

(27) *hano latyo **nošo**, əlla hano kšobəh, d-kətyo malaxo m d-aloho w qadišo*

hano	*latyo*	*nošo*	*əlla*	*hano*	*k-šobəh*
this.M	NEG.COP.3S	human	but	this.M	PRS-be_like.IPFV.3MS

5 Both words can also mean 'somebody'.

d-kət-yo *malaxo* *m* *d-aloho* *w* *qadišo*
that-COP-3S angel from of-god and saint

'He is not **a human**, but he looks like a holy angel of God.' (35:47, ʿIwardo)

In the contemporary usage of Ṭuroyo speakers, *nošo* is gaining ground as an exponent of MAN (HUMAN BEING). Some speakers use exclusively *nošo* in this meaning, some employ both words and some still use *ənsān*.

Note that *noše* may be used as a plural of *ənsān*, alongside *ənsanat*. Thus a speaker who invariably uses *ənsān* for HUMAN BEING employs *noše* as its plural:

(28) ***u=ənsan*** *d-lo maye laybe ʿoyəš*

u=ənsān *d-lo* *maye* *layb-e* *ʿoyəš*
ART.MS=human without water NEG.can-3MS live.IPFV.3MS

'**Man** cannot live without water.' (Midyat)

(29) ***an=noše*** *kibən məġġoli, aḥ=ḥayewən laybən məġġoli*

an=noše *kib-ən* *məġġol-i*
ART.PL=people can-3PL speak.IPFV-3PL

aḥ=ḥăyewən *layb-ən* *məġġol-i*
ART.PL=animals NEG.can-3PL speak.IPFV-3PL

'**People** can speak, but animals cannot.' (Midyat)

5. Sun

The concept SUN has two exponents in the language, the inherited *šəmšo* (RW 496) and an innovative one that also means DAY, *yawmo* (RW 575). They are attested in the corpus conveying two different meanings: *šəmšo* is the source of warmth and sunshine, while *yawmo* is the source of daylight.

The basic meaning of the Ṭuroyo word *yawmo* is DAY. In addition *yawmo* is used in published texts in connection with the sun's movement across the sky, i.e. sunset and sunrise. In other words, *yawmo* denotes SUN as a moving celestial body, which is responsible for alternation of day and night. It is, therefore, closely associated with the idea of DAYTIME. In this meaning, *yawmo* occurs only within the following collocations:

5.1. Verbs

(30) *ʕly* 'to go up':

u=yawmo	*ʕali*
ART.MS=sun	rise.PRET.3MS

'The sun rose.' (8:4; 28:105)

(31) *gny* 'to set (about sun)':

gani	*yawmo*
set.PRET.3MS	sun

'The sun set.' (28:103; 65:451; 88:80; 90:24, 34)

(32) *nfq* 'to go out':

awwəl d	*nofəq*	*u=yawmo*
as soon as	go_out.IPFV.3MS	ART.MS=sun

'As soon as the sun rose.' (29:349; 58:201)

(33) *qlb* 'to roll over':

qaləb	*u=yawmo*
roll_over.PRET.3MS	ART.MS=sun

The sun set.' (8:13)

(34) *slq* 'to ascend':

ko-saləq	*u=yawmo*
PRS-ascend.PRET.3MS	ART.MS=sun

'The sun is going to rise.' (LB 251)

(35) *ṭwʿ* 'to sink':

ṭawəʿ	*u=yawmo*
set.PRET.3MS	ART.MS=sun

'The sun set' (61:149; 62:273; 69:407, 525; 89:34, 35, 36; 97:64; 98:44; 102:47, 48; 112:12, 78)

Consider a few examples:

(36) *mḥawrable me ṣafrayto, hul ṭawəʿ* ***u=yawmo***

mḥawrab-le	*me*	*ṣafrayto*	*hul*
fight.PRET-3MS	from	morning	till

ṭawəʿ	*u=yawmo*
set.PRET.3MS	ART.MS=sun

'He was fighting from morning till **sunset**.' (98:44, Arkaḥ)

(37) *gani* ***u=yawmo,*** *l=aṯyo i=tərto*

gani	*u=yawmo*	*l=aṯy-o*
set.PRET.3MS	ART.MS=sun	NEG=come.PRET-3FS

i=tərto
ART.FS=COW

'**The sun** set, but the cow had not yet come.' (90:24, unknown)

5.2. Nouns

(38) *gneto/gnayto:*

gnete/gnayte d-yawmo 'sunset' (11:51; 65:299)

(39) *ġyoṭo:*

ġyoṭe d-yawmo 'sunset' (LB 75)

(40) *sloqo:*

sloqe d-yawmo 'sunrise' (73:353)

(41) *ṭwoʿo/twaḥto:*

ṭwoʿe/twaḥte d-yawmo 'sunset' (11:171; 29:274; 58:201; 63:15; 69:31, 148, 407, 487, 519, 522, 524; 91:8; 23; 96:136, 157; 113:83)

Cardinal points can be expressed with *yawmo*-collocations as well:

(42) 'east':

nfəqte d-yawmo (11:22, 24; 26:145; 61:241; 91:53; 92:10);

sloqe d-yawmo (74:49; 75:53, 54; 115:1, 162)

(43) 'west':

ṭwoʿe/twaḥte d-yawmo (61:241; 92:12);

gnete d-yawmo (26:145);

ġyoṭe d-yawmo (73:240; 75:53; 78:190)

5.3. From Day to Sun

We must admit that the semantic boundary between the concepts of DAY and SUN as a source of daylight is very blurred. *Yawmo* in all the examples above can also be interpreted as 'day, daylight' in a metaphorical sense.

The only case where the features of *šəmšo*, i.e. the sunshine, are attributed to *yawmo* is an expression used for describing the outstanding beauty of a human being.

(44) *kətle ḥḏo barṯo bəlḥuḏe. kəmmo* ***lu=yawmo:*** *"taxər d-ubono šawq ʿal i=mamlake m-darbux!"*

kət-le	*ḥḏo*	*barṯo*	*bəlḥuḏe*
EXIST-DAT.3MS	one.F	daughter	alone

k-əmm-o	*l-u=yawmo*	*taxə́r*
PRS-say.IPFV-3FS	to-ART.MS=sun	mover_over.IMP.S

d-ub-o-no	*šawq*	*ʿal*	*i=mamlake*
that-give.IPFV-F-1S	sunshine	over	ART.FS= country

m-darb-ux

in_place-POSSI.2MS

'He had only one daughter. [She was so beautiful that she could] tell the **sun**: "Move over so that I can give sunshine to the country in place of you!"' (28:71, Midyat)

(45) *kale xort, ʿumre arbaḥṣar=əšne, hama, komalle* ***lu=yawmo****: "nḥat, d-oṯeno l-dukṯux!"*

kal-e	*xōrt*	*ʿumr-e*	*arbaḥṣar=əšne*
PRES-3MS	boy	life-POSSI.3MS	fourteen=years

hama	*ko-mal-le*	*l-u=yawmo*
DM	PRS-say.IPFV.3MS-DAT.3MS	to-ART.MS=sun

nḥat	*d-oṯe-no*	*l-dukṯ-ux*
descend.IMP.S	that-come.IPFV-1MS	to-place-POSSI.2MS

'There was a boy of fourteen years old, [he was so handsome that he could] tell **the sun**: "Come down so that I can occupy your place!"' (95:87, Xarabe Kafre).

As for *šəmšo*, it conveys the sense of 'the source of warmth and sunshine':

(46) *yawmo d-qayṭo-yo, hawa basəmto-yo.* ***i=šəmšo*** *kmabrqo w kobo šḥanṯo l-hawír*

yawmo	*d-qayṭo-yo*	*hawa*	*basəm-to-yo*
day	of-summer-COP.3S	weather	pleasant-FS-COP.3S

i=šəmšo	*k-mabrq-o*	*w*	*k-ob-o*
ART.FS=sun	PRS-shine.INFECT-3FS	and	PRS-give.IPFV-3FS

šḥanṯo	*l-hawīr*
warmth	to-around

'It is a summer day. The weather is pleasant. The **sun** shines and heats up the air.' (4:11, Midyat)

(47) *u=sawko kəmḥafəḏ u=qarʿo* ***mi=šəmšo****, mu=maṭro w šmənto maḏ̣=ḏ̣arbat w mu=ğroḥo*

u=sawko	*kə-mḥafəḏ̣*	*u=qarʿo*
ART.MS=hair	PRS-protect.IPFV.3MS	ART.MS=head

m-i=šəmšo	*m-u=maṭro*	*w*	*šmənto*
from-ART.FS=sun	from-ART.MS=rain	and	little

m-aḏ̣=ḏ̣arbat	*w*	*m-u=ğroḥo*
from-ART.PL=blows	and	from-ART.MS=injury

'The hair protects the head from **the sun**, the rain and, to some extent, from blows and injury.' (3:5, Midyat)

Moreover, *šəmšo* by itself can mean 'shine', e.g., in *i=šəmšo du=ṣahro* 'the shining of the moon' (115:128, Midən; JL 7:7:9, Midən).

These two components of the sun concept are in complementary distribution in the published texts: *šəmšo* is never used in the collocations associated with *yawmo*; *yawmo* almost never means 'the warmth and the shining of the sun' (except for the set expression mentioned above).

As for the answers from our informants, the usage varies. The word *šəmšo* can be used in the *yawmo*-collocations and, moreover, *yawmo* can mean a celestial body. Consider their translations of the following sentences:

(48) ‘**The sun** set, but the cow had not yet come home.’

gani ***yawmo*** *w heš tərto lə=maḥwela* (Midyat)

gani	*yawmo*	*w*	*hēš*	*tərto*
set.PRET.3MS	sun	and	yet	cow

lə=maḥwe-la
NEG=appear.PRET-3FS

ṭawəʿ ***u=yawmo*** *i=tərto heš lo=daʿiro lu=bayto* (Midyat)

ṭawəʿ	*u=yawmo*	*i=tərto*	*hēš*
set.PRET.3MS	ART.MS=sun	ART.FS=cow	yet

lo=daʿir-o	*l-u=bayto*
NEG=return.PRET-3FS	to-ART.MS=house

u=yawmo *ṭawəʿ elo i=tərto he lo=daʿiro lu=bayto* (Mzizaḥ)

u=yawmo	*ṭawəʿ*	*elo*	*i=tərto*	*he*
ART.MS=sun	set.PRET.3MS	but	ART.FS=cow	yet

lo=daʿir-o	*l-u=bayto*
NEG=return.PRET-3FS	to-ART.MS=house

i=šəmšo *ṭawiʿo bas i-tərto l=aṯyo lu=bayto* (Arkaḥ)

i=šəmšo	*ṭawiʿ-o*	*bas*	*i=tərto*
ART.FS=sun	set.PRET-3FS	but	ART.FS=cow

l=aṯy-o	*l-u=bayto*
NEG=come.PRET-3FS	to-ART.MS=house

(49) ‘**The sun** rose.’

w saləq ***yawmo*** (Midyat)

w	*saləq*	*yawmo*
and	ascend.PRET.3MS	sun

nafiqo ***i=šəmšo*** (Midyat)

nafiq-o	*i=šəmšo*
go_out.PRET-3FS	ART.FS=sun

u=yawmo *nafəq=ste* (Mzizaḥ)

u=yawmo	*nafəq-ste*
ART.MS=sun	go_out.PRET.3MS-too

i=šəmšo *saliqo* (Arkaḥ)

i=šəmšo	*saliq-o*
ART.FS=sun	ascend.PRET-3FS

(50) 'The **Sun** is one of the stars.'

i=šəmšo*-ste kəkwo mak=kəkwe di=šmayo-yo* (Midyat)

i=šəmšo-ste	*kəkwo*	*m-ak=kəkwe*
ART.FS=sun-too	star	from-ART.PL=stars

d-i=šmayo-yo
of-ART.FS=sky-COP.3S

i=šəmšo *kəkwo-yo bayne d-kəkwe* (Midyat)

i=šəmšo	*kəkwo-yo*	*bayne d*	*kəkwe*
ART.FS=sun	star-COP.3S	among	stars

u=yawmo *kəkwo-yo bayne d-kəkwe* (Mzizaḥ)

u=yawmo	*kəkwo-yo*	*bayne d*	*kəkwe*
ART.MS=sun	star-COP.3S	among	stars

i*=*šəmšo *kəkwo-yo b-bayn d-kəkwe* (Arkaḥ)

i=*šəmšo*	*kəkwo-yo*	*b-bayn d*	*kəkwe*
ART.FS=sun	star-COP.3S	in-among	stars

A semantic shift DAY > SUN is known in various languages of the world, in particular in Kurmanji, where *roj* is the basic word for both DAY and SUN (Chyet 521, 733, 826). In some of NENA, the MEA **yawmā* also acquired the meaning 'sun': Barwar *yoma* (Khan 2008, 1451); C. Urmi *yuma* (Khan 2016, vol. 3, 342). In Modern South Arabian languages PS **yawm-* DAY has become the main word for SUN (Kogan 2015, 541).

6. Woman and Wife

The Midyat (*məḏyoyo*) and the village (*quryoyo*) dialects of Ṭuroyo have their own sets of basic words for the concepts of WOMAN and WIFE. These notions can often be rendered by the same words. However, the relationship between the words for WOMAN and WIFE within both sets is complex. Through a few illustrative passages we shall discuss the meaning and the dialectal distribution of the words *aṯto* (RW 39), *ḥurma* (RW 246), *žənəke* (RW 257) and *pire* (RW 382).

6.1. Midyat Dialect

The basic *məḏyoyo* word for WIFE is *aṯto*. However, *aṯto* is almost never used as a form of address in direct speech when the speaker addresses his wife. For this purpose the word *žənəke*, which usually means WOMAN, is used as in the example below:

(51) *ʿaṣriye aṯi lu*=*bayto. mə́llela* ***li*=*aṯto***, *omər:* ***"žənəke!"***

ʿaṣriye	*aṯi*	*lu*=*bayto*
evening	come.PRET.3MS	to-ART.MS=house

mə́l-le-la	*l-i = at̠to*	*omər*
say.PRET-3MS-DAT.3FS	to-ART.FS = wife	say.IPFV.3MS

žənəke
woman

'In the evening, he came home and called **his wife**: "**Wife!**"' (PrS 12/21)

It should be noted that *žənəke* is a general form of address that can refer to any female person.

At̠to is a generic term for a human female, WOMAN (FEMALE), but it is only rarely used to denote a referential female person, WOMAN (PERSON). This function is performed by *žənəke*.

(52) *l = əd̠ʿiwo, d-kətyo* ***at̠to,*** *ḥəšwiwola gawro. mu = sabab d-ağ = ğule d-u = gawro aʕla-wayye*

l = əd̠ʿ-i-wo	*d-kət-yo*	*at̠to*
NEG = know.IPFV-3P-PST	that-COP-3S	woman

ḥəšw-í-wo-la	*gawro*	*m-u = sabab*
think.IPFV-3PL-PST-3FS.P	man	from-ART.MS = reason

d-ağ = ğule	*d-u = gawro*	*aʕl-a-wayye*
that-ART.PL = clothes	of-ART.MS = man	on-POSSI.3FS-COP.3PL

'They did not know that she was a **woman**, they were thinking [she was] a man, because she dressed in men's clothes.' (24:178, Midyat)

(53) *u = ḥa yawmo at̠yo žənəke sawto w faqərto, mlaʿela w ṭləbla meni i = odayat̠e*

u = ḥa	*yawmo*	*at̠y-o*	*žənəke*
ART.MS = one.M	day	come.PRET-3FS	woman

saw-to	*w*	*faqər-to*	*mlaʿe-la*
old-FS	and	poor-FS	beg.PRET-3FS

w	*ṭləb-la*	*men-i*	*i=oday-aṯe*
and	ask.PRET-3FS	from-POSSI.1S	ART.FS=room-this.F

'One day an old and poor **woman** came, begging and asking me [to rent out] this room.' (2:64, Midyat)

Compare, however, also:

(54) *qayəm u=Bardawil, azzé li=walay, mšayele m-ḥḏo* ***aṯto****, omər: "l-ma mahzamle an=nišayḏan?"*

qayəm	*u=Bardawil*	*azzé*	*l-i=walay*
get_up.PRET.3MS	ART.MS=PN	go.PRET.3MS	to-ART.FS=town

mšaye-le	*m-ḥḏo*	*aṯto*	*omər*
ask.PRET-3MS	from-one.F	woman	say.IPFV.3MS

l-ma	*mahzam-le*	*an=niš-ayḏan*
why	abduct.PRET-3MS	ART.PL=women-POSSII.1PL

'Bardawil came to the town and asked **one woman**: "Who has abducted our wives?"' (PrS 40/12-14)

Niše/neše is a suppletive plural used for both WOMAN and WIFE in the Midyat dialect of Ṭuroyo.

Ḥurma occurs two times in Ritter's corpus meaning WOMAN. *Pire* is found in the Prym-Socin collection only with the meaning of OLD WOMAN.

6.2. Village Dialects

There are two prominent words for WIFE in *quryoyo*: *at̠to* and *ḥurma*. Though *ḥurma* occurs quite often in the published corpus, *at̠to* is attested in the meaning of WIFE at least twice as much as *ḥurma* is:

Table 2: WIFE in other dialects

	Midən	**ʿIwardo**	**Kfarze**	**Anḥil**
at̠to 'wife'	65	55	80	13
ḥurma 'wife'	21	10	34	8

An exception is constituted by two villages of the Raite region dialectal cluster—Xarabe Məška and Xarabe Kafre—where *ḥurma* is a basic word for WIFE, as shown in Table 3.

Table 3: WIFE in the Raite dialectal cluster

	Raite				
	XM	S	Ḥwo	XK	A
at̠to 'wife'	12	22	13	1	12
ḥurma 'wife'	35	6	4	4	8

As in *məd̠yoyo*, *at̠to* is not used as a form of address for WIFE in direct speech. *Ḥurma* takes on this function. Consider the following example:

(55) *qayəm sġəd̠le* ***li=at̠to*** *d-ruḥe, məlle: "ya* ***ḥurma!*** *ḥaṭino qumax, kobaʿno d-ʿofatli"*

qayəm	*sġəd̠-le*	*l-i=at̠to*
get_up.PRET.3MS	bow.PRET-3MS	to-ART.FS=wife

d-ruḥ-e	*məl-le*	*ya*	*ḥurma*
of-REFL-POSSI.3MS	say.PRET-3MS	VOC	woman

ḥaṭi-no	*qum-ax*	*k-obaʿ-no*
sin.PRET-1MS	before-POSSI.2FS	PRS-want.IPFV-1MS

d-ʿof-at-li
that-forgive.IPFV-2S-1S.P

'He got up, bowed **to** his own **wife** and said: "**Wife**! I've sinned against you, I want you to forgive me."' (62:349, Kfarze)

Ḥurma is used as a general form of address for any female person (wife, mother, familiar or unfamiliar woman).

Occasionally, *pire* and *žənəke* can also mean WIFE.

The basic word for WOMAN (FEMALE) as well as for WOMAN (PERSON) in the village dialects is *ḥurma*. Consider the following examples:

(56) *mqadamla l-gab Farxuṣaf, məlla: "ya i=ḥoṯayḏi! hawo d-mamṭelelax, ono* ***ḥurma****-no"*

mqadam-la	*l-gab*	*Farxuṣaf*
come_near.PRET-3FS	to-side	PN

məl-la	*ya*	*i=ḥoṯ-ayḏi*
say.PRET-3FS	VOC	ART.FS=sister-POSSII.1S

hawo	*d-mamṭé-le-lax*	*ono*	*ḥurma-no*
this.M	that-bring.PRET-3MS-2FS.P	I	woman-COP.1S

'She came near to Farxuṣaf and said: "O, my sister! The man who brought you [there], [i.e.] I, is [actually] a woman."' (62:350, Kfarze)

(57) *kətwa ḥḏo* ***ḥurma,*** *kurdiye, əmmíwayle Ḥore*

kət-wa	*ḥḏo*	*ḥurma*	*kurdiye*
exist-PST	one.F	woman	Kurdish.f

əmm-í-way-la	*Ḥore*
say.IPFV-3PL-PST-3FS.P	PN

'There was a Kurdish woman, named Ḥore.' (80:2, Midən)

The word *pire* can hardly have a claim on the status of basic word for WOMAN in any of the village varieties in Ritter's corpus. Though it is more popular in the dialects of the Raite region, as shown in Table 4 below, *ḥurma* still holds its position as the main word for WOMAN. The more typical meaning of *pire* is OLD WOMAN. It should be noted, however, that *pire* is the only word for WOMAN found in Jastrow's Lehrbuch (JL) texts, which represent the Midən variety of Ṭuroyo. Two of our informants, one from Midən and the other from Bsorino, consistently used *pire* in their replies.

Table 4: *pire* across dialects

	Raite					Midən	Kfarze
	XM	S	Ḥwo	XK	A		
pire 'old woman'	5	4	0	0	8	1	58
pire 'woman'	2	5	1	2	6	0	0

Žənəke is yet another secondary word for WOMAN (PERSON) in *quryoyo*. It is worth mentioning that in Anḥil, it is used even more frequently than *ḥurma* (11 tokens of *žənəke* vs. 4 tokens of *ḥurma*).

Niše/neše and *pirat* are suppletive plurals for both WOMAN and WIFE. *Pirat* is more common in the dialects of the Raite region.

Niše/neše is attested in all the village varieties, especially in Kfarze and Anḥil, where *pirat* is only rarely used. In the dialects where both *niše/neše* and *pirat* are present, the former word stands for WOMAN and WIFE, while the latter one merely means WOMAN.

6.3. Summary

To summarise, *at̠to* is the basic word for WIFE and WOMAN (FEMALE) in the Midyat dialect. *Žənəke* is the main word for WOMAN (PERSON) which can also be used as a form of address for any female person, including a wife. *Niše/neše* are suppletive plurals for both WOMAN and WIFE.

In the village dialects, the basic words for WIFE are *at̠to* and *ḥurma* depending on the variety. *Ḥurma* is the main exponent of the notions WOMAN (FEMALE) and WOMAN (PERSON), which can be used as a form of address for female persons including wife. *Pire* is the main word for WOMAN (both FEMALE and PERSON) in some modern Ṭuroyo dialects (Midən, Bsorino). *Niše/neše* and *pirat* are suppletive plurals for WOMAN and WIFE.

7. Etymology

The following list shows our suggested etymologies of the lexemes in the previous discussion:

(1) BIRD

safruno < MEA: *ṣeprōnā* 'little bird' (SL 1299); *ṣipronā* 'bird, fowl' (DJBA 962); *ṣipra* 'little bird, sparrow' (MD 394), *ṣupra, ṣuprina* idem, colloq. dimin. (MD 390).

ṭayro < MEA: Syriac *ṭayrā* 'bird' (SL 528).

(2) HEAD

rišo, rešo < MEA: *rēšā* 'head' (SL 1462); *rēšā* 'head, top part' (DJBA 1078); *riša* 'head, top' (MD 434).

qarʿo: see Arab. *qarʿ* 'gourd' and *qarʿa* 'gourd, skull, head' (DMWA 887–888), *qarʿa* 'Kürbis' (VW II 116), *qarʿa* 'Kürbis" (Kinderib 113) and Syriac *qarʿā* 'gourd' and *qarʿṯā* 'skull' (SL 1414), the latter is considered a borrowing from Arabic. Tezel (2003, 119) assumes *qarʿo* to be an Arabic loanword. See also a discussion in Tezel (2003, 117ff).

(3) MAN, HUSBAND

gawro < MEA: *gaḇrā* 'man, person, husband' (SL 202); *gaḇrā* 'man, husband' (DJBA 258); *gabra* 'man' (MD 73).

zlām < Kurd. *zilam* 'man' (Chyet 691). The Kurdish word must be a borrowing from Arabic, see EALL II: 606.

(4) HUMAN BEING

ənsān < Arab.: *insān* 'man, human being' (DMWA 39).

nošo < MEA: *nāšā* 'man, human beings' (SL 65); *ināšā* 'man' (DJBA 120); *(a)naša* 'human being' (MD 24).

(5) SUN

šəmšo < MEA: *šemšā* 'sun' (SL 1576); *šimšā* 'sun, sunlight' (DJBA 1136); *šamšā* 'sun' (MD 443).

yawmo < MEA: *yawmā* 'day' (SL 568); *yōmā* 'day, sun' (DJBA 529); *iuma* 'day' (MD 190).

(6) WOMAN, WIFE

aṯto < MEA: *aṯṯā* 'woman, wife' (SL 66); *ittəṯā* (DJBA 128); *ʿnta* 'woman, wife' (MD 354). Nöldeke (§ 146) posits *attā* for Syriac (as against *aṯṯā*, expected etymologically), yet the Ṭuroyo form is not the expected regular descendant (in terms of historical phonology) of any of the aforementioned MEA words.

ḥurma < Arab.: *ḥurma* 'that which is holy, inviolable; woman, lady, wife' (DMWA 201); *ḥərme* (pl. *ḥarīm*) 'femme (appartenant à un homme)' in Mardin Arabic (Grigore 2007, 196); *ḥərme*, pl. *ḥəram* 'femme', lat. fœmina, mulier, uxor (DAS 154).

pire < Kurd.: *pîr* 'old woman; wife' (Chyet 464).

žənəke < Kurd.: *jin* 'woman; wife, married woman' (Chyet 290). The source form must be the indefinite oblique *jinekê*.

Abbreviations

Languages and Dialects

Arab.	Arabic
Ḥwo	Iḥwo
Kurd.	Kurdish (Kurmanji)
MEA	Middle Eastern Aramaic
NENA	North Eastern Neo-Aramaic
PS	Proto-Semitic
S	Sedari
Tur.	Ṭuroyo
A	Arkaḥ
XK	Xarabe Kafre
XM	Xarabe Məška

Glossing Abbreviations not in the Leipzig Glossing List

DM	discourse marker
EXIST	existential
EZ	ezafe
PN	personal name
POSS	possessive suffix
PRET	preterite

Bibliographical Abbreviations

Chyet	Chyet, Michael L. 2003. *Kurdish-English Dictionary*. New Haven and London: Yale University Press.
DAS	Barthélemy, Adrien. 1969. *Dictionnaire Arabe-Français*. Dialectes de Syrie: Alep, Damas, Liban, Jérusalem. Paris: Librairie Orientaliste Paul Geuthner.
DJBA	Sokoloff, Michael. 2002. *A Dictionary of Jewish Babylonian Aramaic of the Talmudic and Geonic Periods*. Ramat-Gan, Israel: Bar Ilan University Press; Baltimore; London: The John Hopkins University Press.
DMWA	Wehr, Hans. 1979. *A Dictionary of Modern Written Arabic*. Edited by J. Milton Cowan. 4th edition. Wiesbaden: Harrassowitz.
EALL	*Encyclopedia of Arabic Language and Linguistics*. Leiden, Boston: Brill. 2006–2009.
JL	Jastrow, Otto. 2002. *Lehrbuch der Ṭuroyo-Sprache*. Wiesbaden: Harrasowitz Verlag.
Kinderib	Jastrow, Otto. 2005. *Glossar zu Kinderib (Anatolisches Arabisch)*. Wiesbaden: Harrasowitz Verlag.

LB	Talay, Shabo. 2004. *Lebendig Begraben*. Münster: Lit Verlag.
MD	Drower, Ethel Stefana and Rudolf Macuch. 1962. *A Mandaic Dictionary*. Oxford: Clarendon Press.
Nöldeke	Nöldeke, Theodor. 1966. *Kurzgefasste syrische Grammatik*. Darmstadt: Wissenschaftliche Buchgesellschaft. Reprint.
PrS	Prym, Eugen and Albert Socin. 1881. *Der Neu-Aramaeische Dialekt des Ṭûr 'Abdîn*. Göttingen: Vandenhoeck & Ruprecht.
RW	Ritter, Hellmut. 1979. *Ṭūrōyo. Die Volkssprache der syrischen Christen des Ṭūr ʿAbdîn*. B: Wörterbuch, Beirut: Franz Steiner Verlag.
SL	Sokoloff, Michael. 2009. *A Syriac Lexicon*. Winona Lake, Indiana: Eisenbrauns.
VW	Vocke Sibylle and Wolfram Waldner. 1981. *Der Wortschatz des Anatolischen Arabisch*. 1981. Tl. I–II. Nürnberg.

Bibliography

Barsky, Eugene, Yulia Furman and Sergey Loesov. 2018. 'Two-Hundred-Word Swadesh List for a Modern Aramaic Variety (Ṭuroyo)'. In *Aula Orientalis* 36/1: 75–110.

Beyer, Klaus. 1984. *Die aramäischen Texte vom Toten Meer: samt den Inschriften aus Palästina, dem Testament Levis aus der Kairoer Genisa, der Fastenrolle und den alten talmudischen Zitaten*. Göttingen: Vandenhoeck & Ruprecht.

Fitzmyer, Joseph. 1979. 'The Phases of the Aramaic Language'. In *A Wandering Aramean: Collected Aramaic Essays by Joseph A. Fitzmyer*, pp. 57–84. Missoula, MT: Scholars Press.

Grigore, George 2007. *L'arabe parlé à Mardin: Monographie d'un parler arabe «périphérique»*. Bucureşti: Editura Universității din Bucureşti.

Khan, Geoffrey. 2008. *The Neo-Aramaic Dialect of Barwar*. Leiden, Boston: Brill.

———. 2016. *The Neo-Aramaic Dialect of the Assyrian Christians of Urmi*. Leiden, Boston: Brill.

Kogan, Leonid. 2015. *Genealogical Classification of Semitic. The Lexical Isoglosses*. Boston; Berlin: De Gruyter.

Ritter, Hellmut. 1967. *Ṭūrōyo. Die Volkssprache der syrischen Christen des Ṭūr ʿAbdîn*. A: *Texte*. Band I. Beirut: Franz Steiner Verlag.

———. 1969. Ṭūrōyo. *Die Volkssprache der syrischen Christen des Ṭūr ʿAbdîn*. A: *Texte*. Band II. Beirut: Franz Steiner Verlag.

———. 1971. *Ṭūrōyo. Die Volkssprache der syrischen Christen des Ṭūr ʿAbdîn*. A: *Texte*. Band III. Beirut: Franz Steiner Verlag.

Tezel, Aziz. 2003. *Comparative Etymological Studies in the Western Neo-Syriac (Ṭūrōyo) Lexicon*. Uppsala: Uppsala Universitet.

NEO-ARAMAIC ANIMAL NAMES

Hezy Mutzafi

1. Aspects of Neo-Aramaic Animal Names in Scholarly Literature[1]

The topic of animal names in the field of Neo-Aramaic (NA) has hardly attracted any scholarly interest, nor is there any lexicological work dedicated to this topic. This is in contrast with the better investigated subject of some animal names in pre-modern Aramaic languages, the most noteworthy works in this respect being Löw's comparative studies in Aramaic names of fishes, reptiles and amphibians (Löw 1906, 1909a, 1909b, 1912a, 1912b), and Talshir's comparative work on animal names in the Samaritan Aramaic version of the Pentateuch (Talshir 1981). These works contain some references to NENA animal names mentioned in scholarly literature, primarily in Maclean's

1 Data on Neo-Aramaic regional varieties is fieldwork-based, unless a reference is adduced, and except for Western Neo-Aramaic, based on Arnold (2019). Abbreviations: Ar. = Arabic, Aram. = Aramaic, BH = Biblical Hebrew, C. = Christian (NENA dialect), dim.suff. = diminutive suffix, J. = Jewish (NENA dialect), JBA = Jewish Babylonian Aramaic, JPA = Jewish Palestinian Aramaic, Kurd. = Kurdish, lit. = literally, NA = Neo-Aramaic, NENA = North-Eastern Neo-Aramaic, NM = Neo-Mandaic, post-cl. M = post-classical (literary) Mandaic, pre-mod. = pre-modern, NA = Neo-Aramaic, Pers. = (modern) Persian, Sam.Aram. = Samaritan Aramaic, st. abs. = status absolutus, st. emph. = status emphaticus, Syr. = Syriac, Trg.O = Targum Onkelos, Ṭur. = Ṭuroyo, WNA = Western Neo-Aramaic. Main sources for pre-modern Aramaic are Cook (2008), *DJBA, DJPA, LS, SL, Thesaurus*; for Akkadian *CAD, AHw*; and for Kurdish Chyet (2003), İzoli (1992) and Omar (1992).

 https://doi.org/10.11647/OBP.0209.13

dictionary of 'vernacular Syriac' (Maclean 1901). Additionally, some NA animal names inherited from older Semitic layers and attested in the literature are adduced in volume 2 of *Semitic Etymological Dictionary* by Militarev and Kogan (2005).

Various inherited and borrowed animal names in a large number of Neo-Aramaic varieties are attested in grammars, texts and especially dictionaries and glossaries pertaining to these varieties. Still, the inventory of NA animal names published to date remains partial, and some of these zoonyms did not receive accurate zoological definitions. Examples related to the former point, taken from the NENA dialects, are the following hitherto unattested animal names:[2]

Table 1: Hitherto unattested Neo-Aramaic animal names

	NENA dialect and animal name	Compare
1.	Hertevin *parḥadüdək* 'bat'	Syr. *praḥdūḏā* 'bat; a flying insect'[3]
2.	Tisqopa *yaʾta* (pl. *yaʾə*) 'sandgrouse'	Syr. *yaʿʿā* 'sandgrouse or quail'[4]
3.	Haṣṣan *mašoṭa* 'caterpillar'	Syr. *māšōṭā* 'caterpillar' +[5]

2 Notes on transcription: *č̭, k̭, ṱ* are unaspirated phonemes whereas *č, k, t* are aspirated. Vowel length is indicated only where it is phonemic, i.e., for *ā* vs. *a*. Superscript + indicates word-emphasis. Stress is penultimate unless otherwise indicated (transcription of NENA words quoted from scholarly works is adapted to this method).

3 Hertevin evinces restructuring by analogy with *parḥa* 'bird, fowl', as well as what seems to be a Kurdish diminutive ending *ək* (although the local Kurdish parallel is, according to Hertevin informants, *çêlêçêlê*).

4 Cf. also *yaʿʿā, yaʿṯā* 'sandgrouse; wood pigeon; turtledove or ringdove' in Gewargis Ashitha (2018, 399a), which is one of the many imports from Manna's Syriac-Arabic dictionary (Manna 1975, 313b) in Gewargis Ashitha's dictionary, and by no means represents any genuine NA forms, nor are the definitions related to pigeons and doves relevant to NENA.

5 Note also that *māšōṭā* 'caterpillar of locust' in Gewargis Ashitha (2018, 528b) is highly inaccurate, given genuine NENA *mašoṭa* 'caterpillar' and the fact that the larva of a locust, called 'nymph', is not a caterpillar, the latter being strictly the larva of a butterfly or a moth.

	NENA dialect and animal name	Compare
4.	Telkepe *xargəlta* 'Saga pedo'	Syr. *ḥargālā* 'large wingless locust'[6]
5.	Jinet *peḥu* 'mosquito'	Gaznakh *xepo* 'mosquito', Syr. *ḥē(ʾ)pay* 'a kind of gnat'

The following are three examples of inaccurate definitions in the literature: In Maclean's dictionary *pašuwa* is defined 'foul smelling black centipede' (Maclean 1901, 260a) instead of '(black) millipede',[7] *yoša* is defined 'a large bird like a goose, inhabiting the lake shore' (ibid., 118b) instead of simply 'bustard',[8] and *ṭoya* is defined 'deer' (ibid., 109a) instead of 'gazelle'.

Another problematic aspect related to Neo-Aramaic animal names in lexicological works concerns Classical Syriac animal names that have nothing to do with vernacular Aramaic and nonetheless occur in dictionaries from the 19th century and the first half of the 20th century. Syriac animal names in Maclean's dictionary, such as—to take a few names of reptiles—*ʾamaqta* 'gecko' (Maclean 1901, 14b), *yadyāda* 'chameleon' (ibid., 94b; cf. Syr. *yaḏyāḏa* 'millipede; hoopoe') and *patna* 'asp, adder' (ibid., 261b), were imported into this dictionary from the C. Urmi translation of the Bible, in particular of the Hebrew Bible, which includes quite a few Classical Syriac zoonyms not used in

6 For this definition, based on medieval lexicons, see *Thesaurus,* 1367 (followed by Payne Smith 1903, 156a).

7 Originally a nomen agentis of the verbal root *pšy* 'to fart inaudibly' (**pāšōyā*), it is related to informants' description of the millipede as curling itself into a coil and emitting a foul brown secretion when touched or threatened (and see Hutchins 2004, vol. 2, 364–365).

8 As already in Bar Bahlul's 10th century lexicon, where *yaḇšā* 'bustard' is referred to as a dialectal Mesopotamian word (Duval 1888–1891, vol. 1, 711/9, 835), hence likely an early NENA vernacularism in that lexicon. The correct NENA meaning is adduced, as regards C. Urmi *yoša,* in Khan (2016, vol. 3, 342). An older form, *yawša,* is found in the NENA dialect clusters of Baz and Ṭyare.

colloquial speech.[9] Some other animal names imported from the Urmi Bible into Maclean's dictionary are *qāqa* 'pelican' (ibid., 284a), *deṣa* 'wild goat' (ibid., 65b), *yaxmur, yaxmura* 'antelope, roebuck' (ibid., 119a) and *rema* 'wild ox, or unicorn' (ibid., 293a).

These aforementioned classicisms, their sources and vernacular C. Urmi parallels, are presented in what follows:

Table 2: C. Urmi classicisms and vernacular parallels

	Animal name (Maclean 1901)	**C. Urmi Bible**	**Cf. vernacular C. Urmi**
1.	*ʾamaqta* 'gecko'	Lev. 11.30	+*mazuzta* '(any) lizard'
2.	*yadyāda* 'chameleon'	Lev. 11.30	(no chameleons in Urmi area)[10]
3.	*patna* 'asp, adder'	Deut. 32.33	+*corāmal* 'viper'
4.	*qāqa* 'pelican'	Lev. 11.18	+*sak̭k̭av* 'pelican'[11]
5.	*deṣa* 'wild goat'	Deut. 14.5	+*ʾəzzət*/+*ɟečit* +*ṯuyra* 'wild goat'
6.	*yaxmur(a)* 'antelope, roebuck'	Deut. 14.5	+*jeyran* 'gazelle, roe deer'
7.	*rema* 'wild ox or unicorn'	Job 39.9 +	the aurochs is extinct

9 The Peshiṭta vocables *ʾāmaqṯā*, *yaḏyāḏā* and *paṯnā* appear side by side in a parallel column with the C. Urmi literary classicisms derived thereof — *ʾāmaqtā, yadyādā, patnē* (pl.) — in Perkins 1852, Lev. 11: 30 (lizards), Deut. 32: 33 (snake). The pl. form *patnē* in the C. Urmi version diverges from the singular *paṯnā* in the Peshiṭta by virtue of the former being a translation of BH *pəṯånim* 'asps'. The same vocables appear in the revised version of the C. Urmi Bible (1893), which was published in New York by the American Bible Society, and includes only the 'modern Syriac' part.

10 Another case of infelicitous definition 'chameleon', despite the absence of this reptile from the area, is *xulda* 'chameleon' in Sabar's dictionary (2002, 194a), rather than the genuine meaning 'mole-rat'.

11 See Khan (2016, vol. 3, 281).

These imports from the Urmi Bible are listed in Stoddard's unpublished dictionary of 'Modern Syriac'[12] as well,[13] and three of them, taken from Stoddard's dictionary, are cited in *Thesaurus Syriacus* as 'Neo-Syriac' words.[14]

All these Syriac words are not marked in Maclean's dictionary with an asterisk, which is the regular symbol in this work for marking 'ecclesiastical or literary, but not colloquial [words]' (Maclean 1901, xxii). There are, however, a few animal names in Maclean's dictionary which do appear with an asterisk, including Syriac terms such as *garsa* 'adder, basilisk' (ibid., 57b) and *xarmāna* 'adder' (ibid., 106b), as well as Biblical Hebrew animal names copied intact, and independently of the Peshiṭtā, into the Urmi Neo-Aramaic Bible, such as *xāġaw* 'type of locust or grasshopper' (ibid., 92a; BH חָגָב, Peshiṭta *ḥargālā*) and *ʿāġor* 'crane' (ibid., 235a; BH עָגוּר 'type of bird', Peshiṭta *snōnīṯā*)

Oraham's Dictionary is teeming with Classical Syriac words, which the author incorporated zealously as part of his policy of rendering his dictionary 'enriched'. In Oraham's dictionary *ʾamaqta* 'lizard' (Oraham 1943, 24b), *yadyāda* 'hoopoe' (ibid., 98b), *pattāna* (!) 'asp' (ibid., 422a), *qāqa* 'pelican' (ibid., 461a), *dayṣa* 'ibex' (ibid., 111b), *yaxmur* 'fallow-deer, bubal' (ibid., 202a) and *rayma* 'buffalo, water buffalo; unicorn' (ibid., 479b) are all classicisms, mostly copied from Payne Smith 1903.

Based on these dictionaries, one might be inclined to assume that the animal names *ʾamaqta, yadyāda, patna, qāqa, deṣa/ dayṣa yaxmur/yaxmura* and *rema/rayma* are genuine modern Aramaic words that exist in C. Urmi or some other Christian NENA dialect(s), but no such vocables are known to occur in any modern Aramaic variety.[15]

---

12 Yale University ms. AOS Rn St 64m; written between the publication of the Urmi Bible in 1852 and Stoddard's death in 1857.

13 P. 12 *ʾamaqta* 'weasel' (!), marked as 'anc[ient]', p. 153a *yadyāda* 'hyena' (!), p. 348a *patna* 'a kind of serpent', p. 397a *qāqa* 'pelican', p. 80a *dayṣa* 'wild goat', 155b *yaxmora* 'wild buffalo', 391a *rayma* 'wild ox'.

14 See Thesaurus, 1554 *yadyādā*, 3345 *patnā*, 3897 *raymā*.

15 Consider Militarev and Kogan (2005, 90, 249, 172, 319) where 'Neo-Syriac' *patnâ, rémâ, ḳâḳâ* and *yakhmûrâ* are derived from Maclean's

2. Chronological Strata of Neo-Aramaic Animal Names

Neo-Aramaic animal names can be classified into three major chronological strata, starting with reflexes of the oldest names harking back to Proto-Aramaic, and in most cases to an earlier Semitic layer, if not Proto-Semitic, followed by terms inherited from a later Aramaic layer, mostly regional words, and ending in the layer of modern innovations and recent loanwords. Indeed, it seems that the entire lexical stock of any modern Aramaic variety can be chronologically stratified in this way. The following are selected examples of NA animal names in each of the three layers:

2.1. Oldest Stratum: Neo-Aramaic Vocables Inherited From Proto-Aramaic

Among the oldest inherited animal names are the ones within the first group shown in Table 3 below. All five selected pre-modern Aramaic lexical items have Semitic cognates which justify their classification as belonging to a Semitic chronological layer that pre-dated Proto-Aramaic. The first item, *tawlʿā, tawlaʿtā,* already attested in Old (Ancient) Aramaic as *twlʿh* (f. form in st. abs., see *DNWSI*, vol. 2, 1206), has reflexes in all four major NA dialect groups, as well as Semitic cognates such as Akk. *tūltu*, Harari *tuluʾ*, Soddo *təlä*, Soqotri *taʿáleh* and Mehri *təwālōt.*[16] Likewise, the inherited Aramaic words for 'dove', 'hare', 'gazelle' and 'ass foal' and their cognates in other Semitic languages must be of ancient Semitic pedigree.[17]

dictionary. Löw, however, realised that Maclean's *ʾamaqta* is not genuine NA but Syriac (Löw 1912a, 127); whilst he thought that *patna* did exist in 'Neo-Syriac' (Löw 1908, 42).

16 For these and further cognates see Militarev and Kogan (2005, 294–295).

17 See Militarev and Kogan (2005, 321–322; 20–21; 310–312; 65–66).

Table 3: Common Aramaic animal names

	Pre-modern Aramaic	WNA	Ṭuroyo	NENA	Neo-Mandaic
1.	*tawlaʿtā, tawlʿā* 'worm'	*ṭawlaʿča*	*tlawʿo*	*tawəlʾa*[18]	*tollɔ*[19]
2.	*yāwnā* 'dove'	*yawna*[20]	*yawno*	*yawna*[21]	*həyunɔ*
3.	*ʾarnəḇā* 'hare'	*ʾarᵊnba*	*arnuwo*[22]	*ʾarnuwa*[23]	*arwɔ*[24]
4.	*ṭaḇyā* 'gazelle'	*ṭabya*	—	*ṭoya*[25]	*ṭawyɔ*
5.	*ʿīlā* 'ass foal'	*ʿila*	*ʿilo*	*ʾila*[26]	—

As a matter of course, there are inherited Aramaic animal names that did not survive in every NA language or dialect. Thus, for instance, Ṭuroyo does not preserve the native name for 'gazelle', having replaced it with the Arabic loanword *ġazāle*, and

18 In Hertevin. Among NENA dialectal cognates are J. Dohok *toleʾṭa* (also 'caterpillar'), Chamba d-Mallik-Ṭyare *tlolāṯa*, Tkhuma *tawəlṭa*, Timur *⁺tuwəlla* and Sat *⁺tolta*.

19 Also 'caterpillar'.

20 Thus in Maʿlula. In Jubbʿadin: *žawna*.

21 In various C. NENA varieties, e.g. Baz, C. Aradhin, Harbole. Contracted to *yona* in some other NENA dialects, e.g. Ashitha, C. Urmi and Tkhuma-Gáwaya.

22 In the Rayite-Ṭuroyo dialects *arnowo* (Ritter 1971, 284/244, 300/344); and another NA cognate is Mlaḥsô *arabbó* (Jastrow 1994, 138(15), 169, on the latter page with a question mark).

23 E.g. in Haṣṣan, Betanure; in some dialects, e.g. Ashitha, *haṛnuwa*; also *ʿaṛnuwa*, with *ʿ* by assimilation to *ṛ*, e.g. in Telkepe, J. Dohok.

24 < **ʾárənḇā*. First attested in Macuch (1965, 214:16, mistranscribed *ārβa*), this is an obsolescent term marginally used amongst the oldest generation of speakers alongside the dominant Arabic loanword *ʾarnab*. The latter is already attested in post-classical Mandaic (see Drower and Macuch 1963, 38a).

25 Restricted to ʿAnkawa and some C. NENA dialects of the area of Mosul, e.g. Telkepe and Qaraqosh. An older form *ṭawya* manifests itself in Chamba d-Mallik-Ṭyare in the phrase *gəldət ṭawya* 'parchment made of gazelle hide'.

26 In Qaraqosh, Bariṭle and ʿAnkawa.

Neo-Mandaic resorted to the phrase *jihəl al-bəhimɔ* 'offspring of a donkey' as the term for 'ass foal'.

2.2. Later Stratum: Neo-Aramaic Vocables Inherited From Late Aramaic

The second layer involves NA animal names that are inherited from a later stage in the history of Aramaic, and cannot be ascribed to Proto-Aramaic. Their antecedents are either loanwords or late innovations. Most are not widely attested in Late Aramaic, but appear to be regional vocables, being confined to some Aramaic languages of either the eastern or western branch. Thus in the following examples, listed in Table 4.

Table 4: Region-specific animal names

	Pre-modern Aramaic	WNA	Ṭuroyo	NENA	Neo-Mandaic
	Eastern				
1.	*zāġā* 'chick of hen'	—	*zoġo* 'cock'	*zāʾa* 'chick' +	*zɔġɔ* 'cock'
2.	*kurpā* 'viper'	—	*kərfo* 'snake'	*kərpa* 'viper'	—
3.	**māʾeṣ ʿezzē* 'lizard'	—	—	*māṣəzze*	—
4.	*peqʿā* 'frog'	—	—	*pəqʾa, paqeʾṯa*	*paqettɔ*
	Western				
5.	*ʾurdʿānā* 'frog'	*wurtaʿna*	—	—	—
6.	*ṭabzā* 'hyrax'	—	*ṭabzo* 'badger'	—	—

(1) *zāġā* (cf. Syriac *zāġā*[27] 'chick of hen', JBA אגז 'cock', post-cl. M **zaga** 'cock') is considered an Iranian loanword,[28] and has reflexes in all major divisions of Eastern NA. The meaning 'cock' in Ṭuroyo and NM, as already in JBA and post-cl. M, may have evolved from *'cockerel'. Indeed, in Bariṭle *zāʾa* is 'chick of a hen; cockerel', but it is unclear whether Bariṭle 'cockerel' exhibits an inherited meaning or an independent dialectal innovation. In some NENA dialects *zāʾa* (e.g. in Tisqopa and Telkepe) or *zaʾa* (e.g. in Karimlash) is 'chick of a hen', as in Syriac; whereas some other dialects evince semantic broadening, either to any chick (e.g. J. Zakho and Qaraqosh *zāʾa*), or even to the offspring of a bird or animal in general (e.g. as regards Ko d-Chalwe-Ṭyare *zāʾa*, Geramun *zāya*, C. Salmas ⁺*zāya*).

(2) *kurpā*, of uncertain origin,[29] is attested in Syriac, where it denotes 'viper'—as is evident from the synonym *ʾāḵeḏnā* 'viper' and the Arabic gloss *ʾafʿa(y)* 'ditto' in medieval Syriac lexicons[30]—as well as some other kinds of snakes.[31] The only known reflex in NENA is Hertevin *kərpa*, which preserves the meaning 'viper',

27 Vocalisation is according to Audo (1897, vol. 1, 253a).

28 For the different possible Iranian etyma of this word see Ciancaglini (2008, 171, *DJBA*, 399a, *SL*, 364b).

29 Perhaps from Akk. *kuppû* as (*inter alia*) a kind of snake (see *CAD* K, 551b-552a).

30 See Hoffman (1874, 657, 4669); Duval (1888–1891, vol. 1, 883). Accordingly, it is glossed 'viper' in *Thesaurus*, 1837–1838.

31 See Löw (1908, 39–40), where also 'deaf snake' (unknown species), '*Eryx jaculus*', 'adder' (*Vipera berus*, a viper not found in the Middle East) and 'female serpent' are mentioned. The latter is the definition of *kurpā* in *LS*, 349a (followed by *SL*, 615a), and is based on the Arabic gloss *ʾal-ʾunṯa(y)* 'the female'. However, the epithet *ʾal-ʾunṯa(y)* may well be related to the fact that *kurpā* is a feminine noun. Consider also the NENA epithets *dādé-ḥuwa* (Hertevin) and *yəmmət xuwwe* (Ashitha, Betanure), both referring to the viper (Hertevin *kərpa*, Ashitha, Betanure *šəlya*) as 'mother of snake'. All three epithets may be related to the fact that local vipers bring forth live young, unlike other local snakes, which lay eggs.

whereas Ṭuroyo expanded the denotation of *kərfo* into a generic term for 'snake'.[32]

(3) **mā'eṣ ʿezzē* 'lizard', more precisely 'monitor lizard', lit. 'goat sucker', is in accordance with the emendation of Bar Bahlul's *mā'eṣ ʿērā* 'monitor lizard', offered by Löw[33] and, recently, Sokoloff.[34] There can be little doubt that *ʿērā* is indeed corrupt and that this emendation is justified, given the following considerations:

(i) Bar Bahlul's lexicon is replete with words derived from local Mesopotamian—quite possibly early NENA—vernaculars.[35] Unlike *'mā'eṣ ʿērā'*, with the second component not related to any known Aramaic or foreign root or noun, **mā'eṣ ʿezzē,* lit. 'goat sucker', is clearly the antecedent of NENA dialectal forms such as *māṣəzze* (Marga), *maṣəzze* (Ko d-Chalwe-Ṭyare), *miẓaẓẓe* (Bariṭle), *māč̣əẓẓe* (Geramun), all 'lizard' (genus *Lacerta*) and +*mazuzta* (C. Urmi) 'lizard' (generic).[36] Synchronically more transparent forms, based on the same myth of lizards sucking milk from goats, are Mer *mayṣa-'əzze* and Barwar *mɛṣa-'əzze*[37] 'lizard' (genus *Lacerta*), lit. 'she sucks [milk from] goats'.[38]

---

32 For 'viper' > 'snake' cf. the case of NENA *šəlya* below §3.

33 See the corrupt form in Duval (1888–1891, vol. 1, 668, line 22) and the emendation in Löw (1912a, 129), where also the vocables *mn ṣʿr'* and *mā ṣʿr'* in Bar ʿAli's 9th century lexicon and in Bar Bahlul's 10th century lexicon, respectively—already considered 'most corrupt' in *Thesaurus,* 1070—were emended by Löw to *mā'eṣ ʿezzē.*

34 See *DJBA,* 533b, s.v. יילא. In *SL,* 703b, however, the form *ʿērā* remains unaltered.

35 Most vernacular words mentioned in Mutzafi (2016, 511–512) concerning Bar ʿAli's lexicon apply to Bar Bahlul's lexicon as well.

36 Indeed, Löw (1912a, 139–140) connected medieval *mā'eṣ ʿezzē* to NA forms furnished in Maclean (1901: 152b) and Stoddard's unpublished dictionary (the later cited in *Thesaurus*); and Sokoloff (*DJBA,* 533b, s.v. יילא) adduces the NENA form transcribed *miṣʿizî* in Maclean (1901, 152b, s.v. *mā'eṣ ʿezzē).*

37 Also *mɛṣantət 'əzze* (Khan 2008, vol. 2, 1077, 1334).

38 There is also a NENA form with *š,* more specifically in the Christian dialect of Ardishay, Urmi plain, mentioned in Maclean (1901, 203b) as '*mîsh'izzî*'

(ii) The folk belief that monitor lizards suck milk from livestock, particularly cows, is already evident in the Babylonian Talmud (Shabbat 54b).[39]

(iii) The noun **maṣuṣta** (< **māṣōṣtā* 'sucker'), in all likelihood signifying 'lizard' or some kind of lizard), is manifest in a Mandaic incantation dated to the 5th-7th centuries (Abudraham and Morgenstern 2017, 757).

(iv) Syrian Ar. *raḍḍāʿ il-maʿiz* 'salamander', lit. 'goat sucker' (Behnstedt and Woidich 2010, 370a) may well be a calque on pre-mod. Aram. **māʾeṣ ʿezzē.*[40]

(4) *peqʿā* 'frog' is attested in Bar ʿAli's and Bar Bahlul's Syriac lexicons of the 9th and 10th centuries,[41] most probably as a regional vernacularism, possibly an early NENA word.[42] Its etymology is uncertain, but it is likely related to Syr. *paqʿā* 'noise, din, thunderbolt', as well as the verbs *paqqaʿ* 'make a noise of breaking, rattle, crackle', *ʾap̄qaʿ* 'make a noise', in connection with noisy anuran croaks.[43]

(apparently *+mišəzzə*).

39 Cf. *DJBA*, 533b, s.v. ײלא.

40 Consider also dialectal Moroccan Ar. *rṭēṭaʿ əl-bqaṛ* 'gecko', lit. 'little cow-sucker' (Behnstedt and Woidich 2010, 367, 369c) and similar Maghrebin lexemes (ibid., 370a; also in Dozy 1967, vol. 1, 534b as *raḍḍāʿat ʾal-baqar* 'red-spotted lizard'), as well as Palestinian Ar. *raḍḍāʿa* 'skink' (Dalman 1923, 72, No. 72) and 'reptile similar to stellion lizard with soft, smooth skin, famous for sneaking and sucking milk from small cattle' (Barghouthi 2001, 511). Similar terms, referring to the monitor lizard, are Kurmanji *bizinmêj*, lit. 'goat-sucker', *pezmijok*, lit. 'sucker of small cattle' and *mangemijok*, lit. 'cow-sucker'. At least some of these terms may ultimately be the outcomes of an early Aramaic influence. English *goatsucker* 'nightjar', modelled on Latin *caprimulgus* 'nightjar', lit. 'goat milker', is a similar case, albeit related to a bird.

41 See Hoffmann (1874, 404); Duval (1888–1891, vol. 1: 87, line 23).

42 See Mutzafi (2014, 121), Mutzafi (2016, 511–512).

43 Cf. *LS*, 590a and *SL*, 1224a where *peqʿā* 'split, gorge, seaweed, frog' is regarded as a polysemic derivative of *pqʿ* 'to split'. Other suggestions in

Among the NENA reflexes of *peqʿā* are the dialectal cognates *pəqʿa* (Qaraqosh),[44] *pəqʾa* (Hertevin), *pəqqa* (e.g. in Telkepe), *p̭ək̭k̭a* (C. Urmi),[45] *piqqa* (e.g. in Tin), *peqa* (Mer), *pəqa* (e.g. in Harbole), *pŭqa* (Bariṭle), *paqa* (Inishke) and *paqeʾṯa* (Betanure), all denoting 'frog, toad'. Betanure (northernmost Iraq) *paqeʾṯa* and NM (south-western Iran) *paqettɔ* 'frog, toad' appear to have each evolved independently as reflexes of **paqəʿṯā* (< **paqʿəṯā* < **peqʿəṯā*), a feminine derivative of *peqʿā*.

(5) Trg.O. עורדען, JPA עורדען, אורדען and Sam.Aram. ערדען, ארדען 'frog' exhibit an innovation whereby the forms **ʿurdʿā, ʾurdʿā* (or rather their alternants in st. abs.)—the latter, *ʾurdʿā,* being attested in Syriac—were expanded by the ending *-ān* in these three Aramaic varieties of Palestine. Modern reflexes of the Western Aramaic innovation אורדען (or rather its alternant in st. emph.) are Maʿlula *wurtaʿna* and Jubbʿadin *burṭaʿnṯa* (< **wurtaʿnṯa*).

A NA cognate is likely Midyat-Ṭur. *gurdaʿdaʿ* (informants), *gurdaʿa* (Ritter 1979, 180). Assuming that these forms represent a native Ṭuroyo word,[46] its etymon would seem to be identical to Western Syriac *ʾurdʿō* 'frog', whence **wurdʿo* (by partial assimilation of *ʾ* to *u*) > **gurdʿo* (with a highly irregular change

scholarly literature: *Thesaurus*, 3222 hesitantly compared *peqʿā* 'frog' to Ar. *faqʿ* 'red(dish) worms', which is hardly likely; whereas Löw (1909, 395) derives *peqʿā* 'frog' from Pers. *pak, bak* 'frog' and compared *peqʿā* to NENA *piqqa, bāqa*, etc. 'frog'. Similarly, Maclean (1901, 255b) derived *pəqqa* 'frog' from Kurd. *beq* and Pers. *pak* 'id.', Fox (2009, 158) derives Borb-Ruma *pəqa* 'frog' from Kurd. *beq* 'id.' and Napiorkowska (2015, 506b) derives Diyana-Zariwaw *piqqa* 'frog' from Kurdish. Medieval Mesopotamian Aramaic *peqʿā* is obviously the etymon, however, and the similar sounding Iranian parallels might have only reinforced or facilitated the ousting of older Aramaic *ʾurdʿā* by the innovation *peqʿā*.

44 See Khan (2002, 533, 740a).

45 See Khan (2016, 54, 262).

46 No such word is known to exist in any neighbouring language—consider local Arabic *ʿaqṛōqa* (informant and Behnstedt and Woidich 2010, map 129b and p. 383c) and Kurdish *beq* (> rural Ṭur. *baqqe, baqe*).

w > *g*) > *gurdaʿa* (with final *a* found in a small number of native nouns—see Tezel 2003, 32, 222) > partial reduplication: *gurdaʿdaʿ*.[47] It is nevertheless only in WNA that the Western Aramaic form with *-ān(ā)* has modern reflexes.

(6) Ṭuroyo *ṭabzo* 'badger', used at least in the southern dialect of Ba-Dibbe, is most probably a reflex of *ṭabzā* 'hyrax', attested in JPA as טבזא alongside טפזא and טפסא (st. abs. טבז, טפז, טפס), which are cognate with Sam.Aram. טפסה (st. abs. טפס) 'hyrax'.[48] The earliest occurrences appear in Trg.O as טפזא and טבזא. Therefore, although Ṭuroyo is an Eastern NA language, it inherited a Western Aramaic word as a result of diffusion northward and eastward. Since the northernmost distribution of the hyrax is in Lebanon, the original meaning of the term *ṭabzā* could not have been preserved in Ṭuroyo, and the reflex *ṭabzo* came to refer to another chubby, short-limbed mammal, the badger.[49]

2.3. Latest Stratum: Modern Innovations

The latest stratum is that of Neo-Aramaic lexical innovations, many of which are new creations based on inherited Aramaic etyma moulded by mechanisms of word formation. Some of these innovations are highly imaginative and picturesque. Selected examples from NENA are furnished in what follows:

NENA dialect	**1. 'ladybird'**	**2. 'snail'**
Ishshi	*tawərtət bābí-ʾalāha*	*saṭāna*
Harbole	*ktɛtət bābí-ʾalāha*	*šeda*
Qaraqosh	*sustət ʾabuna*	*nəṯyaṯṯəd mar daniyel*

47 Cf. Tezel (2003, 221–222).

48 For a linguistic and zoological treatment of the latter word and its cognates see Talshir (1981, 102–103).

49 Note also that the Qalamun mountains, where WNA is spoken, are outside the geographical distribution of the hyrax, hence it has no name in WNA (Prof. Werner Arnold, e-mail).

NENA dialect	1. 'ladybird'	2. 'snail'
C. Urmi	*ʾurxət ⁺xālu*	*spaditət xuvva*
Chamba d-Mallik	*baṭibāṭo*	*šarro*

NENA dialect	3. 'guinea-fowl'
Telkepe	*kṯeṯət pərʿon*
C. Urmi	*ctetət haštarxan*
Lizin-Ṭyare	*məštarxa*
Bne Romta-Ṭyare	*kṯɛšət qāna*

(1) As for some of the dialectal NENA terms for the 'ladybird', in Ishshi creative imagination forged the name *tawərtət bābí-ʾalāha,* lit. 'cow of my Father God', which has striking parallels in some of the Slavic languages, e.g. Polish *boża krówka,* lit. 'God's little cow'.[50] These are outcomes of the same human imagination of this plump spotted creature as a tiny cow,[51] that is considered to be a godsend for farmers by virtue of the fact that ladybirds mainly feed on aphids. In Harbole, however, the chubby ladybird was compared to a hen and the parallel term is *ktɛtət bābí-ʾalāha* 'hen of my Father God'.[52]

Perhaps no less picturesque is Qaraqosh *sustət ʾabuna,*[53] lit. 'our priest's mare', which in some other C. NENA dialects

---

50 See further terms in Merkin (1993, 130).

51 Hence also regional English *ladycow* and Spanish *vaca de San Antón* 'Saint Anthony's cow' (Merkin 1993: 130; and see *ladycow* also in OED Online), as well as modern Irish *bóín Dé* 'God's little cow' (*bóín* < *bó* 'cow' + dim. suff. ín).

52 Cf. Danish *mariehøne,* Norwegian *marihøne,* lit. '[Virgin] Mary's hen'; as well as dialectal Catalan *gallineta,* lit. 'little hen', *gallineta de Nostre Senyor,* lit. 'little hen of Our Lord' (and similar terms)—see Veny and Pons i Griera (2014, map and p. 1546 (=http://aldc.espais.iec.cat/files/2015/03/Mapa-1546.pdf).

53 Thus according to my informants. In Khan (2002, 743b *susta l-abuna*).

designates the praying mantis (e.g. C. Aradhin *sustət ʾabona,* lit. 'bishop's mare'). C. Urmi *ʾurxət* ⁺*xalu* is literally 'way of uncle', to be precise 'the way to the maternal uncle', and is based on a tradition of telling children that if they made this beetle fly, their uncle would come.[54] *ʾurxət* ⁺*xalu* may have also been influenced by Kurdish *xalxalok* 'ladybird', lit. 'spotty', which is based on the Kurdish noun *xal* (< Ar.) 'birthmark, freckle'. 'Spotty' is also the basic meaning of *baṭibāṭo* in the Chamba d-Mallik dialect of Ṭyare and some other C. NENA dialects, derived from *bəṭṭa* 'spot' (cf. Syr. *beṭṭā* 'spark') or from a reduplicative form thereof, akin to Syr. *baṭbāṭā* 'spark'.[55]

(2) As for NENA words for 'snail', in some Christian dialects (e.g. Ishshi, Telkepe and Ashitha) the snail is referred to as *saṭāna,* 'Satan, devil', which is a semantic parallel of Harbole *šeda* 'demon; snail', Jilu *šida* 'snail', Ṭur. *šiḏo* 'Satan, devil; snail' and Kurd. *şeytanok* 'snail', lit. 'little devil'. Similarly, ⁺*ʾaynət šida* 'snail', lit. 'devil's eye' is listed in Maclean (1901, 238b) as a C. Urmi term, but, unknown to informants from the city of Urmi itself, is perhaps to be found in some village(s) in the vicinity, or has gone obsolete by now. Semantically related is *šarro* 'snail' in the Ṭyare dialect of Chamba d-Mallik, ultimately from Arabic *šarr* 'wicked'.

The semantic background of these terms might be related to the snail's eyestalks, which a fanciful mind may relate to the

54 See Khan (2016, vol. 3, 85).

55 There is also *biṭibāṭu* 'brightness, sheen' in *LS* 66a, followed by *SL,* 140b, but this is based on the occurrence of the word *biṭibāṭo* in Budge's edition of the Syriac book of medicines, a manuscript replete with NENA words and forms. The text, referring to a type of glowing or sparkling flowers, reads *ʾa(y)ḵ biṭibāṭo d-nahrā b-qayṭā* (Budge 1913, vol. 1, 598/6), and this was mistranslated by Budge (1913, vol. 2, 711/10) 'like the sparkling of the waters of a river in the summer'. It seems to me that *nahrā* 'river' is a miscopying of *nāhrā* 'it glows', and that the correct translation should be 'like a firefly that glows in summer', with *biṭibāṭo* being a dialectal NENA word (cf. Telkepe *biṭubāṭu* 'firefly'). Consider also the translation '[like] fireflies by the river in summer' in Margoliouth (1927, 53b), based upon the Chaldean priest and native NENA speaker Alphonse Mingana (for the latter's contributions to Margoliouth's work see ibid., vii, viii).

demonic horns of Satan. Indeed, in the Ṭyare dialect of Bne Belatha the snail is called *qanānət saṭāna*, lit. 'Satan's horns'.

By contrast, in Qaraqosh the snail has a positive name, *nəṯyaṯṯəd mar daniyel* 'Saint Daniel's ear', apparently referring to a Mesopotamian monk of the fifth century, Daniel the Stylite. Informants could offer no explanation as to the connection to that saint, but at least one can find a faint resemblance between a snail shell and the human ear.[56]

A rather neutral, yet no less picturesque name for 'snail' (and 'snail shell') is the C. Urmi term *spaditət xuvva* ~ *spaditət xuvvə*,[57] lit. 'snake's pillow'. The surreal image of a sleepy snake using a snail shell as a pillow might have ultimately been taken from a folktale, but informants know of no such tale, nor could they offer any other background for this rather quaint term. It may well be that this term is a calque on some unattested Kurdish construction denoting 'snake's pillow', given Kurmanji *balif* 'pillow; snail'.[58] This postulated Kurdish term would also be the model on which the term *sariná-xiwá* 'snail' (< *sariná* 'pillow' < Kurd. *serîn* + inherited NENA *xiwá* 'snake') was coined in the Jewish NENA dialect of Kerend.

(3) Some dialectal NENA innovations refer to new species of animals introduced into NENA-speaking areas, such as the guinea-fowl, more accurately the helmeted guinea-fowl, which was raised in some C. NENA-speaking villages for its meat and eggs. Telkepe *kṯeṯət pərʿon* 'Pharaoh's hen' has a striking parallel in Italian, namely *faraona*, an ellipsis of *gallina faraona* 'Pharaonic hen'.[59] The connection to the Pharaohs is, presumably, the African

56 Cf. J. Urmi ⁺*nahaltət* ⁺*šeytan* 'snail, snail shell', a calque on Kurd. *guhşeytan* 'snail', both literally denote 'Satan's ear'; and consider also the zoological term *auriculella* for a genus of snail endemic to Hawaii (see Cowie et al. 2016, 248–250, 252, 262–263, including photos), literally 'little ear', a diminutive form of Latin *auris* 'ear'.

57 First attested in Sargis (1909, 587, s.v. улитка).

58 See İzoli (1992: 41b).

59 Cortelazzo and Zolli (2004, 430a).

origin of the bird and possibly the idea that it was one of the delicacies served to the rulers of ancient Egypt.

C. Urmi *ctetət haštarxan* 'guinea-fowl'[60] is a hen from Hashtar Khan, which is one of the old names of Astrakhan near the Caspian Sea (I could not find any information about guinea-fowl breeding in Astrakhan, though). Lizin-Ṭyare *məštarxa* must be an ellipsis of **kṯɛša mən ʾəštarxan* 'hen from Astrakhan', especially in the light of Chamba d-Mallik-Ṭyare *ʾəštarxən* ~ *kṯɛšət ʾəštarxən* 'guinea-fowl'. The innovation in Bne Romta-Ṭyare *kṯɛšət qāna* 'hen of horn, horned hen' is after the fowl's horn-like protrusion.

Numerous other dialectal NENA innovations of animal names could be added to the terms above, among which are Bne Belatha-Ṭyare *čale-miya* 'water-bride' and Harbole *xasla-məṭre* 'weaner of rains' as unique names for the salamander (the latter term, *xasla-məṭre,* is related to the appearance of [full-grown] salamanders in May and early June, when rainfall ceases).

3. Semantic Differences in Dialectal Cognates of Animal Names

In some cases the same animal name refers to different referents across specific NA varieties. Selected cases taken from the NENA dialects are the following:

Invertebrates

Syriac	Lizin-Ṭyare	Shwawwa-Baz
1. *naddālā* 'centipede'	*madāla* 'centipede'	*madāla* 'earthworm'

Birds

	Borb-Ruma	Qaraqosh
2. *bakkā* 'cock'	*buka* 'cock'	*buka* 'male dove'

60 Already attested in Sargis (1909, 633, s.v. цесарка).

Reptiles

Postulated etymon	Haṣṣan	Tilla
3. **šālyā* 'she draws [fangs]'	*šəlya* 'viper'	*šəlya* 'snake'

Mammals

	Ṭyare	Jilu
4. **kakkeš(t)ā* 'weasel'	*kakəšta* 'weasel'	*kakša* 'vole'

Birds, Insects

	Lizin-Ṭyare	Bne romta-Ṭyare
5. *qāša* 'priest' + 2 dim.suff.	*qašonik̭a* 'tit'	*qašonik̭a* 'antlion'

(1) Pre-mod. Aram. *naddālā* 'centipede', as, e.g., in Syriac, has reflexes in various C .NENA dialects, mostly referring to the centipede or millipede, such as Lizin-Ṭyare *madāla* 'centipede',[61] Barwar *madāla* 'millipede' (Khan 2008, vol. 2, 1324), Bne Romta-Ṭyare *nadāla* 'centipede, millipede', Sat *medāla* 'id.'. Some other Christian NENA dialects and cognates evince a semantic shift to another elongated creeping invertebrate, the earthworm. Thus, e.g., Shwawwa-Baz *madāla,* Timur and Upper Barwar (Hakkâri) *midāla.* In the dialect of Geramun *madāla* signifies both 'centipede, millipede' and 'earthworm'.

(2) Some of the north-western NENA dialects in the area of Bohtan preserve an inherited NENA word for 'cock, rooster' closely related to Syr. *bakkā* 'cock', a by-form of *ʾāḇakkā* (also אבכא 'id.'

61 The direct antecedent *maddālā* is already attested in Bar ʿAli's 9th century lexicon (Hoffmann 1874, 212, No. 5438) and in Bar Bahlul's 10th century lexicon, in the latter as a word in the (early NENA?) dialect of Tikrit (Duval 1888–1891, 836, s.v. *yadyādā*).

in the Judaeo-Syriac Targum to Proverbs 30.31).[62] Thus *buka* in Borb-Ruma and Hertevin and *büka* in Qurich, stemming from the antecedent **bukkā*. In Qaraqosh *buka* exhibits a semantic change into 'male dove'.

(3) Various C. NENA dialects exhibit the zoonym *šəlya* 'viper', e.g. Haṣṣan, C. Aradhin, Iṣṣin, the dialect cluster of Ṭyare and Sharmen. In all these dialects *šəlya* is a feminine noun. I postulate the etymon **šālyā,* a fs. participle of the pre-modern Aramaic verbal root *šly* 'to draw, pull out', hence *šəlya* is a snake that 'draws' its fangs and bites. The connection between *šly* 'to draw, pull out' and a venomous snake is attested in JPA: שדיי שלח לחוויה דאשלי לארס 'God sent the snake, which drew out the venom.' (*DJPA* 553a, s.v. $_{2}$שלי). For the vowel change **a* > *ə* in **šālyā* > **šalya* > *šəlya* compare *ləxma, ləxmá* 'bread' in some NENA varieties (e.g. Ṭyare and Arbel, respectively).

In the NENA dialect of Tilla the denotation of *šəlya* was expanded to include any snake, followed by the ousting of inherited NENA *xuwwe* 'snake' out of the dialect's lexical system.[63]

(4) Ṭyare *kakəšta* 'weasel' is etymologically related to JBA כרכושתא 'weasel' and Syr. *kāḵuštā* 'weasel, ferret, mongoose, cat' (*'weasel' > 'mice-eating mammal'), among other cognates. The antecedent of the Ṭyare form appears to have been **kakkeštā,* closely akin to **kakkuštā,* the postulated precursor of the JBA cognate. Another cognate form is *kākšā* 'weasel' in a late Nestorian manuscript.[64] In the light of C. Salmas and Van *kakša* 'weasel' and the fact that this manuscript includes a number of NENA vocables,[65] *kākšā* is

62 Perhaps the feminine form בכתה already occurs in Old Aramaic, if its meaning is 'hen'—see *DNWSI*, vol. 1, 192.

63 Cf. *kurpā* 'viper' > Ṭur. *kərfo* 'snake' above §2.2.

64 Hoffmann (1880, 90: 19), where the reading *ḵākšā* (!) with initial *ḵ (x)* appears to be the result of an inadvertent speck of ink under the first letter *kap* (cf. Nöldeke 1914–1915, 240). Indeed, *LS* 326b, followed by *SL*, 621b, read *kākšā*.

65 E.g. *ḵyārē* 'cucumbers' (Hoffmann 1880, 92/19) < NENA *xiyāre* or *⁺xyārə* < Ar.; and *slāwlyō* 'weasel' (ibid., 90/19), as in C. Aradhin *slawəlyo*

likely an interpolation of a NENA word into that Syriac text. In addition, Jilu *kakša* evinces a change of meaning into another small, short-legged, agile mammal, the vole.[66]

Further cognates are *kakča* 'mole, rat' (Maclean 1901, 131b), *kaška* 'field mouse' (Tsereteli 1980, 44) and 'mole' (David 1924, English-NA part, 64). All these pre-modern and modern cognates might hark back to Akkadian *kakkišu,* which appears to have denoted 'weasel',[67] in which case the form closest to the etymon is modern *kakša* (< **kakkəšā*) rather than the pre-modern cognates.

(5) Oddly enough, in Ṭyare *qašoniḵ̭a* is a term for two entirely different creatures according to dialect, denoting 'tit' (a songbird) in Lizin and 'antlion' in Bne romta. Informants construe the literal meaning of this word as 'little priest'. Indeed, *qašoniḵ̭a* is synchronically, and probably also etymologically, based on inherited NENA *qāša* (consider Syriac *qaššā* < *qaššīšā*) 'priest' with two diminutive suffixes, native *-on* and *iḵ̭a.* The latter is based on the Kurdish diminutive suffix *ik.* The connection to 'priest' eludes me, however, and is completely opaque as far as the speakers are concerned.

'weasel', with a typical NENA ending *o* found in many animal names (including *baṭibāṭo* 'ladybird' and *šarro* 'snail' above, §2.3., as well as *gāṛo* 'weasel; vole, rat' in n. 66 below).

66 Similar cognates involving a weasel or another musteline animal and a rodent are NENA *gāṛo* 'weasel' (e.g. in Mer, Rekan), 'vole, rat' (e.g. in Betanure, Halmun); BH *ḥolɛḏ,* Mishnaic Hebrew *ḥuldå* 'marten, weasel and closely related mammals' and Ar. *xuld,* Syr. *ḥuldā* 'mole-rat' (Talshir 2012, 95–106); quite possibly Akk. *akbaru* 'jerboa', Hebrew *ʿaḵbår* 'mouse' and Tigre *ʿerkib* 'badger' (assuming metathesis; see Militarev and Kogan 2005, 47); and, farther afield, Classical Armenian ak'is 'weasel; rat' (Martirosyan 2010, 159).

67 See *AHw* vol. 1, 422a *kakkišu* 'weasel', compared to Aram. *ka(r)kuštā,* whereas *CAD* K, 50a defines it as a small animal, possibly a rodent. The Aramaic forms denoting 'weasel', including NENA *kakša,* support *AHw.*

References

Abudraham, Ohad and Morgenstern, Matthew. 2017. 'Mandaic Incantation(s) on lead scrolls from the Schøyen Collection'. *Journal of the American Oriental Society* 137: 737–765.

AHw—Soden, Wolfram von. 1965–1981. *Akkadisches Handwörterbuch*. 3 vols. Wiesbaden: Harrassowitz.

Arnold, Werner. 2019. *Das Neuwestaramäische. Teil VI: Wörterbuch: Neuwestaramäisch–Deutsch*. Semitica Viva 4.6. Wiesbaden: Harrassowitz.

Audo, Toma. 1897. *Simtā d-Leššānā Suryāyā* [*Treasure of the Syriac Language*]. 2 vols. Mosul: Imprimerie des Pères Dominicains.

Behnstedt, Peter and Woidich, Manfred. 2011. *Wortatlas der arabischen Dialekte. Band 1: Mensch, Natur, Fauna und Flora.* Leiden: Brill.

Budge, Ernest A.W. 1913. *Syrian Anatomy, Pathology and Therapeutics, or The Book of Medicines.* 2 vols., London: Oxford University Press.

CAD—Gelb, Ignace J. et al (eds.). 1956–2010. *Chicago Assyrian Dictionary (The Assyrian Dictionary of the Oriental Institute of the University of Chicago)*. 26 vols., Chicago: Oriental Institute.

Chyet, Michael L. 2003. *Kurdish-English Dictionary. Ferhenga Kurmancî-Inglîzî.* New Haven, CT: Yale University Press.

Ciancaglini, Claudia A. 2008. *Iranian Loanwords in Syriac*. Wiesbaden: L. Reichert.

Cook, Edward M. 2008. *A Glossary of Targum Onkelos.* Leiden: Brill.

Cortelazzo, Manlio and Zolli, Paolo. 2004. *l'Etimologico minore. DELI, Dizionario etimologico della lingua italiana.* Bologna: Zanichelli.

Cowie, Robert H. et al. 2016. 'Annotated Catalogue of Types of Hawaiian Land and Freshwater Snails (Mollusca: Gastropoda) in the Muséum national d'histoire naturelle, Paris, with Lectotype Designations'. *Zoosystema* 38: 245–266.

Dalman, Gustaf. 1923. 'Palästinische Tiernamen'. *Zeitschrift des Deutschen Palästina-Vereins* 46: 65–78.

David, Shmuel. 1924. *The First Chaldean-English Dictionary.* Chicago: n.p.

DJBA—Sokoloff, Michael. 2002. *A Dictionary of Jewish Babylonian Aramaic of the Talmudic and Geonic Periods*. Ramat-Gan: Bar-Ilan University Press.

DJPA—Sokoloff, Michael. 2017. *A Dictionary of Jewish Palestinian Aramaic of the Byzantine Period*. 3rd. ed., Ramat-Gan: Bar-Ilan University Press.

DNWSI—Hoftijzer, Jacob and Jongeling, Karel. 1995. *Dictionary of the North-West Semitic Inscriptions*. 2 vols., 2nd. ed., Leiden: Brill.

Dozy, Reinhart P. 1967. *Supplement aux dictionnaires arabes*. 3rd. ed., Leiden: Brill.

Drower, Ethel S. and Macuch, Rudolf. 1963. *A Mandaic Dictionary*. Oxford: Clarendon Press.

Duval, Rubens. (ed.). 1888–1891. *Lexicon syriacum auctore Hassano bar Bahlule*, 3 vols., Paris: Reipublicæ Typographæ.

Fox, Samuel E. 2009. *The Neo-Aramaic Dialect of Bohtan*. Piscataway, NJ: Gorgias Press.

Gewargis Ashitha, Odisho M. 2018. *Hilqa de Leshana: Assyrian-Arabic Dictionary*. 2nd edition. Dohok: n.p.

Hoffmann, Georg (ed.). 1874. *Syrisch-arabische Glossen: Autographie einer Gothaischen Handschrift enthaltend Bar Ali's Lexikon von Alif bis Mim*. Kiel: Schwers'sche Buchhandlung.

———. 1880. *Opuscula Nestoriana Syriace Tradidit*. Kiel: G. von Maack.

Hutchins, Michael et al. (eds.). 2004. *Grzimek's Animal Life Encyclopedia*. 2nd. ed., 17 vols., Farmington Hills, MI: Gale.

İzoli, D. 1992. *Ferheng Kurdi-Tırki*. Istanbul: Deng Yayınları.

Jastrow, Otto. 1994. *Der neuaramäische Dialekt von Mlaḥsô*. Wiesbaden: Harrassowitz.

Khan, Geoffrey. 2002. *The Neo-Aramaic Dialect of Qaraqosh*. Leiden: Brill.

———. 2016. *The Neo-Aramaic Dialect of the Assyrian Christians of Urmi*. 4 vols., Leiden: Brill.

Löw, Immanuel. 1906. 'Aramäische Fischnamen'. In *Orientalische Studien: Theodor Nöldeke zum siebzigsten Geburtstag (2. März 1906) gewidmet von Freunden und Schülern*. 2 vols., edited by Carl Bezold, 549–570. Giessen: A. Töpelmann.

———. 1909a. 'Aramäische Schlangennamen', In *Festschrift zu Ehren des Dr. A. Harkavy aus Anlass seines am 20. November 1905 vollendeten siebzigsten Lebensjahres*. 3 vols., edited by David Günzburg and Isaac Markon, vol. 1: 27–52. St. Petersburg: H. Itzkowski,.

———. 1909b. 'Aramäische Lurchnamen (Frosch und Salamander).' In *Florilegium ou recueil de travaux d'érudition dédiés à Mosieur le Marqis Melchior de Vogüé à l'occasion du quatre-vingtième anniversaire de sa naissance, 18 octobre 1909*, edited by Melchior Vogüé, 391–406. Paris: Imprimerie nationale.

———. 1912a. 'Aramäische Lurchnamen. 1. Eidechsen.' *Zeitschrift für Assyriologie und verwandte Gebiete* 26: 126–147.

———. 1912b. 'Aramäische Lurchnamen. 2. Wurmzüngler (Chamäleon); 4. Panzerechsen (Krokodil); 5. Schildkröten', in *Judaica: Festschrift zu Hermann Cohens siebzigstem Geburtstage*, edited by Hermann Cohen, 333–346. Berlin: B. Kassirer.

LS—Brockelmann, Carl. 1928. *Lexicon Syriacum*. 2nd. ed., Halle: Max Niemeyer.

Maclean, Arthur J. 1901. *A Dictionary of the Dialects of Vernacular Syriac*. Oxford: Clarendon press.

Macuch, Rudolf. 1965. *Handbook of Classical and Modern Mandaic*. Berlin: W. de Gruyter.

Manna, Yaqub E. 1975. *Chaldean-Arabic Dictionary, Printed with a New Appendix by Dr. Raphael J. Bidawid.* Beirut: Babel Center Publications.

Margoliouth, Jessie. 1927. *Supplement to the Thesaurus Syriacus*. Oxford: Clarendon Press.

Martirosyan, Hrach K. 2010. *Etymological Dictionary of the Armenian Inherited Lexicon.* Leiden: Brill.

Merkin, Reuven. 1993. 'פרת משה רבנו (= Ladybird)'. *Lešonenu Laʿam* 44.3: 129–134.

Militarev, Alexander and Kogan, Leonid. 2005. *Semitic Etymological Dictionary, vol. II: Animal Names.* Münster: Ugarit-Verlag.

Mutzafi, Hezy. 2014. *Comparative Lexical Studies in Neo-Mandaic.* Leiden: Brill.

———. 2016. 'The Origin of the Neo-Aramaic Verb *dʿr* 'To Return' and Its Cognates: A New Proposal'. *Journal of Semitic Studies* 61.2: 507–525.

Napiorkowska, Lidia. 2015. *A Grammar of the Christian Neo-Aramaic Dialect of Diyana-Zariwaw*. Leiden: Brill.

Nöldeke, Theodor. 1914–1915. 'כרכושת'. *Zeitschrift für Assyriologie und verwandte Gebiete* 29: 239–246.

Omar, Feryad F. 1992. *Kurdisch-deutsches Wörterbuch (Kurmancî)*. Berlin: Institut für Iranistik der Freien Universität Berlin.

Oraham, Alexander J. 1943. *Dictionary of the Stabilized and Enriched Assyrian Language and English*. Chicago: Consolidated Press.

Payne Smith, Jessie. 1903. *A Compendious Syriac Dictionary*. Oxford: Clarendon Press.

Perkins, Justin. 1852. *Kṯāḇā Qaddīšā hānaw da-Ḏyattēqē ʿAttīqtā. Suryāʾīṯ wPuššāqā d-men ʿEḇrāʾīṯ* (The Holy Scriptures, i.e. of the Old Testament. Syriac and Translation from Hebrew). Urmi.

Ritter, Hellmut. 1971. *Ṭūrōyo: die Volkssprache der syrischen Christen des Ṭūr ʿAbdîn, A. Texte, Band III*. Beirut: In Kommission bei Franz Steiner Verlag, Wiesbaden.

———. 1979. *Ṭūrōyo: die Volkssprache der syrischen Christen des Ṭūr ʿAbdîn, B. Wörterbuch*. Beirut: Orient-Institut der Deutschen Morgenländischen Gesellschaft.

Sabar, Yona. 2002. *A Jewish Neo-Aramaic Dictionary: Dialects of Amidya, Dihok, Nerwa and Zakho, northwestern Iraq*. Wiesbaden: Harrassowitz.

Sargis (Лавров, Алексей Петрович), Arḵimandrit. 1909. *Lēqsiqon d-Lišānā Rusnāyā Pušqā l-Suryāyā* (Dictionary of Russian Language Translated into [Neo-]Syriac). Urmi: Maṭbaʿtā də-Šlixē Rusnāyē.

SL—Sokoloff, Michael. 2009. *A Syriac Lexicon: A Translation from the Latin, Correction, Expansion, and Update of C. Brockelmann's Lexicon Syriacum*. Winona Lake, Ind.: Eisenbrauns.

Tal, Abraham. 2000. *A Dictionary of Samaritan Aramaic*. Leiden: Brill.

Talshir, David. 1981. *The Nomenclature of the Fauna in the Samaritan Targum*. Jerusalem: Hebrew University (in Hebrew).

———. 2012. *Living Names: Fauna, Places and Humans*. Jerusalem: The Bialik Institute (in Hebrew).

Tezel, Aziz. 2003. *Comparative Etymological Studies in the Western Neo-Syriac (Ṭūrōyo) Lexicon*. Uppsala: Uppsala Universitet.

Thesaurus—Payne Smith, Robert et al. 1868–1901. *Thesaurus Syriacus*. 2 vols., Oxford: Clarendon Press.

Tsereteli, Konstantin. 1980. Хрестоматия современного Ассирийского яазыка со словарем. (A Reader of the Modern Assyrian Language with a Dictionary). 2nd ed., Tbilisi: Tbilisi University Press.

Veny, Joan and Pons i Griera Lídia. 2014. *Atles Lingüístic del Domini Català, VII, 14. Insectes i altres invertebrats. Ocells. Animal salvatges, 15. Oficis*. Barcelona: Institut d'Estudis Catalans.

A CORPUS-BASED SWADESH WORD LIST FOR LITERARY CHRISTIAN URMI (NEW ALPHABET TEXTS)

Alexey Lyavdansky[1]

1. Introduction

The aim of this paper is to compile a basic word list for the literary Neo-Aramaic dialect of the Christians of Urmi and establish their etymologies. This study is intended as a starting point for a comparison of the lexicon in all dialects of the North-Eastern Neo-Aramaic (NENA) subgroup. Literary Christian Urmi is chosen for this study because it is attested in a very large corpus of texts.

Research of Neo-Aramaic in recent decades has produced descriptions of many dialects, especially within the NENA dialect subgroup.[2] We are now, therefore, in a good position to attempt to understand the genealogical relationships between the dialects.

Hoberman (1988) has suggested a reconstruction of the proto-NENA pronominal system. One of the conclusions of Hoberman's study was that the dialects of Northern Iraqi Kurdistan share some morphological innovations, which may help to single them out as a cohesive subgroup. Fox (1994) attempts to explore relationships within NENA according to selected phonological, morphological and lexical features. The outcome of Fox's study was the identification of three major

1 HSE University, Moscow. The research has been supported by RFBR grant No. 17-04-00472.

2 For a bibliography of these dialect descriptions see: Napiorkowska (2015, 583–594). There are 137 NENA dialects listed in (https://nena.ames.cam.ac.uk/dialects/ Date of Access 28.01.2018).

 https://doi.org/10.11647/OBP.0209.14

clusters of isoglosses, which, however, need to be checked with a broader range of data.[3]

In this paper I shall present a Swadesh list of 110 basic words (following the version of Kassian et al. 2010) that are attested in a corpus of literary Christian Urmi.

The corpus used for this purpose consists of a collection of books and newspapers issued in the latinised alphabet in Soviet Russia and Georgia from 1929 to 1938. This corpus was chosen on the assumption that these textual data provide sufficient documentation needed to create a basic word list. There are certain drawbacks in using literary texts for this purpose, because the language of literature and journalism may not reflect the true usage of a natural spoken language. The lexical features of the literary register, however, usually do not affect the usage within the scope of word lists consisting of 100 or even 200 words. It is important to note, however, that data collected from fieldwork are usually restricted in volume. The currently largest collection of spoken narrative texts of a Neo-Aramaic dialect (Khan 2016) amounts to approximately 70,000 words.

2. The Corpus[4]

The books and newspapers in the Assyrian new alphabet (Novij Alfavit, henceforth NA) were published in Moscow and Tbilisi from 1929 to 1938. This project was an integral part of the latinisation campaign in the Soviet Union (Smith 1998, 121–42). After 1938 the publication of Assyrian books and the newspaper in NA ceased because most of the authors, editors and translators had been condemned to death by the Stalinist regime.

It is important to note that the books dated 1929–1931 were printed using the earlier variety of the Assyrian new alphabet, which is basically Cyrillic with the admixture of some Latin letters (*t, d, j, l*). A modified variety of the Assyrian NA was introduced in 1931 and was used later as a standard, with some further changes adopted in 1933. A table of correspondences

3 Fox (1994) uses data from a sample of only eleven NENA dialects.

4 For a detailed discussion of this corpus, see Lyavdansky, (forthcoming).

between the transcription notations used by various scholars and the graphemes of the Assyrian NA is given in the appendix to this paper.

The corpus includes 172 books and approximately 270 issues of the newspaper *Kokhva d Madinkha* with the texts in NA.[5] The genres of the books are the following: translations of Russian literary texts (the largest part of the corpus), original literary fiction in Assyrian Neo-Aramaic, school textbooks, popular scientific texts, Soviet propagandistic and atheistic literature. Currently the corpus of digitised texts amounts to approximately 630,000 words from the 46 books.[6] The word 'digitised' here means that the texts are available in the doc/txt formats and electronically searchable. Recently the morphologically tagged corpus of the texts in NA has been made available for queries at: http://neo-aramaic.web-corpora.net/index_en.html.

3. The Method of Presentation of the Results

Two kinds of queries were performed in order to determine the exponents of the meanings of the basic word list. First, the meanings of the word list were searched for in the Russian originals of the translated texts.[7] The corresponding exponent was checked in the Neo-Aramaic translation. Second, the word count of the exponents was performed on the basis of the textual database of approximately 630,000 words. In some cases I searched in the literature beyond the digitised corpus. I did this, for example, for anatomical terms such as FOOT. They were found in a school textbook on natural science. In the case of the words with high frequency, the word count was made on a sample textual file of 37,000 words.

Each entry in the following list of basic words consists of:

1. the meaning

---

5 Most of the texts in this newspaper are printed in Syriac script.

6 The expected volume of the textual corpus after its full digitisation is more than 2 million words.

7 More than 80 percent of the searchable textual corpus are translations from Russian into Neo-Aramaic.

2. the exponent
3. the etymological data on the exponent
4. textual examples
5. discussion

For the lexemes with clear Aramaic origin the comparative data are adduced in the following order: Classical Syriac, Jewish Babylonian Aramaic, Classical Mandaic. These three languages are subsumed under the term 'Middle Eastern Aramaic' (henceforth MEA).[8]

4. The 110 Swadesh List

The 110 Swadesh word list for the corpus of Neo-Aramaic texts in the New Alphabet is as follows.

(1) ALL

kul, kull-. > 50×.

MEA: *kul, kol* 'all' (SL 622); *kullā* (DJBA 559); *kul* (MD 206).

(2) ASH

qьṭma. 34×.

MEA: *qeṭmā* 'ash' (SL 1353); *qiṭmā* 'ash' (DJBA 1011); *giṭma, gaṭma* 'ash' (MD 89).

(3) BARK

qəlpə. 16×.

MEA: *qlāp̄tā* 'bark, shell' (SL 1375); *qlāp̄ṭā* 'peel, shell' (DJBA 1022); *qlapta* 'shell, hard casing' (MD 413).

8 The term is based on one of the classifications of Aramaic languages which divides the Aramaic languages of the Middle period into Western and Eastern branches (Rosenthal 1939).

çuluxtə. 4×.

< Kurd. *çûlik* 'peau, pelure, coquille, écorce' (DKF 318).

In most of its uses *qəlpə* refers to objects similar to the bark of the tree: eggshell, nutshell, watermelon rinds, or, metaphorically, the turtle shell. There is only one clear usage of *qəlpə* in a translated text: *Kirvijşi d meşə ʙ leləvəti ki axlьj* ***qəlpə*** *d ijləni* 'The hares feed at night on tree **bark**' (THH 21/1). The other one renders original Russian кора 'bark', but the text speaks metaphorically about the turtle shell (THH 10/4).

(4) BELLY

kisə. > 50×.

MEA: *karsā* 'belly, stomach' (SL 655); *karsā* 'stomach, rumen, womb' (DJBA 603); *karsa* 'belly, stomach; womb, uterus' (MD 201). For the loss of the consonant **r* in the same position, cf. *qənə* 'horn' < MEA *qarnā*.[9]

(5) BIG

gura. > 50×.

< ? Kurd. (K) *gir* 'gros, grand' (DKF 568); *gir, gur* 'large, big' (Chyet 213); Kurd. (S) *gewre* 'grand, gros' (DKF 557). The Kurdish etymology for C. Urmi *gura* is suggested in (Khan 2016, vol. 3, 169) with a question mark.

(6) BIRD

ţera. > 50×.

MEA: *ṭayrā* 'bird' (SL 528).

---

9 Cf. the attestations of this word in other NENA dialects: J. Challa *kāsa* (Fassberg 2010, 282), J. Lishana Deni *kāsa* (JNAD 180), J. Betanure *kāsa* (Mutzafi 2008, 356), C. Tiyari *časa* (Talay 2008, 100), C. Txuma *časa* (Talay 2008, 101), C. Qočanəṣ *kisa* (Talay 2008, 339).

(7) TO BITE

qraṭa. 10 ×.

MEA: *qrṭ* pe.'to gnaw, to wound with the beak' (SL 1405); *ṭrq* pe. 'to hit, sting, bite' (DJBA 519).

njasa. 4 ×.

The etymology is uncertain. Cf. *ngs* pe. 'to eat' (DJPA 340; Mutzafi 2004, 234).

(8) BLACK

kumə. > 50 ×.

MEA: *kōmā* 'black' (SL 608); *ʾukkāmā* 'black' (SL 15); *ʾukkām* 'black' (DJBA 88); *ʿukma* 'blackness' (MD 343).

(9) BLOOD

dimmə. > 50 ×.

MEA: *dmā* 'blood' (SL 307); *dmā* 'blood' (DJBA 340); *dma, adma* 'blood' (MD 111, 8).

(10) BONE

gərmə. > 50 ×.

MEA: *garmā* 'bone' (SL 261); *garmā* 'bone' (DJBA 302); *girma* (MD 92).

(11) BREAST (CHEST)

sadra. > 50 ×.

Pers. *ṣadr* 'breast' (CPED 783) < Arab. *ṣadr* 'Brust' (AWSG 701).

(12) TO BURN (intr.)

qjədə. > 50 ×.

MEA: *yqd* 'to burn' (intr.) (MD 193); *yqd* af 'to burn' (tr.) (SL 580); *yqd* af 'to set on fire' (DJBA 540).

(13) CLOUD

ajva. > 50×.

MEA: *ʿaybā* 'obnubilatio, nubes humidae' (TS 2824); *ʿēḇā* 'dark cloud, cloudiness' (DJBA 850); *aiba* 'cloud, fog, mist, darkness' (MD 14).

(14) COLD

qajra. > 50×.

MEA: *qrr* pe. 'to be cold, frosty' (SL 1417); *qrr* pe. 'to cool down' (DJBA 1047).

qarʙjra. 23×.

MEA: *qarrirā* 'cold' (SL 1409); *qarrīr* 'cold' (DJBA 1043); *qarir* (MD 403).

(15) TO COME

təjə. > 50×.

MEA: *ʾty* 'to come' (SL 110); *ʾty* 'to come' (DJBA 176); *ata* (MD 41).

(16) TO DIE

mjətə. > 50×.

MEA: *mwt* 'to die' (SL 731); *mwt* 'to die' (DJBA 650); *mut* 'to die' (MD 263).

(17) DOG

kəlʙə. > 50×.

MEA: *kalbā* 'dog' (SL 622); *kalbā* 'dog' (DJBA 580); *kalba* 'dog' (MD 197).

(18) TO DRINK

ştəjə. > 50×.

MEA: *šty* 'to drink' (SL 1614); *šty* 'to drink' (DJBA 1184); *šta* 'to drink' (MD 476).

(19) DRY

ʙəruzə. > 50 ×.

The etymology is uncertain. Cf. Arab. *barāz-* 'champ, vaste plaine sans arbres' (BK 110; Mutzafi 2008, 340).

(20) EAR

nətə. > 50 ×.

Syr. *ʾeḏnāṯā*, pl. of *ʾeḏnā* 'ear' (SL 10); cf. 17 cent. Telkepe *nhāṯa* < Syr. *ʾeḏnāhāṯā* (Mutzafi 2005, 84, n. 5; Mutzafi 2008, 366).

(21) EARTH

uprə. > 50 ×.

MEA: *ʿap̄rā* 'dust; earth, soil' (SL 1124); *ʿap̄rā* 'earth, dust, powder' (DJBA 875); *apra* 'dust, ashes' (MD 32).

(22) TO EAT

xala. > 50 ×.

MEA: *ʾkl* 'to eat' (SL 41), *ʾkl* 'to eat' (DJBA 129); *akl* 'to eat' (MD 16).

(23) EGG

ʙitə. 24 ×.

MEA: *bēʿṯā* 'egg' (SL 143); *bayʿṯā*, *bēṯā* 'egg' (DJBA 204); *bita* 'egg' (MD 64).

(24) EYE

ajna. > 50 ×.

MEA: *ʿaynā* 'eye' (SL 1097); *ʿēnā* 'eye, sight' (DJBA 855); *ayna* 'eye' (MD 15).

(25) FAR

rixqə. > 50 ×.

< MEA: *rḥq* 'to go away' (SL 1458); *rḥq* 'to be far away' (DJBA 1071); *rhq* 'to be far' (MD 427).

(26) FAT

tərʙə. 8×.

< MEA: *tarbā* 'fat' (SL 1663f.); *tarbā* 'fat' (DJBA 1230); *tirba* 'fat of animals' (MD 486).

(27) FEATHER

pərrə. 14×.

< Pers. *par, parr* 'a wing, a feather' (CPED 239); Kurd. *p'eř* 'feather, wing' (Chyet 439); Azer. *pər* 'Flügel' (ADW 512).

(28) FIRE

nurə. > 50×.

MEA: *nūrā* 'fire' (SL 904); *nūrā* 'fire' (DJBA 738); *nura* 'fire' (MD 294).

(29) FISH

nunə. > 50×.

MEA: *nūnā* 'fish' (SL 900); *nūnā* 'fish' (DJBA 737); *nuna* 'fish' (MD 294).

(30) TO FLY

prəxə. > 50×.

MEA: *prḥ* pe. 'to fly' (SL 1235); *prḥ* pe. 'to fly' (DJBA 930); *phr* pe. 'to fly', *pra* pe. 'to fly' (MD 366, 377).

(31) FOOT

pənçə. 3×.

< Pers. *panj* 'five' (CPED 256). For this etymology, see Khan (2016, vol. 3, 249). *əqlə itlə ьţma, şəqə u pənçə.* 'The leg consists of the thigh, the shin and the foot' (TEK II 74/23).

(32) FULL

miljə. > 50×.

MEA: *mly* 'to fill up' (SL 768); *mly* 'to be full' (DJBA 678); *mla* 'to fill, be full' (MD 272).

(33) TO GIVE

jəvə. > 50 ×.

MEA: *yhb* 'to give' (SL 565); *yhb 'to give'* (DJBA 526); *yhb* 'to give' (MD 189).

(34) TO GO

zələ. > 50 ×.

MEA: *ʾzl* 'to go' (SL 24); *ʾzl* 'to go, travel' (DJBA 100); *azl* 'to go, move on' (MD 12).

(35) GOOD

spaj. > 50 ×.

< Kurd. *spehî* 'beau, belle, joli' (DKF 1539).

(36) GREEN

qijnə. > 50 ×.

The etymology is unclear.

mijlənə. 10 ×.

< Pers. *mīnā* 'a blue, blueish green, green colour' (CPED 1364; Khan 2016, vol. 3, 220).

(37) HAIR

kosə. 37 ×.

< Syriac *sawkā* 'branch, twig' (SL 978f.).[10]

mьsta. 27 ×.

MEA: *mezṯā* 'hair' (SL 736); *mazzyā* '(coll.) hair' (DJBA 652); *manza* 'hair' (MD 248). In some cases *mьsta* is used as nomen unitatis for 'hair'.

(38) HAND

ijdə. > 50 ×.

MEA: *īḏā* 'hand' (SL 31); *yḏā* 'hand, possession' (DJBA 523); *ʿda* 'hand' (MD 341).

10 See Mutzafi (2006, 89–9).

(39) HEAD

rişə. > 50 ×.

MEA: *rēšā* 'head' (SL 1462); *rēšā* 'head, top part' (DJBA 1078); *riša* 'head, top' (MD 434).

(40) TO HEAR

şmaja. > 50 ×.

MEA: *šmʿ* 'to hear, listen to' (SL 1574); *šmʿ* 'to hear' (DJBA 1158); *šma* 'to hear, listen' (MD 469).

(41) HEART

liʙʙə. > 50 ×.

MEA: *lebbā* 'heart' (SL 666); *libbā* 'heart' (DJBA 623); *liba* 'heart' (MD 234).

(42) HEAVY

jaqura. > 50 ×.

MEA: *yqr* 'to be heavy' (SL 582); *yqr* 'to increase in value' (DJBA 540); MD *yqr* 'to honor, respect'.

(43) HORN

qənə. 41 ×.[11]

MEA: *qarnā* 'horn' (SL 1412); *qarnā* 'horn' (DJBA 1044); *qarna* 'horn' (MD 403).

(44) I

ənə. > 50 ×.

MEA: *enā* 'I' (SL 58); *ănā* 'I' (DJBA 143); *ana* 'I' (MD 24).

(45) TO KILL

qţala. > 50 ×.

MEA: *qṭl* 'to kill' (SL 1352); *qṭl* 'to kill' (DJBA 1006); *gṭl* 'to kill' (MD 87).

11 Two attestations were found beyond the digitised corpus: MPX 13/6, VEG 44/17.

(46) KNEE

вirkə. > 50 × .

MEA: *burkā* ‘knee’ (SL 131); *birkā* ‘knee’ (DJBA 206); *burka* ‘knee’ (MD 57).

(47) TO KNOW

daja. > 50 × .

MEA: *ydʿ* ‘to know’ (SL 563); *ydʿ* ‘to know’ (DJBA 525); *yda* ‘to know’ (MD 188).

(48) LEAF

ţarpa. 22 × .

MEA: *ṭarpā* ‘leaf’ (SL 555); *ătarpā* ‘leaf’ (DJBA 108); *aṭirpa* ‘leaf’ (MD 13).

(49) TO LIE (a stative situation)

dməxə. > 50 × .

MEA: *dmk* ‘to sleep’ (SL 310); *dmk* ‘to lie’ (DJBA 343).

(50) LIVER

çigar. 2 × .[12]

< Azer. *ciyər*, *qara ciyər* ‘Leber’ (ADW 184).

(51) LONG

jarъjxa. 51 × .

MEA: *arrīḵ* ‘long’ (SL 99); *arīḵ* ‘tall, long’ (DJBA 167); *arika* ‘long’ (MD 37).

(52) LOUSE

qəlmə. 6 × .

MEA: *qalmā* ‘louse’ (SL 1372); *qalmṯā* ‘vermin’ (DJBA 1021).

---

12 The only attestation is MXM 63/25, which is currently outside the digitised corpus.

(53) MAN (MALE)

urzə. > 50 ×.

The etymology is uncertain. For the suggestion to derive it from Sanskrit *vr̥ṣán* 'big, strong, male, ox', see Nöldeke (1868, 385).[13]

gorə. It is not yet clear, perhaps *gorə* should be included as a synonym, but it refers to 'husband' in most cases.

(54) MAN (HUMAN BEING)

nəşə. > 50 ×.

MEA: *nāšā* 'man, human beings' (SL 65); *ināšā* 'man' (DJBA 120); *(a)naša* 'human being' (MD 24).

ʙarnəşə. > 50 ×.

The ratio of the usage of *nəşə* to *ʙarnəşə* is 10:1. Therefore, *nəşə* is the main exponent of the meaning in question.

(55) MANY

raʙa. > 50 ×.

MEA: *rābā* 'great, large' (SL 1425).

(56) MEAT

ʙьsra. > 50 ×.

MEA: *besrā* 'flesh, meat' (SL 167); *bisrā* 'flesh, meat' (DJBA 207); *bisra* 'flesh, meat' (MD 62).

(57) MOON

sara. > 50 ×.

MEA: *sahrā* 'moon' (SL 974); *sehrā* 'moon' (DJBA 800); *sira* 'moon' (MD 329).

13 The etymological note of Yona Sabar on this word (K < Sanskrit *vrśa*) may be interpreted that the author in fact proposes a Kurdish etymon derived from O.Ind. *vr̥ṣán* (JNAD 91).

(58) MOUNTAIN

ţura. > 50×.

MEA: *ṭūrā* 'mountain' (SL 521); *ṭūrā* 'mountain' (DJBA 498); *ṭura* 'mountain, hill' (MD 178).

(59) MOUTH

pummə. > 50×.

MEA: *pūmā* 'mouth' (SL 1165); *pūmā* 'mouth' (DJBA 889); *puma* 'mouth' (MD 368).

(60) NAIL

ţupurta. 14×.

MEA: *ṭep̄rā* 'nail, claw, talon' (SL 548); *ṭup̄rā* 'fingernail, toenail' (DJBA 498); *ṭupra* 'claw, nail' (MD 178).

(61) NAME

şimmə. > 50×.

MEA: *šmā* 'name' (SL 1569); *šmā* 'name' (DJBA 1153); *šuma* 'name, reputation' (MD 454).

(62) NEAR

qurʙə. 10×.

MEA: *qrb* 'to approach to, be near' (SL 1400); *qrb* 'to come near, bring near' (DJBA 1037); *qrb* 'to approach, draw near' (MD 415).

(63) NECK

qdələ. > 50×.

MEA: *qḏālā* 'neck' (SL 1317); *qḏālā* 'neck' (DJBA 984).

(64) NEW

xətə. > 50×.

MEA: *ḥaṯā* 'new' (SL 418); *ḥăḏaṯ* 'new' (DJBA 433); *hadta* 'new' (MD 116).

(65) NIGHT

leli. > 50 × .

MEA: *lelyā* 'night' (SL 691); *lelyā* 'night' (DJBA 626); *lilia* 'night' (MD 236).

(66) NOSE

nəxijrə. 34 × .

MEA: *nḥīrā* 'nasus' (TS 2340); *nḥīrā* 'nostril' (DJBA 741); *nhira* 'nose' (MD 291).

(67) NOT

lə, le. > 50 × .

MEA: *lā* 'no' (SL 665); *lā* 'no' (DJBA 613); *lā* 'no, not' (MD 227).

(68) ONE

xə. > 50 × .

MEA: *ḥaḏ* 'one' (SL 413); *ḥaḏ* 'one' (DJBA 430); *had* 'one, single' (MD 116).

(69) RAIN

mьţra. > 50 × .

MEA: *meṭrā* 'rain' (SL 749); *miṭrā* 'rain' (DJBA 665); *miṭra* 'rain' (MD 266).

(70) RED

smuqə. > 50 × .

MEA: *summāqā* 'red' (SL 981); *summāq* 'red object, redness' (DJBA 794); *s(u)maq(a)* 'red, ruddy' (MD 322).

(71) ROAD

urxə. > 50 × .

MEA: *ʾurḥā* 'road' (SL 21).

(72) ROOT

ьqra. 17×.

MEA: *ʿeqqārā* 'root' (SL 1132).

(73) ROUND

glulə. 32×.

MEA: *glālā* 'round' (SL 238);[14] *glālā* 'stone-shaped object' (DJBA 288); *glala* 1 'stone, rock, hailstone', *glala* 2 'something round, ball' (MD 91).

(74) SALT

milxə. 40×.

MEA: *melḥā* 'salt' (SL 767); *milḥā* 'salt' (DJBA 667); *mihla* 'salt' (MD 266).

(75) SAND

silə. 44×.

< Kurd. *seylak* 'sable' DKF 1495; *sêl* DKF 1498; *sêlak* DKF 1498; *sêlax* DKF 1498; *sêleh* DKF 1498; *sêlix* DKF 1498; *sîlewan* DKF 1524; *sîlik* DKF 1524. The mixed source background of DKF (Sorani-Kurmanji) suggests that the words in question are mostly used by Sorani speakers. The corresponding Kurmanji terms with the basic meaning 'sand' would be *xîz* (Chyet 665) and *qûm* (Chyet 498). Therefore, C. Urmi *silə* must have been borrowed from Sorani Kurdish.

(76) TO SAY

mərə. > 50×.

MEA: *ʾmr* 'to say' (SL 57); *ʾmr* 'to say, tell' (DJBA 140); *amr* 'to say, speak' (MD 23).

14 Syriac *glultā* pl. *glulē* 'pair of compasses; globe, ball' is attested only in the lexicon of Bar Bahlul. It may be a borrowing from Modern Aramaic.

(77) TO SEE

xzəjə. > 50×.

MEA: *ḥzy* 'to see' (SL 438); *ḥzy* 'to see, look at' (DJBA 444); *hza* 'to see, look' (MD 138).

(78) SEED

ɞarzarra. 8×.

MEA: *bar zarʿā* 'seed' (SL 180); *bazrā, bizrā* 'seed' (DJBA 195); *bazira, bazra* 'seed' (MD 46).

(79) SHORT

kirjə. > 50×.

MEA: *karyā* 'short' (SL 651).

(80) TO SIT

tjəvə. > 50×.

MEA: *ytb* 'to sit' (SL 587); *ytb* 'to sit' (DJBA 545); *ytb* 'to sit, stay' (MD 193).

(81) SKIN

gildə. > 50×.

MEA: *geldā* 'skin, leather' (SL 233); *gildā* 'scab, hide' (DJBA 280); *gilda* 'leather' (MD 90).

(82) TO SLEEP

dməxə. > 50×.

MEA: *dmk* 'to sleep' (SL 310); *dmk* 'to lie' (DJBA 343).

ṭləjə >50×.

MEA: *ṭlʿ* etpa. 'to suffer from sleepiness' (SL 534); *ṭulāʿā* 'deep sleep, torpor' (SL 517); *mṭalaʿ* 'heavy (sleep)' (SL 747), *mṭalʿānā* 'soporific' (SL 747).

The character of the Classical Syriac sources that use derivatives of *ṭlʿ* with the meanings relating 'to sleep' (Bar Bahlul dictionary, *The Book of Medicines*) point to a probable Neo-Aramaic background of these terms in these dictionaries of CS.

The verb *ţlaja* has the meaning 'to fall asleep' in most of its uses. Nevertheless, the verb *ţlaja* clearly has the meaning 'to sleep' in a number of instances: *Lə gəşəqtə l dəhə, в leləvəti Fritjof qujə вьţlajьva* 'Despite that, at night Fritjof was sound asleep' (FNA 27/2); *Bopre go otax al qaravat ţьljьva b şintə dlə gnəhə.* '[At this moment] Bopre was innocently sleeping in the room on the bed' (PBQ 7/22).

(83) SMALL

surə. > 50×.

MEA: *zāʿorā* 'small' (SL 390); *zʿer* 'small, young' (DJBA 418).

(84) SMOKE

tinnə. > 50×.

MEA: *tennānā* 'smoke' (SL 1656); *tnnʾ* 'smoke' (DJBA 1223).

(85) SNAKE

xuvvi. 24×.

MEA: *ḥewyā* 'snake' (SL 424); *ḥiwyā* 'snake' (DJBA 450); *hiuia* 'serpent, snake' (MD 142).

(86) TO STAND

kləjə. > 50×.

MEA: *kly* 'to impede, prevent' (SL 624); *kly* 'to be finished' (DJBA 582); *kla* 'to keep enclosed, hold back' (MD 216).

(87) STAR

koxvə. > 50×.

MEA: *kawkḇā* 'star' (SL 606); *koḵḇā* 'star' (DJBA 558); *kukba* 'star' (MD 206).

(88) STONE

kipə. > 50 × .

MEA: *kēp̄ā* 'stone' (SL 594); *kēp̄ā* 'stone' (DJBA 577).

(89) SUN

şimşə. > 50 × .

MEA: *šemšā* 'sun' (SL 1576); *šimšā* 'sun, sunlight' (DJBA 1136); *šamšā* 'sun' (MD 443).

(90) TO SWIM

mxəjə sьxvь/sьxva. 29 × .

sьxvь < MEA: *sḥy* 'to wash o.s., bathe' (SL 992); *sḥy* 'to wash oneself, bathe' (DJBA 797); *saa* 'to wash, perform ablutions' (MD 308). The periphrastic verb is modelled after Kurmanji *ajnê kirin* (Chyet 3) or Sorani *mele kirin* (DKF 972).

(91) TAIL

ţuprə. 27 × .

There is no clear etymology. Possibly related to MEA: *ṭep̄rā/ṭup̄rā* 'nail, claw'.[15]

(92) THAT (ms.)

av. > 50 × .

MEA: *haw* 'that one' (SL 333).

(93) THIN

nəqijdə. 20 × .

Cf. MEA *nqd*: *naqḏā* 'clean; (gramm.) tenuis' (SL), *naqdonā* 'delicate' (SL 945); *nquḏtā* 'dot' (DJBA 772).

15 For references, see no. 60.

(94) THIS (ms.)

əhə. > 50×.

For the etymology of this see Khan (2016, vol. 1, 239) and also Militarev (2014, 172).

(95) TONGUE

lişənə. > 50×.

MEA: *leššānā* 'tongue' (SL 698); *liššānā* 'tongue' (DJBA 627); *lišana* 'tongue' (MD 237).

(96) TOOTH

kikə. > 50×.

MEA: *kakkā* 'molar tooth' (SL 621). On this word, see Mutzafi (2014, 113).

(97) TREE

ijlənə. > 50×.

MEA: *ʾīlānā* 'tree' (SL 35).

(98) TWO

tre. > 50×.

MEA: *trēn* 'two' (SL 1666); *trē(n)* 'two' (DJBA 1233); *trin* 'two' (MD 490)

(99) WARM

şəxijnə. > 50×.

MEA: *šḥn* 'to be inflamed', pa. 'to warm, heat' (SL 1544); *šḥn* 'be inflamed, heat' (DJBA 1128); *šḥn* 'to become hot' (MD 451).

(100) WATER

mijə. > 50×.

MEA: *mayyā* 'water' (SL 750); *mayyā* 'water' (DJBA 662); *mai* 'water' (MD 242).

(101) WE

əxnən. > 50×.

MEA: *ḥnan, ʾnḥnn* 'we' (SL 472, 60); *ănan* 'we' (DJBA 145); *anin, anʿn* 'we' (MD 27).

(102) WHAT?

mudij, mu. > 50×.

MEA: *mā* 'what?' (SL 700), *dēn* 'then' (SL 296), see Nöldeke (1868, 82).

(103) WHITE

xvara. > 50×.

MEA: *ḥewwārā* 'white' (SL 432); *ḥiwwār* 'white' (DJBA 450); *hiuara* 'white' (MD 142).

(104) WIND

poxə. > 50×.

MEA: *pwḥ* pe. 'to blow, to breathe' (SL 1160), *pāwḥā* 'odour, smell' (SL 1161); *pwḥ* pe. 'to breathe, blow up' (DJBA 888).

(105) WHO?

mən, mənij. > 50×.

MEA: *man* 'who?' (SL 778); *man* 'who' (DJBA 636); *man* 'who' (MD 246).

(106) WOMAN

ʙəxtə. > 50×.

There is no clear etymology. For the discussion of the possible origin of this word see Khan (1999, 146–147).

(107) WORM

tьvьlta. 5×.[16]

MEA: *tawlʿā* 'worm' (SL 1630); *tōlaʿtā* 'worm' (DJBA 1197); *tulita* 'worm, embryo' (MD 483).

(108) YEAR

şitə. > 50×.

MEA: *šattā* 'year' (SL 1581); *šattā* 'year' (DJBA 1183); *šita* 'year' (MD 464).

(109) YELLOW

zərdə. > 50×.

< Pers. *zard* 'yellow' (CPED 614)

(110) YOU (s.)

ət. > 50×.

MEA: *at* 'you (s.)' (SL 66); *ant* 'you (ms.) (DJBA 146); *anat* 'thou' (MD 24).

5. Conclusions

The digitised corpus for literary Christian Urmi of approximately 630,000 words has been shown to be sufficient to establish the basic 110 word list with 117 exponents. More than 70 percent of the entries (87/117) have more than 50 attestations in the corpus.

There are seven meanings that have two exponents: BARK (*qəlpə, çuluxtə*), TO BITE (*qraţa, njasa*), COLD (*qajra, qarьjra*), GREEN (*qijnə, mijlənə*), HAIR (*kosə, mьsta*), MAN (*nəşə, ɞarnəşə*); TO SLEEP (*dməxə*, ţlaja). In the cases of COLD and GREEN the problem may be solved by statistical data: the exponents *qajra* for

16 One of the attestations of this word was found in the text MPX 90/28, which is not yet digitised.

COLD and *qijnə* for GREEN have considerably more attestations in the corpus than the alternative exponents *qarьjra* and *mijlənə*. On the other hand, bare statistical data do not help in the case of BARK (see the discussion of no. 3).

More than 90 percent of the meanings (94/110) have exponents with reliable Middle Eastern Aramaic etymologies. Four meanings have exponents that originate from Persian (*sadra* 'breast' < Pers. *ṣadr*; *pərrə* 'feather' < Pers. *par*; *pənçə* 'foot' < Pers. *panc*; *zərdə* 'yellow' < Pers. *zard*). The exponents of two meanings have Kurdish etymologies (*spaj* 'good' < Kurd. *spehî*; *silə* 'sand' < Kurd. *sêl*). One meaning is expressed by a word originating from Azeri Turkish (*çigar* 'liver' < Azer. *ciyər*). Three meanings have each two exponents with different etymologies: BARK (*qəlpə* MEA; *çuluxtə* < Kurd. *çûlik*), BITE (*qraţa* MEA, *njasa*—of uncertain etymology), GREEN (*qijnə*—of uncertain etymology; *mijlənə* < Pers. *mīnā*). A special case is the meaning TO SWIM, which is expressed by a compound verb *mxəjə sьxvь/sьxva*. Both members of this construction have Aramaic origin, but this verb is a loan translation from Kurdish (no. 90). Six meanings have exponents with uncertain or unknown etymologies (5. BIG *gurə*; 22. DRY *вəruzə*; 53. MAN (MALE) *urzə*; 91. TAIL *ţuprə*; 94. THIS *əhə*; 196 WOMAN *вəxtə*).

General Abbreviations

af.	*afʿel*
C.	Christian
J.	Jewish
K	Kurmanji Kurdish
MEA	Middle Eastern Aramaic
NA	New Alphabet
NENA	North-Eastern Neo-Aramaic
pa.	*paʿʿel*
pe.	*peʿal*
S	Sorani Kurdish

Bibliographical Abbreviations

ADW Rahmati, Nemat. 1999. *Aserbaidschanisch-deutsches Wörterbuch: unter Berücksichtigung der Besonderheiten des Nord- und Südaserbaidschanischen*. Engelschoff: Verlag auf dem Ruffel.

AWSG Wehr, Hans. 1985. *Arabisches Wörterbuch für die Schriftsprache der Gegenwart*. Wiesbaden: Harrassowitz.

BK de Biberstein-Kazimirski, Albert. 1860. *Dictionnaire arabe–français*. Paris: Maison-neuve et cie.

Chyet Chyet, Michael L. 2003. *Kurdish-English Dictionary*. New Haven–London: Yale University Press.

CPED Steingass, Francis J. 1892. *A Comprehensive Persian English Dictionary*. London: Routledge & Kegan Paul Limited.

DJBA Sokoloff, Michael. 2002. *A Dictionary of Jewish Babylonian Aramaic of the Talmudic and Geonic Periods*. Ramat-Gan, Israel: Bar Ilan University Press.

DJPA Sokoloff, Michael. 1992. *A Dictionary of Jewish Palestinian Aramaic of the Byzantine Period*. Ramat-Gan, Israel: Bar Ilan University Press.

DKF Bedir Khan, Kamuran A., Joséfa Bertolino and Kendal Nezan. 2017. *Dictionnaire Kurde-Français*. Paris: Riveneuve.

JNAD Sabar. Yona. 2002. *A Jewish Neo-Aramaic Dictionary. Dialects of Amidya, Dihok, Nerwa and Zakho, Northwestern Iraq*. Wiesbaden: Harrassowitz.

MD Drower, Ethel S. and Rudolph Macuch. 1962. *A Mandaic Dictionary*. Oxford: Clarendon.

MXM Marogulov, Qonstantin. 1935. *Xrestomatija d saprajuta*. Moskva: Ucpedgiz.

MPX Marogulov, Qonstantin. u Petrosov, Dəvid. 1935. *Xrestomatija d saprajuta. Qə mədrəsə d şuraja*. Səmə I. Moskva: Ucpedgiz.

SL Sokoloff, Michael. 2009. *A Syriac Lexicon*. Winona Lake & Piscataway: Gorgias Press.

TEK II Tetjurev, Vladimir. 1937. *Elm kjənetə. Səmə II. Qə klas rvƅeta d mədrəsə d şuraja*. Puşəqə d U. A. Bedrojev. Moskva: Detizdat.

THH Tolstoj, Lev N. 1935. *Həqətti but hejvanƅ*. Puşəqə d A. Minasov. Moskva: OGIZ-Detgiz.

TS Payne Smith, Roberth. 1879–1901. *Thesaurus Syriacus,* T. 1–2. Oxford: Clarendon.

VEG Vegin, Sergej. 1933. *Go səmi ƅllajƅ d'Diqlət. Puşəqə d'Bedrojev.* Moskva: GIXL.

References

Fischer, Wolfdietrich. 2002. *A Grammar of Classical Arabic*, 3rd edition, New Haven and London: Yale University Press.

Fassberg, Steven. 2010. *The Jewish Neo-Aramaic Dialect of Challa*. Studies in Semitic Languages and Linguistics 54. Leiden: Brill.

Fox, Samuel. 1994. 'The Relationship of the Eastern Neo-Aramaic Dialects'. *Journal of the American Oriental Society* 114: 154–162.

———. 1997. *The Neo-Aramaic Dialect of Jilu.* Semitica Viva 16. Wiesbaden: Harrassowitz.

Hoberman, Robert D. 1988. 'The history of the Modern Aramaic pronouns and pronominal suffixes'. *Journal of the American Oriental Society* 108.4: 557–75.

Jastrow, Otto. 1990. 'Personal and Demonstrative Pronouns in Central Neo-Aramaic'. In *Studies in Neo-Aramaic*, edited by Wolfhart Heinrichs, 89–103. Atlanta, GA: Scholars Press.

Kassian, Alexei, George Starostin, Anna Dybo, and Vasiliy Chernov. 2010. 'The Swadesh Word List. An Attempt at Semantic Specification'. *Journal of Language Relationship* 4: 46–89.

Khan, Geoffrey. 1999. *A Grammar of Neo-Aramaic: The Dialect of the Jews of Arbel.* Boston, MA: Brill.

———. 2008. *The Neo-Aramaic Dialect of Barwar.* 3 vols. Leiden–Boston: Brill.

———. 2016. *The Neo-Aramaic Dialect of the Assyrian Christians of Urmi.* 4 vols. Studies in Semitic Languages and Linguistics 86. Leiden–Boston: Brill.

Lyavdansky, Alexey. Forthcoming. 'Neo-Aramaic Texts in the New Alphabet Published in the Soviet Union 1929–1938'. In *A Handbook of Neo-Aramaic*, edited by Steven E. Fassberg, Simon Hopkins and Hezy Mutzafi.

Marogulov, Qonstantin I. 1976. *Grammaire néo-syriaque pour écoles d'adultes (dialecte d'Urmia)*. Translated by Olga Kapeliuk. Comptes rendus du Groupe Linguistique d'Études Chamito-Sémitiques, 5. Paris: Librairie Orientaliste P. Geuthner.

Militarev, Alexander. 2014. 'A Complete Etymology-based Hundred Word List of Semitic Updated: Items 75–100'. *Journal of Language Relationship* 11: 159–185.

Mutzafi, Hezy. 2004. *The Jewish Neo-Aramaic Dialect of Koy Sanjaq (Iraqi Kurdistan)*. Semitica Viva 32. Wiesbaden: Harrassowitz.

———. 2005. 'Etymological Notes on North-Eastern Neo-Aramaic'. *Aramaic Studies* 3 (1): 83–107.

———. 2006. 'On the Etymology of Some Enigmatic Words in North-Eastern Neo-Aramaic'. *Aramaic Studies* 4 (1): 83–99.

———. 2008. *The Jewish Neo-Aramaic Dialect of Betanure (Province of Dihok)*. Semitica Viva 43. Wiesbaden: Harrassowitz.

———. 2014. *Comparative Lexical Studies in Neo-Mandaic*. Studies in Semitic Languages and Linguistics 73. Leiden: Brill.

Napiorkowska, Lidia. 2015. *A Grammar of the Christian Neo-Aramaic Dialect of Diyana-Zariwaw*. Studies in Semitic Languages and Linguistics 81. Leiden: Brill.

Nöldeke, Theodor. 1868. *Grammatik des Neusyrischen Sprache am Urmia-See und in Kurdistan.* Leipzig: T. O. Weigel.

Rosenthal, Franz. 1939. *Die Aramaistische Forschung seit Th. Nöldeke's Veröffentlichungen*. Leiden: Brill. 1939.

Smith, Michael G. 1998. *Language and Power in the Creation of the USSR, 1917–1953*. Berlin–New York: Mouton de Gruyter.

Talay. Shabo. 2008. *Die Neuaramäischen Dialekte der Khabur-Assyrer in Nordostsyrien: Einführung, Phonologie und Morphologie.* Semitica Viva 40. Wiesbaden: Harrassowitz.

Appendix: Correspondences of Transcriptions

New Alphabet	Kapeliuk[17]	Khan (2008)[18]	Khan (2016)
a	*a*	*a*	*a*
в, b	*b*	*b*	*b*
c	*č*	*č*	*č, č̭*
ç	*ǧ*	*j*	*j*
d	*d*	*d*	*d*
e	*e*	*e*	*e*
ə	*ä*	*a*	*a*
f	*f*	*f*	*f*
g	*g*	*g*	*ɟ*
h	*h*	*h*	*h*
i	*i*	*i*	*i*
j	*y*	*y*	*y*
ь	*ə*	*ə*	*ị, ə*
k	*k*	*k*	*c, c̭*
l	*l*	*l*	*l*
m	*m*	*m*	*m*

17 Marogulov (1976).

18 The transcription in Khan (2008 and 2016) is representative of the transcriptions used in the descriptions of Neo-Aramaic dialects.

New Alphabet	**Kapeliuk**[17]	**Khan** (2008)[18]	**Khan** (2016)
n	*n*	*n*	*n*
o	*o*	*o*	*o*
p	*p*	*p*	*p*
q	*q*	*q*	*k̭*
r	*r*	*r*	*r*
s	*s*	*s*	*s*
ş	*š*	*š*	*š*
t	*t*	*t*	*t*
ţ	*ṭ*	*ṭ*	*ṱ*
u	*u*	*u*	*u*
v	*v*	*v*	*v*
x	*kh*	*x*	*x*
z	*z*	*z*	*z*
ƶ	*ž*	*ž*	*ž*

LEXICAL ITEMS RELATING TO MATERIAL CULTURE IN THE NENA DIALECTS OF THE AQRA REGION

Aziz Emmanuel Eliya Al-Zebari

(in collaboration with Anjuman M. Sabir)

This article is based on my research on the Neo-Aramaic dialects of the Aqra (Akre) region, which are spoken across the Aqra mountain in Iraqi Kurdistan. Some details about these dialects have been discussed in previous publications, notably by Coghill (2008, 102–104). No systematic documentation of these dialects has, however, so far been published.

The Neo-Aramaic dialects of Aqra belong to the North-Eastern Neo-Aramaic (NENA) subgroup, which is the largest and most diverse branch of Neo-Aramaic.

The informants for this project come from various areas of the Aqra region, where different dialects were spoken. These dialects can be classified broadly into those of the villages lying to the North of the Aqra mountain and those of the inhabitants of the region to the South of the mountain. Those lying to the North are situated in an area known as Nexla (henceforth Nx.) and include the villages of Dinarta, Upper Girbish, and Sanaye. The inhabitants of these are descendants of families from the villages of Geppa, Arena and Qalunta (known in Kurdish as Shkafte, Harene, and Kalate respectively), which were abandoned in the 1880s. The dialect area lying to the South of the Aqra mountain (referred to by the abbreviation Sam.) includes the town of Aqra and the villages of Kherpa, Kharjawa, Nuhawa, Barrake, Sharmen and Malaberwan. The most conspicuous differences between these two dialect areas are (i) the reflexes of the historical interdentals **θ* and **ð* and (ii) the pronunciation of long */u/*.

 https://doi.org/10.11647/OBP.0209.15

In the Nexla area in the North the historical unvoiced *θ is debuccalised to /*h*/, e.g. Dinarta *beha* (< **bayθa*) 'house', as in some NENA dialects of the Baz region (Mutzafi 2000). In the southern area, on the other hand, it is realised as a sibilant /*s*/, e.g. Kherpa *besa* 'house'. The reflex of the historical voiced interndental *ð is the voiced sibilant /*z*/ in both areas, e.g. Dinarta *ʾiza* (< *ʾiða*) 'hand'. The dialect spoken in the town of Aqra is an exception to this generalisation, since the reflex of historical *θ is /θ/ or /*s*/, e.g. *beθa* ~ *besa* 'house', and the reflex of historical *ð is the stop /*d*/, e.g. *ʾida* 'hand'. This is summarised in Table 1 below:

Table 1: Reflexes of Interdentals

Location	*θ	*ð
Nexla area		
Dinarta	/h/	/z/
Girbish	/h/	/z/
Sanaye	/h/	/z/
South of the Aqra mountain		
Aqra town	/θ/ ~ /s/	/d/
Kherpa	/s/	/z/
Kharjawa	/s/	/z/
Nuhawa	/s/	/z/
Barrake	/s/	/z/
Sharmen	/s/	/z/
Malaberwan	/s/	/z/

The other conspicuous feature that distinguishes the two dialect areas is the pronunciation of the long /*u*/ as a fronted rounded vowel (represented here as /*ü*/) in the northern Nx. area and as a back /*u*/ in the southern area,[1] e.g. *güza* (Nx.), *guza* (Sam.) 'skin churn' (< **guđa*).

In this paper I shall present a collection of lexical items relating to material culture that are used in the dialects of the area. The classification of the semantics fields is based on Khan's lexical lists in his grammar of the Barwar dialect (2008, vol. 2).

Lexical items are cited in the variant forms that occur in the two dialect areas, reflecting the phonological differences that have just been described. The gender of the nouns is indicated and their plural form(s). The two plural inflections *-aha* and *-asa* represent the two regional variations in the realisation of historical **θ* (< **-aθa*) across the dialects of Nexla and south Aqra mountain (Sam.) respectively. The plural inflection *-aθa* is used by some speakers in the town of Aqra (At.). When the words are loans from other languages, this is indicated by the abbreviations Kurd. (Kurdish), Arab. (Arabic) and Turk. (Turkish) respectively. The transcription system follows the practice of Khan's (2008) grammar of the Barwar dialect. Short vowels in closed syllables and long vowels in open syllables are left without diacritical marks. A long vowel in a closed syllable is marked by a macron and a short vowel in an open syllable is marked by a breve. The character /ə/ in all syllables represents a short centralised vowel, which is realised as [ɪ] or [ə] according to the phonetic context.

1. Buildings and Structures

1.1. Houses and their Appurtenances

beha, besa m. (pl. *behane, besane, bāte*) house

darta f. (pl. *dartaha, dartasa*) courtyard, residential enclosure

ḥawš m. (pl. *ḥawšane*) (Kurd.) courtyard, residential enclosure

gare m. (pl. *garawaha, garawasa*) roof

---

1 For the fronting of /*u*/ in many languages of the region see Haig and Khan (2018, 13–14).

qaṛiyya f. (pl. *qaṛyaha, qaṛyasa*) beam

sapətka m. (pl. *sapətke*) small beam

stüna (Nx.), *stunta, stuna* (Sam.) f. (pl. *stunyaha, stunyasa*) wooden pole that supports the ceiling

sterka m. (pl. *sterke*) (Kurd.) scaffold on which food is kept

swane m. (pl. *swanane*) overhanging eaves of roof

mandarüne (Nx.), *mandarune* (Sam.) m. (pl. *mandarünyaha, mandarunyasa*) roller for flattening roof

güda (Nx.), *guda* (Sam.) m. (pl. *güdane, gudane*) wall

taqa m. (pl. *taqane*) (Kurd.) face of the wall

bərbawa m. (pl. *bərbawe*) a hole made on the roof for lowering straw into the straw store

btüne (Nx.), *btune* (Sam.) m. straw store

ṣalmət-güda (Nx.) *ṣalmət guda* (Sam.) m. front of wall facing outwards

quṛṣulta f. (pl.*quṛṣulyaha, quṛṣulyasa*) outer angle of house

ṭaṛa m. (pl. *ṭaṛane*) door

ṭareha, ṭaresa f. small door

dəsqət-ṭaṛa f. (pl. *dəsqe*) handle of a door

darga m. (pl. *darge*) (Kurd.) main door (with two leaves)

spuqta f. (pl. *spuqyaha, spuqyasa*) lintel

qulqulta m. (pl. *qulquyaha,qulqulyasa*) rods in wooden door lock

qzila, qdila (At.) f. (pl. *qzile, qdile*) key

qufla m. (pl. *qufle*) metal lock

kaylun m. (pl. *kaylone*) (Kurd.) metal lock of a door

panjara m. (pl. *panjare*) (Kurd.) window

čawiyya f. (pl. *čawyaha, čawyasa*) airhole of clay oven

kullina f. (pl. *kulline*) small opening at the top of a room without glass

ṛazunta (pl. *ṛazunyasa*) (Kherpa) small opening at the top of a room without glass

barbānka f. (pl. *barbānke*) (Kurd.) balcony, low structure attached to outside of house for people to sit on

parda m. (pl. *pardaha, pardasa, parde*) (Kurd.) curtain; cloth blind

qam-ṭaṛa f. (pl. *qam-ṭaṛane*) open space in front of house

tăbaqa m. (pl. *tăbaqe*) (Arab.) storey

ʾăra f. floor

ʾăsās m. (pl. *ʾăsāse*) (Arab.) foundation

benaġa m. (pl. *benaġe*) (Kurd.) foundation

ləbna m. (pl. *ləbne*) mud brick

sarʾuli f. (pl. *sarʾuliyye*) (Kurd.) upper floor

ʾoda f./m. (pl. *ʾodaha, ʾodasa*) (Kurd./Turk.) room

ʾodəd dmaxa f. (pl. *ʾodahəd dmaxa, ʾodasəd dmaxa*) sleeping room

ʾodət ʾitawa f. (pl. *ʾodahət ʾitawa, ʾodasət ʾitawa*) sitting room

ʾodət ʾarzāq f. (pl. *ʾodahət ʾarzāq, ʾodoasət ʾarzāq*) store room for cereals

ʾoda leha, ʾuda lesa f. (pl. *ʾudaha laye, ʾudasa laye)* upper room, room on first floor of a house

ʾoda xteha ʾuda xtesa f. (pl. *ʾudaha xtaye, ʾudasa xtaye*) lower room

manzal f. (pl. *manzale*) (Arab./Kurd.) room

manzalət ʾitawa f. sitting room

kočəka f. (pl. *kočəkyaha, kočəkyasa*) (Kurd.) guest room

jăṛade f. (pl. *jaradāyha, jaradyasa*) ladder

səllamta f. (pl *səllamyaha, səllamyasa*) wooden ladder

pepalānka f. (pl. *pepalānke*) (Kurd.) flight of steps, staircase

došəka, došəksa f. (pl. *došəkyaha, došəkyasa*) outer low structure attached to the entrance of a house used for sitting

ṣüpa (Nx.), *ṣupa* (Sam.) m. outer shed opening outwards

ṣupaniyya, ṣupanisa f. small outer shed opening outwards

ṣoba f. (pl. *ṣobaha, ṣobasa*) large stove with a chimney fuelled by wood

došăka (pl. *došăke, došakyaha, došakyasa*) (Kurd.) mattress

marša m. (pl. *marše*) thin mattress for sitting

maršəka, maršəksa f. (pl. *maršəkyaha, maršəkyasa*) small mattress for sitting

kursi m. (pl. *kursiyye*) (Arab.) chair

šwiyya, šwisa f. (pl. *šəwyaha, šəwyasa*) bed, bedding

spadiyya, stabiyya f. (pl. *spadyaha, spadyasa, stabyaha, stabyasa*) pillow, cushion

taxta f. (pl. *taxtaha, taxtasa*) wooden bed

kulla m. (pl. *kulle*) mosquito net

boriyya, borisa m. (pl. *boryaha, boryasa*) smoke duct of stove

quprana f. (pl. *qupranane*) summer bed on roof mounted on wood poles

qupraniyya, qupranisa f. (pl. *qupranyaha qupranyasa*) small wooden trellis *tanüra, tanura* m. (pl. *tanüre, tanure*) oven (for baking bread)

bnüre, bnu:re m. out-door horseshoe-like hearth built of stones and clay for cooking

bükare, bkare (Kherpa) m. (pl. *bükarane, bkarane*) animal shed usually annexed to the house

kolita f. (pl. *kolite*) hen-house

ʾoṛṛe f. (pl. *ʾoṛṛaha, ʾoṛṛasa*) a box or trough in a stable or barn from which horses or cattle eat

koska m. (pl. *koske*) a fenced area where sheep and cattle are kept in summer

dünga, dunga m. (pl. *dünge, dunge*) winter shelter for sheep and goats

koxa m. (pl. *koxe*) (Kurd.) hut

küra, kura m. (pl. *küre, kure*) furnace, kiln

gərba f. (pl. *gərbe*) beehive (cylindrical)

šana m. (pl. *šanaha, šanasa*) honeycomb

1.2. Church and its Appurtenances

ʾeta m. (pl. *ʾetaha, ʾetasa*) church

maðəbḥa m. (pl. *maðəbḥe*) altar

guṛna f. (pl. *gorne*) baptismal font

qəṭṛa m. (pl. *qəṭṛe*) arch, dome

kasa m. (pl. *kase*) chalice

pəṛma m. (pl. *pəṛme*) incense burner

ṛaza m. (pl. *ṛaze*) mass

quṛbana m. holy communion; host

kaṛuzuwwa, kaṛuzusa m. sermon, preaching

ʾəngaliyyun m. Gospel

bṛuksa m. blessing

bəsqüṛe, bəsquṛe m. (pl. *bəsqüṛawaha, bəsquṛawasa*) cemetery

qawṛa f. (pl. *qawṛaha, qawṛasa*) grave

naqoša m. (pl. *naqoše*) bell

ṣuṛta f. (pl. *suṛyaha, suṛyasa*) painting

kursi d-mawdoye m. confessional

ẓəngloka m. (pl. *ẓəngloke*) (Kurd.) small bell

sətra m. curtain

jullət-ṛaze m. mass vestments

jullət-šamaše n.pl. deacon apparel

huṛaṛa m. stole of deacon

ṣliwa m. (pl. *ṣliwe*) cross

quṛbana m. holy communion, host

ṣaṛḥaṣṣa m. deacon belt

fənda m. (pl. *fənde*) burning wick

ḥuðṛa m. (pl. *ḥuðṛe*) prayer book of liturgical calendar

qdamasər m. liturgical book of prayer

1.3. Watermill

ʾarxəl f. (pl. *ʾarxəlwaha, ʾarxəlwasa*) watermill

kepət reša m. upper grindstone

kepət səssa m. lower grindstone

kotăla m. (pl. *kotăle*) raised tank attached to a water-mill which fills with water from a channel and releases water flow at a high pressure to drive the mill

boṭəka m. (pl. *boṭəkyaha, boṭəkyasa*) large wooden channel that carries water at high speed to drive water-mill

parwana m. (pl. *parwane, parwanāt*) propeller

paṛṛe n.pl. blades of propeller

dulaba m. wooden wheel to which propellers are attached

dawla m. open box over a water-mill containing wheat, with a hole in the bottom through which wheat comes out onto the grindstone

čaqčaqa m. wooden wheel shaking and dispensing slowly grain to be ground by a water-mill

suṛṛəka f. lip in the ridge of the lower grindstone of a water-mill where sesame oil pours off

bəsta m. driving rod

1.4. Churn

güza, guza m. (pl. *güze, guze*) skin bag used for churning

mayoya m. (pl. *mayoye*) long wooden rod running the length of the frame carrying the churn bag

lawlaba m. (pl. *lawlabe*) wooden stick at the two ends of the frame carrying the churn bag

1.5. Cradle

dodiyya f. (pl. *dodiyye, dudyaha, dudyasa*) cradle

dazbenka m. (pl.*dazbenke*) (Kurd.) swaddling bands

qasrika m. (pl. *qasrike*) pot for collecting urine and excrement of baby

šaruqta f. (pl. *šaruqyaha, šaruqyasa)* pipe for taking away urine of baby

2. Containers

2.1. Miscellaneous Vessels

badiyya m. (pl. *badiyye*) brass vessel (for water and *dawwe*)

dana f. (pl. *dane*) water jar

margəlta f. (pl. *margəlyaha, margəlyasa*) pan for cooking

maqle f. (Arab.) frying-pan

talma m. (pl. *talme*) (Kurd./Arab.) water pot

manjaloke f. (pl. *manjalukyaha, manjalukyasa*) (Kurd.) pail for milk or yoghurt

kawaza f. (pl. *kawaze*) earthenware pot for water

kwara f. (pl. *kwarane*) storage bin for corn

lagana f. (pl. *lagane*) brass container for food

lina f. (pl. *line*) large conical-shaped pot

linta f. (pl. *linyaha, linyasa*) small conical-shaped pot

majmaʿa f. (pl. *majmaʿe*) (Arab.) tray

maṛəgla m. (pl. *maṛəgle*) brass pan for heating water

masina f. (pl. *masine*) earthenware or brass pot with spout, dish for washing hands

qaṭxa m. (pl. *qaṭxe*) cup measure for grain and flour

qapüla, qapula m. (pl. *qapüle, qapule*) a small measure used by the owner of water-mill to measure out his share as a fee for milling flour or sesame oil

qoqa m. (pl. *qoqe*) water pot

quqta f. (pl. *quqyaha, quqyasa*) small water pot

qasrika m. (pl. *qasrike*) (Kurd.) pot under a cradle for collecting urine and excrement of a baby

ṣəṭla f. (pl. *ṣəṭle*) brass or aluminium bucket

seniyya f. (pl. *seniyye*) (Kurd./Arab.) large metal plate

senika f. (pl. *senikyaha, senikyasa*) (Kurd./Arab.) small metal plate

koka m. (pl. *koke*) large pot for cooking oil and fried meat

šarba f. (pl. *šarbe*) earthenware jug

šüša, šuša m. (pl. *šüše, šuše*) bottle

tănăka m. (pl. *tănăke*) tin

ṭašta f. (pl. *ṭašyaha, tašyasa*) (Kurd.) brass bowl (for kneading dough)

lüliyya, luliyya m. (pl. *lüliyye, luliyye*) spout (on a pot)

kofka, kuwwa m. (pl. *kuwwe*) funnel

2.3. Cups and Glasses

glās m. (pl. *glase*) (Kurd./English) glass

kasa m. (pl. *kase*) chalice (in church)

stikana m. (pl. *stikane*) (Kurd.) small tea glass

samawar m. (Kurd.) samovar

bardaġ m. (pl. *bardaġe*) glass for drinking water

čapaste, čapaske f. (pl. *čapaskyaha, čapaskyasa, čapastyaha, čapastyasa*) (Kurd.) teapot

2.3. Bags and Baskets

məziyya f. (pl. *məziyaha, məziyasa*) large skin bag for storing grains

kisa m. (pl. *kise*) (Arab.) small bag of cloth for keeping grains

kista m. (pl. *kisyaha, kisyasa*) (Arab) small bag of cloth

buqča m. (pl. *boqčəkyaha, buqčəkyasa*) (Kurd.) a piece of cloth used to carry or keep clothes

buqčəka (Nex.), *buqčəksa* (Sam.) m. (pl. *boqčəkyaha, buqčəkyasa*) (Kurd.) small piece of cloth used to carry or keep clothes

ça̜nṭa f. (pl. *ça̜nyaha, ça̜nyasa*) (Kurd.) shoulder bag

güza, guza m. (pl. *güze, guze*) skin bag for churning or carrying liquids

širmaška m. (pl. *širmaške*) small skin bag for carrying milk

goniyya f. (pl. *goniyye*) (Arab.) sack (made of flax)

jawala f. (pl. *jawalane*) (Kurd.) sack (made of animal hair)

pa̜ruzun m. (Kurd.) woolen knapsack carried by women

pista f. (pl. *pisyaha, pisyasa*) bag usually of sheep skin for keeping cheese and *jajək*

qəṛṭala f. (pl. *qəṛṭalane*) pannier bag on the back of an animal

qupiyya, qupisa f. (pl. *qupiyaha qupyasa*) small pannier bag

ṭəryanta f. (pl. *ṭəryanane*) small basket tray used for bread or new-born babies.

ṭəryana m. (pl. *ṭəryanane*) large basket tray used for storing bread *gərba* m. (pl. *gərbe*) conical basket for keeping bees

kurtana m. (pl. *kurtanane)* saddle-bag especially for donkeys

3. Miscellaneous Instruments and Tools

tarkəsana m. long wooden poker for stirring up the fire of an oven

baxošta f. (pl. *baxošyaha, baxošyasa*) big stirring spoon, ladle

ḅyaṭa m. (pl. *ḅyaṭe*) pickaxe

jalla m. (pl. *jalle*) long stick used for bringing down walnuts from walnut trees

čakuč m. (pl. *čakuče*) (Kurd./Arab.) hammer

čamča f. (pl. *čamče*) spoon (made of wood)

čəngala f. (pl. *čəngale*) (Kurd.) fork

garoma m. (pl. *garome*) large wood rolling pin

garusta f. (pl. *garosyaha, garusyasa*) handmill

geṛa m. (pl. *geṛe*) long thin rolling pin

gəṛkə f. (pl. *gəṛkaha, gəṛkasa*) (Kurd.) handmill used to remove husks from rice

ja'oza f. (pl. *ja'oze*) wood chopper

kanušta f. (pl. *kanušyaha, kanuyasa*) small broom, brush

kallax m. (pl. *kallaxe*) (Kurd.) sheep shears

kalbaṭān m. (pl. *kalbṭane*) (Kurd./Arab.) pincers

gupala f. (pl. *gupale*) (Kurd.) shepherd's stick; walking stick

magla m. (pl. *magle*) sickle

magəsta f. (pl. *magəsyaha, magəsyasa*) small sickle

mandaṛüne, mandaṛune f. (pl. *mandaṛunyaha, mandarunyasa*) roller for flattening roof

məqqara m. (pl. *məqqare*) gouge, chisel

məqqaṣ m. (pl. *məqqaṣe*) (Arab.) scissors

maṛa m. (pl. *maṛe*) metal spade with a piece of wood above the metal part used to press the tool with the leg

maṛuwwa f. (pl. *maṛuwwe*) wooden spade for moving snow

maṛbəl f. (pl. *maṛbele, maṛbəlyaha, maṛbəlyasa*) metal spade

rušta f. wooden spade for cereals

mazraqa f. (pl. *mazraqe*) wooden stick covered in wool used to stick bread to the oven

maṣəxwa m. (pl. *maṣəxwe*) metal scoop with a long handle to carry embers or remove ash from ovens

masasa m. (pl. *masase*) long stick ending in one end with a goad and the other with an iron blade used to goad oxen during ploughing and to remove mud from the plough

maxətwa m. (pl. *maxətwe*) awl (with wooden handle)

məlġawa m. (pl. *məlġawe*) winnowing fork

daqṛa m. (pl. *daqṛe*) two-pronged winnowing fork

məšna f. (pl. *məšne*) whetstone for sharpening blades

məṣapyu f. strainer

ṣapuwwa f. (pl. *ṣapuwwe*) strainer

tarkəsana m. (pl. *tarkəsane*) wooden poker

nara m. (pl. *nare*) axe

nəsurta f. (pl. *nəsuryaha, nəsuryasa*) saw

qaṭu m. big saw mounted on a wooden frame and handled by two people to cut big tree trunks

gupala f. (pl. *gupale*) walking-stick

šawṭa m. (pl. *šawṭe*) long thin flexible stick used like a whip

maʿalləm čiči m. a cross-like shape covered with cloth to frighten away birds in paddy fields and orchards

šapṛa m. (pl. *šapṛe*) large knife

beṭiyya f. (pl. *beṭyaha, beṭyasa*) small metal tool lie an adze for digging up vegetables

xaṣṣina f. (pl. *xaṣṣine*) axe

xaššola m. (pl. *xaššole*) hand-held grinding stone for grinding rice or wheat

maduxta f. a small horizontal stone mortar with a stone to crush wet grains by rubbing them against the mortar by hand

xatoṛa m. (pl. *xatoṛe*) washing board

makinət xyaṭa f. sewing machine

4. Agriculture

4.1. Cultivated Land

ʾara f. (pl. *ʾaraha, ʾarasa*) ground, land

ʾaqaṛa m. (pl. *ʾaqaṛe*) area of open farmland

ʾəpra m. soil, ground; land

bayara f. land left without cultivation for one season

čamma m. (pl. *čammane*) large field near river; plantation *gwānda* m. (pl. *gawānde*) boundary; strip between fields with no cultivation to mark boundary

karma m. (pl. *karmane*) vineyard; orchard

marga m. (pl. *margane*) meadow

praza f. (pl. *prazane, prazaha, prazasa*) stubble field

txüba, txuba m. (pl. *txübe, txu:be*) boundary

zṛota f. planted vegitables and crops

4.2. Paddy Fields

sadda m. (pl. *sadde*) (Arab.) dammed section of paddy field consisting of a row of basins

šella n.pl. (Kurd.) soft mud made in preparation for cultivation of rice

makajo f. (pl. *makajoye*) section of a paddy field, paddy field basin

4.3. Irrigation

šaqiyya f. (pl. *šaqyaha, šaqyasa*) irrigation channel

darawe f. (pl. *darawyaha, darawyasa*) (Kurd.) dam put in an irrigation channel (*šaqiyya*) to stop or redirect the flow of water

ṣəkra m. (pl. *ṣəkre*) (Kurd.) dam put in an irrigation channel (*šaqiyya*) to stop or redirect the flow of water

boṭəka f. (pl. *boṭəkyaha, boṭəkyasa*) long hollow tree trunk split in two used to carry water across a water stream (*šaqiyya*)

kaṛṛaxa m. (pl. *kaṛṛaxe*) irrigation adminstrator, who was concerned principally with regulating the flow of water in a water channel (*šaqiyya*)

4.4. Harvest and Storage

ġzada f. harvest

bədṛa f. (pl. *bədṛaha, bədṛasa*) threshing floor

gurza m. (pl. *gurze*) large tied bundle of grass or produce (usually wheat)

qapla m. (pl. *qaple*) an arm-full amount of grass, produce

dwara m. threshing of grains by animals on the threshing floor

gdiša m. (pl. *gdiše*) pile of harvested rice, wheat or sesame

kartət ṛəzza f. (pl. *karahət rəzza, karasət rəzza*) load of harvested rice carried on the back in a piece of cloth

dṛaya m. to winnow, to separate threshed wheat from straw with wind and rakes

qayne m. metal finger covers worn by harvesters

səmmala f. (pl. *səmmale*) small bundle of grass or produce

ṭaṛpa m. tree (oak) leaves for winter

ṭaṛpušna m. fallen tree leaves

deqa f. (pl. *deqaha, deqasa*) stack of twigs with leaves or harvested rice stalks for animal fodder in winter

deqət ṭaṛpa f. (pl. *deqahət ṭaṛpa, deqasət ṭaṛpa*) stack of oak tree twigs with leaves built around a pole for animal fodder in winter

deqət balma f. (pl. *deqahət balma, deqasət balma*) stack of harvested bundles of rice stalks built around a wood pole or animal fodder in winter

taxa m. (pl. *taxe*) pile, untied bundle of grass and leaves *btüne, btune* m. storage bin for straw

parta f. removed rice husks

püška, puška m. (Kurd.) rice grains with husks

4.5. Plough and Ploughing

bzara f. (pl. *bzarane*) plough

nira m. (pl. *nire*) yoke

lata f. (pl. *latəkyaha, latəkyasa*) furrow

latəka f. (pl. *latəkyaha, latəkyasa*) small furrow

psana f. a ploughed unit of land

šapna f. instrument made of oak twigs for smoothing ground after ploughing and sowing

4.6. Sieves and Sieving

maxəlta f. (pl. *maxəlyaha, maxəlyasa*) sieve with small holes (for flour)

ʾərbala f. (pl. *ʾərbale, ʾərbalane*) sieve with medium sized holes

sarada m. (pl. *sarade*) (Kurd./Arab.) sieve with large holes (for corn)

parta f. husks remaining in sieve after sieving

dəqqa m. fine particles of grains (especially rice) after pounding them in a stone mortar

5. Sewing, Weaving and Spinning

5.1. Sewing

xyaṭa to sew

xayyaṭa m. (pl. *xayyaṭe*) (Arab.) tailor

xayyaṭṭa f. (pl. *xayyaṭe*) (Arab.) seamstress

makinət xyaṭa f. sewing machine

xmaṭa f. (pl. *xmaṭyaha, xmatyasa*) needle

ʾurtəxa f. (pl. *ʾurtəxe, ʾurtəxyaha, ʾurtəxyasa*) long needle

qaṭwa m. (pl. *qaṭwe*) large wooden needle

sənjaqa f. (pl. *sənjaqe*) crochet-hook

kəštaban f. thimble

gzaza, gdada (At.) m. (pl. *gzaze, gdade*) thread

bakara m. (pl. *bakare*) spool for thread

keliyya m. (pl. *keliyye*) loose stitch used to join pieces of fabric together in a preliminary fashion before they are sewed with the final stitching

pṛaṭa to undo a stitching by pulling apart the two sides of the stitched cloth

5.2. Weaving

zqaṛa to weave, to knit

zəqṛa m. (pl. *zəqṛe*) weaving, woven product

5.3. Spinning

ʾzala to spin (wool)

ʾəzla m. yarn

küša, kuša m. (pl. *küše, kuše*) spindle (hanging from a distaff) *masərqa* m. (pl. *masərqe*) large comb for carding wool

gəgla m. (pl. *gəgle*) skein (of wool, thread) spun on a spool

6. Hunting

lāstika f. (pl. *lāstike*) sling

zwəlla m. (pl. *zwəlle*) an elastic strip with which the sling is tied to the pronged piece of wood used for making slings

kawla m. (pl. *kawle*) piece of leather fastened to the sling where the round stone is put and fired at birds

dənjama f. (pl. *denjama*) (Kurd.) screen behind which hunters hide to shoot birds

ṭappəka, ṭappəksa f. (pl. *ṭappəkyaha, ṭappəkyasa*) trap for partridges and sparrows consisting of a broad stone that falls down on a pit once the bird steps on the trigger supporting the stone.

ṭaḷḷe f. (pl. *ṭaḷḷaha, ṭaḷḷasa*) metal springed animal trap

tăfaqa f. (pl. *tăfaqe*) rifle

qeṛma f. (pl. *qeṛme*) shotgun

7. Fires

nüra, nura m. fire

manqušta f. (pl. *manqušyaha, manqušyaha*) metal instrument for striking fire on flint

kepət manqušta m. flint used to strike fire with metal instrument known as *manqušta*

lata f. flame

črüska, čruska m. (pl. *črüske, črüska*) (Kurd.) spark

tənna m. smoke

palla m. (pl. *palle*) (Kurd.) ember of burning wood

qəṭma m. ash

šəmṛa m.soot

šəxṛa m. soot that forms on the surface of cooking pots or chimnies

maṣəxwa f. (pl. *maṣəxwe*) metal scoop with a long handle to remove soot from fire place, carry hot charcoal, or ember.

tarkəsana m. small wooden poker

bnüre, bnure m. fireplace, hearth

sekuča m. (pl. *sekuče*) (Kurd.) metal frame for cooking over a fire with three legs

malhoye to burn, to be kindled

ṭpaya to kindle

draya nüra, nura b- gu- to set fire to (used in an abstract way), e.g. *drele nüra/nura gu-ləbbi* 'he set fire to my heart' (= he made me very sad)

ʾiqaza to burn, *maqoze, mqaza* 'to set fire to'

yuqzana m. fuel

lwaxa to catch fire, to blaze, to get furious at somebody

baṭboṭe to fluctuate when burning from one extreme to another

qmaya to scorch (clothes) (tr. and intr.)

xraxa to singe

xərxa m. singed head, forearms and legs of animal for eating

šy*ara* to stoke (fire)

tarkose to build up embers of a fire in order to keep it burning

ṭyaxa to die down (fire), *maṭyoxe* to dampen down (fire)

8. Clothes and Fabrics

8.1. General Clothes

bahitta f. (pl. *bayaha, bayasa*) men's long sleeve hanging from a white shirt down the hand, women's long sleeves that can be tied from behind above the buttocks.

gəṛwiyya, gəṛwisa f. (pl. *gəṛwe*) socks

bubba m. (pl. *bubbe*) the lower part of a woman's shirt below the breasts used as a pocket

jeba m. (pl. *jebane*) (Arab.) pocket (men)

gəfka m. (pl. *gəfke*) (Kurd.) tassel

šaḷa, m. (pl. *šaḷe*) (Kurd.) traditional thick cloth belt worn by women

čarukta f. (pl. *čarukyaha, čarukyasa*) a traditional piece of cloth worn around one side of the waist by women, usually with sashes

šütka, šutka m. (pl. *šütke, šutke*) (Kurd.) a single strand of cloth used as a belt by women, men's traditional belt of a long piece of cloth worn around the waist in layers.

qupča m. (pl. *qupče*) button

ziqa m. neck of a shirt

8.2. Men's Clothes

kapanak m. (Kurd.) thick woolen cloak of shepherd

šərwala m. (pl. *šərwalane*) (Kurd.) trousers made from white cloth *təka* f. cord for trousers

qayiš m. (pl. *qayiše*) (Kurd.) leather belt

ṣudṛa f. (pl. *ṣudraha, ṣudrasa*) shirt

jamadani f. a decorated cloth made into rolls and tied around a decorated hat

kusiyya, kusisa f. (pl. *kusyaha, kusyasa*) hat with a sash in the middle usually worn under the traditional headdress called *jamadani*

qabaya m. (pl. *qabayane*) (Kurd.) waistcoat

pašma=u barguzta (pl. *pašma=u bargüze/barguze*) (Kurd.) traditional festive suit

saqa m. (pl. *saqe*) legging (covering lower leg)

šütka, šutka (pl. *šütke, šutke*) long cloth belt turned many times around the waist

qundərta f. (pl. *qundəre*) shoes

8.3. Women's Clothes

helaka m. (pl. *helake*) waistcoat without sleeves

ṣudra f. (pl. *ṣudraha, ṣudrasa*) shirt

šala m. (pl. *šale*) (Kurd.) sash wrapped around waist

čarukta (pl. *čarukyaha, čarukyasa*) a traditional piece of cloth worn around one side of the waist by women, usually with sashes

dasmālka (pl. *dasmālke*) coloured piece of cloth worn by women on head, handkerchief

pošiyya f. (pl. *pošyaha, pošiyyasa*) festive head dress

kusiyya f. (pl. *kusyaha, kusyasa*) hat worn under the *pošiyya xürət/xurət ṣuḍra* m. long undergarment ending with a coloured part above the feet)

qundərta f. (pl. *qundəre*) shoes

8.4. Shoes

liyane n.pl. snow shoes

pelawət lāstik n.pl. (Kurd.) rubber shoes

pelawta m. (pl. *pelawe*) (Kurd.) shoes

qundərta f. (pl. *qundəre*) (Kurd./Turk.) leather shoes with heals

qaytan m. (pl. *qaytane*) shoe-lace

jazma f. (pl. *jazma*) long plastic shoes worn in winter

8.5. Fabrics

bara m. (pl. *bare)* (Kurd.) sheet

parča m. (pl. *parče*) (Kurd.) sheet of cloth

baza m. type of fabric

čapan f. white fabric

kənjəṛṛa m. (pl. *kənjəṛṛe*) (Kurd.) piece of (usually useless) cloth

čita m. (Kurd.) type of thin smooth fabric

čoxa f. (Kurd.) broadcloth, thick woolen fabric

grawa m. (Kurd.) off-white cotton fabric

ʾabresəm m. silk

jurjet m. type of velvet fabric

ləhefa m. (pl. *ləhefe*) (Kurd./Arab.) duvet

nəqša m. embroidery

prasta f. cloth spread on floor on which food is laid, spread, covering for floor (such as rug or carpet)

tatiyya m. (pl. *tatiyye*) mat made of compressed wool

maḥfərṭa f. (pl. *maḥfəryaha, maḥfəryasa*) (Kurd.) carpet

matraḥta f. (pl. *matraḥyaha, matraḥyasa*) (Arab.) small mat for sitting

zəqṛa m. (pl. *zəqṛe*) woven fabric

gota f. a ball of woven thread

bakara m. (pl. *bakare*) (Arab.) spool

8.6. Ropes and Ties

xawla m. (pl. *xawle*) rope

xawəlta f. (pl. *xawəlyasa, xawəlyaha*) short rope

patəka f. (pl. *patəkyaha patəkyasa*) (Kurd.) short rope tethering an animal to a stake, shorter than a *xawəlta*

hawsara m. (pl. *hawsare*) (Kurd.) rope for leading an animal

gzaza, gədda, gdāda (At.) m. (pl. *gzāze gədde*) string; thread

rəsta f. (pl. *rəsyaha, rəsyasa*) line (for hanging clothes)

səkka f. (pl. *səkkake*) tether

qəxṛa m. (pl. *qəxṛe*) knot

həmbaluqta f. (pl. *həmbaluqyaha, həmbaluqyasa*) loop, knot (joining two pieces of rope)

hečiyya m. (pl. *hečiyye*) a pronged piece of (oak) wood to used as a loop to tie loads on animals.

Abbreviations

Nx.	Nexla area
Sam.	area South of the Aqra mountain

Bibliography

Coghill, Eleanor. 2008. 'Some Notable Features in North-Eastern Neo-Aramaic Dialects of Iraq'. In *Neo-Aramaic Dialect Studies*, edited by Geoffrey Khan, 91–104. Piscataway: Gorgias.

Haig, Geoffrey, and Geoffrey Khan, eds. 2018. *The Languages and Linguistics of Western Asia: An Areal Perspective*. The World of Linguistics 6. Berlin: De Gruyter.

Khan, Geoffrey. 2008. *The Neo-Aramaic Dialect of Barwar*. 3 vols. Leiden: Brill.

Mutzafi, Hezy. 2000. 'The Neo-Aramaic Dialect of Maha Khtaya d-Baz. Phonology, Morphology and Texts'. *Journal of Semitic Studies* 45 (2): 293–322.

ARABIC LOANWORDS IN THE NEO-ARAMAIC DIALECT OF ANKAWA

Salam Neamah Hirmiz Hakeem

1. Introduction

The Neo-Aramaic dialect of Ankawa belongs to the North-Eastern Neo-Aramaic (NENA) subgroup. It is spoken by a Christian minority in the town adhering to the Chaldean Catholic Church, who refer to it by the term Suret or Sureth. Ankawa is located to the North of the city of Erbil, the capital of Iraqi Kurdistan, where Kurdish is the dominant means of communication.

Aramaic, the ancestor of Sureth, and Arabic are genetically related in that they both belong to the Semitic language family. As we shall see, however, this does not seem to be the primary cause of the introduction of an extensive number of Arabic words in the speech of the Sureth-speakers of Ankawa. This is because there are so many more Arabic words in the speech of the young than in that of the older generation. So the crucial factor must be the current social situation rather than the linguistic affinity of the two languages.

2. Research Data

The source of the majority of the data presented in this paper is my own native-speaker knowledge of the Sureth of Ankawa. I am also a speaker of Arabic as a second language. The data and analyses have been verified through various audio recordings of interviews and spontaneous conversations that have been elicited from other native speakers of Ankawa Sureth of different ages.

 https://doi.org/10.11647/OBP.0209.16

3. Findings and Discussion

Versteegh (2001, 473) states that:

> In borrowing speakers are primarily interested in lexical items from another language, which are either perceived to be more prestigious than the lexical equivalents in their own language, or for which their own language has no equivalents at all.

This seems to be true with regard to a large number of Arabic loanwords that can be heard in the speech of the young Sureth-speakers in Ankawa. The young generation have started to consider Arabic as a more prestigious language than their mother tongue on account of the wider use of Arabic and its richer vocabulary. They have, moreover, studied academic subjects such as physics and biology in Arabic and do not know equivalents to the technical terminology in Sureth. The common genetic origin of the two languages facilitates the process of borrowing, since in many cases the Arabic loanwords do not sound very different from their own native vocabulary, e.g.

Arabic	**Sureth**	
ḥub	*ḥubba*	'love'
zamān	*zawna*	'time'

It is not clear when exactly this process of borrowing started, but we can deduce from the nature of the loanwords that the Arabic public education and local television channels during the middle of the twentieth century played a pivotal role in initiating and facilitating this process. Although nowadays the educational system has shifted to Kurdish instead of Arabic and there is no immediately neighbouring Arab community, we can still notice an increase in the use of Arabic loanwords by the Sureth-speakers of Ankawa. This may be ascribed to the remaining influence of schooling and education, which were predominantly in Arabic until the end of the last century, in addition to the television channels and other media that still involve an extensive use of Arabic. As a result, most of the technical words used in the region, including those used by other sections of the population, such as Kurds, Turkmens, Yezidis, are Arabic. Another more recent and prevailing source for more Arabic loanwords is social media, such as Facebook, Instagram, Snapchat and Twitter, in which Arabic is the predominant means of communication.

It can be observed that in the majority of cases the Arabic loanwords have not undergone any phonological changes. This is in agreement with Thomason and Kaufman's assumption that 'the more the borrowing speakers come to know the foreign language, the more they tend to take over the foreign phonological elements in an unadapted form' (1988, cited in Versteegh, 2001, 476). Furthermore, morphological borrowing occurs in loanwords, particularly in the use of Arabic plural forms of nouns, whether regular or broken, e.g. *ʾiḥtimālāt* 'possibilities' and *ʾaḥwāl* 'conditions'. Sometimes borrowed Arabic nouns are used either with their Arabic plural form or with the Sureth plural inflection (see §4.1 below), e.g. *kutub* ~ *kitābānə* 'books'.

The following sections present a classification and analysis of the most common Arabic loanwords that I have noticed as a native speaker in conversations and in the interviews with Sureth-speakers in Ankawa. The source of loanwords is Modern Standard Arabic rather than Iraqi dialectal Arabic. This is because this is the variety of Arabic that the people of Ankawa have been mostly exposed to. The counterpart of the Arabic words in Ankawa Sureth is provided when available. In some cases, however, there is no counterpart in Ankawa Sureth as far as can be established.

4. Nouns

The vast majority of the Arabic nouns have been borrowed into Sureth in their singular form without any modification or inflection. Those for which a counterpart in Ankawa Sureth can be identified include the following:

Arabic	**Sureth**	
kalima	*tanēθa*	'word'
ḥayāt	*xāyə*	'life'
ḥub	*bʾāya*	'love'
ʾixtilāf	*šuxlāpa*	'difference'
fikir	*xušāwa*	'thought'
xawf	*zdōθa*	'fear'
tartīb	*msazgōrə*	'arrangement'
zamān	*zawna*	'time'
wajih	*poza*	'face'
ʿāʾila	*našwātha*	'family/ relatives'
nāḥiya	*dəpna*	'side/aspect'
šāb	*jwonqa*	'young man'
šābba	*xamθa*	'young woman'
sāʿa	*šēθa*	'hour'
faraḥ	*pəṣxūθa*	'joy'
ḥaṣād	*ġzāda*	'harvest'
najəm	*kawəxwa*	'star'
lāʿəb	*mṭaʿlāna*	'player'
muʿalim	*malpana*	'teacher'
ṭālib	*yālōpa*	'student'
xāliq	*bārōya*	'Creator'

Examples of borrowed Arabic nouns for which there is no clear counterpart in Ankawa Sureth are the following:

fikra	'idea'
ʿaqil	'mind'
taqqabul	'tolerance'
tafāhum	'understanding'
suʾāl	'question'

jawāb	‘answer’
xuṭṭa	‘plan’
ʾihmāl	‘negligence’
ḥurriya	‘freedom’
taḥrīr	‘release’
suhūla	‘ease’
qarār	‘decision’
silāḥ	‘weapon’
θiqa	‘trust’
ʾiḥtirām	‘respect’
xilāf	‘disagreement’
taqlīd	‘imitation’
taḍḥiya	‘sacrifice’
maqbara	‘cemetery’
muškila	‘problem’
marḥala	‘stage’
ṣabir	‘patience’
taḥammul	‘endurance’
nawʿ	‘sort’
ʿilim	‘science’
musāʿid	‘assistant’
qāḍi	‘judge’
maḥkama	‘court’
ḥāl	‘condition’
šikil	‘shape/image’

There are, however, also Arabic roots that are used with Sureth noun patterns (especially as verbal nouns), e.g.

ʿarabana	‘wagon’
nəʿməta	‘grace’

ḥukīθa	'tale'
ḍġaṭa	'pressure/pressing'
mṣalōḥə	'reconciliation'
mjarōbə	'trial/testing'
mbadōlə	'change/changing'
mḥarōkə	'moving/ movement'
maqlōbə	'turning over'
maxlōsə	'saving/salvation'
mḥamōyə	'protecting/ protection'
msafōrə	'travelling'

In some both the original Arabic form and Arabic root with a Sureth morphological pattern are used interchangeably, e.g.

ziyāda ~ *zodāna*	'addition'
naqiṣ ~ *nuqṣāna*	'shortage'
qiṣṣa ~ *qəṣṣəta*	'story'
ṣura ~ *ṣurta*	'picture'
ʾuʿjūba ~ *ʿajibūθa*	'wonder'
xaṭīʾa ~ *xṭīθa*	'sin'.

It is worth mentioning that the majority of borrowed nouns retain their Arabic plural forms, whether sound feminine, sound masculine or broken, e.g.

kalimāt	'words'
taḍḥiyāt	'sacrifices'
xilafāt	'disagreements'
ḥurriyāt	'freedoms'
qararāt	'decisions'

muʿallimīn	'teachers'
musāʿidīn	'assistants'
lāʿibīn	'players'
ʾasliḥa	'weapons'
ʾafkār	'ideas'
ʿuqūl	'minds'
nujūm	'stars'
ʾajwiba	'answers'

There are also a few Arabic nouns that are modified and inflected with Sureth plural suffixes, e.g.

zamānə	'times'
maqbarə	'cemeteries'

Moreover, we can also find various borrowed nouns that have both the Arabic and Sureth plural forms, respectively, e.g.

sāʿāt ~ *saʿāθa*	'hours'
xuṭaṭ ~ *xuṭāθa*	'plans'
muškilāt ~ *muškilāθa*	'problems'
ʾaḥwāl ~ *ḥālə*	'conditions'
ʾaškāl ~ *šəklə*	'shapes/images'

5. Verbs

The Arabic verbs that are borrowed into Sureth involve an Arabic root that is inflected with Sureth morphological patterns. In what follows the verbs are cited in the form of the third person singular masculine past form. In some cases there is a semantic counterpart in the Sureth of Ankawa, e.g.

Arabic verbal root	**Sureth**	
trəklə	*šwəqlə*	'left/gave up'
mṭuwəllə	*yrəxlə*	'lengthened'
mduxəllə	*yə'əllə*	'interfered'

In many cases, however, no exact counterpart in Ankawa Sureth can be identified, e.g.

mufəqlə	'agreed'
qnəˁlə	'was persuaded'
msufērə	'traveled
mḥuləllə	'solved'
mkuməllə	'completed'
mqurērə	'decided'
mjuməˁlə	'gathered'

Furthermore, Sureth speakers of Ankawa often use Arabic nouns preceded or, more often, followed by a Sureth light verb such as *wədlə* 'did' and *wəllə* 'gave' to produce compound verbs, e.g.

Compound verb	**Sureth**	
'istiˁmāl wədlə [use did]	*mupləxlə*	'used'
'istirāḥa wədlə [rest did]	*nəxlə*	'rested'

Examples of such hybrid compound verbs without clear counterparts in Ankawa Sureth include the following:

taḥḥamul wədlə [endurance did]	'endured'
'iˁlān wədlə [announcement did]	'announced'

jawāb wəllə [answer gave]	'answered'
ʾiḥtirām wəllə [respect gave]	'respected'

The Sureth of Ankawa has a basic SVO word order. Such compound verbs, however, generally have the light verb after the object and this suggests that their syntax has been influenced by Kurdish. Sureth speakers in Ankawa also know the local Kurdish, which is an SOV language. In Kurdish also compound verbs with borrowed Arabic nouns and light verbs are in use. The light verb is regularly placed after the noun, in accordance with the normal Kurdish word order, e.g.

taḥammuli kərd [endurance did]	'endured'
jawābi da [answer gave]	'answered'

Arabic verbs with Arabic morphological inflection are occasionally used in Sureth. One example is the expression of attitude *ʾaʿtaqid* 'I think', the Sureth counterpart for which is *xəšboni.*

6. Adjectives

In Arabic the singular masculine is the basic form of the adjective. It is this form that is borrowed by speakers of Ankawa Sureth and used in all contexts, e.g.

Arabic	Sureth	
ʿaṣabi	*ʿīqa*	'nervous/angry'
mayyit	*mīθa*	'dead'
ḥay	*bəxāy*	'alive'
saʿīd	*pṣīxa*	'happy'
waḥīd	*l-xōde*	'alone'

Examples of loaned Arabic adjectives without exact Sureth counterparts include:

rəṣaṣi	‘grey’
burtuqāli	‘orange [colour]’
muḥtaram	‘respectful’
kāmil	‘complete’
ʾiʿtiyādi	‘normal’
mumkin	‘possible’
mustaḥīl	‘impossible’
mutʾakkid	‘certain’
mašġūl	‘busy’
majbūr	‘obliged’
baṣīṭ	‘simple’
ṣarīḥ	‘frank’

Sabar (1984, 206) states that in Neo-Aramaic dialects in general ‘native adjectives agree with the qualified noun or pronoun in singular masculine and feminine, but in plural the masculine form serves both masculine and feminine . . . but in the case of borrowed adjectives, the singular masculine is used invariably with all four categories.’ The same agreement patterns are found in the Sureth of Ankawa. For instance, when using native adjectives, we find examples such as *ʾubra yarīx****a*** ‘tall boy’, *brāta yarix****ta*** ‘tall girl’, *nāšə yarīx****ə*** ‘tall people’. However, when using Arabic loanwords, we would hear forms like *ʾubra baṣīṭ* ‘simple boy’, *brāta baṣīṭ* ‘simple girl’, *nāšə baṣīṭ* ‘simple people’.

To produce the comparative form, the Ankawa Sureth speakers use the word *bəš* ‘more’ followed by the borrowed adjectives, e.g. *bəš baṣīṭ* ‘more simple’, *bəš ṣarīḥ* ‘more frank’. Sometimes, however, they apply the Arabic comparative morphological pattern to the loaned adjective, e.g.

Arabic	Sureth	
ʾakθar	*bəš kabīra*	'more in number/ amount'
ʾaqall	*bəš qəṣa*	'less in number/ amount'
ʾajmal	*bəš čalabi*	'more beautiful'

7. Adverbs

Ankawa Sureth uses borrowed Arabic adverbs of time, place, and manner, e.g.

Arabic	Sureth	
marrāt	*naqlāθa*	'sometimes'
dāʾiman	*kud-ga*	'always/every time'
baʿdēn	*m-xardax*	'later'
xāṛij	*baṛay*	'abroad/outside'
taqrīban	*qarīwa mən*	'roughly'

Cases where there are no clear Sureth equivalents include:

ṭabʿan	'certainly'
ʾiḥtimāl	'maybe/probably'
fajʾatan	'suddenly'
rajaʾan	'please' (used when asking for a favour)

As we can see above, most of the adverbs of manner are expressed by nouns in the accusative case (cf. Sabar 1984, 206). There are also various loaned Arabic adverbs of manner that are composed of nouns preceded by prepositions, e.g.

fī ḥāl	'in case'
ʿala lʾakθar	'most probably'
ʿalā šarṭ	'on a condition'
ʿalā ġafla	'all of a sudden'
bi-lʿakis	'on the contrary'
biz-zōr	'by force'
bilā dāʿi	'without (good) reason'
bilā zaḥma	'without annoyance' (used when asking for a favour = Sureth *zaḥmə l-oya*).

Some of these are used as heads of adverbial clauses, e.g.

fī ḥāl xzelux izdiḥām, dor

'In case you see crowding, return.'

8. Function Words

In addition to the extensive lexical borrowing that has been demonstrated above, various instances of borrowing of grammatical function words can be also found.

Many such borrowed function words are conjunctions or discourse markers, e.g.

liʾannahu	'because'
maʿa ʾannahu	'although'
bas/lākin	'but'
bi-mā ʾannahu	'as long as'
maθalan	'for example'

Arabic ordinal numerals are another group of loanwords that are widely used, especially by the young generation, in preference to the equivalent Sureth forms. This applies to the ordinals first to tenth:

Arabic	**Sureth**	
ʾawwal	*qamāya*	'first'
θāni	*dət-tre*	'second'
θāliθ	*dət-ṭlāθa*	'third'
rābiʿ	*dət ʾarba*	'fourth' etc.

For the ordinal numerals of eleventh and above only the Sureth forms are in use, e.g.

dət-xadesar	'eleventh'
dət-tresar	'twelfth'
dət-ʾəmma	'hundredth'
dət-ʾalpa	'thousandth'.

It is noteworthy that the Arabic forms precede nouns, in accordance with Arabic grammar, whereas the Sureth forms follow the nouns, e.g.

Arabic	**Sureth**	
ʾawwal ḥub	*ḥub qamāya*	'first love'.

Other modifiers relating to ordering and addition that are loaned in Sureth are the following:

Arabic	**Sureth**	
ʾāxir	*xarāya*	'last'
ġēr	*xənna*	'other'

The borrowed and native forms follow the same patterns as above, e.g.

Arabic	**Sureth**	
ʾāxir šuma	*šuma xarāya*	'last name'.

9. The Future of Ankawa Sureth

Khan (2007, 106–7) states that after the Arab conquests most of the Aramaic speakers of Iraq either started to adopt Arabic, or their speech was gradually Arabicised. Although the transition from Aramaic to Arabic was in some cases slow, this was a continuous process which was fastest in the central and southern areas of Iraq. Spoken Aramaic mostly survived among the Christian and Jewish communities in the North of Iraq.

Ankawa is one of the towns in the North where this language has survived to this day. Will, however, this situation remain the same in the future?

Versteegh (2001, 501–2) states that in various cases 'Arabic was taken over [by speakers] in the same process of acculturation that brought Islam, and in most areas Arabic became at first the second, and then the first language of the inhabitants.' Unlike the situation in such cultures, the Sureth speakers of Ankawa seem to have borrowed the Arabic words without being influenced by the Arab Islamic culture, either because they have retained their Christian faith or because they have been influenced by the communist thought that prevailed in the eighties and nineties of the last century as well as the atheistic ideas that are becoming globally more prevalent. The situation is similar to various Christian minorities in the Middle East where, as Bohac (2010, 24) puts it, 'most existing Christian groups resisted Islamization, but they cannot resist Arabization.'

Versteegh points out that in several situations where there was an extensive borrowing and interaction between a minority language and Arabic within Arabic-speaking regions, the minority language became extinct. This applied, for example, to Coptic in Egypt. In fact, this has already happened to many former Sureth speakers in the city of Mosul, who have almost lost not only Sureth their mother tongue but also their identity as Syriacs, since the majority believe that they are Christian Arabs. In reality, the current displacement of these Arabic-speaking Christians from Mosul to Ankawa in the wake of the invasion of ISIS and their fear of returning due to the relative instability of the region has created a new status quo that adds an extra pressure on Sureth speakers in Ankawa, who have no choice but to use Arabic most of the time when they are outside. Thus, gradually and subconsciously, they are replacing more and more Sureth words with Arabic ones. Besides, many Ankawi families have emigrated to Europe, the USA or Australia because of the instability of the region. This has created even further pressure on this vulnerable dialect.

Could what happened to Mosul be repeated in Ankawa if the rate of the Arabic loanwords continues to increase with the coming generations, or will they be speaking a hybrid variety that basically has Arabic lexical items inflected with Sureth morphology?

10. Conclusion

O'Connor (1986, 220) states that 'the vast majority of loans in any language are nouns.' As it can be seen from the material that is presented above, nouns make up the majority of the Arabic loanwords in the Sureth of Ankawa. The next most common set of loanwords are Arabic verbal roots and Arabic nouns within compound verbal constructions with light verbs. Adjectives follow as the third group of loanwords in terms of their frequency and adverbs are the last.

In addition to the extensive borrowing of Arabic content words, Ankawa Sureth speakers have borrowed various Arabic function words, such as conjunctions and ordinals, which have become integral parts of the dialect.

It is interesting that though Ankawa is within the confines of a neighbouring Kurdish-speaking community, Ankawa Sureth is full of Arabic loans and has only a relatively small number of Kurdish ones. This is a result of the fact that education was entirely in Arabic until the last decade. This is reflected in particular in the fact that most of the Arabic loanwords are technical terms used in education, which in general do not have any counterparts in Ankawa Sureth. Another more recent source for these Arabic loanwords are the media, especially television programmes and social media, such as Facebook, Instagram, Snapchat and Twitter, in which Arabic is the major means of communication. Moreover, the recent displacement of many Arabic-speaking Christians from Mosul to Ankawa has added a new stimulus for borrowing. This has been accompanied by the immigration of numerous Ankawi people abroad, making the situation even more difficult for Sureth to thrive.

Could this dialect survive under the pressure of the increasing number of Arabic words used by the new generation in Ankawa? As a matter of fact, there have been several attempts to encourage the use of Sureth vocabulary and reduce the number of Arabic loanwords, but they do not seem to have had any effect on the increasing preference for the use of Arabic words, which are considered more expressive and versatile. The proportion of Arabic loanwords is, therefore, constantly increasing and the Sureth of Ankawa should be considered an endangered dialect of NENA.

References

Boháč, Artur. 2010. 'Problems of Studying Christian Minorities in the Islamic Middle East'. *Folia Geographica* 15: 15–26.

Khan, Geoffrey. 2007. 'Aramaic in the Medieval and Modern Periods'. In *Languages of Iraq, Ancient and Modern*, edited by Nicholas Postgate, 95–114. Cambridge: The British School of Archaeology in Iraq.

O'Connor, Michael. 1986. 'The Arabic Loanwords in Nabatean Aramaic'. *Journal of Near Eastern Studies* 45 (3): 213–29.

Sabar, Yona. 1984. 'The Arabic Elements in the Jewish Neo-Aramaic Texts of Nerwa and ʿAmādīya, Iraqi Kurdistan'. *Journal of the American Oriental Society* 104 (1): 201–211.

Versteegh, Kees. 2001. 'Linguistic Contacts between Arabic and Other Languages'. *Arabica* 48 (4): 470–508.

LANGUAGE LOSS IN THE ṢŪRAYT/ ṬŪRŌYO-SPEAKING COMMUNITIES OF THE DIASPORA IN SWEDEN

Sina Tezel

1. Ṭūr ʿAbdīn—the Language Situation

Before describing the state of Ṣūrayt/Ṭūrōyo in the diaspora in Sweden, I shall give a brief account of the language situation in Ṭūr ʿAbdīn (SE Turkey) by way of background.

Nowadays, there are only a few villages, where the population speak only Ṣūrayt/Ṭūrōyo. These are Mīdən, Bsōrīno, Sāre (returning people from the diaspora), Bēqusyōno, Dayro du-ṣlībo (a few families), Kafro, Xarābāle and the villages around Xarābāle, namely Arbo, Eḥwo, Bādəbe, Kharabemiška.

The current inhabitants of Kafro, with its impressive newly built houses, consist of only returning people. It was previously completely uninhabited due to migrations to Europe. The same is more or less true of the aforementioned villages around Xarābāle. The only village in the area known as Rāyīte that has remained inhabited is Xarābāle, nowadays also known as Arkaḥ among Suryōye (i.e. the Christian speakers of Ṣūrayt/Ṭūrōyo).

There are also a few villages that each have a few Ṣūrayt/ Ṭūrōyo-speaking families but where the majority of the population are Kurds. These are: Mzīhaḥ, ʿIwardo, Kfarze and Anḥəl. Finally, there is the chief town in the area, Mədyad̠ (Midyat), where today the Ṣūrayt/Ṭūrōyo-speakers are mixed. They consist of families who speak the original Mədyad̠ dialect and Ṣūrayt/Ṭūrōyo-speaking families who have moved to Mədyad̠ from different villages around it.

 https://doi.org/10.11647/OBP.0209.17

2. Dialectal Differences

As is the case with any language, there were and are dialectal differences in Ṣūrayt/Ṭūrōyo. What is noteworthy about this dialectal diversity is that the Ṣūrayt/Ṭūrōyo language area is relatively small. Two villages only two kilometres apart from each other may have dialectal differences. The rural village dialects as a whole can, however, be classified together in a group that contrasts with the urban dialect of Mədyaḏ.

Many of the dialectal differences in Ṣūrayt/Ṭūrōyo are due to influences from the neighbouring languages such as Arabic, Kurdish and Turkish. Geographically, Ṭūr ʿAbdīn is surrounded by the Mesopotamian Arabic dialect area and Kurdish-speaking villages. Among the Arabic dialects in the area the dialect of Mardin, the chief town, was and still is the most important one. Between Mardin and Ṭūr ʿAbdīn there are several Arabic-speaking centres, including, among others, Bnēbīl, Ṣawro, Maʿsarte and Qeleṯ. Around Ṭūr ʿAbdīn, especially near Mədyaḏ, one finds the Mḥallami-Arabic dialects, which are spoken today only by Muslims. Beyond Mīdən eastwards there were three Arabic dialects, namely Āzəx, Espes and Bābake, whose original population consisted of Suryōye. There are also some Kurdish-speaking villages in Ṭūr ʿAbdīn, namely Kerburan, ʿArbāye, Ḥaḥ, Kafro ʿĒlayto and Yardo, all had Suryōyo inhabitants. Today, among these villages only Ḥaḥ is populated by Suryōye, who today also speak Ṣūrayt/Ṭūrōyo alongside Kurdish.

We do not know with any certainty what the historical depth was of the aforementioned influence on Ṣūrayt/Ṭūrōyo. An interesting statement concerning this question is found in Ritter (1967, *19*).[1] He refers to his informant Besim Akdemir speaking

1 See Ritter (1967, *19*) writing:

Der Metropolit von Mardin, Ḥasyo Ḥanna Dölapönü, sagte Besim Akdemir, der ihn danach fragte, der Einfluß des Arabischen und Kurdischen habe im 12. jahrhundert eingesetzt. Der Patriarch ʿazîz bar Sabṯo (Ignaz VII, 1466–1488, Spuler, *Die Morgenländischen Kirchen*, Leipzig 1964, p. 214) habe den Gebrauch der fremden Sprachen verboten, sei aber damit nicht

to Ḥasyo Yuḥanon Dolabani saying that the influence from Arabic and Kurdish began during the 13th century and, as a consequence of this, the Patriarch Aziz Bar Sabṯo tried to forbid the people from speaking foreign languages (Arabic and Kurdish), but then it was too late since they had already lost many native words.

With this background, I shall now examine the current language situation in the diaspora. To the best of my knowledge, no systematic studies have been of this topic, so we cannot establish the full details. We can, however, obtain a general picture.

3. The Challenge of New Social and Cultural Terminology

The Ṣūrayt/Ṭūrōyo-lexicon in Ṭūr ʿAbdīn was characterised by agricultural, narrative and religious terms. During the 1960s and the 1970s the majority of Suryōye migrated from Ṭūr ʿAbdīn, mostly first to Istanbul and then to different countries in Western Europe. Previously, emigration from Ṭūr ʿAbdīn was mostly to the Arabic-speaking countries in the region, especially Syria, Lebanon and Iraq.

The emigration after the 1950s was far more intense than the earlier trend of emigration. It took place during a short period and resulted in the emptying of Ṭūr ʿAbdīn of the majority of Suryōye. Furthermore, the migrants settled in countries that were far more advanced than Ṭūr ʿAbdīn and the neighbouring areas in terms of their economic, political, cultural, social, technological and educational development.

In their new countries of residence in Western Europe the Suryōyo community became familiar with the concept of 'mother tongue education' and for the first time in their history Syriac and Ṣūrayt/Ṭūrōyo were taught in official schools. This was an unexpected event in their history.

---

durchgedrungen. Man habe damals schon viele syrische Worte vergessen und statt dessen fremde gebraucht.

One serious challenge was the need to find linguistic equivalents to the social and cultural terminology of the Western European countries. This was difficult for a minority group from countries with very different social systems.[2]

4. Neologisms

During the period in which the Suryōyō community has been in the diaspora many neologisms have been formed. There was a need to create terms for the new cultural phenomena that the Suryōye encountered in Western European societies. These neologisms were formed almost entirely from lexical items of literary Western Syriac, which were given new meanings. As a result they were not considered as borrowings into Ṣūrayt/Ṭūrōyo.

A situation of diglossia similar to that between Modern Standard Arabic and Arabic dialects exists between Western Syriac and Ṣūrayt/Ṭūrōyo. The Ṣūrayt/Ṭūrōyo speakers in general view Ṣūrayt/Ṭūrōyo as the everyday language of communication, while they consider Western Syriac as the prestigious cultural and ecclesiastical language.

A large number of such neologisms are in use today in Ṣūrayt/Ṭūrōyo. Most of these probably did not exist before the 1950s, judging by their absence in Ritter's Ṭūrōyo collection. They appear to have been first introduced at the beginning of the 1970s, when Ṣūrayt/Ṭūrōyo-speakers began to emigrate to Sweden and other Western European countries. The formation of their own clubs and associations in these countries, and the publication of their own newsletters and magazines have played an important role. They did not have the freedom to engage in such communal activities to the same extent in their homeland. The exact number of neologisms and their diffusion among the Ṣūrayt/Ṭūrōyo-speakers are not known. At any rate, it is clear that the neologisms are used by purists in clubs and associations, in television programs and in newspapers. They are disseminated

2 Ehrnebo (2013, 174–175).

through these means. These neologisms in Ṣūrayt/Ṭūrōyo have been created not only for describing new phenomena in society but also to replace foreign words.[3]

5. Language Loss

While the language has acquired many neologisms, the use of which is prestigious among the Ṣūrayt/Ṭūrōyo speakers, the language has at the same time lost or is in the process of losing many native words.

5.1. Dialect Mixing and the Loss of Dialectal Diversity

The dialectal differences found in Ṭūr ʿAbdīn do not exist in a consistent manner in the diaspora. A Ṣūrayt/Ṭūrōyo-speaking community in a Swedish or a German town consists of people from very different dialectal areas. Consequently, the children born in these circumstances learn and develop their mother tongue in a linguistically mixed environment.

The mixing of the dialects results in a more homogenous language, which is an advantage for the diaspora communities. It has, however, the regrettable consequence of the loss of much dialectal native vocabulary.

I present here a few examples demonstrating the dialectal differences pertaining to the Ṣūrayt/Ṭūrōyo lexicon in Ṭūr ʿAbdīn:

(1) 'street'

There are four dialectal words for the word 'street', namely *šūqo* (Mīdən), *bašqūqo* (Bēqusyōno and Bsōrīno), *basyōġo* (Rāyīte) and *zābūqo*. The last one is a borrowing from local Arabic into the dialect of Mədyad, while the others are native words found in the village dialects. Today *šūqo* has a new common meaning in the diaspora, namely 'a market place, a shopping centre'. The

3 For details and treatment of a great numbers of these neologisms, see S. Tezel (2015, 100–109).

Ṣūrayt/Ṭūrōyo-speakers in the diaspora use *darbo* for ‘street’, which used to refer to a road outside the villages in Ṭūr ʿAbdīn.

(2) ‘axe’

There are at least three words for ‘axe’, *nargo, ʿašfo* ~ *ʿağfo* and *maʿwōlo*. The last of these, which is derived from Arabic *miʿwāl*, is used in the Rāyīte-dialects.[4]

(3) ‘water-pitcher’

At least three dialectal words *gḏōno* (< **kaddōnō*), *mxōlo* (< Western Syriac *mḵōrō*?) and *ğarra* (Arabic) denote a normal ‘water-pitcher’, a smaller one being termed *dgušto* (cf. NENA *gādušta* and Levantine Arabic *dakkūše*) in Məḏyaḏ and *kädūne* in villages.[5]

(4) ‘vineyard guard’

The word for ‘vineyard guard’ is *nōṭūro* in most dialects. Some dialects use the word *naḥtōr*, which is a loan from Kurdish. The Kurdish word is, in turn, a loan from Arabic *nāṭōr*, which itself is a loan from earlier Aramaic *nāṭōrā*.[6] The form *naḥtōr* is in the process of disappearing in the diaspora.

(5) ‘to buy’

The verb for ‘to buy’, *zwənle*, which used to be common to all the village dialects in Ṭūr ʿAbdīn, is in the process of being replaced by *šqīle*, which was and still is a typical Məḏyaḏ-word in Ṭūr ʿAbdīn. Nowadays *šqīle* is the common word for ‘to buy’ among almost all Ṣūrayt/Ṭūrōyo speakers in the diaspora.

(6) ‘hair’

In Ṭūr ʿAbdīn, the village dialects use(d) the word *ṣaʿro* (< **saʿrō*) for denoting ‘hair’, while Məḏyaḏ uses *sawko*. In the diaspora the

4 For details, see A. Tezel (2003, 175).

5 For details, see A. Tezel (2003, 161–163).

6 For details, see A. Tezel (2003, 178).

use of *ṣaʿro* among the Ṣūrayt/Ṭūrōyo speakers from the villages has decreased and they tend to use instead the Mədyōyo word *sawko*.

(7) 'good'

There is a similar situation with regard to the words for 'good', namely *ṭōwo* in the village dialects and *kāyīso* in the dialect of Mədyad. Though the word *ṭōwo* is native and *kāyīso* is foreign, the foreign word *kāyīso* is in the process of being adopted even among the Ṣūrayt/Ṭūrōyo speakers from the villages.

5.2. The Loss of Original Lexemes and Semantics

(1) 'to change'

The village dialects in Ṭūr ʿAbdīn used the native verb *mḥālafle* 'to change'. Today in the diaspora this has almost entirely been replaced by three foreign verbs, namely *mġāyarle*, *mbādēle* and *mdāgašle*. The first two are of Arabic origin and the last one is of Turkish origin.

(2) 'to flee'

Likewise, the native verb 'to flee, run away', *ʿārəq*, has been replaced by the foreign verb *mahzamle*, which is of Arabic origin. The use of the native word *ʿārəq* was restricted to a few dialects in Ṭūr ʿAbdīn and the foreign word *mahzamle* seems to have entered some varieties in Ṭūr ʿAbdīn at an early date.

(3) 'to close'

The native verb for 'to close', *ṣxərle*, was a common word in Ṭūr ʿAbdīn. Today many Ṣūrayt/Ṭūrōyo speakers living in or coming from Turkey have replaced it with the Turkish foreign verb *mqāpaṭle*.

(4) 'to be informed'

A common expression that used to be in wide use and can still be heard in the speech of the older generation is *ʿal ū-mamro*, 'according to what I have heard/been informed'. Today, the expression in question has been replaced by two foreign words. Ṣūrayt/Ṭūrōyo speakers from Turkey use *gōya/gūya* and those from Arabic-speaking countries use *ʿala bana*.

(5) 'to be surprised'

The word expressing surprise, *dūmōro*, and its verb *mdāmar* (mostly used with first personal pronouns *mdāmarno/mdamrōno*) has been replaced by the Arabic *ʿəğbo* and its verb *mʿāğabno/mʿağbōno*.

(6) *fulḥōno* 'an arable land' > 'political activities'

Sometimes a word loses its original meaning and acquires a new meaning in the diaspora. A case in point is *fulḥōno*. Today it usually denotes 'activities' in an association or 'political activities' in general in the diaspora. In Ṭūr ʿAbdīn the word denoted 'an arable land'.

(7) *ḥāṣo* 'back; belt' > 'back'

In some cases the semantic range of a word is restricted. For example, *ḥāṣo* had both the meaning 'back' and also the meaning 'a belt of cloth' in Ṭūr ʿAbdīn. In the diaspora, however, the younger generation is only aware of the meaning 'back'.

5.3. Phraseology and Idioms

Each language contains cultural-specific metaphors, phrases alluding to historical events or religious and social phenomena. Such phraseology is conditioned by the physical, cultural and religious environment of the language community. This is best described by the following quote in an article by Fishman (1996) entitled 'What do you lose when you lose your language?', where he (ibid., 72) writes:

> Take it [language] away from the culture, and you take away its greetings, its curses, its praises, its laws, its literature, its songs, its riddles, its proverbs, its cures, its wisdom, its prayers.

In the case of Ṣūrayt/Ṭūrōyo, the language has not entirely been extracted from its culture and religion, but it has been removed from its physical environment, which has influenced the language in different ways. I shall demonstrate this by a few illustrative examples.

In Ṭūr ʿAbdīn, for example, stones were a very important feature of life and constituted a crucial building material. This is evident from the phrases people formed with the word for 'a stone' *kēfo*, for instance:

(1)	*hāwən*	*kēfo*	*w-kalšo*
	became.they	stone	and-lime

'They became inseparable friends.' (Literally: 'They became stone and lime.')

The phrase is, of course, used figuratively. It is used when you are very good friends. The phrase *dāʿīri hāwən kēfo w-kalšo* can also be used when one is on bad terms with another person and then find their way back to each other, *dāʿīri* meaning literally 'they returned'.

When one built houses, the most important components were stone and lime and then people experienced concretely how stone and lime were composed:

(2)	*mḥē-le*	*kēfe*	*mīn-e*
	threw-he	stones	at (from)-him

'to insult someone in an indirect way' (Literally: 'He threw stones at him.')

(3) *hawyō-no kēfo kamto lō səm-le b-dīḏ-i*

became-I stone black not did-he in-my (mine)

'Whatever I did, he did not do as I said.' (Literally: 'I became a black stone and he did not do in accordance with me.')

(4) *ʾī-kēfo yāqurto b-dukṯ-a ṭawtō=yo*

the-stone heavy in-place-its good=is

'The value of a person lies in his serious-mindedness.' (This was said of a person who does not laugh or smile, literally: 'The heavy stone is good in its place.')

In Ṣūrayt/Ṭūrōyo body parts are used in the formation of metaphorical phrases. Many such phrases contain the words *lēbo* 'heart' and *mēne* (pl.) 'hair' (or *manṯo* 'a single hair'). For example:

(5) *m-ū lēbo (kəmmət)*

from-the heart saying.you

'Are you serious? (Literally: '[Are you saying] from the heart?')'

(6) *twər-le lēb-e*

broke-he heart-his

'He hurt his feelings.' (Literally: 'He broke his heart.')

(7) *lat-le lēbo*

is.not-to.him a heart

'He does not feel like it.' (Literally: 'He does not have a heart.')

(8)	*lēb-e*	*qīṣ*
	heart-his	was.cut

'He is suspicious.' (literally: 'His heart was cut.')

(9)	*ʾāṯi*	*mēne*	*b-līšōn-i*
	came.he	hair	on-tongue-my

'I am sick of saying it over and over again.' (Literally: 'Hair came on my tongue.')

(10)	*kō-ṣōləḥ*	*ʾī-manṯo*
	IND-he.splits	the-hair

'He is very clever.' (Literally: 'He splits the single hair.')

Religion played and still plays an important part in the life of the Suryōye and there are many phrases relating to this, such as:

(11)	*šubḥo*	*l-ālo*
	praise	to-God

'Oh my God!' (Literally: 'Praise be to God!')

(12)	*ʾālo*	*ṭōrē-l-ux*
	God	keep-ACC-you

'May God keep you!'

(13)	*moryo*	*w-aq-qādīše*	*hōwən*	*ʾaʿm-ux*
	Lord	and-the-saints	be.they	with-you

'May the Lord and the saints be with you!'

(14)	*mḥālaq-le*	*rūḥe*	*qəm*	*raġl-e*	*d-ū-qādīšo*
	threw-he	himself	at	feet-his	of-the-saint

'He sought protection or help from the saint by [visiting his tomb or church].' (Literally: 'He threw himself at the feet of the saint.')

Many oaths of a religious content were used in the community, e.g. *b-ālōho* '[I swear] by God'; *bə-mšīḥo* '[I swear] by Jesus'; *b-ū-mgalyun* '[I swear] by the Bible'; *b-aq-qādīše* '[I swear] by the saints'; *b-ū-ṣlībo* '[I swear] by the Cross'; *b-ū-qabro* '[I swear] by the grave [of Jesus]'; *b-indāṯ-ālo* (< **yōldaṯ ʾalōhō*) '[I swear] by the Virgin Mary'.

Except for the phrases *b-ū-ṣlībo* and *b-ū-mgalyun* all these expressions of oaths are in the process of disappearing among the younger generation of speakers. In Sweden, for instance, the younger generation frequently make use of the Swedish phrase *Jag lovar* 'I promise'.

6. Language Attrition and Codeswitching

The fact that many original words and meanings are being lost in the diaspora is due to the imperfect learning of the language by younger speakers and the lack of planning on the part of the older generation as to how to pass on the language to the younger generation. I shall illustrate this by two concrete examples.

The native verb *mṭāwēle*, which was used in many villages in Ṭūr ʿAbdīn with the sense of 'to grill', has been almost entirely replaced by the Arabic loanword *mšāwēle* in the diaspora or by the mixed Ṣūrayt/Ṭūrōyo and Swedish phrase *səmle grilla*, which literally means 'he did the grill'.

Another example is as follows. Once I was in a lift and somebody told me to press the button by saying *səm trycka!*, which consists of Ṣūrayt/Ṭūrōyo *səm* 'do, make' and Swedish *trycka* 'press'. The phrase could easily be expressed by the Ṣūrayt/Ṭūrōyo phrase *dəš ʿal u-zraʿlo* 'press the button!'

The younger generation uses codeswitching, which is, of course, very common among bilinguals. They begin a conversation in Ṣūrayt/Ṭūrōyo and then they suddenly switch over to Swedish for various reasons. This is partly because the words required in the conversation are lacking in Ṣūrayt/Ṭūrōyo or they have not mastered them.

7. Phonology and Hypercorrection

The previous discussion concerned changes relating to the vocabulary of the language. There has also been an important change in phonology in the diaspora. Many of the children born in the diaspora pronounce the interdentals /*ṯ*/ [θ] and /*ḏ*/ [ð] as [s] and [z]. For example, *qrīṯo* 'a village' is pronounced [qrīso], and *ʿēḏo* (m.) 'a feast' [ʕēzo]. The latter coincides with *ʿēzo* (f.) 'a she-goat'.

A shift from interdentals to sibilants is not a recent phenomenon among the Ṣūrayt/Ṭūrōyo speakers. The dialects of two villages, namely Bēqusyōno and Dayro du-ṣlībo, had undergone this shift long ago. Interestingly, in Ṭūr ʿAbdīn today the shift in question has spread to the dialects of other villages. There is a phonetic motivation behind the changes *ṯ* > *s* and *ḏ* > *z*, in that it is easier to articulate *s* and *z* than the original interdental fricatives *ṯ* and *ḏ*. The phenomenon is also known from Mlaḥsô and some dialects in (NENA). The same is true in many Arabic dialects.

When some Ṣūrayt/Ṭūrōyo speakers try to correct their pronunciation, they create hypercorrections. They pronounce interdentals where sibilants are correct. For example the correct word for 'a bishop', *hasyo*, becomes instead [haθyo].

8. Bilingualism, Multilingualism and the Future

Many among the younger generation grow up as bilingual or multilingual. The younger generation born in the diaspora are not normally familiar with a large part of the Ṣūrayt/Ṭūrōyo vocabulary that was originally used in Ṭūr ʿAbdīn. All the younger generation in the diaspora normally speak the national language with each other. They speak Ṣūrayt/Ṭūrōyo with their parents, relatives and elderly people.

Many of the younger Ṣūrayt/Ṭūrōyo generation have difficulties in making themselves understood in Ṣūrayt/Ṭūrōyo. This is a gradual process, but eventually the younger generation will lose so much of the language that they will inevitably shift entirely to the national language. This situation is, of course, a common phenomenon in minority groups, especially with minority groups of stateless immigrants.

Fishman (1996) writes about a story told by John MacNamara, who studied Irish all his childhood in school. He was scolded one day when he was buying sweets by the woman who ran the shop. He began speaking English to his sister and the woman asked him why he did not speak Irish with her. When they came out, his sister asked him: 'Is Irish really for talking?' It did not occur to them that Irish was for talking. They considered it rather to be a school subject. This is also what is happening among the Ṣūrayt/Ṭūrōyo-speaking younger generation. It is no longer natural for them to speak Ṣūrayt/Ṭūrōyo among each other, despite the efforts to teach the language in schools. This confirms the view of Fishman (1996, 79) that a real—not institutional—social space has to be created for a language to survive.

References

Ehrnebo, Paula. 2013. 'Terminologiarbete på minoritetsspråk'. In *Från ett språk till ett annat-om översättning och tolkning*: 174–75. Språkrådet, Falun: Norstedts.

Fishman, Joshua A. 1996. 'What *Do You Lose* When *You Lose Your Language?*'. In *Stabilizing Indigenous Languages*, edited by Gina Cantoni, 71–81. Flagstaff: Center for Excellence in Education, Northern Arizona University.

Tezel, Aziz. 2003. *Comparative Etymological Studies in the Western Neo-Syriac* (*Ṭūrōyo*) Lexicon. *With Special Reference to Homonyms, Related Words and Borrowings with Cultural Siginification*. Studia Semitica Upsaliensia 18. Elanders Gotab: Stockholm.

Tezel, Sina. 2015. 'Neologisms in Ṣūrayt/Ṭūrōyo'. In *Neo-Aramaic and its Linguistic Context*, edited by Geoffrey Khan & Lidia Napiorkowska, 100–09. Piscataway: Gorgias Press.

ABOUT THE PUBLISHING TEAM

Alessandra Tosi was the managing editor for this book.

Anna Gatti designed the cover using InDesign. The cover was produced in InDesign using Fontin (titles) and Calibri (text body) fonts.

Luca Baffa typeset the book in InDesign. The text font is Tex Gyre Pagella; the heading font is Californian FB. Luca created all of the editions — paperback, hardback, EPUB, MOBI, PDF, HTML, and XML — the conversion is performed with open source software freely available on our GitHub page (https://github.com/OpenBookPublishers).

INDEX

ʿAyn et-Tīne 245, 254–256, 260–261, 263, 265–266, 270, 272–273

ʿIwardo 40, 47, 56, 60, 66, 78, 354–355, 359, 367, 487

affectedness 31, 45–47, 58–59, 61, 63, 83, 85–87

agent 18, 30, 37, 39–40, 45–46, 66, 68, 72, 82–87, 134

agentivity 30, 45

agreement 34, 37–40, 43, 64, 66, 71, 75–76, 119, 200, 471, 478

agreement, verbal 32, 34, 36, 38–39, 42, 44, 53, 62–63, 66, 68, 70, 86–87, 237

Akkadian 219, 301, 339, 343, 348, 389, 408

alignment, split 41

Alqosh 91, 137

Amedia, Jewish 37–38, 73, 96, 139

Anḥil 363, 379, 381–382

Ankawa 395, 469–472, 475–479, 482–484

annexation 54, 302, 305, 314

anterior 11, 100, 174, 185

Aqra 443–445, 468

Arabic 3–5, 25, 72, 76, 83, 90, 93, 96, 102, 140, 188–190, 192–193, 221, 224–227, 229–231, 235–265, 267–272, 275, 277–281, 284–285, 289–292, 295, 297–299, 335–337, 339, 341–343, 345–347, 349–350, 383–385, 389–390, 395, 397, 400, 403, 410–411, 445, 469–479, 481–485, 488–494, 498–499

Arabic, Anatolian 225, 227, 230–231, 340, 342–344, 346

Arabic, Classical 4, 193, 254, 256, 301, 439

Arabic, Damascene 272

Arabic, Iraqi 341–342

Arabic, Levantine 337, 492

Arabic, Moroccan 188

Arabic, Palmyrene 295

Arabic, Syrian 29, 88–89, 235–273, 275–285

Aradhin, Christian 395, 403, 407

Arbel 38, 62–63, 90, 135, 285, 407, 439

Ardishay 398

Arena 443

Arkaḥ 356, 363, 365–366, 369, 374–376, 384, 487

Armenian 408, 411

articulatory phonology 326

Ashitha 390, 395, 397, 403, 410

aspect 45, 57, 86, 95, 97, 134–136, 138, 156–157, 162, 184, 235, 264, 267, 277, 279, 281–282, 391, 472

Azeri Turkish 437

Āzəx 227, 231, 233

Azran 319–326, 329

Bariṭle 395, 397–398, 400

Barrake 443–444

Barwar 28, 69, 73, 84, 90, 130, 134, 140, 143–146, 162, 166, 168–169, 177–178, 180–181, 184–186, 191, 195, 219, 225, 229–230, 232, 308–310, 317, 336, 340, 348–349, 376, 387, 398, 406, 439, 445, 468

basic word list 415–417

Baxʿa 250, 254–255, 257, 259–260, 267, 270, 275, 283, 288, 292, 294, 296

Baz 391, 395, 444, 468

beneficiary 45–47, 50, 73

Betanure 73, 77, 84, 91, 96, 395, 397, 400, 408, 419, 440

Billin 169

Bne Belatha-Ṭyare 405

Bne Romta-Ṭyare 402, 405–406

Bohtan 44, 89, 292, 297, 406, 410

Borb-Ruma 405, 407

Bsorino 337, 357, 365, 381–382

case marking, prepositional 29–34, 36–40, 43–44, 55, 62, 64–67, 69–70, 79–80, 82, 85, 87, 312

case marking, zero 32–33, 55, 57, 63–64, 70, 76, 80, 85, 87

Catalan 167, 176, 191, 402

Central Semitic 2, 4–5, 21, 236, 254, 282

Challa 96, 284, 419, 439

Chamba d-Mallik-Ṭyare 395, 405

Christian Palestinian Aramaic 258, 271, 287, 293–294, 298, 357

circumstantial clause 221–228, 230–231

cognate 5, 188, 235, 238–241, 246, 248, 253–254, 257–258, 262–265, 267–269, 271, 277–278, 280–282, 341, 343, 345, 394–395, 400–401, 406–408

complement clause 208, 210, 235, 269, 271, 279–280

concessive 195, 205–206, 208, 218

conditional 149–150, 154, 158–159, 177, 188, 195, 198, 200–203, 205–209, 211–218, 235, 271, 275, 279–280

conservatism 235, 278

construct state 27, 214, 302–303, 305–307, 313–314

continuous 3, 100, 134–138, 264, 282, 482

copula 10, 42, 63–64, 70, 87, 100–101, 116, 119, 132–137, 139, 178, 180, 204, 214, 224–227, 231

Cudi 169, 340

cycle, linguistic 165, 301–302, 313–315

Damascus 26, 236, 284

Danish 402

dative 29–30, 32, 34, 36, 45, 54, 64–66, 85–87, 259

dative, ethical 32, 45, 51, 53, 85–86

definite article 165, 247

definiteness 165, 247, 257

deontic modality 139, 144, 146–148, 154, 156–158, 165, 173, 188, 196–198, 256, 279–280

dependency 143, 146, 150, 153, 158–163, 174, 187–189, 216–217, 302

Dêrxas 225

deverbal adjective 1, 3–4, 25, 37

diaspora 35, 487, 489–494, 498–499

differential object marking 30, 32, 38, 66, 68, 247

Dinarta 443–444

Diyana 320–321, 332, 412, 440

Diyana-Zariwaw 320, 332, 412, 440

Dobe, Jewish 143, 188

Dohok, Jewish 41, 45–46, 59, 61, 69, 76–78, 84, 95–98, 101, 105, 115, 118, 128, 130, 132–133, 135–139, 395

English 29, 66, 69, 73, 141, 159, 163, 220, 233, 285, 316–317, 331, 339,

347, 349–350, 385, 399, 402, 408–409, 412, 438, 453, 500

epistemic modality 131, 158, 195–198, 200–201, 216–218

etymology 23, 116, 291, 345, 348, 399, 419–422, 424, 427, 433–434, 437

eventive 16

existential constructions 30, 55, 57, 63, 87, 385

experiencer 29–30, 32–34, 36, 71–73, 75–86

fientive 16

focus 46

French 23, 86, 167–168, 233, 347

future, immediate 167, 169–170, 172–173, 183

Gargarnaye 320, 333

Gaznakh 391

genitive case 302–303, 306, 314–315

Georgia 416

Geppa 443

Geramun 397–398, 406

gestures (phonological) 320, 322–323, 326, 330

Geʾez 306

grammaticalisation 30, 76, 130, 137–139, 144, 148, 169

Greek 8–15, 17–18, 20–21, 26, 335, 338

Halmun 408

Harari 394

Harbole 169–170, 173, 176, 395, 400–403, 405

Harene 443

Hasköy 225, 233

Haṣṣan 44, 89, 390, 395, 406–407

Hawdiyan 320

Hebrew 5, 29, 61, 65, 88, 90–91, 102, 292, 296–297, 299, 316, 339, 343, 347–349, 391, 408, 412

Hebrew, Biblical 4–5, 189, 292, 389, 393

Hebrew, Mishnaic 93, 298, 408

Hebrew, Modern 29–30

Hertevin 41, 68, 79, 81, 83–84, 90, 390, 395, 397, 400, 407

Iḥwo 360–361, 384

imperfective 37, 47, 49–51, 84–85, 157, 162, 173, 199, 354

impersonal constructions 29–32, 34, 36, 53, 57, 59, 63, 66, 71, 73, 75, 77–79, 83–84, 87, 112, 264, 267

Inishke 400

interdentals 443, 499

intransitive 1–3, 7, 18, 21, 23, 25, 30, 37, 52–53, 62, 77–79, 85, 115, 169, 171, 176, 289, 292, 294

inversion 37

Irish 402, 500

Ishshi 401–403

Iṣṣin 407

Italian 18, 23, 28, 91, 140, 317, 404

Jewish Babylonian Aramaic 27, 88, 336, 343–345, 350, 357, 385, 389, 410, 418, 438

Jewish Palestinian Aramaic 1, 271, 287, 293–294, 298–299, 343–344, 350, 357, 389, 410, 438

Jənnet 44, 68

Jilu 403, 406, 408, 439

Jinet 391

Jrēǧir (Ğrēğir) 258–259, 269

Jubbʿadin 28, 76, 250, 259–261, 275, 283, 288, 292, 294, 395, 400

Judaeo-Syriac 407

Kalate 443
Karimlash 397
Kerend 404
Kfarze 2, 353, 356, 362, 365, 379–382, 487
Kharjawa 443–444
Kherpa 443–444, 447, 449
Kinderib 225–227, 230, 232, 349, 383, 385
Ko d-Chalwe-Ṭyare 397–398
Koy Sanjak, Christian 166
Kurdish xxv, 72, 89, 96, 102, 112, 117, 189, 221, 225, 229, 231, 238, 244, 285, 304, 310–312, 316–317, 320, 329, 335, 341–343, 345, 381, 383–385, 389–390, 400, 403–404, 408–409, 419, 427, 430, 437–438, 443, 445, 469–470, 477, 484, 488–489, 492
Kurdish, Behdini 72
Kurmanji 105, 189, 304, 307, 310–312, 320, 329, 376, 384, 399, 404, 430, 433, 437

language contact 189, 221, 237–238, 253, 264, 277, 280, 310, 320, 329–330
Late Aramaic 32, 236, 254, 256, 265, 277, 287–288, 293–294, 357, 396
Latin 26, 339, 341, 350, 399, 404, 412, 416
lexical innovation 401
Lishana Deni Jewish Neo-Aramaic 41, 45, 59, 84, 419
Lizin-Ṭyare 402, 405–406
loanword 102, 117, 238, 242–244, 260, 275, 335, 338, 340–341, 347, 383, 394–397, 470–471, 478, 481, 483–484, 498
L-suffix 34, 36–47, 49–53, 55, 57–63, 65–66, 68–70, 73, 75–80, 82–87

Malaberwan 443–444
Mandaic 1, 28, 292, 357, 386, 389, 395, 399, 409–411, 418, 438
Mardin 225, 232, 384, 386, 488
Marga 40–42, 44, 59, 71, 75, 81, 398
Mawana 160–161
Maʿlula 2, 27–28, 51–52, 72, 243, 245, 249–250, 254, 256–261, 263, 266, 270–271, 275, 284–285, 287–292, 294–296, 298, 395, 400
Mehri 394
Mer 340, 398, 400, 408
Meze 168
Mḥallami 225, 227, 488
Middle Aramaic 1–2, 6, 23, 25, 287, 357
Middle Eastern Aramaic 357, 376, 382–384, 418–437
Midin 2, 46, 48, 62, 64, 70, 74–75, 90, 93, 233, 244, 285, 337–338, 341, 347, 357–358, 360–361, 365, 373, 379, 381–382, 487
Midyat 2, 46–49, 54–56, 58, 62, 75, 82, 335, 341–342, 344, 347, 353, 355, 359–360, 363, 365–367, 372–378, 382, 400, 487–488, 491–493
mixing of dialects 319
Mlaḥso 2, 35, 50, 61, 64–65, 90, 395, 410
modality 131, 139, 158, 162, 195–198, 200, 203, 205, 214, 217–218, 256, 279–280
mood 57, 95, 97, 128–130, 235, 255, 263, 279
morphosyntax 30, 36, 66, 86, 238, 241, 246, 257–258, 261–262, 269, 271, 277, 280, 282, 288, 301
Mosul plain 50, 52, 143, 350, 395, 409, 483–484

Mzizaḥ 73–74, 354, 356, 365, 374–375

narrative 16, 21, 97, 134–135, 138, 164, 166, 170, 172, 176, 178, 181, 183–189, 213–214, 218, 222, 416, 489

neologisms 490–491

Neo-Mandaic 1–3, 237, 285, 389, 395–396, 411, 440

Nerwa 96, 141, 412, 438, 485

Nexla 443–445, 468

nominal pattern 288

non-verbal clause 225

Norwegian 402

Nuhawa 443–444

obligatorisation 34

Old (Ancient) Aramaic 394

palatalisation 329

Palmyrene Aramaic 295

participle 3, 36, 45, 76, 100, 132, 139, 180, 228, 236–237, 240, 248–249, 253, 259, 261, 263, 265, 271, 275, 278, 281–283, 288–289, 407

passive 16, 18, 236–237, 251, 289, 293

perfect 11, 16, 19, 21–22, 45, 50, 86, 100, 133–134, 139, 224, 231, 264, 267–268, 277, 281–282, 294

perfective 20, 37–38, 41, 44–45, 48–51, 59, 61, 66, 68, 74–75, 84–87, 97, 99–100, 134–135, 156–157, 166, 175–176, 178

Persian xxv, 25, 72, 90, 231, 285, 335–336, 339–340, 350, 389, 437–438

person marking 36, 44, 68, 87, 237

phonetics 322, 330

pivot 237, 254

pluperfect 16, 21–22

Polish 402

possessee 30–31, 59–60, 64, 66–70

possessor 29–33, 35, 45, 54–55, 57, 59, 61–66, 68–69, 71–73, 82, 85–87

possessor, external 31, 59, 61–62

possessor, predicative 29, 32, 34, 36, 57, 59, 61, 64–65, 68–69, 73, 84, 87, 204

prefix conjugation 236, 240, 248–249, 253, 255–258, 260, 262–264, 267–272, 274–275, 277–283

preterite 40, 45, 50, 59, 66, 68, 83–86, 134, 199, 203, 208–209, 240, 290, 294, 385

progressive 99, 130, 135–137, 139, 177–178, 180–181, 183, 186–187, 255, 264, 282

pronoun, dependent 66–67, 171, 176

pronoun, independent 32, 46, 55, 67, 69, 74, 85, 312

proto-Semitic 5, 301

purpose clause 168, 177, 181–184, 187, 260

Qalamun 236, 264, 401

Qalunta 443

Qaraqosh 51–52, 90, 135, 144, 156, 166, 191, 308, 317, 336, 349, 395, 397, 400–402, 404–405, 407, 410

Qurich 407

Raite 39, 50, 82, 379, 381

realis 98–100, 104, 128–131, 135, 139, 197

recipient 45–47, 55, 58–59, 61–62, 65, 73, 75, 82–83, 85–87

Rekan 408

relative tense 16, 21, 173–174

replication 221, 237–240, 243–247, 250–254, 257–259, 262, 267,

277–278, 280–282, 307, 310–312, 317
resultative 8, 10, 16, 45, 76, 100, 132–135, 139, 236–237, 248–249, 253, 259, 261, 265, 271, 275, 282–283
resultative participle 7, 16–17, 45, 248, 253, 265–267, 271, 275–277, 279, 281–283
Russia 416

Salamas 44
Salamas, Christian 397, 407
Samaritan Aramaic 287, 293, 299, 357, 389, 412
Samʾal inscriptions 302
Sanandaj, Christian 82, 166
Sanandaj, Jewish 63
Sanaye 443–444
Saqqiz 53, 63, 71, 79–80, 90
Sat 395, 406
Sedari 362, 364, 384
Semitic 29, 32, 236, 277, 292, 302, 343, 345, 394
Shaqlawa 67, 132, 177
Sharmen 407, 443–444
Shkafte 443
Shwawwa-Baz 405–406
Soddo 394
Soqotri 356, 394
Sorani 189, 304, 312, 430, 433, 437
Spanish 190, 402
Sprachbund
  Caucasian 329
  Eastern Anatolian 329
stative 3, 7–8, 10, 16, 45, 74, 99–100, 133–136, 139, 426
stem 1–2, 37, 83, 99, 135, 177–178, 242, 244, 248–252, 257–258, 264–265, 267, 270–271, 278, 289–290, 292, 294, 304, 335–336
subject, non-canonical 30, 32, 86–87
subjunctive 57, 166–168, 177–178, 180–181, 183–187, 189, 199–200, 203–204, 206–209, 211, 240, 354
suffix conjugation 1, 27, 236, 240, 248–251, 253–254, 256, 262, 267–268, 271–272, 275–279, 281–283
Sulemaniyya, Christian 166
Ṣurayt (Ṭuroyo) 335–340, 342–343, 345–346, 348
Sureth 469–484
Swadesh list 353, 416
Syria 51, 72, 76, 236, 240, 287, 290, 293, 295, 489
Syriac 1, 3–4, 6–7, 10, 15–16, 18–28, 32–33, 88, 90–92, 225, 228, 230–232, 292, 296–297, 304–307, 313–314, 317, 335–340, 343, 345–351, 355, 357, 382–383, 386–387, 389–393, 397, 399–400, 403, 405–406, 408–409, 411–413, 417–418, 424, 430–431, 438, 489–490, 500

TAM 55, 57, 86, 98, 235, 238, 248, 252–253, 255, 262, 267–268, 277, 279, 281–282
Targum Onkelos 389, 409
telic 8, 18–19, 21–22, 47, 53
Telkepe 88, 91, 137, 391, 395, 397, 400, 402–404, 422
tense 1–2, 10–11, 18, 23, 40, 45, 55, 57, 86, 95, 97, 105, 129–130, 146, 154, 156, 166, 173–174, 223–224, 231, 235, 240, 254, 277, 281
Tigre 408
Tilla 406–407
Timur 395, 406
Tin 400
Tisqopa 390, 397

Tkhuma 395
Tkhuma-Gáwaya 395
topic 160, 162–164, 389, 489
topicalisation 33–34, 87
transitive 1–2, 16, 18, 67–68, 83–84, 86, 133, 139, 169, 176, 292, 294
transitivisation 30, 34, 66–67, 84, 86
Trans-Zab Jewish Neo-Aramaic 53, 61–62, 79, 244
trigger effect 230
Turkish 303, 316, 320, 335, 445, 488, 493
Ṭuroyo 21, 24–25, 335–338, 340–343, 346, 348, 350–351, 500
Ṭūr ʿAbdīn 350
Ṭyare 134, 391, 403–404, 406–408

Umṛa 44, 68, 79, 81
Upper Barwar (Hakkâri) 406
Urmi, Christian 34–35, 50, 56, 58–59, 67, 70, 77, 83–84, 135, 143, 181, 183–184, 186–187, 321, 329, 343, 376, 391–393, 395, 398, 400, 402–405, 415–416, 419, 430, 436
Urmi, Jewish 404

Van 285, 407
verbalisation 3, 10, 87
verboid 69, 84–85

Western Neo-Aramaic 2, 35, 51–52, 55, 57, 65, 72, 76, 85, 235–243, 245–254, 257–260, 262–264, 267–271, 275, 277–284, 287–288, 290–292, 294–295, 389
Western Syriac 337–338, 347, 400, 490, 492

Xarabe Kafre 372, 379, 384
Xarabe Məška 361, 364, 379, 384

Zakho, Jewish 88–89, 96, 98, 117–118, 136, 139–141, 195, 201, 217, 219–220, 309, 313, 315, 397, 412, 438
Zariwaw 320, 332, 412, 440
Zaz 365

Cambridge Semitic Languages and Cultures

General Editor Geoffrey Khan

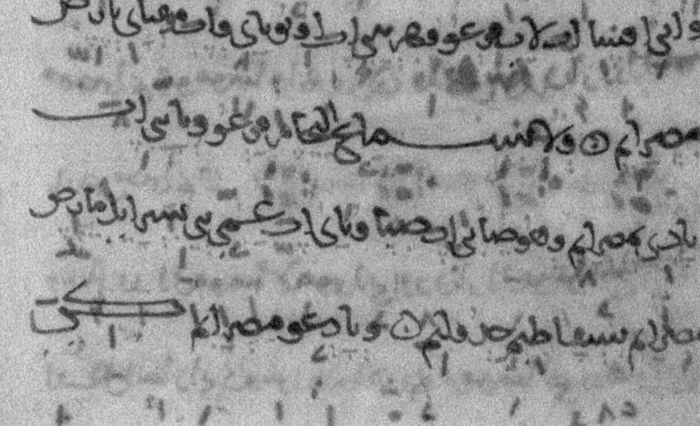

Cambridge Semitic Languages and Cultures

About the series

This series is published by Open Book Publishers in collaboration with the Faculty of Asian and Middle Eastern Studies of the University of Cambridge. The aim of the series is to publish in open-access form monographs in the field of Semitic languages and the cultures associated with speakers of Semitic languages. It is hoped that this will help disseminate research in this field to academic researchers around the world and also open up this research to the communities whose languages and cultures the volumes concern. This series includes philological and linguistic studies of Semitic languages and editions of Semitic texts. Titles in the series will cover all periods, traditions and methodological approaches to the field. The editorial board comprises Geoffrey Khan, Aaron Hornkohl, and Esther-Miriam Wagner.

This is the first Open Access book series in the field; it combines the high peer-review and editorial standards with the fair Open Access model offered by OBP. Open Access (that is, making texts free to read and reuse) helps spread research results and other educational materials to everyone everywhere, not just to those who can afford it or have access to well-endowed university libraries.

Copyrights stay where they belong, with the authors. Authors are encouraged to secure funding to offset the publication costs and thereby sustain the publishing model, but if no institutional funding is available, authors are not charged for publication. Any grant secured covers the actual costs of publishing and is not taken as profit. In short: we support publishing that respects the authors and serves the public interest.

Other titles in the series

Jewish-Muslim Intellectual History Entangled

Camilla Adang, Bruno Chiesa, Omar Hamdan, Wilferd Madelung, Sabine Schmidtke and Jan Thiele (eds)

doi.org/10.11647/OBP.0214

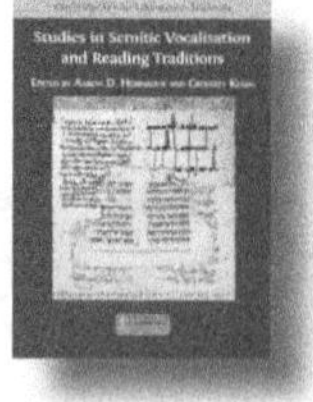

Studies in Semitic Vocalisation and Reading Traditions

Aaron Hornkohl and Geoffrey Khan (eds.)

doi.org/10.11647/OBP.0207

You can find more information about this serie at:
http://www.openbookpublishers.com/section/107/1

www.ingramcontent.com/pod-product-compliance
Lightning Source LLC
LaVergne TN
LVHW020501100826
845148LV00003B/685

* 9 7 8 1 7 8 3 7 4 9 4 7 8 *